Applying OMT

ADVANCES IN OBJECT TECHNOLOGY SERIES

Dr. Richard S. Wiener
Series Editor

Editor
Journal of Object-Oriented Programming
Report on Object Analysis and Design
SIGS Publications, Inc.
New York, New York

and

Department of Computer Science
University of Colorado
Colorado Springs, Colorado

Additional Volumes in Preparation

Applying OMT

A Practical Step-by-Step Guide to Using the Object Modeling Technique

Kurt W. Derr

Idaho National Engineering Laboratory
Lockheed Martin Idaho Technologies
Eagle Rock Technologies
University of Idaho

Idaho Falls, Idaho

SIGS
BOOKS
New York

Library of Congress Cataloging-in-Publication Data

Derr, Kurt W., 1949-
  Applying OMT : a practical step-by-step guide to using the object
modeling technique / Kurt W. Derr.
     p.   cm. -- (Advances in object technology series ; 8)
  Includes bibliographical references and index.
  ISBN 1-884842-10-0 (pbk. : alk. paper)
  1. Object-oriented programming (Computer science) 2. Computer
software--Development.   I. Title. II. Series: Advances in object
technology ; 8.
  QA76.64.D463 1995
  005.1'1--dc20   95-19076
                                                                        CIP

PUBLISHED BY
SIGS Books
71 W. 23rd Street, Third Floor
New York, New York 10010

Design and composition by Susan Culligan, Pilgrim Road, Ltd. Set in Bembo.
Printed on acid-free paper.

SIGS Books ISBN 1–884842–10–0
Prentice Hall ISBN 0-13-231390-1

Printed in the United States of America
99 98 97 96   10 9 8 7 6 5 4 3 2

About the Author

Kurt Derr is a veteran of software development. He has worked on software and systems projects in capacities ranging from individual contributor to technical manager. Since 1972, Derr has held positions at companies such as Datapoint Corp., NCR Corp., and EG&G Idaho, Inc., contributing to object-oriented methodologies and to a variety of software and hardware configurations. Currently, Derr is object technologist with the Lockheed Idaho Technologies Company at the Idaho National Engineering Laboratory, Idaho Falls, Idaho. He is also chief technologist for Eagle Rock Technologies, Idaho Falls, Idaho, a company that provides vital object technology products and services.

Derr received a bachelor's degree in electrical engineering (1971) from the Florida Institute of Technology, Melbourne, Florida, and a master's degree in computer science (1980) from the University of Idaho, Moscow, Idaho. As adjunct professor at the University of Idaho, Derr teaches courses on programming in Smalltalk and on object-oriented analysis and design.

Foreword

THIS BOOK IS a detailed case study using the Object Modeling Technique (OMT) as a foundation. The publication of this book is a sign that OMT is maturing, and I am pleased to have the chance to write its forward. OMT is not proprietary; it was placed in the public domain to survive on its own merits and to evolve to fit software engineering needs.

Kurt presents a complete case study in two of the most commonly used object-oriented programming languages, C++ and Smalltalk. He has a good grasp of OMT, including both basic concepts and advanced ones. For example, in places, he has applied reification to include controller objects and agents in the object model of the case study. A large number of appendices follow the main part of the book with documentation of the products of the case study, including C++ and Smalltalk code. One of the appendices addresses the important issue of metrics.

Also, there are a couple of object-oriented principles that I feel strongly about that this book reinforces. The power of abstraction that an object-oriented approach offers is valuable during all phases of software development, not just during programming. One of the reasons we (Rumbaugh, Blaha, Premerlani, Eddy, and Lorensen) wrote our book on OMT *(Object Oriented Modeling and Design,* Prentice Hall, 1991) was because, at the time, there was a disproportionate emphasis on programming. Furthermore, it is important that design precedes implementation, even in an iterative approach. There is nothing wrong with building a system incrementally or with rapid prototyping, providing that there is an architecture for the overall system and that each part of the system is designed before it is implemented. Most of the problems that I have seen encountered during software development are caused by ad hoc designs created during implementation. In many places, there is still a management view that unless code is being written, there is no progress.

This book follows the extended OMT methodology fairly closely, with respect to both the process and the products. Furthermore, although Kurt has made some contributions, he has not invented yet another methodology. The object-oriented industry suffers from having too many methodologies carrying their inventors' names. My hope is that a single unified view of object-oriented technology will eventually emerge and be the subject of many books, similar to the way that unified views evolved in, for example, physics and mathematics. Kurt's book is a step in that direction. I would like to see more.

— William Premerlani

Dr. William Premerlani has spent over 20 years at the General Electric Research and Development Center in Schenectady, New York, where he has applied his interests in object-oriented methodologies, applications of metamodels, and database technology to a number of software projects. Dr. Premerlani is a coauthor of *Object-Oriented Modeling and Design,* Prentice Hall, 1991. He is currently writing a book with Michael Blaha, "Object-Oriented Modeling and Design for Database Applications," forthcoming from Prentice Hall in 1996. His present addresses are GE CR&D, P.O. Box 8, Schenectady, NY 12301, and premerlani@crd.ge.com.

Preface

Several years ago, I began teaching object-oriented analysis and design classes at the University of Idaho. After surveying the literature and texts available, it became apparent that there was a lack of complete examples showing a developer how to start with a problem statement and then analyze, design, and actually build an application using the object-oriented approach. Furthermore, no complete examples existed using any well-known object-oriented methodology (such as Rumbaugh et al., Booch, Wirfs-Brock, Meyer, Coad and Yourdon, Shlaer, etc.) along with the use of well-known class libraries and development tools (such as Borlands' C++ and Application Frameworks, or Digitalk's Smalltalk/V) to guide a software engineer in developing an application.

This book represents an intent to fill that void by providing a thorough example of the development of an application, of electronic filing from analysis through design, and of coding and testing using a popular and well-known object-oriented analysis and design approach; i.e., the Object Modeling Technique (OMT). In addition, the example in the text will show how popular class libraries and tools are used to develop an application. The Borland implementation is developed in a Windows environment using ProtoGen to generate the user interface code. The Smalltalk/V implementation is also developed in a Windows environment, using WindowBuilder to generate the user interface code.

The goals of this book are as follows: to help software developers make the shift from object-oriented theory to actual practice of the technology; to show how to apply a well-known comprehensive object-oriented analysis and design technique in building a real world application (i.e., to express the thought process on how to apply the Object Modeling Technique); to help students and professionals make the "paradigm shift" from traditional development techniques to object-oriented development; and to demonstrate the use of well-known class libraries and development tools in building an application.

This book is written for the student, software engineering professional, or anyone else who wants to learn how to apply object-oriented technology (OT). At present, there are no books I know of covering a complete example which in detail analyzes, designs, and implements an application using OMT. In fact, there are few books, if any, that develop a complete, detailed example using any object-oriented analysis and design methodologies.

Applying OMT is suitable for short courses, undergraduate/graduate courses in engineering or computer science, or for self learning. This is not a book on theory, but rather a how-to book illustrating the building of an application using OMT. The OMT approach is put into practice for the purpose of analyzing, designing, and implementing an application. In addition, there is a focus on the thought process involved in implementing OMT for a particular application. Since this text covers analysis, design, and C++ and Smalltalk implementations, many opportunities exist for student exercises. These exercises can include exploring different analysis and design models and evaluating the adequacy of those models; extending the existing analysis, design, and code to include additional features in the application; changing the C++/Smalltalk code to focus more on reuse of code in existing class libraries; performing your own metrics analysis on the existing analysis, design, and/or implementation artifacts and exploring how the quality can be improved; and improving the process described in the text.

This book is designed to be read from cover to cover. Each chapter builds upon the material covered in previous chapters. However, if you are most interested in the design of an application, you can review the analysis model in the appendices and then skip over to Part 2 of the text. If you only care about actual implementation and testing, you can review the design model in the appendices and then skip to Part 3 of the text.

All of the chapters in this book have something in common. However, each chapter is also unique from the rest. In the flavor of object technology, each chapter may be viewed as an instance of a chapter class. The chapter class has attributes that are the main topics of the chapter. The main topics for each chapter type may be different or the same. The operations or methods of each chapter class are the processes that take place on the attribute values or chapter topics. At the beginning of each chapter, there will be a listing of the main topics of that chapter and the questions/explanations (operations/methods) that will be provided about those topics. A page number will precede each of the questions/explanations to quickly orient the reader and facilitate locating specific topics.

In addition, changes/differences between class diagrams will be highlighted in italics; i.e., changes to the previous class diagram are shown in italics in the current class diagram to enable the reader to quickly identify differences between the diagrams. This highlighting of differences will be followed throughout the text for all class diagrams.

Applying OMT contains four parts beyond the first introductory chapter. Part 1 (chapters 2-6) centers around analysis and presents an approach for building a real-world model of the problem we are trying to solve using the OMT approach. This consists of building the initial object, dynamic, and functional models that make up OMT. The OMT notation is used both here and throughout the text. An analysis document tracks the results of the analysis process. The analysis document consists of the problem statement, object model (data dictionary, object model diagrams, traversals of access paths), dynamic model (user interface formats, scenarios, event trace, event flow diagram for electronic filing, state diagrams), and functional model (context diagram, data dictionary, data flow diagrams, constraints, and descriptions of atomic processes).

Part 2 (chapters 7-8) discusses the design of the system, subsystems, and individual objects within the system. Reusability is one of the key benefits promised by the proponents of OT. The application built in this text demonstrates how to use commercial off-the-shelf class libraries to maximize code reuse.

Metrics is a new field in software engineering that is not yet fully developed. A software metric enables you to measure some aspect of the development process or the product, potentially leading you to a better software development process and/or product. Although there is no general agreement about what metrics are really useful, some authors recommend that we start to collect them and then refine the metrics as the software industry learns more about them. We will follow their recommendation and collect data for specific process and product-related metrics noted by other authors as interesting.

A discussion of basic windowing concepts that will be used throughout the text is referenced in this part of the book and included in an appendix. Also, breaking a system into subsystems, building a detailed user interface from the dynamic model, combining the three models to obtain operations for objects by major application function, and a process for flushing out algorithms to implement operations are discussed in this section of the book. In addition, the use of informal English description, or grammatical inspection, as the initial technique for identifying objects is demonstrated.

The user interface implemented in Part 2 is used as the driver for testing scenarios, as objects and behavior are incrementally added to the application. The user interface is loosely coupled to the rest of the application to facilitate porting the application to different environments and to minimize changes to the application as either the user interface changes or as new interfaces are developed to suit the needs of the user community.

Each class is discussed in terms of how it will be represented using both the Smalltalk and C++ class libraries. Each association between classes is discussed in terms of how the association will be represented in the implementation. The object, dynamic, and functional models are examined in detail for obtaining operations on classes.

Part 3 of the text (chapter 9) shows how the application is built using popular commercial off-the-shelf object-oriented development tools and class libraries. Borlands' C++ with Application Frameworks and Protogen are used to build the application in C++. The Digitalk Smalltalk/V environment (with its extensive class library) and WindowBuilder are used to build the application in the Smalltalk language. The protocol for each class in the electronic filing application is discussed in terms of both Smalltalk (instance and class variables and methods) and C++ (data members, member functions, levels of program access) implementations. Programming style and differences between the design and the implementation are also discussed for each Smalltalk and C++ application class.

Part 4 of the book (chapter 10) discusses the lessons learned during the development of the electronic filing application using object-oriented technology. In addition to experience with commercial-off-the-shelf class libraries, these lessons learned include an understanding of what graphical user interface development tools do and do not do for the developer; how to keep your documentation in synchronization with your application development; the importance of inheritance as well as analysis, design, and code walkthroughs; good coding style guidelines; how much iteration to expect during application development; and the advantages of implementations in Smalltalk or C++, etc.

The appendices contain the analysis document, systems design document, and object design document, the Smalltalk and C++ code for the application on a subsystem by subsystem basis, the pseudo code for the operations of many of the classes, a discussion of process and product metrics using the specific data collected, and more. The Smalltalk and C++ code is also contained on a diskette in the back of the book.

This book also incorporates my interpretation of OMT extensions/changes since the publication of *Object-Oriented Modeling And Design* (Rumbaugh et al., 1991). These extensions/changes to the OMT were introduced by James Rumbaugh and/or Michael Blaha in various articles on modeling and design in the *Journal Of Object-Oriented Programming* (JOOP). The changes involve using object interaction diagrams for design purposes, using logical design models and implementation models during design and implementation, using solid circles at an end of an association and 1+ to denote one or more multiplicity, using "use cases" at the front-end of the OMT process to capture requirements, and using the phrase class diagram to denote a diagram showing the classes in a system. (The phrase object diagram will refer to an object instance diagram. Object model will refer to collections of both types of diagrams.)

There are a number of things which *Applying OMT* is not. First, this book is not a tutorial or an authoritative guide for the OMT approach. It covers only the concepts of the OMT approach that apply to building the electronic filing application. Furthermore, the example in this text represents only my interpretation of how to put the Object Modeling Technique into practice. For a tutorial on the OMT methodology, see *Object-Oriented Modeling and Design* by James Rumbaugh, Michael Blaha, William Premerlani, Frederick Eddy, and William Lorensen.

Second, I do not provide a tutorial of C++ or Borland's Application Frameworks, although a discussion of the basic organization of Application Frameworks is included in the text to provide readers with some familiarity of the C++ class library that is used to construct the application. Third, this is not a tutorial of Smalltalk/V or the Smalltalk/V for Windows Encyclopedia of classes, although a discussion of the basic organization of the Smalltalk/V for Windows Encyclopedia of classes is included in the text to provide readers with some familiarity of the Smalltalk/V class library that is used to construct the application. A basic knowledge of C++ or Smalltalk is necessary to understand the implementation of the electronic filing application. Fourth, this book is not a tutorial of GUI builders or diagramming tools for object-oriented development, although several tools that were used to construct the application are included in the text to show how tools may be a part of the O-O life cycle and improve productivity.

This book shows how I have interpreted the OMT approach to develop an application. Some of the important concepts of the OMT approach that are covered in this book include: an explanation as to how to construct the object, dynamic, and functional models; a detailed description of the object, dynamic, and functional models; a detailed analysis of the three models to obtain operations for objects; the use of a data dictionary; and an iterative approach for refining and improving the analysis, design, and implementation of our application.

In regard to the object model, I explain the approach for discarding unnecessary and incorrect classes, associations, and attributes, as well as the use of a grammatical approach, or informal English description, as an initial technique for identifying objects. For the functional model, I teach the use of pseudocode in flushing out algorithms and the use of an object-oriented pseudocode to describe algorithms for each method. When detailing the dynamic model, I delve into the use of "use cases" to capture requirements, the important role that scenarios play in the development and testing of an object-oriented application, and the importance of event traces in the development and testing of an application. When dealing with design and implementation, I present the use of subsystems in design and implementation, the use of delegation rather than implementation inheritance, and a discussion of programming style and design vs. implementation differences.

In addition, I have defined some approaches to building an object-oriented application or borrowed from others to enhance the construction of the electronic filing application using OMT. These concepts or approaches include class libraries, user interfaces, and modeling. In defining class libraries, I discuss how to choose or represent your application classes using existing classes from commercial off-the-shelf class libraries and provide a detailed discussion of the applications classes for both the Smalltalk and C++ implementations. The user interface is discussed in terms of using commercial off-the-shelf GUI tools for generating Smalltalk and C++ code. Here I provide a discussion of basic windowing concepts and a process for building a detailed user interface from the dynamic model. I also explain a procedure for combining the three models to identify operations for each object, by use case.

I would be happy to receive constructive as well as destructive critiques on the content of this book. Electronic mail may be sent to k_derr@acm.org.

A lot of work went into producing this book. I hope that it answers some of the questions you may have about developing applications using OT. I am very excited about object-oriented technology and the hope that it holds for dealing with complexity and improving productivity in the software industry. I hope that you find the contents of this text useful in learning how to apply the object-oriented approach in solving real-world problems.

I would like to thank Scott Matthews and Kurt Welker for their contributions to the style, presentation, and technical content of this book. On a personal note, I would like to thank my wife, Jill, for her support and understanding and my children, Shannon, Justin, and Corey, for putting up with their dad always being busy.

Contents

xiii

CHAPTER 1

Introduction

Main Chapter Topics	Topic Questions/Explanations
object-oriented development process (OODP)	1 what is the OODP
Object Modeling Technique (OMT) specification	3 what is the OMT specification
	3 what are the different phases of the OODP
	3 what are the inputs and outputs of the OODP
tools	6 what tools are used in the development of this application
metrics	7 what role will metrics play in our process and product development

Object-oriented technology (OOT) is becoming a popular approach for building applications because it deals better with complexity and addresses the software productivity issue more effectively than any other approach known to date. The object-oriented approach is a new way of thinking about solving problems and modeling those problems with a computer.

The popular Object Modeling Technique (OMT) by Rumbaugh, Blaha, Premerlani, Eddy, and Lorensen (1991) has been used in many real-world problems. The OMT will be the approach used in this text to develop an electronic filing application. But I have also augmented the OMT approach with techniques I have found valuable that are prescribed by other authors in the object-oriented world. These techniques by other authors are specifically identified as they apply throughout the book. Borland's C++ and Application Frameworks is one of the most popular tools for developing object-oriented applications today. Examples are provided in the text on how the electronic filing design is implemented using Borland's Integrated Development Environment with Application Frameworks. An implementation using Digitalk's Smalltalk/V for Windows is also presented.

1.1 THE OBJECT-ORIENTED DEVELOPMENT PROCESS

The iterative object-oriented development process (OODP), shown in Figure 1.1, consists of the traditional analysis, design, code, and test activities (Winblad, 1990). The object-oriented paradigm, using the Object Modeling Technique, spans the entire development process, so there is no need to transform from one type of model to another. This is a key benefit of the Object Modeling Technique. Some other object-oriented approaches use different notations for their analysis and design stages of the process.

Object–oriented programs grow incrementally, with additional classes and message flow between classes being added as the program evolves. As shown in Figure 1.1, development in an object-oriented environment, as in most software development environments, is iterative in nature; i.e., problems may be found during testing that require a change to the product design, users may request additional features after viewing a preliminary version of the product, and programmers may discover new opportunities for reuse during the coding phase that necessitate a change to the design. At any stage in the development process, one or two steps backward may need to be taken before any further progress is made in the development of the program.

Object-oriented development typically follows the "analyze a little, design a little, code a little, test a little" philosophy. An experimental approach to program development is the norm, rather than the exception. Although development is iterative, it is important to record all development decisions as product development progresses. For example, if during the analysis phase the scheduler for a computerized traffic control system is modeled as a single class but someone develops an idea for how the actual scheduling should take place, then this information should be

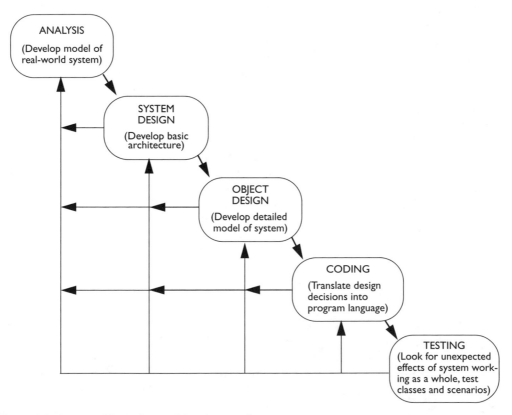

Figure 1.1. Iterative Object-Oriented Development Process.

recorded, ideally using a CASE tool, so that the idea is not lost. Later when the design of the scheduler is being addressed, previous ideas can be resurrected, analyzed, and built upon.

1.1.1 The Object Modeling Technique Specification

All of the results and decisions in building a product are captured in the OMT specification. The OMT specification consists of analysis, systems design, object design, and implementation results or documents, which are developed in various parts of this text. The OMT approach supports incremental development, wherein a portion of the software is developed, evaluated through use, and then built upon over time, or the more traditional life-cycle approach, wherein the first release of a software product is built in one pass.

1.1.2 Phases of the Object-Oriented Development Process

Figure 1.2 is a data flow diagram (DFD) for the object-oriented development process using the OMT, which shows the inputs and outputs from each phase of the process. Each phase of the process transforms some inputs to outputs, starting at a high level of abstraction and progressing to a more detailed level of abstraction that ultimately represents the problem solution. For example, the circle labeled System Design represents a transformation. It has several inputs, an object model, dynamic model, function model, and previous system design results from the same and similar

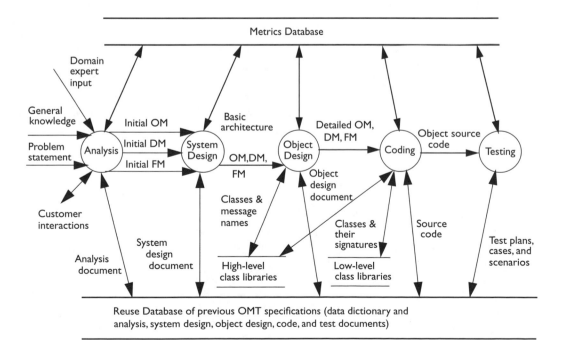

Figure 1.2. Inputs and Outputs of the Object-Oriented Development Process Using The OMT.

problem domains. The process of system design takes these inputs and transforms them into a basic architecture for the system. Object, dynamic, and functional models are updated as necessary to accommodate the system architecture.

The types of output, or deliverables, that are produced in the analysis, system design, and object design stages of the development process (Rumbaugh et al., 1991) are:

- ❑ **Analysis**—document consisting of the problem statement, object model, dynamic model, and functional model

- ❑ **System Design**—document describing the basic architecture for the system and high-level strategic decisions

- ❑ **Object Design**—document consisting of the detailed object model, detailed dynamic model, and detailed functional model

In addition, previous analysis, systems design, and object design documents may be examined for potential reuse in the development of the new system. Configuration management and version control tools such as Team/V by Digitalk and ENVY by Object Technology International, Inc., will be key in managing the artifacts of the development process.

The output of a development phase in the OMT may include some type of pictorial representation, such as an object model, functional model, or dynamic model. These pictorial models reduce the level of complexity of the representation of the system because human beings assimilate graphical information much faster than verbal or textual information (Jones, 1980).

During the analysis phase, a model of the real-world system is being developed. A problem statement, customer interactions, information about the application domain, general knowledge, and previous analysis results from same or similar problem domains captured in other OMT specifications are used to develop this real-world model. In many cases a problem statement will not have been developed by the user, and the object-oriented software developer will have to glean this information from users and write the problem statement. This may necessitate the use of prototyping to help gather user requirements. The software developer should research the problem domain to learn as much as possible about it, so that he or she knows what questions to ask the user and is effective in modeling the real-world environment.

According to Rumbaugh et al. (1991), "the analysis model serves several purposes: It clarifies the requirements, it provides a basis for agreement between the software requestor and the software developer, and it becomes the framework for later design and implementation." The work done during the analysis phase forms the beginning of the OMT specification. The OMT specification will be refined and added to at each stage of the development process. This specification should be used to document your work as you progress and should not be developed after the fact. The reason for developing a specification is to think through the analysis and design of an application before actually building it—similar to developing blueprints before actually building a house. Analysis results from the same or similar problem domains documented in OMT specifications should be examined for potential reuse of their results. The output of the analysis phase is an analysis document consisting of initial object, functional, and dynamic models along with a data dictionary. The data dictionary describes all of the object classes in the program/system. The analysis document represents the developers' model of the real-world system. The analysis document, as part of the OMT specification, will be updated as required throughout the OODP as decisions are made that impact it.

The system design phase takes the real-world model of the system and develops a high-level strategy for solving the problem. This includes organizing a system into subsystems, allocating subsystems to processors (if this is a distributed system) and tasks, choosing an approach for management of data stores. and handling boundary conditions. Systems design results from the same or similar problem domains documented in OMT specifications should be examined for potential reuse. A system design document is the output of the system design phase. This document specifies the structure of the basic architecture of the proposed system. Like the analysis document, this document will be updated as required as the iterative development process continues.

During the object design phase the full definitions of the classes, interfaces, associations, and operations will be developed. At this point we shift the focus of the model from application domain concepts toward computer concepts. Everything that has been done to date is examined and fleshed out in detail. Sometimes this means going back and adding or modifying classes, changing associations or basic structure of the model, or moving attributes or operations from one class to another. Class libraries previously developed for this problem domain are examined for potential reuse in the application. Object design results from the same or similar problem domains documented in OMT specifications should be examined for potential reuse. An object design document, as part of the OMT specification, is the output of the object design phase. This document represents a detailed model of the system and provides the basis for implementation. The object design document will be updated as required as the iterative development process continues.

One major difference between the object-oriented development process and the traditional development process is that during the design and coding phases of an OO project, much time is spent in reviewing, reusing, and extending existing code from class libraries (generic or problem domain types, low level or high level) instead of writing new code from scratch. This is a difficult and time-consuming process because programmers must understand code before they can use it. Learning the ins and outs of a class library is something that can take many months to do. This is one reason why a project manager of a reasonable size software development effort might assign a specific individual(s) to play the role of the class library/reuse specialist. Another difference between the object-oriented development process and the traditional development process is that a cleaner conceptualization of ideas and design occurs. In the object-oriented approach the program is a model of the application domain, whereas in the traditional procedural development process the program is a stream of actions that constitutes a solution to the target problem.

When the design phase is completed, writing code should be fairly straightforward, almost mechanical—a simple translation of design decisions into the target language chosen for implementation. Although decisions do have to be made during the coding process, they should only affect a small part of the program unless something major has been overlooked.

Testing in the OODP is still required to assure a high-quality product. Implementation obstacles, no matter what development process is being used, can cause some rethinking of the original design. However, as in traditional approaches to software development, quality cannot be tested into the product. A quality product is built by understanding user requirements and having a sound design and implementation based on those requirements.

Object-oriented program testing begins at the unit or object level and then continues with testing classes that are closely related to one another. Untested objects are added to tested objects in an incremental fashion, with each additional object being tested before adding a new object. So in the OODP, integration testing is carried out at an early stage in the development process because communication between objects is crucial for program development. Scenarios developed for the dynamic model form the basis for the testing processes. Also, test operations or test member functions may be developed for each class that exercise the functionality of the class.

The testing approach taken for the Electronic Filing application is to first develop the code for the user interface, and then to use this code as a scenario driver for other objects integrated into the program—top down. At the same time, code will be developed and tested for the search and file mechanisms (i.e., on a scenario basis)—bottom up. Then by the time the actual testing phase is reached, we are only looking for unexpected effects of the system working as a whole. Testing may begin earlier in the OODP than in the traditional approach to development.

Finally, remember that the first few times you develop object, dynamic, or functional models to describe some problem domain, you will probably end up with models that are not correct. The objects and their relationships, the control flows, and the data flows will not seem quite right. Everything will probably not play well together. DeMarco (1978) expresses this concept best: "if you wait for a complete and perfect concept to germinate in your mind, you are likely to wait forever. Perfect ideas do not germinate, they evolve. So you put your lousy ideas down on paper, rout out its faults one by one, and gradually come up with a good product. There is a name for this careful improvement of a faulted concept into a desired result: It is called engineering."

1.1.3 Tools Used for Application Development

Figure 1.3 shows several tools that will be used throughout the OODP to build the electronic filing application. FrameMaker, a desktop publishing tool from Frame Technology Corporation, will be used throughout the development process to plan and document the work and to record the results. FrameMaker will also be used to develop the object model during the analysis, system design, and object design phases. Borlands' Application Frameworks, Digitalks' Smalltalk/V Windows class library, and Class Hierarchy Browsers will be used during object design and coding phases. Borlands' C++ Integrated Development Environment and Digitalks' Smalltalk/V Windows Environment will be used throughout the coding and testing phases. In addition, WindowBuilder by Object Share Systems Inc. and Protogen by Proto-View Development Company will be used to build the user interfaces in Smalltalk/V and the C++ languages, respectively.

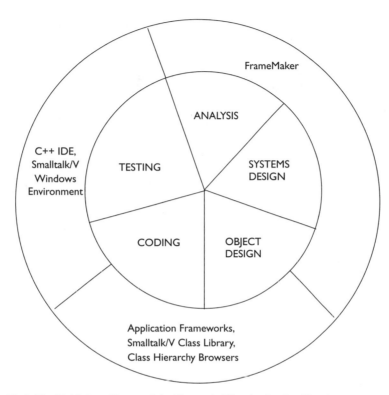

Figure 1.3. Tools Used in Various Phases of the Electronic Filing Application Development.

1.2 USING METRICS TO IMPROVE THE OODP OR PRODUCT

Metrics is a new field in software engineering that is not yet fully developed. A software metric enables you to measure some aspect of the development process or the product; i.e., metrics can be either product or process related. Process and product metrics may emerge from any or all phases of the OODP. There is much more experience in industry with process-related metrics (e.g., total development time, time spent in each phase of software development, number of faults found during code inspections, number of faults found during design reviews, cost for introducing new tools, time spent on inspections and/or walkthroughs, etc.) than product related metrics (e.g., number of classes, number of associations, number of scenarios, etc.) (Jacobson et al., 1992). Metrics can be directly measurable, such as lines of code, or can be computed, such as number of source statements per engineer per week (Grady and Caswell, 1987).

The use of metrics can lead to a better software-development process (Wiegers, 1994) and a better product (Jacobson et al., 1992). However, because metrics are not widely used today (Jacobson et al., 1992), we do not have much data on them, and therefore they have not been validated or calibrated. Due to these factors, no general agreement exists on what are really useful metrics. Jacobson recommends breaking this vicious cycle by starting to collect metrics and then refining the metrics as the software industry learns more about them. We will follow Jacobson's recommendation and collect data for specific process- and product-related metrics (see Appendix K). Ideally, the data from these metrics may be used over time to improve the OODP, the electronic filing application itself, or other products or applications that we develop.

Building the Electronic Filing Object Model

THE MAIN PURPOSE OF this book is to illustrate how an application may be developed using object-oriented technology, from analysis and design through coding and testing. Something to keep in mind while reading the book is that there is more than one solution to any problem. This book presents just one view. The design presented in the text is not the only possible design and may not be the best possible design.

Applying OOT requires a "paradigm shift" in our thinking. An effective way to make this paradigm shift is to learn from examples. The example used in this book, *electronic filing* or *document database,* was inspired by application development that I had done while working at Datapoint Corporation. *Electronic filing* is a problem that just about everybody should be able to understand because manual filing systems are probably part of every office environment in the world. The problem is also large enough to be meaningful to both students and practicing professionals, but not so large as to be unmanageable.

2.1 ELECTRONIC DOCUMENT PROCESSING

Electronic document processing refers to all the things that might be done to a document, e.g., creation, deletion, editing, storage, retrieval, tracking progress or workflow, version tracking, or archival. An electronic document-management system (EDMS) includes aspects of all of these features and more. An EDMS typically would enable a user to control and access documents and help company administrators manage documents in a distributed computing environment.

Many different components may be part of an electronic document management or processing system, such as:

❑ scanners

❑ storage devices

❑ printers

❑ monitors

❑ computers

❑ software

❑ networks

Scanners may be used to input documents and convert them to text using optical character-recognition software. Storage devices could be optical disks, magnetic disks, and/or optical jukeboxes. Monitors and printers are used to view or produce copies of documents. Computers are used to coordinate and control the processing of documents. In a distributed computing environment, an EDMS might consist of multiple server computers, linked via a network, for managing the processing of documents. Client computers or workstations would also be linked to the network and provide administrative and user access to the document-management system.

A variety of technologies can fall under the electronic document-management umbrella:

❑ text storage and retrieval

❑ image storage and retrieval

❑ workflow processing

❑ relational database management system

Some or all of these technologies can be developed into products themselves, or they can be combined in some form as an EDMS.

Text storage and retrieval software builds an index of an ASCII text document. The index may be based on attributes of the text document and/or of the content of the text document itself. Users can access those documents, or portions of a document, that they have an interest in by specifying some search criteria. The software then uses the search criteria and the indexes of documents it has built to locate the information that is of interest. The sophistication and performance of the search capability is dependent upon the extent and form of the index and the retrieval techniques used in the software.

Imaging technology transforms information in paper form, such as text, graphics, signatures, and drawings, into manageable electronic forms. Images are typically tagged with descriptions for future search and retrievals. Image storage and retrieval software may perform such functions as indexing, storage, image compression/decompression, retrieval, scaling, and editing.

Workflow-processing software automates the processing associated with documents. The company processes that guide the flow of documents through an organization are automated in software. These software systems support the routing of work in the organization.

Relational database management systems (RDBMS) have been used traditionally to manage structured information. The handling of unstructured information, such as text documents, is still not dealt with effectively in most cases. Some RDBMS vendors have implemented the concept of a Binary Large OBject (BLOB) to permit variable-length multimedia-type objects to be included as a field in a table. However, in many cases no index or search capability is provided by the vendor for a BLOB text field. The indexing and searching of this field is left to the application. However, an RDBMS would be useful for handling many other aspects of an EDMS, such as keywords, authors, versions, document types, document routes, etc.

2.1.1 The Domain of the Electronic Filing Problem

The electronic filing application in this text is not an EDMS. The electronic filing example described herein is a simple text storage and retrieval system. Text storage and retrieval is only one aspect of an EDMS. One approach to implementing an EDMS is to use a relational database that can handle unstructured information. This electronic filing application is *not* designed and implemented using relational database technology. The electronic filing application uses simple but efficient text storage and retrieval algorithms (see Knuth, 1993, for definitions).

The description of methods of putting documents into electronic form is outside the domain of this electronic filing problem. Documents could be scanned in and converted to text using optical character-recognition software, received via electronic mail, typed in, etc. Documents may be viewed using a text window—part of the applications user interface—that is a standard part of a graphical user interface toolkit. The use of commercial word processors or editors to create, edit, or view a document is also outside the domain of the electronic filing problem. This electronic filing application processes ASCII text files only. However, filters could be added to the program to enable it to store and retrieve any commercial off-the-shelf word-processing document.

2.1.2 What Is Electronic Filing?

The purpose of electronic filing is to solve the storage and retrieval problem of office automation information. Electronic filing is the technically enhanced storage and recall of data or information. It promotes the straightforward and accurate management of information, regardless of the recording medium. Filing costs are one of the biggest hidden costs in an office today: it can cost $20 to file a single paper document. Electronic filing programs/systems provide fast and accurate retrieval of information and promote lower costs.

Manual filing systems can be replaced with electronic filing systems by converting existing documents to and creating new documents in electronic form. The goal of electronic filing is to enable the storage and retrieval of documents in such a way that documents can be located quickly and easily.

Electronic filing is for anyone who has ever had problems finding a letter, a file, a research paper written years ago, personnel information, company rules and regulations, federal codes, or business contracts regarding a particular subject. Electronic filing is meant to solve such problems by providing timely access to information, which can be retrieved using a variety of techniques. For example, a document stored in an electronic filing system can be found by one or more of the following mechanisms to search for it: a particular word or phrase, multiple words or phrases, user-defined keywords, date range, description, author, document type, etc.

Some of the advantages of electronic filing include faster access to information, reduction in misfiling, reduction in amount of storage space required, portability of files, storage efficiency through shared access, geographic and time transparency for access, and limited dependence on human knowledge of filing techniques. Applications for electronic filing include word processing, electronic mail, publishing, archives, information management, medical libraries, bibliographic information, legal records, and any type of business that creates, uses, and processes a large number of documents. Electronic filing systems are available today on platforms ranging from PCs to Mainframes.

2.1.3 Brief Scenarios of Interaction for the Electronic Filing Problem

Some brief scenarios depicting how the electronic filing program would be used on a PC follow. The purpose of these scenarios is to give the reader who is unfamiliar with electronic filing systems an idea of how such a program is used to manage information. These scenarios assume that a user is using a PC in an environment where many documents must be managed, necessitating the use of an electronic filing application. Also, the user may electronically connect to many other users via the Internet or any other network.

1. User Creating a Document Using a Word Processor or Editor:
   - ❑ user invokes favorite editor or word processor
   - ❑ user enters the text of a document
   - ❑ user saves the document in ASCII format and quits editor/word processor
   - ❑ user invokes the electronic filing program
   - ❑ user files the document using the electronic filing program

2. User Looking for Any Documents Related to a Particular Subject:
   - ❑ user invokes the electronic filing program
   - ❑ user selects the search capability in the electronic filing program
   - ❑ user specifies some type of search request/criteria/query, such as find all documents that contain the word phrase, "object-oriented technology"
   - ❑ the electronic filing program presents the user with a list of file names (documents) that satisfy the search request, commonly known as a *search hit list* or *document name list*
   - ❑ user selects one of the file names and views the contents of the document
   - ❑ user selects another of the file names and views the contents of the document
   - ❑ user prints the document

3. User Filing an Electronic Mail Message:
   - ❑ user receives an electronic mail message and saves it
   - ❑ user invokes the electronic filing program
   - ❑ user files the message using the electronic filing program

The electronic filing application can be used in any scenario having electronic documents that need to be managed.

2.2 USING THE OBJECT MODELING TECHNIQUE

The OODP using the OMT (extracted from Figure 1.2) is shown in Figure 2.1. The highlighted portion of the diagram shows where we are now. Note that the OMT process itself does not address testing. However, testing is an integral part of the software development process and is included in the diagram for completeness.

The first step of the OMT is concerned with developing a correct model of the real-world problem so that it can be understood. This is analysis. The analysis model states what must be done and avoids implementation decisions. The analysis model consists of the object, dynamic, and functional models.

The analysis phase of the OMT process is concerned with developing a model of what the system will do. The OMT analysis process is shown in Figure 2.2. The first step in the analysis process is to build the object model (see highlighted area of Figure 2.2). The object model identifies the object classes in the system and their relationships, as well as their attributes and operations. It represents the static structure of the system. The static structure of the system is developed first because it is easier to understand than those aspects of the system concerned with changes to the objects and their relationships over time. Also, the static structure of the system is more stable, less vulnerable to change, and better grounded in reality.

However, before building something, the requirements must be understood. The problem statement is a statement of the requirements. It states what the application is supposed to do, but not how it is to be done. The problem statement might be generated by a client, but in many cases it will be generated by the developer working with the client to discover what is desired. The problem statement may be used as the basis for discovering what the initial object classes in a system may be.

The OMT identifies the following steps in constructing an object model:

1. Develop a problem statement.
2. Identify the object classes.
3. Discard unnecessary and incorrect classes.
4. Prepare a data dictionary.
5. Identify associations between object classes.
6. Discard unnecessary and incorrect associations.
7. Identify attributes of the object classes.
8. Discard unnecessary and incorrect attributes.
9. Use inheritance to share common structure.
10. Traverse access paths to identify deficiencies.

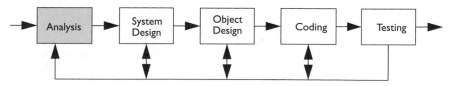

Figure 2.1. OMT Process and Testing.

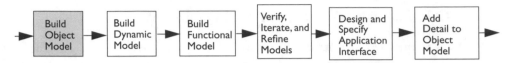

Figure 2.2. OMT Analysis Process.

We will follow these same steps to construct an object model of the electronic filing application.

The OMT approach previously used the phrase *object diagram* to refer to a diagram showing the classes in a system (Rumbaugh et. al, 1991). As of the June 1994 issue of the *Journal of Object-Oriented Programming,* Rumbaugh has decided to call this diagram a *class diagram,* which is consistent with the terminology used by other authors. An object diagram is a diagram that shows object instances—the same thing as an object instance diagram. An *object model* may consist of collections of both class diagrams and object diagrams. We will also use this new terminology throughout this text.

So let's begin applying the OMT to solving the electronic filing problem. Although the text goes through each of the OMT steps in building a solution to the problem, as you become more fluent in OMT you will often combine several steps and move back and forth between the steps until you achieve the desired result. However, as with any methodology, it is advisable to go through each of the steps for the first few projects until you develop a good understanding of how to apply the technique.

2.3 STATING THE PROBLEM

The following problem statement for an electronic filing program will be used throughout this book to demonstrate the author's application of the OMT to building a real-world application.

Problem Statement

An electronic filing program (EFP) can be used to store and retrieve text documents. Any document created by a word processor, editor, or other means may be stored in the electronic filing system. Documents may be filed along with keywords, authors, and/or a document description or abstract describing the document. Documents filed in the system may also be removed or deleted.

Documents stored using the EFP are indexed to enable rapid retrieval. Documents are retrievable according to convenient schemes not found in conventional classifications; e.g., users may retrieve or locate documents based on their content, description, author(s), or user-defined keywords. Therefore, the document description, authors, keywords, and/or the actual text document itself may be searched.

A user may specify search criteria, which results in a number of documents being found that meet the specified search criteria. The user may then continue to specify additional search criteria, successively narrowing down the search until the required documents are found. Documents found that meet the user's search criteria may then be viewed or printed.

The user is provided with the capability of specifying any extraneous or "junk" words, which if found in the content of the document will not be searched or indexed—for example, and, or, not, the, if. The user can also specify which alphanumeric characters in the text document will be indexed and searchable (the filing character set), thereby limiting the search and index to only portions of a document(s).

2.4 IDENTIFYING OBJECT CLASSES

Potential objects and classes are first identified in the application domain. Objects and classes may be physical or conceptual entities. Some object classes will be found in the problem statement, while others will be discovered in the application domain and by general knowledge.

Object classes will also be discovered during the design phase when we are figuring out how to implement the solution to this problem. For example, object classes will be discovered by studying class libraries in your computing environment to see which object classes will be appropriate for your implementation. However, that is something that we will postpone until later. Right now we are just interested in developing a real-world model of the problem.

2.4.1 Objects Found in the Problem Domain Using Grammatical Inspection

Using grammatical inspection or informal English description to identify potential object classes is a technique first proposed by Abbott (1983). Abbott proposed that an English description of the problem be written and that the noun/noun phrases be identified by underlining them. The nouns/noun phrases represent candidate objects/classes. This technique is not precise, due to the ambiguities of the English language and its dependence upon the writing skills of the author of the problem statement. However, it is a good way to get started. Besides, writing things down is a good way to discipline your thinking. If you can't express your ideas clearly in writing, then you probably have not thought them through well enough yet. An initial pass over the problem statement produces a list of potential object classes, which have been identified as noun/noun phrases:

Potential Object Classes

abstract	description	index	system
alphanumeric character	document	junk word	text document
author	document description	keyword	user
content	EFP	number of documents	user-defined keyword
convenient schemes	editor	portion of the document	word processor
conventional	electronic filing system	search	
classifications	filing character set	search criteria	

Some other techniques used to initially identify objects include scripting in *Object Behavior Analysis* (Goldberg and Rubin, 1992) and the use case model in *Object-Oriented Software Engineering* (Jacobson et al., 1992). These techniques stress the examination of system behavior as a means of identifying potential objects in the system.

2.4.2 Objects Discovered in the Problem Domain by General Knowledge

Additional classes that do not directly appear in the problem statement, but can be identified from our knowledge of the problem domain or are implied (referred to but not explicitly stated) in the problem statement, are *line, word,* and *page.* An experienced object-oriented analysis and design (OOA&D) person might discard the obvious nonsense object classes at this point. However, in the interest of making the process as clear as possible, I will discuss the rationale for discarding each unnecessary and incorrect object class according to the OMT criteria.

2.5 DISCARDING UNNECESSARY AND INCORRECT CLASSES

Potential object classes may be discarded because they are redundant, irrelevant, vague; are actually object attributes; are operations or implementation constructs; or because they reflect roles.

1. Redundant Classes: The guideline here is to keep the most descriptive object-class name for object classes that express the same information.

   Since the EFP only processes text documents, *document* and *text document* are redundant. *Text document* is retained because it is more descriptive. Also, *content* refers to the document itself and is redundant with *text document*. Therefore, the more descriptive object class, *text document*, will be retained.

   Filing character set and *alphanumeric characters* are redundant. *Filing character set* is retained because it is more descriptive and makes more sense in the application domain.

   Description, document description, and *abstract* are redundant. *Abstract* is retained because it is a document description and is a familiar term in business and academia, i.e., *abstract* represents the concept more clearly.

   User-defined keyword and *keyword* are redundant. *User-defined keyword* is an adjective-noun phrase. All keywords, documents, and authors must be specified by the user in the EFP. Therefore, *user-defined* is not relevant and *keyword* will be retained as the tentative object-class.

2. Irrelevant Classes: Classes that have little or nothing to do with the problem domain should be eliminated. In the context of this problem, *word processor* and *editor* are irrelevant. The creation of a document is outside the scope of the EFP software.

   Portion of the document and *number of documents* have nothing to do with the problem and will also be eliminated as potential object classes.

   User also has little or nothing to do with the problem. All systems (i.e., nonembedded) have users, and so later on we will need to create a user interface. *User* is eliminated as a potential object class.

3. Vague Classes: Classes should be specific, i.e., should not have ill-defined boundaries or be too broad in scope. *System* is too broad in scope. The *system* is really the EFP. *System* will be discarded as a potential object class.

   Conventional classifications and *convenient schemes* are also rather vague terms. They have ill-defined boundaries and are therefore dropped as potential object classes.

   EFP and *electronic filing system* are rather broad in scope. It is the application we are attempting to build, and not an object class in itself. The *EFP* or *electronic filing system* is a program of interacting objects. *EFP* and *electronic filing system* are therefore dropped as potential object classes.

4. Attributes: Attributes are properties of object classes and not object classes themselves. However, if the independent existence of a property is important, then make it a class and not an attribute. A search operation requires *search criteria* in order to perform the search, but beyond that *search criteria* does not affect the problem. So *search criteria* should be treated as an attribute of a search operation. *Search criteria* is discarded as a potential object class.

5. Operations: A name that is not manipulated in its own right and actually describes an operation that is applied to objects should be discarded as a potential object class. *Search* involves a sequence of actions to locate one or more documents satisfying some search criteria. *Search* is discarded as a potential object class.

6. Roles: The name of a class should not reflect a role it plays in an association. The name should reflect the fundamental nature of the class. No candidate object classes fall in this category.

7. Implementation Constructs: Anything that is not a part of the real-world problem domain but has to do with how the problem is solved should not be a part of the analysis model. *Filing character set* is also an implementation construct. The exact representation of the collection of filing characters is a design issue. *Filing character set* is renamed *filing character*.

A preliminary analysis yields the following candidate classes from the initial list of potential object classes:

Candidate Object Classes

abstract	keyword
author	line
filing character	page
index	text document
junk word	word

Our initial list of potential object classes has been narrowed down considerably. New object classes will emerge as we begin designing the system in more detail. Also, more object classes may be eliminated as we progress through the design and implementation of the EFP.

2.6 PREPARING THE DATA DICTIONARY

A data dictionary should be prepared for all modeling entities to clarify the role each entity plays in the system. The English language and isolated words can be subject to many interpretations. The data dictionary provides a place to collect information about an object class that is considered important and to clarify the meaning of the object class.

Any assumptions or restrictions on the use of the object class are also specified. Each modeling entity or object class would have an entry or specification in the data dictionary consisting of the following

- ❑ Name
- ❑ Description
- ❑ Assumptions or restrictions
- ❑ Associations
- ❑ Attributes
- ❑ Operations/Methods

The data dictionary entry for each object class will be expanded as we progress from analysis to design to include additional information pertinent to the actual implementation. Also, each entry will include more and more detail as our development progresses. The initial data dictionary for the classes in the electronic filing program is as follows:

Abstract—Brief statement of the essential thoughts of the document. The abstract may consist of several sentences describing what the specific document is all about.

Author—Name of the person who wrote or originated the document. More than one author may be associated with a document.

Filing character—An alphanumeric character that is recognized by the EFP. Some applications in which electronic filing is used may require that only specific characters or numbers be indexed and retrievable. Only electronic filing characters are indexed and retrievable.

Index—Each document is indexed in some manner to enable rapid retrieval of data. The indexing technique is not specified at this point in time.

Junk (or noise) word—A word that is common in the vocabulary of the language and is not of any value for retrieval purposes. Junk words are therefore not indexed. Examples of junk words are the following: and, the, or, if, is, are.

Keyword—A word that helps the user to uniquely identify a document. Multiple keywords may be associated with a document.

Line—Text documents are made up of lines of words. A document must have at least one line. Each line in a text document may contain zero or more words.

Page—A text document that is not an empty document is made up of one or more pages. Each page consists of one or more lines.

Text document—Document possibly created by an editor, word processor, desktop publishing tool, etc. A text document is divided into pages. A document must have one or more pages. A page may consist of multiple lines. Each line may consist of multiple words. A word consists of one or more letters.

Word—An alphabetic character or some meaningful combination of alphabetic characters that represents a unit of language.

2.7 ADDING ASSOCIATIONS BETWEEN CLASSES

Associations model relationships or dependencies between classes. Associations are bidirectional. However, the name of the association is what establishes the direction for traversal. An association may exist between two classes (binary), three classes (ternary), or more than three classes (higher order). However, the OMT approach indicates that in practice most associations are binary.

One way that programming languages may implement associations is as pointers from one object to another. In the Ada language, when classes are implemented via packages, the "with" clause denotes associations including the direction of the association. Various library classes, such as "set" or "dictionary" can also be used to implement associations. However, at this stage of development we want to preserve our design freedom by keeping any such mechanisms out of the analysis model; i.e., we are interested in only what the associations are and not in the form of their implementation.

2.7.1 Associations Found in the Problem Domain Using Grammatical Inspection

Associations can be identified in the problem statement in a manner similar to the way that potential object classes were identified using grammatical inspection. The verb/verb phrases in the problem statement represent potential associations between object classes. All of the potential associations are first extracted from the problem statement, and then we systematically discard unnecessary and incorrect associations using the OMT criteria.

The following list shows all of the potential associations, only some of which are identified directly from the problem statement. Note that the verb phrases in the problem statement may be explicit or implicit. Also, some associations may depend on our general knowledge of the problem domain and may not be stated in the problem statement. Associations that do not come directly from the problem statement should be verified with the user and the problem domain expert.

Explicit verb phrases:

Documents filed in system	EFP retrieves text documents
Documents filed with abstract	EFP stores text documents
Documents filed with author	User prints documents
Documents filed with keyword	User specifies indexable/searchable characters
Documents removed/deleted from system	User specifies junk words
Documents retrievable with convenient schemes	User specifies search criteria
Editor creates document	User views documents
EFP indexes documents	Word processor creates document

Implicit verb phrases:

Document referenced by index	Documents retrievable by keyword
Documents created external to EFP	Search criteria has abstract
Documents must be text only	Search criteria has author
Documents retrievable by abstract	Search criteria has keyword
Documents retrievable by author	Search criteria has word
Documents retrievable by content	

Knowledge of problem domain:

Abstract describes document

Documents contain pages

Keyword identifies document

Lines contain words

Pages contain lines

Text document identified by author

Words contain alphanumeric characters

2.8 DISCARDING UNNECESSARY AND INCORRECT ASSOCIATIONS

Some of the potential associations we have identified so far may be discarded because they are associations between eliminated classes or are irrelevant or implementation associations, actions, ternary associations, or derived associations (Rumbaugh et al., 1991).

1. Associations Between Eliminated Classes: A number of potential classes have been eliminated through our analysis. Any association stated in terms of one of these classes must also be eliminated or restated in terms of some other class.

    The *EFP* was eliminated as a potential object class because it is the program itself and represents a number of interacting objects. Therefore, we can eliminate *EFP stores text documents, EFP retrieves text documents, EFP indexes documents,* and *documents created external to EFP.*

    User was also eliminated as a potential object class. Therefore, *user specifies search criteria, user specifies indexable/searchable characters, user views documents, user prints documents,* and *user specifies junk words* are also discarded.

    Word processor and *editor* were discarded as irrelevant object classes since the creation of a document is outside the scope of the EFP software. *Word processor creates document* and *editor creates document* are eliminated as potential associations.

    System and *convenient schemes* were discarded as potential object classes because of their vagueness. The potential associations *documents filed in system, documents retrievable with convenient schemes,* and *documents removed/deleted from system* are eliminated.

    Content was discarded as a potential object class because it was redundant. Therefore, *documents retrievable by content* is eliminated as an association.

    Search criteria was discarded as a potential object class because it represented an attribute of the search operation. The associations *search criteria has author, search criteria has keyword, search criteria has word,* and *search criteria has abstract* are dropped as potential associations.

    Any associations specifying *document* are changed to *text document. Text document* was retained rather than *document* because it was more descriptive.

2. Irrelevant or Implementation Associations: Just like object classes, any associations dealing with implementation constructs or any associations that are outside the problem domain (i.e., irrelevant) are eliminated.

    Documents must be text only is eliminated because it is outside the domain of the problem. Documents are created by programs other than the EFP, such as editors, desktop publishing systems, or word processors. Documents that are not recognized as text will be rejected by the EFP.

3. Actions: Potential associations describing transient events are discarded. Only those associations that describe a permanent relationship between object classes or a structural property of the application domain should be retained.

   Documents filed with keyword, documents filed with author, documents filed with abstract, documents retrievable by abstract, documents retrievable by author, and *documents retrievable by keyword* describe interactions between the user and the EFP and not permanent relationships. They are all eliminated as potential associations.

   Index created from document also represents a transient event. A document is created from an index at one short moment in time. However, the document is always referenced by an index. *Document referenced by index* represents a more permanent relationship between object classes. *Index created from document* is also eliminated as a potential association.

4. Ternary Associations: Ternary associations are associations between three or more classes. No ternary associations have been identified in the electronic filing problem domain at this point in time.

5. Derived Associations: Derived associations are associations that are defined in terms of other associations. Derived associations don't add any new information to the problem domain but are useful in design. No derived associations have been identified for the EFP so far.

This preliminary analysis yields the candidate associations shown in the following list. Note that a number of these associations actually represent aggregation. Aggregation is a special form of association with some additional semantics.

Abstract describes document	Lines contain words
Documents contain pages	Pages contain lines
Document referenced by index	Text document identified by author
Keyword identifies document	Words contain alphanumeric characters

Our initial list of potential associations has been narrowed down considerably, just as our potential list of object classes was narrowed down by analyzing each item against a set of heuristics to see if it met the criteria. New associations will emerge as we begin designing the system in more detail, while more associations may be eliminated.

An initial object diagram showing the selected candidate object classes and their associations is shown in Figure 2.3 (see Rumbaugh et al., 1991, for description of notation used in object, dynamic, and functional models). Multiplicity is used in this model to denote how many instances of one class may relate to each instance of another class. At this stage of our development we do not have to be precise in our definitions of multiplicity in the model. However, any obvious multiplicity should be included now. As we progress from analysis to design to coding, the multiplicity specification will become increasingly important. Overestimating our multiplicity requirements will lead to extra code and complexity. Underestimating our multiplicity requirements will restrict our flexibility and our program's extensibility.

Note that a new object class—*alphanumeric character*—was discovered while analyzing potential associations between object classes. *Alphanumeric character* was previously discarded as a potential object class in favor of *filing character*. *Alphanumeric character* now seems more relevant in light of the discovery of other new object classes and associations. The following entry is added to the data dictionary as a result of this discovery.

> Alphanumeric character—An alphabetic or numeric character.

The discovery of new object classes also means the discovery of new associations, since associations are relationships among object classes. An object class that does not have a relationship with any other object class in the object model is possibly named inappropriately or is not part of the problem domain.

The new association identified by the addition of the *alphanumeric character* object class is *word contains alphanumeric character*. Associations that were missed during the initial analysis are *abstract contains lines*, *line contains junk words*, and *index references text document*. A revised list of candidate associations including these newly discovered associations is shown in the following list. These associations are included in the initial class diagram shown in Figure 2.3.

Abstract contains lines	Lines contain words
Abstract describes document	Pages contain lines
Document referenced by index	Phrase contains words
Documents contain pages	Text document identified by author
Index references text document	Word contains alphanumeric character
Keyword identifies document	Words contain alphanumeric characters
Line contains junk words	

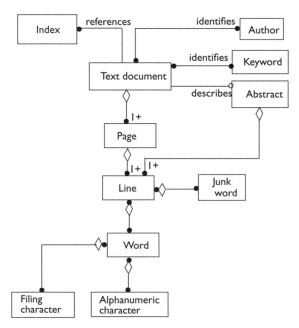

Figure 2.3. Initial Electronic Filing Class Diagram.

2.9 ADDING ATTRIBUTES FOR OBJECTS AND LINKS

Attributes are data values that are held by the objects in a class. Each attribute has a name that is unique within a class. Attributes define the state of an object. Look for nouns followed by possessive phrases (e.g., the length of the bridge, the width of the road, the voltage of the computer, the number of characters in the document) in the problem statement to identify attributes. Attributes are usually found more easily by drawing on your knowledge of the application domain and the real world. The following table lists the potential attributes and their objects for the EFP.

Potential Attribute (Based on knowledge of application domain)	**Object**
Author name	Author
Character	Filing character
Character	Alphanumeric character
Date created	Text document
Document description	Abstract
Document file name	Text document
Document size	Text document
Index file name	Index
Index size	Index
Keyword name	Keyword
Line number	Line
Number of characters	Word
Page number	Page
String	Word
Word	Junk word

Many attributes do not stand out at this point in our modeling. Additional attributes will become obvious as we progress through our analysis and design. Both the dynamic and functional models will help to identify additional attributes for our object classes. At this point we are trying to avoid including those attributes that are solely for implementation.

2.10 DISCARDING UNNECESSARY AND INCORRECT ATTRIBUTES

We now go through the list of potential attributes applying some heuristics to determine which of them will become candidate attributes. The following criteria are used to discard unnecessary and incorrect attributes (Rumbaugh et al., 1991).

1. Objects: Entities that have features of their own in the electronic filing program are objects and not attributes. Attributes are pure data values and do not have identity. If the independent existence of the entity is important, then it is not an attribute, it is an object.

   No objects disguising themselves as attributes have been identified in the electronic filing problem domain at this point in time.

2. Qualifiers: A qualifier is a special attribute whose value depends on a particular context. Any attributes that appear to be qualifiers should be restated as such.

    Author name, keyword name, and *index file name* qualify the associations *author identifies text document, keyword identifies text document,* and *index references text document,* respectively. *Author name, keyword name,* and *index file name* are changed to qualifiers. Note that the use of these qualifiers reduces the effective multiplicity of the specified associations.

3. Names: When names do not depend on context and may be duplicated, then they are likely to be attributes. However, names should generally be modeled as qualifiers. *Document file name* may be duplicated and is therefore left as an attribute.

4. Identifiers: Object identifiers that are generated by object-oriented programming languages should not be listed as attributes.

    We have only identified attributes that exist in the application domain, so no attributes meet this criterion.

5. Link Attributes: Link attributes should not be specified as object attributes. If an attribute depends on the presence of the link, then it is a link attribute and not an object attribute. Link attributes and object attributes are modeled differently. However, the implementation of the link attribute depends on the multiplicity.

    No link attributes masquerading as object attributes are found in our list of potential attributes.

6. Internal Values: Attributes that describe the internal state of an object and are invisible outside the object should not be part of the object model during analysis. Postpone this level of detail until design.

    Size of the index object and *size* of the text document object fall in this category. They are both eliminated from our analysis model but are added to the data dictionary so that they may be incorporated later into our object design model. The data dictionary may act as our design folder, holding information pertinent to the design of specific objects that is not relevant at this point in time.

    Number of characters in the word object is also an attribute that describes the internal state of the object (may be used by private methods to perform various operations on a word) and is not visible outside of the object—at least at this point in time. *Number of characters* may be derived from the *string* attribute in the word object. *Number of characters* is eliminated from the analysis model.

7. Fine Detail: Minor attributes that don't affect most operations for the object class should be omitted at this point in time.

    No attributes are found matching this criterion.

8. Discordant Attributes: Classes should be cohesive. The attributes and methods should be highly cohesive and should not have extra or unused attributes or methods. An attribute that seems unrelated to other attributes in the same class may be out of place and should be in a different class.

    No attributes are found matching this criterion.

A revised list of candidate attributes and their objects is shown in the following table. Several attributes have been eliminated from our initial list of potential attributes.

Candidate Attribute	Object
Character	ASCII character
Date created	Text document
Document description	Abstract
Document file name	Text document
String	Word
Word	Junk word

2.11 USE INHERITANCE TO SHARE COMMON STRUCTURE

The OMT refers to inheritance as the mechanism of sharing attributes and operations using the generalization relationship. Generalization is the relationship among classes. We can refine our object model to capitalize on inheritance by taking a bottom-up or a top-down approach. In the class diagram shown in Figure 2.3, one top-down specialization is apparent from the application domain. Each word is shown to consist of filing characters and alphanumeric characters. This is a mistake because filing characters will most likely be alphanumeric characters. Therefore, a word should actually consist of filing and nonfiling characters. *Filing character* and *nonfiling character* are both noun phrases with adjectives on a class name. Both filing and nonfiling characters are ASCII characters.

Therefore, a more appropriate representation is to show a word consisting of many ASCII characters. A filing character is an ASCII character, and a nonfiling character is an ASCII character. However, showing *filing character* and *nonfiling character* as subclasses of ASCII character would be trivial inheritance. The *filing character* and *nonfiling character* subclasses would not have distinctive attributes, associations, or behavior. We choose the representation to show ASCII character as having an attribute, *character*, which is of the type filing or nonfiling. The class diagram in Figure 2.4 reflects these changes.

2.12 TRAVERSING ACCESS PATHS TO IDENTIFY DEFICIENCIES

Figure 2.4 shows the EFP class diagram with attributes and associations identified to date. (Note that changes to the previous class diagram are shown in italics in the current class diagram to enable the reader to quickly identify differences between the diagrams. This highlighting of differences will be followed throughout the text for all class diagrams.) The model should now be tested by tracing access paths through the object model to see if they yield sensible results. White (1994) refers to this as validating the model, i.e., checking to see if the object classes, attributes, operations, and associations are sufficient to implement a system that satisfies the problem statement. We are basically validating the model by picking one or more use cases/scenarios and by tracing access paths through the object model to see if anything is missing.

The approach taken here is to think of tasks you would like to accomplish and then see if you achieve the results that you would expect. The objective is to make sure that the model can handle all of the situations that you expect it to. If not, then probably something is amiss in the model. There should be ways to pick out unique values that you expect; i.e., the access paths should exist and one out of a multitude of values should be selectable.

Some of the tasks that I believe the EFP object model should accomplish are the following:

1. Name all of the documents that have been indexed by this program.

2. Given an author name, find all of the documents written by this author.

3. Given a keyword, find all of the documents identified by this keyword.

4. Given a word, find all of the documents identified by this word.

5. Given an author name, keyword, and word, find all of the documents identified by these queries.

6. Given a date range, find all of the documents created within this date range.

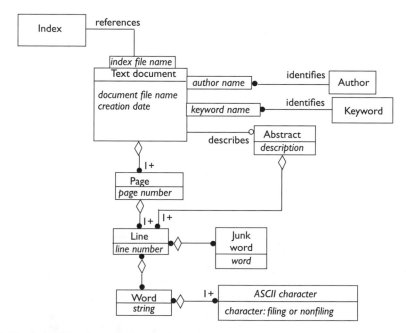

Figure 2.4. Electronic Filing Class Diagram with Attributes.

Most of these tasks involve a search criterion or query to retrieve documents (search use case/ scenario), with the exception of the first task. We will augment text explanation with pseudocode to try to accomplish these tasks. Pseudocode bridges the gap between the native English language and computer languages. It is an intermediate notation that we can use to express program logic without having to be concerned with the syntax details of the computer language. A pseudocode-like notation is described in Blaha (1994) and in the solutions manual to Rumbaugh et al. (1991) for navigating object models.

1. **Problem:** Find all documents indexed by this program.

   Solution: This is not possible to solve because there is no information in the object model about the indexes or text document objects in the system.

   The class diagram should be modified to have a *filing directory* object class, which has zero or more *index* object classes. A qualifier, *index file name*, may be used to reduce the effective multiplicity of the association. Then the *filing directory* object class plus an *index file name* yields an index. Without the qualifier, a text document would reference *many* index objects. Text documents themselves may be located anywhere. The revised class diagram incorporating this enhancement is shown in Figure 2.5.

   All solutions or responses to the subsequent questions will be based on the revised class diagram shown in this figure.

Explanation of Object Model

A filing directory and an index file name uniquely identify an index. An index or index file refers to or represents a text document that has been filed in the system. If no documents have been filed in the system, then no index files will exist. An index file must exist if a text document has been filed in the system. Each index file refers to one and only one text document. The index file is an index into the content of the text document.

Zero or more authors may have been specified when filing the document into the system. An author may identify one or more text documents.

Zero or more keywords may also have been specified when filing a document into the system. A keyword may identify one or more text documents.

An abstract containing the essential thoughts of the document may also have been specified when filing the document into the system. Either one or no abstract may be associated with a specific document.

Each document contains one or more pages. A page must contain one or more lines. A line consists of zero or more words. Therefore, a document may be a single page with one empty line. The document abstract must also contain one or more lines. However, just as in a document, a line may consist of zero or more words. Therefore, the abstract may contain one line that has no words in it.

A line may contain zero or more junk words or nonjunk words. Junk words are not processed by the system; i.e., they are neither indexed nor may they be used to reference a document. A junk word may be a part of zero or more lines. Nonjunk words that are part of a document are indexed and may be used to identify a specific document. Each word consists of one or more ASCII characters. Each ASCII character may be either a filing or a nonfiling character. An ASCII character may be part of more than one word.

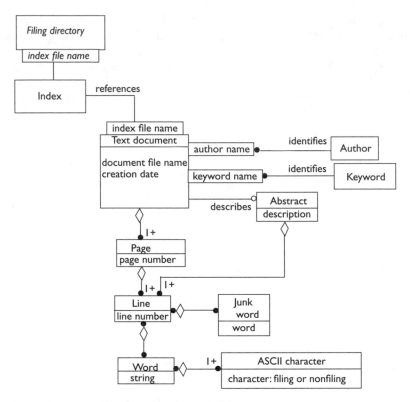

Figure 2.5. Revised Electronic Filing Class Diagram with Enhancements.

2. **Problem:** Given an author name, find all of the documents written by this author.

Solution: The pseudo-variable **self** used here refers to the receiver object of the message that invokes the method. Key pseudocode words, including **self**, are indicated by boldface print.

Each document index in the filing directory will be examined to find all of the documents identified by the given author. An index refers to a specific text document. A text document may then be identified by zero or more authors. All of the authors that identify a specific text document are checked against the given author_name. If the author_name is associated with the specific text document, then the name of the text document is added to the set of documents returned as part of the query.

```
Filing_directory::retrieve_authored_documents (author) returns set of
documents
   documents:= create_empty_set;
   /* check each index */
   for each index in self.index
     /* compare the given author with each author associated with this
document and index */
```

```
for each author in self.index.text_document.author
  if author = self.index.text_document.author then
    add self.index.text_document to set documents;
  end if
end for each author
end for each index
return documents;
```

3. **Problem:** Given a keyword, find all of the documents identified by this keyword.

   Solution: Each document index in the filing directory will be examined to find all of the documents identified by the given keyword. An index refers to a specific text document. A text document may then be identified by zero or more keywords. All of the keywords that identify a specific text document are checked against the given keyword. If the given keyword is associated with the specific text document, then the name of the text document is added to the set of documents returned as part of the query.

```
Filing_directory::retrieve_keyworded_documents (keyword) returns set of
documents
  documents:= create_empty_set;
  /* check each index */
  for each index in self.index
    /* compare the given keyword with each keyword associated with this
document and index */
    for each keyword in self.index.text_document.keyword
      if keyword = self.index.text_document.keyword then
        add self.index.text_document to set documents;
      end if
    end for each keyword
  end for each index
  return documents;
```

4. **Problem:** Given a word, find all of the documents containing this word.

   Solution: Each document index in the filing directory will be examined to find all of the documents containing the given word. An index refers to a specific text document. A text document may contain zero or more occurrences of the given word. The mechanism by which a document index refers to each word contained within the text document has not yet been specified. How the actual indexing will work is a design issue. At this point we are interested in showing that a check will be made to determine if a given word is in the index of a text document. If the given word is part of the index of a text document, then the name of the text document is added to the set of documents that is returned as part of the query.

```
Filing_directory::retrieve_worded_documents (word) returns set of
documents
  documents:= create_empty_set;
  /* check each index */
  for each index in self.index
    /* check if this word is in the document index */
    if word is in self.index then
```

```
          add self.index.text_document to set documents;
      end if
  end for each
```

5. Problem: Given an author name, keyword, and word, find all of the documents identified by these queries. We will assume that each specified search criterion is connected by a logical AND.

Solution: Each document index in the filing directory will be examined to find all of the documents identified by the given author AND given keyword AND given word. If a text document is identified by the given author AND given keyword, then the index will be checked to see if it contains the given word. If all of these conditions are satisfied, then the name of the text document is added to the set of documents that is returned as part of the query.

```
Filing_directory::retrieve_documents (author, keyword, word) returns set
of documents
   documents:= create_empty_set;
   /* check each index */
   for each index in self.index
   /* compare this author with each author associated with this document
      and index */
      for each author in self.index.text_document.author
         if author = self.index.text_document.author then
              /* compare this keyword with each keyword associated with this
                 document and index */
            for each keyword in self.index.text_document.keyword
              if keyword = self.index.text_document.keyword then
                 /* check if this word is in the document index */
                 /* save document information if search criteria met */
                 if word is in self.index then
                    add self.index.text_document to set documents;
                 end if
              end if
            end for each
         end if
      end for each
   end for each
   return documents;
```

6. Problem: Given a date range, find all of the documents created within this date range.

Solution: Each document index in the filing directory will be examined to find all of the documents that have a creation date within the given date_range. A text document has one and only one creation date. The creation date of each text document is examined to determine if it falls within the given date range. If the creation date is within the given date range, then the name of the text document is added to the set of documents returned as part of the query.

```
Filing_directory::retrieve_documents_in_date_range (date_range) returns
set of documents
   documents:= create_empty_set;
   /* check each indexed document */
   for each index in self.index
```

```
/* compare the specified date_range with the creation_date of each
   document */
   if self.index.text_document.creation_date is within date_range then
           add self.index.text_document to set documents;
   end if
 end for each
return documents;
```

Our traversal of the object model to answer some basic questions has identified several deficiencies in our model. This points out the fact that object models are rarely correct after the first pass. The object-oriented development process is one of continual iteration. As we find a deficiency in our modeling, we will go back and make the necessary changes to reflect any updates—so that the model we are working from will always represent our latest thoughts. Additional refinements to our object model can also be expected after the dynamic and functional models are completed.

2.13 SUMMARY OF PROCESS AND DELIVERABLES

The first step in the analysis process of Figure 2.2 has now been completed—developing an object model. The deliverables for this phase of analysis are

- ❑ the object model (class diagrams and object diagrams)
- ❑ the problem statement
- ❑ the initial data dictionary

These deliverables will be part of the analysis document that will be captured in our reuse database of OMT specifications. All of the deliverables required to develop an object model will be contained within the analysis document. No OMT specifications from the same or similar problem domains were available to examine for reuse.

Our process for producing these deliverables was to follow the steps identified by the OMT in constructing an object model, i.e., identifying object classes, preparing a data dictionary, identifying associations between objects, identifying attributes of objects, and verifying access paths. We have used domain expert input from the author, general knowledge of the problem domain, a problem statement that we developed, and customer interactions with the author acting as the customer.

The next step in the object-oriented development process is to develop the dynamic model for the problem if the time-dependent behavior of objects in the system is nontrivial.

CHAPTER 3

Developing a Dynamic
Model for Electronic Filing

"THE DYNAMIC MODEL shows the time-dependent behavior of the system and the objects in it" (Rumbaugh et al., 1991). The dynamic model is more important for some types of system architecture than for others; e.g., the dynamic model is important for interactive and real-time systems but is insignificant for a batch-transformation type of system. The dynamic model is concerned with changes to objects and their relationships over time. It shows possible control flows through the application, while the object model shows possible information flows. The dynamic model is crucial in applications in which collecting input from user interactions, sensors, other applications, etc. is a major task in the system.

The electronic filing program will have an interactive interface, and interactive interfaces are dominated by the dynamic model. The dynamic model is used to define the protocol of the user interaction. However, the dynamic model is simple for the development of the EFP. As we will see later, the search and file operations require significant computation. Therefore, the functional model is relevant to the algorithm for indexing and retrieving documents.

Figure 3.1 shows where we are in the analysis process so far (see the highlighted area)—building the dynamic model. We will go through the following steps to build the dynamic model:

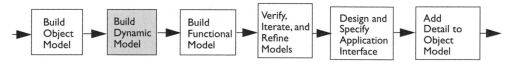

Figure 3.1. OMT Analysis Process.

1. Identify use cases and prepare scenarios of typical interaction sequences.
2. Identify events between objects and prepare an event trace diagram for each scenario.
3. Prepare an event flow diagram for the system.
4. Develop state diagrams for classes with important dynamic behavior.
5. Check for completeness and consistency of events.

3.1 IDENTIFYING USE CASES AND PREPARING SCENARIOS OF TYPICAL INTERACTION SEQUENCES

The first step in building a dynamic model is to construct normal scenarios of interactions between the system and entities outside of the systems boundaries (such as an end user, database administrator, computer operator, another computer system application, or other entity needing to exchange information with the system). Jacobson et al. (1992) refer to these entities outside of the systems boundaries as "actors." They also refer to these sequences of interactions between actors and the system as "use cases." A use case may consist of many scenarios of interactions between actors and the system. The OMT also refers to actors in the context of both data flow diagrams and the dynamic model (Rumbaugh et al., 1991). We will use the term "actor" also.

A scenario is just a sequence of events. An event represents an incident that causes an object to change state, e.g., an object exchanging information with another object, sensor, user, etc. An event occurs any time information comes into the system or goes out from the system.

A scenario represents a sequence of related transactions between an actor and the system itself in the form of a dialogue. However, a scenario may also include interactions among internal objects that are part of the system/program in addition to actors. The scenarios we develop depict how we expect the system to be used. They will also be used later in the development process as test cases to make sure that the system functions as intended.

The next step is to prepare abnormal scenarios, or scenarios with exceptions. Scenarios with exceptions include error conditions, incorrect inputs by the user, omitted inputs (or no responses) where time-outs will occur, data values outside the range of valid values, etc. These types of condition always occur in the real world and are generally the most difficult part of the application to deal with.

The major actor in the context of the electronic filing program is the user. No physical devices (other than the parts of the computer system itself) or other computer applications are involved. Our scenarios will therefore be based on interactions between the user and the EFP.

A use case is a description for a set of scenarios (see Jacobson, 1992 or 1995, for more information on use cases). Rumbaugh (1994b) notes that in order to really understand what a system/application does, you must be able to enumerate all of its use cases. The use cases partition the functionality of the problem. A set of use cases for electronic filing has been identified based on our general knowledge of the problem domain and discussions with end users. The use cases are

1. filing a document
2. searching for, or finding, a document(s)
3. deleting a document

4. changing the filing character set
5. changing the junk words

Multiple scenarios, a normal scenario, and scenario with exceptions will be developed for each use case. During analysis we don't care if the program will use pop-up menus or a dumb CRT. All we care about during analysis is the information being exchanged. During design we will worry about *how* the information is presented to the user. However, an illustration of an interaction format for each use case will be presented to ensure that no important information is left out of the dynamic model.

3.1.1 Filing a Document

Scenario 1 shows a normal scenario for filing a document, while Scenario 2 shows a filing scenario with exceptions. These are only examples of normal and exception scenarios. Other permutations and combinations of events are possible. The information specified includes the directory and the name of the existing document file. Some possible scenarios include the user just filing the document at this point in time, canceling the filing operation, or requesting help information. The user may also continue with the file operation and enter document reference information. Document reference information consists of an abstract/description, author(s), and/or keyword(s) associated with the document. However, document reference information is not required to file a document in the system.

The scenarios developed for the dynamic model are just sequences of events among internal objects and actors. Each event in a scenario is either an English language sentence or an abbreviated form of a sentence. However, the events need only be described in terms of a verb and a noun. The verb must imply some type of action that is taken.

The events listed in the scenario are ordered from top to bottom. The event shown at the top of a scenario is performed first, and the event listed at the bottom of the scenario is performed last.

Scenario 1. Normal Scenario for Filing a Document.

> The user wishes to file a document.
> The user specifies a directory and a document file.
> The user enters an abstract of the document, keywords, and/or authors.
> The user requests the document to be filed.
> The document is filed.

A possible format for the *filing a document* use case is shown in Figures 3.2 and 3.3. The exact details are not important. What is important is the information that is exchanged, not the specific widgets in the interface. The information exchange shown in the scenarios is consistent with the information available in the interaction formats.

Scenario 2. Filing Scenario with Exceptions.

> The user wishes to file a document.
> The user specifies a directory.
> The user requests the document to be filed.
> The EFP displays an error message and asks the user to specify both a directory
> and file name for the document.
> The user cancels the operation.

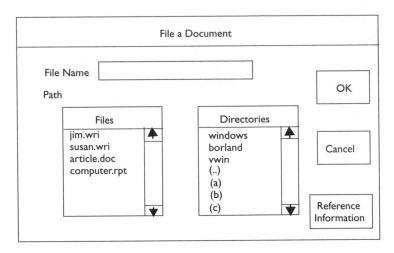

Figure 3.2. Filing a Document Format.

3.1.2 Searching for a Document

A user may retrieve one or more documents based on specific search criteria, which may consist of one or more words or phrases (content query and/or abstract query), authors (author query), and/or keywords (keyword query) associated with the document, as noted in the problem statement. The search may result in a list of document names returned that were found to meet the search criteria. A user may then view or print a document found as the result of a search.

Scenario 3 shows an example of a normal scenario for a single search of a document. Scenario 4 shows an example of a single search scenario with exceptions.

Scenario 3. Normal Scenario Requiring a Single Search for a Document.

    The user wishes to search for a document(s) meeting some specific criteria.
    The user enters an abstract query for an abstract search, a word or phrase for a content search, one or more keywords for a keyword search, and/or one or more authors for an author search.
    The user requests the search to start.
    The EFP returns the names of the documents satisfying the search criteria.
    The user selects a document.
    The user views a document satisfying the search criteria.
    The user ends the request for a search operation.

Scenario 4. Search Scenario with Exceptions.

    The user wishes to search for a document(s) meeting some specific criteria.
    The user requests the search to start.
    A message box is displayed showing an error message and asking the user to enter abstract, content, keyword, and/or author information as a query.
    The user ends the request for a search operation.

```
┌─────────────────────────────────────────────────────────────────┐
│                  Document Reference Information                   │
│                                                                   │
│     Document Name                                                 │
│     Abstract:        _____ │
│                                                                   │
│     Keywords:        _____ │
│                                                                   │
│     Authors:         _____ │
│                                                                   │
│                  ┌──────────┐        ┌──────────┐                 │
│                  │    OK    │        │  Cancel  │                 │
│                  └──────────┘        └──────────┘                 │
└─────────────────────────────────────────────────────────────────┘
```

Figure 3.3. Document Reference Information Format for Filing a Document.

As stated in the problem statement, "a user may specify search criteria, which results in a number of documents being found that meet the specified search criteria. The user may then continue to specify additional search criteria, successively narrowing down the search until the required documents are found. Documents found that meet the user's search criteria may then be viewed or printed." Scenario 5 is a normal scenario depicting how a user might continue narrowing down a search by specifying additional search criteria with each successive search, until the required document is found. The EFP remembers the results of previous searches (i.e., the names of the documents that matched the search criteria) and uses these results in subsequent searches. When a user cancels or ends a search, the results of previous searches are discarded. These are only examples of normal and exception scenarios. Other permutations and combinations of events are possible.

Scenario 5. Normal Scenario Requiring Multiple Searches for a Document.

> The user wishes to search for a document(s) meeting some specific criteria.
> The user enters one or more keywords for a keyword search.
> The user requests the search to start.
> The EFP returns the names of the documents satisfying the search criteria.
> The user selects a document.
> The user views a document satisfying the search criteria.
> The user enters additional keywords to narrow down the search.
> The user requests the search to start.
> The EFP returns the names of the documents satisfying the search criteria.
> The user selects a document.
> The user views a document satisfying the search criteria.
> The user ends the request for a search operation.

Possible interaction formats for searching for a document are shown in Figures 3.4 and 3.5. The information exchange shown in the scenarios is consistent with the information available in interaction format. The search results information is necessary in order to be able to examine a document that is found as a result of a user-specified query.

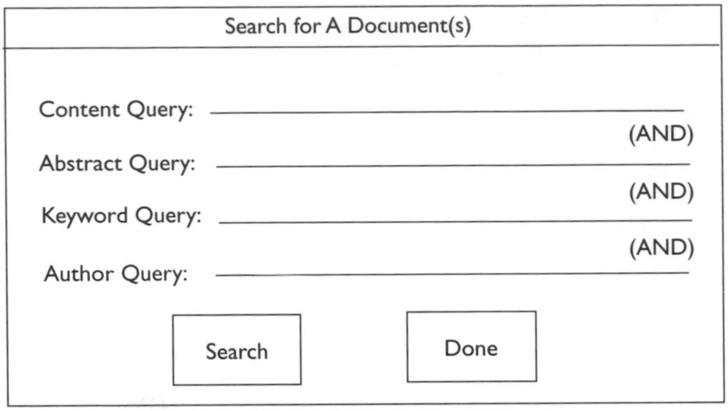

Figure 3.4. Searching for Document(s) Format.

3.1.3 Viewing a Document

Only documents that have been retrieved from a search may be viewed by the EFP. Scenario 3 shows an example of a normal scenario for viewing a document found from a search. Scenario 6 shows an example of a viewing scenario with exceptions.

Scenario 6. Viewing Scenario with Exceptions.

> The user wishes to search for a document(s) meeting some specific criteria.
> The user enters an abstract query for an abstract search, a word or phrase for a content search,
>   one or more keywords for a keyword search, and/or one or more authors for an author search.
> The user requests the search to start.
> The EFP returns the names of the documents satisfying the search criteria.
> The user tries to view a document satisfying the search criteria.
> An error message is displayed indicating that a document must first be selected.
> The user ends the request for a search operation.

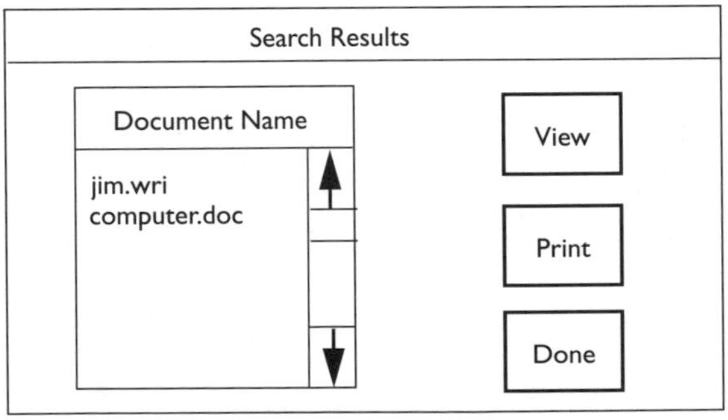

Figure 3.5. Search Results Format.

3.1.4 Deleting a Document

Only documents that have been filed by the EFP may be deleted. The EFP deletes only the index for the document and not the document itself. Scenario 7 shows an example of a normal scenario for deleting a document filed by the electronic filing program. Scenario 8 shows an example of a delete scenario with exceptions.

Scenario 7. Normal Scenario for Deleting a Document.

> The user wishes to delete a document.
> The user specifies a document.
> The user requests the document to be deleted.
> The document index is deleted.

Scenario 8. Delete Scenario with Exceptions.

> The user wishes to delete a document.
> The user requests the document to be deleted.
> An error message is displayed requesting the user to specify a document.
> The user cancels the operation.

A possible interaction format for deleting a document is shown in Figure 3.6. The information exchange shown in the scenarios is consistent with the information available in interaction format.

3.1.5 Printing a Document

A user may also only print a document that has been retrieved as part of a search. Scenarios 3 and 5 may be used to print a document by simply replacing "views" with "prints."

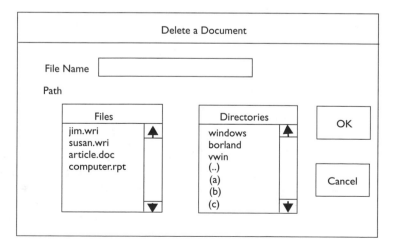

Figure 3.6. Delete a Document Format.

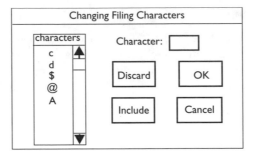

Figure 3.7. Filing Character Format.

3.1.6 Changing the Character Set

As stated in the problem statement, "the user can also specify which alphanumeric characters will be indexed and searchable, thereby limiting the search and index to only portions of a document(s)." Therefore, the user should have the ability to include or discard a filing character used by the electronic filing application. Scenario 9 shows an example of a normal scenario for changing the character set for the EFP. Scenario 10 shows an example of a character set scenario with exceptions.

Scenario 9. Normal Scenario for Changing the Character Set.

> The user wishes to add a character to the filing character set.
> The user specifies a character to include in the filing character set.
> The user requests the character to be included.
> The character is included in the character set.

Scenario 10. Character Set Scenario with Exceptions.

> The user wishes to add a character to the filing character set.
> The user specifies a character to include in the filing character set.
> The user cancels the operation.

A possible interaction format for including/discarding filing characters available for filing and searching for a document is shown in Figure 3.7. The information exchange shown in the scenarios is consistent with the information available in interaction format.

3.1.7 Changing the Junk Words

As stated in the problem statement, "the user is provided with the capability of specifying any 'junk' words, which will not be searched or indexed—for example, and, or, not, the, if." Therefore, the user should have the ability to add or delete a junk word used by the electronic filing application. Eliminating junk words as indexable words in documents reduces the size of the document index and may improve the performance of a search. Scenario 11 shows an example of a normal scenario for changing the junk words in the EFP. Scenario 12 shows an example of a junk word scenario with exceptions.

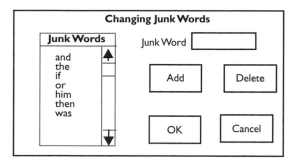

Figure 3.8. Junk Word Format.

Scenario 11. Normal Scenario for Changing Junk Words.

> The user wishes to add a new junk word to the program's set of junk words.
> The user enters a junk word.
> The user requests the word to be added to the junk words.
> The word is added to the junk word set.

Scenario 12. Junk Word Scenario with Exceptions.

> The user wishes to add a new junk word to the program's set of junk words.
> The user enters a junk word.
> The user cancels the operation.

A possible interaction format for adding/deleting junk words available for filing and searching for a document is shown in Figure 3.8. The information exchange shown in the scenarios is consistent with the information available in interaction format.

3.2 IDENTIFYING EVENTS BETWEEN OBJECTS AND PREPARING AN EVENT TRACE FOR EACH SCENARIO

The next step in developing the dynamic model is to identify events between objects and to prepare an event trace for each scenario. The events that may occur in electronic filing include inputs, decisions, or actions from users. An object that transmits information to another object is also an event.

Event traces will be developed for filing, searching for, viewing, deleting, and printing a document and for changing character set and junk words (see Fig. 3.9). The objective here is to show the interactions that take place between various objects in the system for each scenario. Only event traces for normal scenarios will be developed here. Event traces for scenarios with exceptions are variations of the normal scenarios and will be taken into account when we do detailed state diagrams during the design of the user interface.

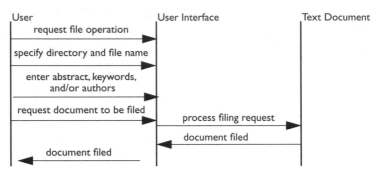

Figure 3.9. Event Trace for Filing a Document.

Each scenario is shown as an event trace. Event traces are constructed by:

1. identifying events in scenarios
2. identifying the actor/object that sends an event
3. identifying the actor/object that receives an event

The event trace is an ordered list of events between different objects for each scenario. The actors and/or objects that send and receive events are shown as columns (i.e., vertical lines) in the event trace diagram. By examining each column you can easily see what events are both received and sent by an object/actor. An event being received by or coming into an object/actor is shown as a horizontal arrow pointing to the vertical line representing the object/actor. An event being sent by or going out of an object/actor is shown as a horizontal arrow pointing to some other vertical line

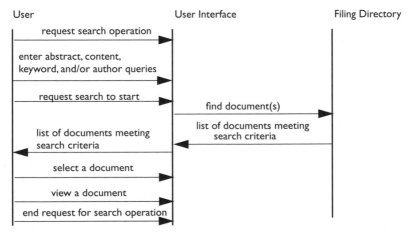

Figure 3.10. Event Trace for Searching for a Document.

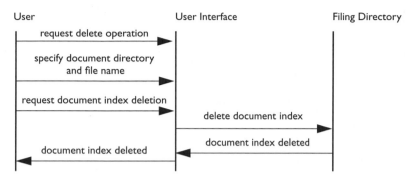

Figure 3.11. Event Trace for Deleting a Document.

representing another object/actor. An event trace might have several objects/actors participating in a scenario, which will be shown as several vertical lines each labeled with the name of an object/actor. Time increases from top to bottom in the event trace diagram.

The interactive interface of the electronic filing program is dominated by the dynamic model. Since multiple application functions are invoked from the user interface, the user interface will be represented as a single object that is part of the system in our event trace diagrams. The intent here is *not* to trivialize the importance of the user interface. The look and feel of the user/application interface can be evaluated while the application is under development. As stressed earlier, the important thing is the information flow and control, not the presentation format. We should strive to decouple the application interface objects from the domain objects as much as possible (see Chapter 6).

The user will also be represented as an instance of an actor that interacts with the system; i.e., the user is actually outside of the context of the system. A text document is also an important object in the system. Many actions are directed at doing something to or with a document.

Figure 3.9 shows an event trace for the normal scenario of filing a document in the system. The event trace shows the flow of control among the user, user interface, and text document objects. Most of the interaction is between the user and the user interface.

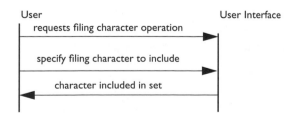

Figure 3.12. Event Trace for Changing Character Set.

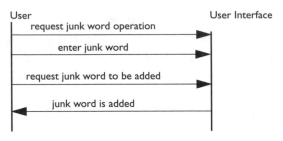

Figure 3.13. Event Trace for Adding Junk Words.

The event trace for a normal scenario of searching for a document(s) based on some search criteria is shown in Figure 3.10. This is also the event trace for viewing a document. Note that only documents that have been located as a result of a search operation may be viewed by the EFP. The main events among the user, user interface, and filing directory objects are shown. The event trace for printing a document is the same as that shown in Figure 3.10 but with "view" replaced by "print."

Figure 3.11 shows the event trace for deleting a document. Deleting a document deletes only the index of the document itself and not the actual document text.

An event trace for excluding one character from the filing character set is shown in Figure 3.12. Figure 3.13 shows an event trace for adding one junk word to the list of filing junk words that are excluded from the indexing of a document.

3.3 PREPARING AN EVENT FLOW DIAGRAM FOR THE SYSTEM

Figure 3.14 shows an event flow diagram for the EFP. The event flow diagram shows the events that flow between several groups of classes, without regard for sequence, at a high level of abstraction. This is an overview diagram for all of the event traces in the system; i.e., the diagram summarizes events between classes. The usefulness of this diagram lies in the fact that it gives a software engineer a high-level picture of some of the possible control flows in a system. The event flow diagram for the EFP clearly shows that there is a significant amount of interaction between the user and the user interface. A "cancel-the-operation" event has been included in the event flow diagram that is not part of the event trace but is part of our scenarios. This is because we previously decided not to show event traces that included exception cases. Additionally, error conditions that are part of exception cases could also be added to the event trace.

The electronic filing event flow diagram is a dynamic counterpart to the electronic filing object model diagram. The paths in the electronic filing event flow diagram show possible control flows within the system, while the paths in the electronic filing object model show possible information flows.

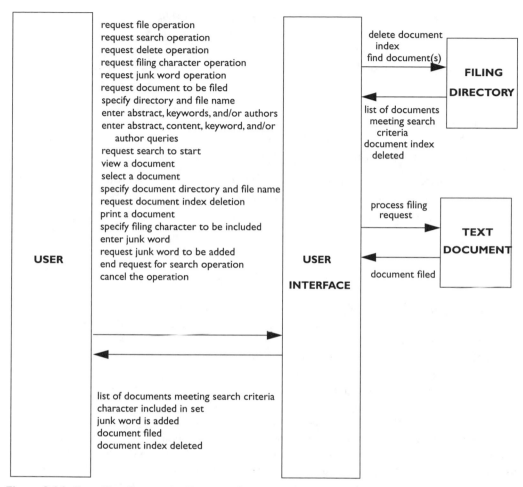

Figure 3.14. Event Flow Diagram for Electronic Filing.

3.4 DEVELOPING STATE DIAGRAMS FOR CLASSES WITH IMPORTANT DYNAMIC BEHAVIOR

State diagrams, or statecharts, will be developed for object classes that have nontrivial dynamic behavior. The process that the OMT specifies for developing state diagrams is as follows:

1. Pick an object class with nontrivial dynamic behavior.

2. Select an event trace diagram depicting a normal scenario that affects the class being modeled.

3. Consider only the events affecting the single object class. The input events are the arrows entering an object. The output events are the arrows exiting an object. Many if not all of the events pointing outward from an object class are either actions or activities. Examine one event at a time and identify the next state of the object class and any actions by objects that transmit information as events.

4. Draw the state diagram as a path of events. A state is the interval between two events. Label each arc representing an event using the input and output events found along one column in the event trace for the object class in question. The state diagram shows a sequence of events with interleaved states.

5. Now select other event trace diagrams depicting normal scenarios that affect the class being modeled, and go through the same process.

6. After including all event trace diagrams depicting normal scenarios, go back and consider all scenarios with exceptions for the object class in question.

7. Repeat this entire process until all object classes with nontrivial dynamic behavior have been included in state diagrams.

Our state diagrams will use the OMT notation, which follows the work of Harel (1987). Any of the Harel notation that is used in the electronic filing state diagrams that is not discussed in Rumbaugh et al. (1991) will be explicitly pointed out to the reader.

Based on the scenarios and event traces, the following objects/actors are the only ones exhibiting dynamic behavior (i.e., having a number of events and states associated with these object classes): user, user interface, text document, and filing directory. Text document and filing directory do not have significant dynamic behavior and will not be included in our state diagrams. The user represents an instance of an actor that is outside the domain of the system and therefore not implemented as part of the system. Therefore, we will develop state diagrams for the user interface class only. State diagrams will be developed that represent each scenario depicting a specific user interface function (i.e., filing, search, print, delete, view, filing character set, and junk words).

The normal scenario is useful for just grasping the basic control flow for each major dialog of the user interface. The abnormal scenarios or scenarios with exceptions include error conditions and exceptions from the normal control flow that complicate the programs logic. Normally we would first develop a normal scenario and then a scenario with exceptions. However, since we are developing state diagrams only for the user interface, and the user interface has minimal exception handling at this point, we will develop one state diagram for each scenario, combining the normal and exception cases. Error handling associated with the mechanics of the user interface will be omitted from the state diagrams at this point in time. At the analysis stage we are interested only in the information flow and control, and not in the specific mechanisms of how the user interface will be implemented and thus need to avoid including such detail. This detail will be provided during the design of the user interface.

A narrative explanation will accompany each state diagram. The state diagram will be explained in terms of the events that drive changes in state in the diagram. Each input event for the user interface object in the event trace also appears as an event in the state diagram. State names begin with a capital letter and appear in **bold** in the state transition diagrams. Both state names and event names will appear as *italics* in the text, with state names beginning with a capital letter.

The state diagrams abstract scenarios and may use both concurrency and generalization. State generalization is used to show patterns of similarity and difference. Generalization and concurrency in state diagrams is discussed in Rumbaugh et al. (1991) and is further expounded upon in Harel (1987). Harel refers to state diagrams that include generalization and concurrency as *statecharts*.

Nested state diagrams are used to show the control flow for the electronic filing problem. These diagrams show concurrency and generalization, economize on the number of arrows, and conceptually make the diagrams clearer than if flat state diagrams had been used. Nested state diagrams are analogous to nested subroutine calls. For example, a subroutine call in your main program may provide some high-level functionality such as retrieving an element from a queue. The details of this subroutine are then provided at a lower level. The lower level is an expansion of code that specifies all of the steps necessary to retrieve the element from the queue. Nested state diagrams work in the same fashion. Activities or events noted in a high-level state diagram may be expanded in subdiagrams. The subdiagram will specify all of the events and states that comprise the higher-level event or state.

3.4.1 User Interface Class State Diagrams

The state diagram for the user interface class is shown in Figure 3.15. When the program is first started, the *User Interface* state is entered. The initial state of the user interface is shown by a solid circle. When in the *User Interface* state, the user may select any function from among file document, delete document, search, junk word, or filing character; the selection moves the program into the respective state. A "selection" could be selecting a menu item with a mouse or via the keyboard or pressing a function key. However, "how" a selection is made is not of our concern during analysis. The mechanisms of how the user interface works will be explored during the design of the user interface. Here

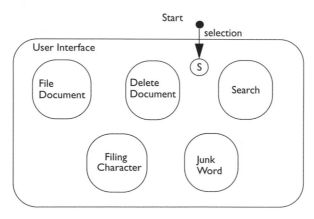

Figure 3.15. User Interface Class Statechart.

we make use of the "selection" entrance to indicate that there is more than one clearly defined option in the *User Interface* state, and we have chosen to model these options as states.

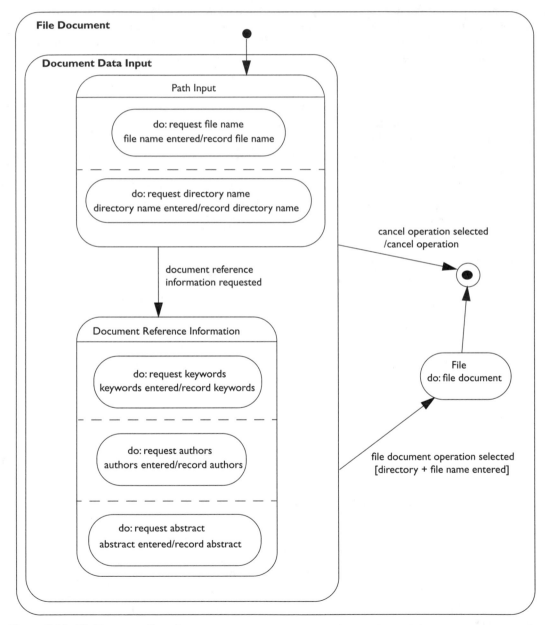

Figure 3.16. File Document Statechart.

The concept of "selection" is discussed in Harel (1987) but is not used in Rumbaugh et al. (1991). This "selection" entrance to substates of a superstate is used to illustrate more complicated entrances than a simple arrow. Selection is again used in Figure 3.15 to show that several substates (*File Document, Delete Document, Search, Filing Character, Junk Word*) are part of the *User Interface*, and any of these states may be entered by the user selecting one of them.

The expanded *File Document* substate is shown in Figure 3.16. This diagram shows two concurrent substates within the *Path Input* substate as indicated by the dashed lines. *Request directory name* and *request file name* are both concurrent activities. During either of the concurrent states in which these activities are being performed, the events *file name entered* and *directory name entered* cause the internal actions *record file name* and *record directory name*, respectively, to occur. These actions are performed without causing a state change.

The order of the *request directory* and *request file name* activities can vary, and both must transition to proceed. Control leaves the *Path Input* state when a *document reference information requested, file document operation selected*, or *cancel operation selected* event occurs. A user may elect to choose to specify document reference information, in which case the *request keywords, request authors*, and *request abstract* activities are all concurrent activities. The *Document Reference Information* substate is exited only when a *file document operation selected* or *cancel operation selected* event occurs. When the event *file document operation selected* occurs, the guarded transition fires only if the guard condition *[directory + file name entered]* is true. Note that in Harel's notation, transitions that leave a superstate also stand for transitions that leave all substates, so the *file document operation selected* and *cancel operation selected* events are transitions that apply to both the *Path Input* and the *Document Reference Information* substate.

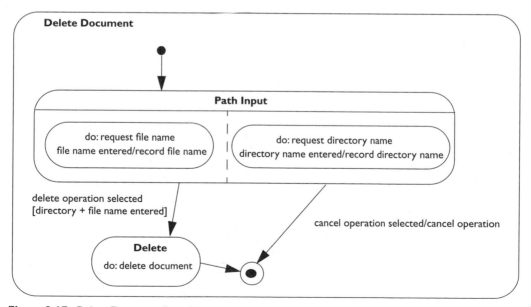

Figure 3.17. Delete Document Statechart.

The *Delete Document* state (see Figure 3.17) may be entered by the user selecting the delete document item *(Event—selection)*. The *Path Input* state is the default state that is initially entered. This diagram shows two concurrent substates within the *Path Input* substate as indicated by the dashed

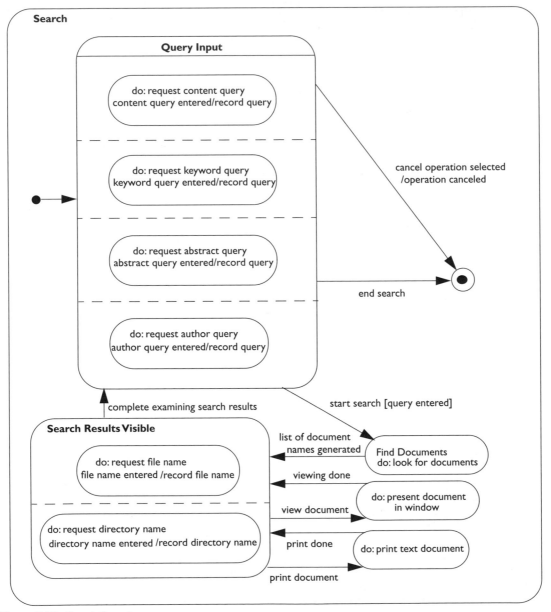

Figure 3.18. Search Statechart.

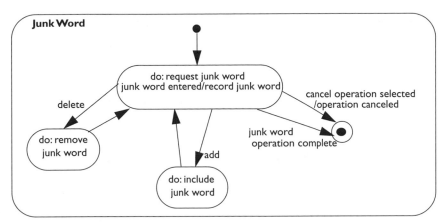

Figure 3.19. Junk Word Statechart.

lines. *Request directory name* and *request file name* are both concurrent activities. The user may transition from this state by deleting the document or canceling the operation, which generates the events *delete operation selected* and *cancel operation selected*, respectively. When the event *delete operation selected* occurs, the guarded transition fires only if the guard condition *[directory + file name entered]* is true.

The *Query Input* state of Figure 3.18 is entered when the user selects the search item. There are a number of concurrent substates within the *Query Input* substate of the superstate *Search. Request content query, request keyword query, request author query,* and *request abstract query* are all concurrent activities. A user may enter any one of the queries and then change his or her mind and reenter a different query before choosing to proceed with the search. A user may elect to end the search after, before, or during the query entry process. A user may also cancel the search process by generating a *cancel operation selected* event.

When a user has completed entry of her or his search query, the user may search for a document(s) meeting the search criteria, signaling a *start search* event. The transition to the *Find Documents* state occurs only if the guard condition *[query entered]* is true. This causes the *do:look for documents* activity in the *Find Documents* state to execute. This results in a *list of document names generated* event meeting the search criteria and causing a transition to the *Search Results Visible* state. The user may then view a document, print a document, or end viewing the search results, generating the events *view document, print document,* or *complete examining search results,* respectively. If the user chooses to end viewing the search results, he or she may continue with the search or end the search process (*Event—end search*).

The *Junk Word* state is expanded in Figure 3.19. The unnamed state with the activity *do: request junk word* is entered as indicated by the arrow with the solid circle. Whenever a *junk word entered* event occurs, the corresponding action is to *record the junk word,* but not to leave the state. The *add, delete, operation canceled,* and *junk word operation complete* events are triggered by the user.

The *Filing Character* state is expanded in Figure 3.20. The unnamed state with the activity *do: request filing character* is entered as indicated by the arrow with the solid circle. Whenever a *filing character*

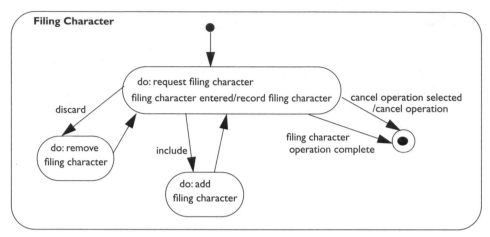

Figure 3.20. Filing Character Statechart.

entered event occurs, the corresponding action is to *record filing character*, but not to leave the state. The *include, discard, operation canceled*, and *filing character operation complete* events are triggered by the user.

3.5 CHECKING FOR COMPLETENESS AND CONSISTENCY OF EVENTS ACROSS STATE DIAGRAMS

After state diagrams have been developed for each object class, we need to ensure that all events are matched between objects, i.e., make sure that events sent and received between objects on different state diagrams are consistent. We also need to ensure that all events have both senders and receivers. No such inconsistencies were found in the state diagrams at this point. The user interface will also be expanded in subsequent chapters to capture implementation details and exception handling.

    Note that no statecharts or state diagrams were developed for the text document or filing directory object classes. These classes do not have significant dynamic behavior and thus are not worth modeling.

3.6 UPDATING THE OBJECT MODEL

User-visible aspects of an application are referred to as application objects (Rumbaugh, 1993). Rumbaugh identifies several types of application objects: presentations, formats, controllers, devices, and interfaces. A controller object is responsible for controlling an application's interactions with the outside world. A user interface is an example of a controller object. Rumbaugh says that the controller object does not need to be included in the initial object model, but should be added

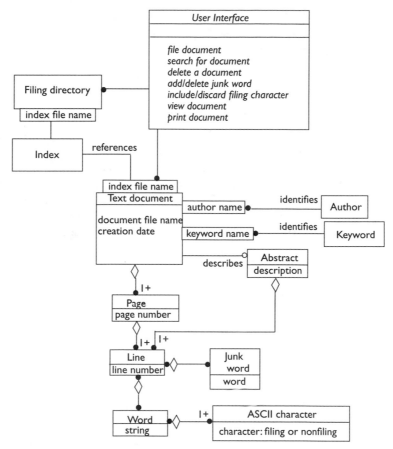

Figure 3.21. Revision 1 of Electronic Filing Object Model.

to the object model after making up the dynamic model. Now that our initial dynamic model has been developed, we are adding the *user interface* object class to the class diagram as shown in Figure 3.21. Based on the scenarios and event traces developed so far, we know that the *user interface* class has associations with the *filing directory* and *text document* classes. All of the interfaces to the *user interface* object class are not known at this time, but will be flushed out as we proceed through the analysis and design of the application.

3.7 SUMMARY OF PROCESS AND DELIVERABLES

The second step in the analysis process of Figure 2.2 has now been completed—developing a dynamic model. The deliverables for developing the dynamic model are:

❑ scenarios of typical interaction sequences

❑ event trace diagrams for each scenario

❑ an event flow diagram for the system

❑ state diagrams or statecharts for those classes with important dynamic behavior

❑ a revised object model (if necessary)

The dynamic model will be part of the analysis document, which will be captured in our reuse database of OMT specifications. All of the deliverables required to develop a dynamic model will be contained within the analysis document. No dynamic models from OMT specifications in the same or similar problem domains were available to examine for reuse.

Our process for producing these deliverables was to follow the steps identified by the OMT in constructing a dynamic model. We used the Harel statechart notation, as noted in Rumbaugh et al. (1991), to show concurrency and generalization and, additionally, included some of the notation described in Harel (1987). We also have used domain expert input from the author, general knowledge of the problem domain, a problem statement developed by the author, and customer interactions with the author acting as the customer.

The next step in the analysis process, as noted in Chapter 11 of Rumbaugh et al. (1991), is to construct a functional model for any significant computations or data transformations in the program or system.

CHAPTER 4

Constructing the Electronic Filing Functional Model

Main Chapter Topics	**Topic Questions/Explanations**
input values	56 what are the input values to electronic filing
output values	56 what are the output values to electronic filing
data flow diagrams	58 how are data flow diagrams developed
	58 what is the top-level data flow diagram
data dictionary	64 what are the elements in the data dictionary

THE FUNCTIONAL MODEL consists entirely of data flow diagrams (DFDs) or graphs and constraints. A DFD is a network representation of the system showing the functional relationships of the values computed by a system. Although some authors do include control information on a DFD, we will restrict the diagramming of control flow to state diagrams as part of the dynamic model. As stated in Rumbaugh et al. (1991), "As a rule, control information should be shown in the dynamic model and not the functional model, although control flows in data flow diagrams are occasionally useful."

Data flow diagrams consist of processes, data flows, actors, and data stores. A process transforms input data values into output data values. We will represent a process in a DFD as an ellipse, as the OMT does, with the name of the process inside the ellipse. A data flow shows the flow of data through a network of processes. Each data flow element is drawn as an arrow both originating from and terminating with a process, actor, or data store. An actor, drawn as a rectangle, lies on the boundary of the DFD and terminates the flow of data as a source or sink of data. Actors are objects. A data store is a repository for the temporary storing of data. A data store is represented in a DFD as a pair of parallel lines containing the name of a data store. Data stores may also be objects. Or a data store could be a file and the actor an external device.

Figure 4.1 shows where we are in the analysis process (see the highlighted area)—building the functional model. A functional model shows the computation that takes place within a program or system.

The electronic filing functional model describes the filing and search computations in the program. These are the only significant computations in our program. The functional model shows how the output values (i.e., a document index and search results) of the program are derived from

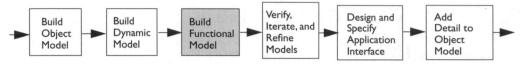

Figure 4.1. OMT Analysis Process.

the input values (i.e., text documents and other user input) of the program. The processes in the DFD correspond to operations in the object model. Data flows may represent objects, values in the object model, or arguments to operations. Rumbaugh et al. (1991) note that it is better to construct the functional model after the object and dynamic models have been developed.

The OMT specifies the following steps in constructing a functional model:

1. Identify input and output values
2. Build data flow diagrams for each input to output transformation
3. Develop descriptions for each process in the DFDs
4. Identify constraints between objects
5. Specify any optimization criteria, e.g., values to be maximized or minimized

We will follow the same steps as the OMT for building data flow diagrams for the electronic filing program.

4.1 IDENTIFYING INPUT AND OUTPUT VALUES

The first step in constructing a functional model is to identify the input and output values. The inputs and outputs for the electronic filing program are shown in Figure 4.2. The actors in the

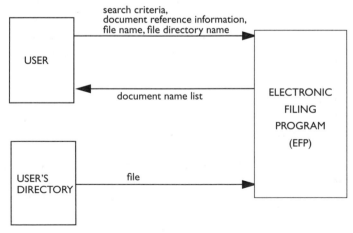

Figure 4.2. Input and Output Values for the EFP.

diagram are the user and the user's directory. The user is both a source and sink of data, while the user's directory is just a source of data. The inputs and outputs determine what the context of study will be for the problem domain. Nothing outside the context of study will be included in our modeling or problem solution: be conservative in your delineation of the problem domain, and include too much rather than too little if you are in doubt. However, make sure that the transformation depicted is possible, i.e., all of the inputs that are necessary to build the outputs have been identified.

The input and output values shown in Figure 4.2 are the parameters of events between the electronic filing application and the outside world. All interactions between the electronic filing program and the outside world pass through the user interface. Therefore, all input and output values are parameters of user interface events. In Chapter 3 we noted that the most important events are a file request and a search request. The input values for the EFP are parameters to these events:

- ❑ file name

- ❑ file directory name

- ❑ document reference information (author, keyword, abstract)

- ❑ search criteria (author, keyword, word, or phrase)

- ❑ a file (the document itself)

The file name and file directory are necessary to locate and read a file (i.e., text document) that is to be filed in the system. The document reference information captures information about the document itself, which can be used to locate the document later on. Search criteria must be specified by a user when trying to search for one or more documents. The last major input is the file, or text document, which the user has put away in the electronic filing system so that it can be retrieved quickly and easily later on when it is needed.

The output values are parameters of the event which signals that the search request has been completed. The output values for the EFP are a document name list (list of document names representing the documents found meeting the search criteria). Remember from Chapter 1 that electronic filing promotes the straightforward and accurate management of information. Users put information, in the form of documents, into the system and expect to be able to retrieve them quickly and easily later on: the major output value of the EFP is a document name list which contains the names of documents that satisfy some search criteria. The user can then either view or print these documents.

4.2 BUILDING DATA FLOW DIAGRAMS

Data flow diagrams are typically shown as layered sets of diagrams because they are generally too large to be shown on a single piece of paper. The EFP shown in Figure 4.2 is decomposed into a network of bubbles/processes and data flows. These processes can in turn be further divided into successively lower-level networks of processes and data flows if the diagram is still too large. We continue decomposing until we end up with processes that describe the functional primitives of the program. The functional primitives are processes that are *not* decomposed any further. They represent transformations that satisfy our requirements and therefore require no further partitioning.

Data flow diagrams can be developed by working from outputs to inputs, inputs to outputs, or from the middle of a process towards both the inputs and outputs. Whatever approach you decide to take, you should concentrate on the data flows first and worry about the processes later. For each data flow you should ask the following question: "What do I need in order to build this item?" (DeMarco, 1978). This will help you to determine what elements a data flow is composed of and where they come from. This exercise also helps to determine what transformations are required of the data flows.

The definitions of data flows should be added to the data dictionary as they are thought of. The data flow definitions and the DFDs will both be necessary later when writing the descriptions of each transformation or process. A data flow may consist of one or more data elements. We will describe the composition of data flows and the meaning of data elements in the data dictionary. Later, when we are designing the system, we will determine what the values of the data elements may be. This information will also be captured in the data dictionary at that time.

4.2.1 Top-Level Data Flow Diagram for Electronic Filing Program

The top-level data flow diagram for the EFP is shown in Figure 4.3; input and output values are supplied and consumed by external objects, such as *User* and *User's Directory*.

The approach that I have used to determine how far to decompose a process is the following: As you decompose a process, try writing a description (i.e., function description in Rumbaugh et al., 1991) for that process. When you do this, focus on what the process does and not how to implement it. If the process is doing many things that make it noncohesive, then decompose the process further. Continue doing this until the process performs as a single function. Very large or

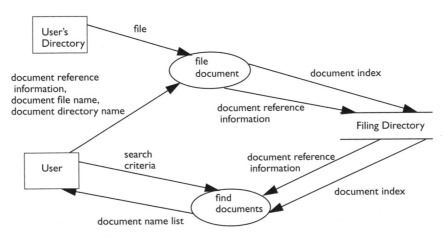

Figure 4.3. Top-Level Data Flow Diagram.

very small processes should be closely scrutinized. The goal is to have processes that are highly cohesive and to minimize coupling between processes. (The coupling between two processes is a measure of how much they depend on one another. Strong coupling complicates a system and makes a process harder to understand or to change. Cohesion is a measure of how closely related the elements in a process are to one another. An element is a statement, group of statements, or subprocess. Strong cohesive processes have elements that are strongly and genuinely related to one another.)

One data store is shown in the top-level data flow diagram: a filing directory. A filing directory, used exclusively by the EFP, maintains document indexes and document reference information. A document index and document reference information are stored in the filing directory when a document is filed in the system. This information is later retrieved from the filing directory and used when searching for documents.

The user represents an actor outside the context of the system. The user provides document reference information, a document file name, and a document directory name when filing a document, and search criteria when the EFP is trying to find a document(s) for the user. A text document in the form of a file comes from a source outside of the filing system—the user's directory.

As the result of the filing process, a document index is created and stored in the filing directory along with document reference information. The document index and document reference information are used to find a document(s) for the user. A list of the names of documents that have satisfied the search request are returned to the user.

The next step is to decompose and expand each nontrivial process in Figure 4.3. If this results in more nontrivial processes, then each nontrivial process should be further decomposed and expanded, resulting in another layer of data flow diagrams.

4.2.2 File Document Process

Figure 4.4 represents the process of filing a document. Note that the net inputs and outputs of this diagram are equivalent to the data flows into and out of the *file document* process in Figure 4.3. This equivalence relation is known as balancing. The balancing rule stated by DeMarco (1979) is:

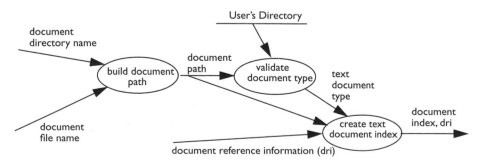

Figure 4.4. DFD for File Document Process.

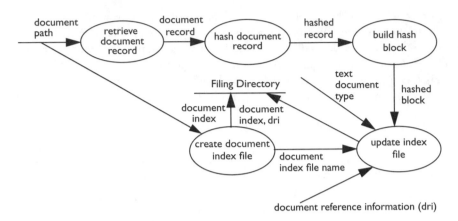

Figure 4.5. DFD for Create Text Document Index Process.

"All data flows entering a child diagram must be represented on the parent by the same data flow into the associated process. Outputs from the child diagram must be the same as outputs from the associated process on the parent with one exception: trivial rejects (reject paths that require no revision of state information) need not be balanced between parent and child."

4.2.2.1 Create Text Document Index

Text document type, document path, and document reference information are the net inputs for the *create text document index* process of Figure 4.5. The net output is a document index. Note that these are the same inputs and outputs as those of the parent process, *create text document index,* in Figure 4.4. Therefore the *create text document index* process of Figure 4.5 is balanced with respect to Figure 4.4. Note that the DFD indicates that a hashing mechanism will be used to create an index of the document file.

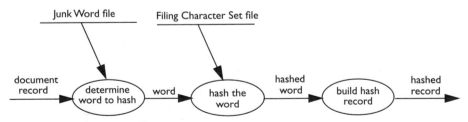

Figure 4.6. DFD for Hash Document Record Process.

4.2.2.2 Hash Document Record Process

The net inputs and outputs to the *hash document record* process, shown in Figure 4.6, are *document record* and *hashed record*, respectively. The *hash document record* process of Figure 4.6 is balanced with respect to the *hash document record* process of Figure 4.5, since the inputs and outputs are the same.

4.2.3 Find Documents Process

Figure 4.7 represents the process of finding one or more documents based on some search criteria. The net inputs to this process are *content query, abstract query, keyword query, author query, logical query operators, document reference information,* and *document index.* Note that these are not exactly the same input data flows for the *find document* process as is shown in the parent diagram of Figure 4.3. However, the *search criteria* input data flow to the *find document* process in Figure 4.3 is equivalent to the content, abstract, keyword, and author queries, and logical query operators of Figure 4.7. Search criteria is just shown in a more detailed representation in the child diagram of Figure 4.7 than in the parent diagram of Figure 4.3. This reflects a top-down partitioning of the data as we move from top-level DFDs to lower-level DFDs. A *document name list* is the output data flow from the *build document name list* process.

4.2.3.1 Build Search Vector Process

The net inputs to the build search vector process are phrase and logical operator (see Figure 4.8). However, the parent process for build search vector (see Figure 4.7) shows content query as the input data flow. Here again we are making use of a parallel decomposition of data and of function. Content query is made up of some combination of phrases and logical operators, so there is a net equivalence or balancing for the build search vector process of Figure 4.7 and Figure 4.8. A search vector represents the output data flow of the *build search vector process.*

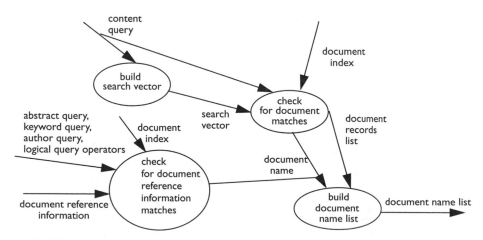

Figure 4.7. DFD for Find Document Process.

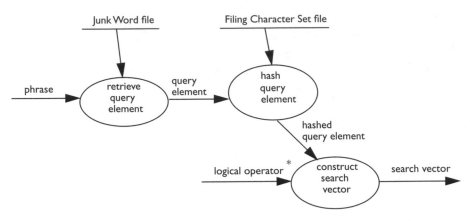

Figure 4.8. DFD for Build Search Vector Process.

4.2.3.2 Check for Document Matches Process

The net inputs to the "check for document matches" DFD of Figure 4.9 are *search vector, content query,* and *document index.* The net outputs are *document name* and *document records list.* These inputs and outputs match the *check for document matches* process of the parent diagram in Figure 4.7. Therefore, the process is balanced in these diagrams.

The *text document* input from the user's directory is relevant only within this process and is not an interface among DFD elements at another level of data flow diagrams. Therefore, this file is not shown in the parent diagram for the *check for document matches* process. It is a data flow that is internal to this process.

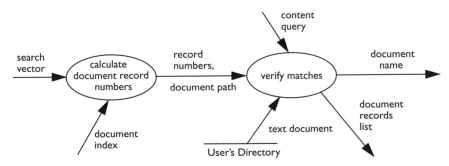

Figure 4.9. DFD for Check for Document Matches Process.

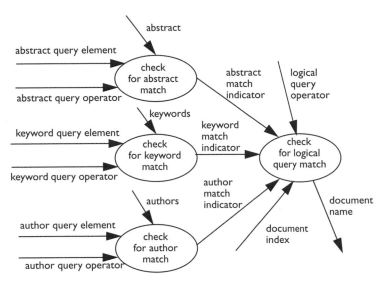

Figure 4.10. DFD for Check for Document Reference Information Matches Process.

4.2.3.3 Check for Document Reference Information Matches Process

The net inputs to the *check for document reference information matches* process are *abstract query, keyword query, author query, abstract, keywords, authors,* and *logical query operators* (see Figure 4.10). However, the parent process for the *check for document reference information matches* process (see Figure 4.7) shows *document reference information* as an input data flow. Here again we are making use of a parallel decomposition of data and of function. *Document reference information* is made up of some combination of *abstract, keywords,* and *authors.* So there is a net equivalence or balancing for the *check for document reference information matches* process of Figure 4.7 and Figure 4.10. A *document name* is the output data flow for the "check for logical query match" process. This is the name of the document that was found as the result of a search.

4.2.4 Data Flow Diagram Definitions in the Data Dictionary

All of the previous data flows that were specified in the building of the data flows diagrams are defined in the data dictionary for the analysis model. All of the definitions in the data dictionary reflect top-down partitioning of data. Entries also exist in the data dictionary for files, processes, and data elements A data element is a component of a data flow that is indivisible. It takes on specific values and may be either discrete or continuous.

The following set of relational operators is used in the data dictionary to explain data flows:

Operator	Meaning
=	is equivalent to
+	and
|	either-or, i.e., select one of the options
{}	**iteration of** the component enclosed; bounds are typically indicated next to the brackets
()	the enclosed component is **optional**

A data flow will be described in the data dictionary using the following entry:

Dataflow Name:

Aliases:

Composition:

Notes:

An alias is a synonymous name for the data flow name or element. The composition section is left blank if the entry is for an alias data flow. The composition section describes the definition of the data flow name or element using data flows and elements combined with the previously defined set of relational operators. The notes section can be used to record information about the entry that you would like to keep track of, except for its physical character.

A data element will be described in the data dictionary using the following entry:

Data Element Name:

Aliases:

Values and Meanings:

Notes:

The values and meanings portion of the data element entry is used to record what values the data element may take on and what those values mean.

A file or database name will be described in the data dictionary using the following entry:

File or Database Name:

Aliases:

Composition:

Organization:

Notes:

The organization portion of the file or database name entry is used to record information on how the file or database is organized and therefore accessed.

The entries in the data dictionary are presented in alphabetical order to facilitate easy lookup.

Dataflow Name:	abstract
Composition:	$_1\{phrase\}^n$
Notes:	A brief statement of the essential thoughts of a document. This is carried over from the initial data dictionary described in Chapter 2.

Data Element Name:	abstract match indicator
Values and Meanings:	match, nomatch
Notes:	

Dataflow Name:	abstract query
Composition:	(word | phrase) + $_0${query operator + (word | phrase)}^{n}
Notes:	An abstract query must have at least one word or phrase.Additional words or phrases require a query operator between them.An abstract query is used to search for similar words or phrases in the abstract of a document(s).

Dataflow Name:	author
Aliases:	author name
Composition:	The name of a person associated with a document.
Notes:	This is carried over from the initial data dictionary described in Chapter 2.

Data Element Name:	author match indicator
Values and Meanings:	match, nomatch
Notes:	

Dataflow Name:	author query
Composition:	author name + $_0${query operator + author name}^{n}
Notes:	An author query must have at least one author name. Additional author names require a query operator between them. An author query is used to search for author names in the authors portion of document reference information for a document(s).

Dataflow Name:	authors
Composition:	$_0${author}^{n}
Notes:	The authors specified as part of document reference information.

Dataflow Name:	content query
Composition:	(word | phrase) + $_0${query operator + (word | phrase)}^{n}
Notes:	A content query must have at least one word or phrase. Additional words or phrases require a query operator between them.

Dataflow Name:	document directory name
Composition:	$_1${alphanumeric characters}^{n}
Notes:	A string of ASCII characters representing the name of a directory for the location of a document. The maximum number of characters in the name, n, is dependent upon the operating software platform.

Dataflow Name:	document file name
Composition:	$_1${alphanumeric characters}^{n}

Notes:	A string of ASCII characters representing the name of a file that is a document. The maximum number of characters in the name, n, is dependent upon the operating software platform.
Dataflow Name:	document index
Composition:	An index of all of the words in a document text file.
Notes:	The document index facilitates rapid retrieval of any nonjunk word in the content of the document. The document index is a file.
Dataflow Name:	document index file name
Composition:	$_1\{$alphanumeric characters$\}^n$
Notes:	An ASCII string of characters representing the name of the document index file. The maximum number of characters in the name, n, is dependent upon the operating software platform.
Dataflow Name:	document name
Composition:	$_1\{$alphanumeric characters$\}^n$
Notes:	An ASCII string of characters used to identify the name of a document. The maximum number of characters in the name, n, is dependent upon the operating software platform.
Dataflow Name:	document name list
Composition:	$_0\{$document name$\}^n$
Notes:	This represents a list of document names that have satisfied some search criteria.
Dataflow Name:	document path
Composition:	document directory name + document file name
Notes:	A document path is a document file name concatenated to a document directory name.
Dataflow Name:	document record
Composition:	$_1\{$word$\}^n$
Notes:	A document consists of one or more records. Each record must contain one or more words.
Dataflow Name:	document reference information
Composition:	(abstract) + (keywords) + (authors)
Notes:	Each text document may have document reference information associated with it.
Dataflow Name:	file
Composition:	program or data
Notes:	Files organize information used by a computer. A program or data is stored as a file on disk.

Dataflow Name:	file directory name
Composition:	$_1\{\text{alphanumeric characters}\}^n$
Notes:	A directory name specifying the location of a file. The maximum number of characters in the name, n, is dependent upon the operating software platform.

Dataflow Name:	file name
Composition:	$_1\{\text{alphanumeric characters}\}^n$
Notes:	A name of a file. The maximum number of characters in the name, n, is dependent upon the operating software platform.

File or Database Name:	Filing Character Set file
Composition:	string of filing characters
Organization:	sequential based on ASCII ordering
Notes:	

File or Database Name:	Filing Directory
Composition:	$_0\{\text{document index}\}^n$
Organization:	Based on the operating system.
Notes:	

Dataflow Name:	hashed block
Composition:	$_1\{\text{hashed record}\}^n$
Notes:	A collection of some number of hashed records representing a portion of a document. A document index typically will have a number of hashed blocks, n, depending on the size of the text document.

Dataflow Name:	hashed query element
Composition:	A string of bits based on a hashing of a word or phrase.
Notes:	

Dataflow Name:	hashed record
Composition:	A string of bits based on a hashing of all of the records in a document.
Notes:	

Dataflow Name:	hashed word
Composition:	A string of bits based on a hashing of all of the filing characters in a word.
Notes:	

File or Database Name:	Junk Word file
Composition:	$_0\{\text{word}\}^n$
Organization:	listing of words in alphabetic order
Notes:	

Dataflow Name:	keyword

Composition:	${}_1\{$alphanumeric character$\}^n$
Notes:	A keyword is a word that helps the user to uniquely identify a document. This is carried over from the initial data dictionary described in Chapter 2.

Data Element Name:	keyword match indicator
Values and Meanings:	match, nomatch
Notes:	

Dataflow Name:	keyword query
Composition:	keyword + ${}_0\{$query operator + keyword$\}^n$
Notes:	A keyword query must have at least one keyword. Additional keywords require a query operator between them. A keyword query is used to search for keywords in the keywords portion of document reference information for a document(s).

Dataflow Name:	keywords
Composition:	${}_0\{$keyword$\}^n$
Notes:	The keywords specified as part of document reference information.

Data Element Name:	logical query operator
Aliases:	query operator, logical operator
Values and Meanings:	and | or
Notes:	

Dataflow Name:	phrase
Composition:	word + ${}_1\{$space + word$\}^n$
Notes:	A phrase is a sequence of two or more words that convey a single thought.

Dataflow Name:	query element
Composition:	a non–junk word of a phrase
Notes:	

Data Element Name:	record number
Values and Meanings:	From 0 to n-1, where n = the maximum number of fixed data records in the file
Notes:	

Dataflow Name:	search criteria
Composition:	(content query) + (logical query operator + abstract query) + (logical query operator + keyword query) + (logical query operator + author query)
Notes:	All the elements of a search criteria are optional. However, one element must be present in order for a search criterion to exist. Logical query operators must separate the elements of the search criterion.

Dataflow Name:	search vector

Composition:	A string of bits based on a hashing of all of the elements in a content query.
Notes:	A search vector is used to determine the records of the document index that should be read. The document index is then read to determine the data records of the document file to read. Specific records of the document file are then read to determine if there is a match between the content query and the content of a document.

Dataflow Name:	text document record
Composition:	$_1\{\text{alphanumeric character}\}^{80}$
Notes:	The data record of a text file, or document, represented by a string of ASCII characters.

Dataflow Name:	text document type
Composition:	$_1\{\text{alphanumeric character}\}^n$
Notes:	An alphanumeric string of characters representing a type of text document.

Data Element Name:	word
Values and Meanings:	$_1\{\text{alphanumeric character}\}^n$
Notes:	An alphanumeric character or some meaningful combination of alphanumeric characters that represent a unit of language. This is carried over from the initial data dictionary described in Chapter 2

4.3 REMAINING STEPS IN CONSTRUCTING FUNCTIONAL MODEL

The remaining steps in constructing a functional model consist of:

❑ develop descriptions for each process in the DFDs

❑ identify constraints between objects

❑ specify any optimization criteria, e.g., values to be maximized or minimized

The descriptions for each process in the DFDs are shown in Appendix A. Any constraints between objects are identified in the descriptions for each process or function. Also, any values to be optimized are also specified in Appendix A.

4.4 SUMMARY OF PROCESS AND DELIVERABLES

The third step in the analysis process of Figure 1.2 has now been completed—developing a functional model. The deliverables for developing the functional model are

❑ data flow diagrams

❑ updated data dictionary

❑ process or function descriptions, including constraints between objects and values to be optimized

The functional model will be part of the analysis document, which will be captured in our reuse database of OMT specifications. All of the deliverables required to develop a functional model will be contained within the analysis document. No functional models from OMT specifications in the same or similar problem domains were available to examine for reuse.

Our process for producing these deliverables was to follow the steps identified by the OMT in constructing a functional model. The program or system input and output values drove the development of the functional model. The input and output values are the parameters of events (file request and search request) between the electronic filing application and the outside world.

The next step in our analysis process (see Rumbaugh et al., 1991) is to verify, iterate, and refine the three models (object, dynamic, and functional).

CHAPTER 5

Summarizing Key Operations and Iterating the Analysis

No ANALYSIS MODEL is complete after the first pass. During the development of the object, dynamic, and functional models, several iterations were shown. Deficiencies were found in some of these models at some point in time, which we had to go back and correct. This iterative process of refinement and improvement will continue throughout the development of the electronic filing program. Our goal throughout the development of the analysis model has been to develop an accurate and complete model of what our program will do, i.e., understand and model the problem to be solved. This chapter is a continuation of that theme, refining and improving the model of our application.

The next step in our analysis process is to summarize key operations in the object model and to verify, iterate, and refine the three models (see highlighted area of Figure 5.1). The key operations will be discovered from the object model, dynamic model (from events, state actions, and activities), and functional model (operations from functions/processes). After summarizing key operations in the object model, we will iterate our analysis. At this stage of analysis we are looking for inconsistencies and imbalances across the object, dynamic, and functional models.

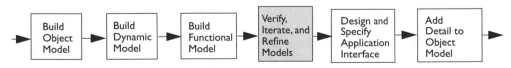

Figure 5.1. OMT Analysis Process.

5.1 REFINING THE OBJECT, DYNAMIC, AND FUNCTIONAL MODELS

The process that we will use to verify, iterate, and refine the three models is shown in Figure 5.2. The process consists of the following steps:

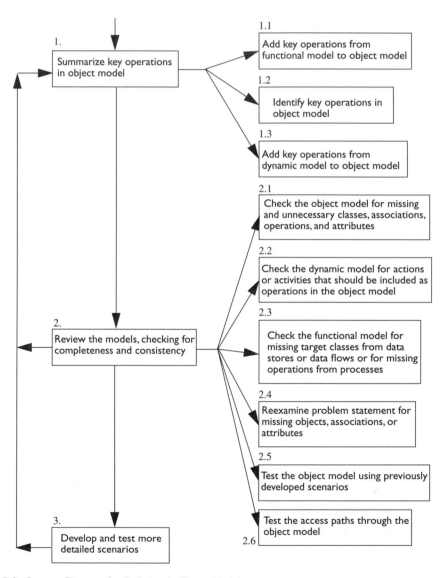

Figure 5.2. Process Diagram for Refining the Three Models.

1. Identify and categorize key operations from the three models, summarizing the key operations in the object model. Key operations found in the functional and dynamic models will be added to the object model. Assign all key operations to objects.

2. Review the three models to check if any classes, associations, attributes, or operations should change (i.e., check for completeness and consistency). This includes retesting the model with previously developed scenarios. Also, review the problem statement and see if it needs revision in light of the three models. As noted in Rumbaugh et al. (1991), "the original problem statement should be revised to incorporate corrections and understanding discovered during analysis."

3. Develop more detailed normal scenarios and scenarios with exceptions, and verify the models against these scenarios.

4. Repeat the above steps, staying at a chosen level of abstraction, until we feel comfortable with the analysis (i.e., the problem is fully specified and is sufficient to serve as the basis for system architecture, design, and implementation).

The process diagram of Figure 5.2 will be shown at several points in this chapter to help orient the reader. The current step under discussion will be highlighted in the diagram.

5.1.1 Summarizing Key Operations in the Object Model

The OMT places less emphasis during object-oriented analysis (OOA) on defining operations or responsibilities of object classes than do other approaches to OOA. Up to this point we have been concerned with developing static and dynamic views of our program and also showing the information flow through the program. Very few operations have been specified to date. Now we will review our models and pick out the key operations. These key operations will then be summarized in the object model. We will also look for the real-world behavior of classes that might suggest operations. These operations will also be included in our object model. We will attempt to simplify operations in the object model by looking for similar operations and variations of the same operation. Later, during the course of object design, we will use the dynamic and functional models to find *all* of the operations that must be associated with each object.

Operations can come from the object, functional, and dynamic models. Operations in the object model may be implied by the presence of an attribute. Some operation must be provided to read and write attribute values. Events in the dynamic model may be represented as operations on objects. Actions and activities in the state diagrams or statecharts of the dynamic model may be functions that should be modeled as operations in the object model if they perform nontrivial computations. Processes/functions in a functional model correspond to operations on classes in the object model. We will identify *key* operations that may come from all of these sources.

5.1.1.1 Adding Key Operations from the Functional Model to the Object Model

We will start by examining the functional model with the top-level data flow diagram from Chapter 4. *File* and *find* are the two major functions of the system—they are key operations. Electronic filing consists mainly of storing/filing documents in the system and then retrieving/finding these documents using techniques that are not available in manual filing systems. These are the only operations that have interesting computational structure. Our system is dominated by interactions between the user and the program. Therefore not many application functions have significant computational structure. However, many trivial operations exist in the program, which will be identified during object design. The pseudocode for each process developed in Chapter 4 will be used to determine if a process is trivial or has enough computation to be called a key operation.

For the *file* operation, the processes at the next level of abstraction are:

❑ *validate document type*

❑ *create text document index*

Validate document type is a fairly trivial process. However, the *create text document index* process is complicated and a key process for the *file* operation. The *create text document index* process is necessary to describe how the *file* operation works. Therefore, the *file* and *create text document index* operations are included in a revised object model showing operations.

At the next level of abstraction, the *hash document record* process has significant computation. The *hash document record* process operates on a record that is part of the text document. This process creates a hashed record and could be assigned to the text document object or to a hash record object. However, the hashing operation has features of its own and will be modeled as a class. We'll call this class the *hash engine*. The *hash engine* class will collect all of the hashing functions together in one place. These functions are likely to change in the future as the hashing algorithms are optimized. Grouping the hashing functions together in one class will minimize the impact on the system as these algorithms are optimized (i.e., reification of behavior).

For the *find* operation, the processes at the next level of abstraction are:

❑ *build search vector*

❑ *check for document matches*

❑ *build document name list*

❑ *check for document reference information matches*

The *build document name list* process combines the *document name* and *document records list* into a new object class. We will consider this a key operation since it creates a new object and is pertinent to understanding the search process. The other processes, *build search vector, check for document matches,* and *check for document reference information matches* are also necessary to describe how the *find* operation works. Therefore, they are also included in a revised object model showing key operations.

At the next level of abstraction, the *build search vector* process is also a key operation. *Build search vector* is a top-level process that is implemented by several low-level processes. *Build search vector* takes a content query and builds a search vector. This process is part of a find document, or search, operation. This process could be assigned to content query or to search vector objects. However, the search operation has features of its own and will be modeled as a class. We'll call this class the *search engine*. The *search engine* class will collect the high-level search functions together in one place. These functions are likely to change in the future as the search operation is enhanced to include additional parameters, e.g., multiple directories from one or more computer systems are included in the search, the electronic filing program is enhanced to store and retrieve multimedia objects, etc. Making the search operation an entity in itself will help to localize any changes that must occur as the search operation is enhanced in the future. Build search vector is an operation of the *search engine* object.

Now that the key operations from the functional model have been identified, the next step is to assign responsibility for those operations to objects. This step may be repeated in the object design phase of our development for some of the operations in the system. The following criteria are used to determine the target object of a suboperation in the functional model (Rumbaugh et al., 1991):

❑ If a process extracts a value from an input flow, then the input flow is the target.

❑ If a process has an input flow and an output flow of the same type, and the output value is substantially an updated version of the input flow, then the input/output flow is the target.

❑ If a process constructs an output value from several input flows, then the operation is a class operation (constructor) on the output class.

❑ If a process has an input from or an output to a data store or to an actor, then the data store or actor is a target of the process. (In some cases, such a process must be broken into two operations, one for the actor or data store and one for a flow value.)

Operations should be assigned to objects that play the lead role in an operation. If there is still some question as to what class owns an operation, ask yourself the following questions (Rumbaugh et al., 1991):

❑ Is one object acted on while the other performs the action? In general, it is best to associate the operation with the target of the operation, rather than the initiator.

❑ Is one object modified by the operation, while other objects are only queried for the information they contain? The object that is changed is the target of the operation.

❑ Looking at the classes and associations that are involved in the operation, which class is the most centrally located in this subnetwork of the object model? If the classes and associations form a star about a single central class, it is the target of the operation.

❑ If the objects were not software, but were the real-world objects being represented internally, what real object would you push, move, activate, or otherwise manipulate to initiate the operation?

Some additional guidelines for assigning responsibilities (i.e., operations to object classes) come from Wirfs-Brock et al., 1990:

❑ Operations should be kept with the data or attributes they operate upon.

❑ Multiple objects should not share the responsibility for maintaining specific data or attributes. This can lead to inconsistencies and the loss of data integrity. Keep related data or attributes in one place.

Now we will start assigning responsibility for operations to objects by looking at each input and output data flow associated with a key operation.

A *text document,* in the form of a file, is the major input flow for the *file* process. The *file* process extracts data values from this input flow and then produces a substantially different output flow. The *file* operation belongs to the *text document* object because the input flow is the target (i.e., it operates on the text document itself). The *file* process will create a *document index* object. We'll rename the *file* operation to *file document* because it is more meaningful.

The *find* operation previously operated on the *filing directory* object, which is a data store, searching appropriate document indexes for some user-specified criteria. With the introduction of the *search engine* object class, the *find* operation is more appropriately placed with the *search engine.* The *search engine* object class is the target of the *find* process and is responsible for any and all search requests. We'll rename the *find* operation *find document* because it is more meaningful.

The *create text document index* process has several input flows. This process takes *document reference information, text document type,* and *document path* and produces a new output flow, *document index.* The *create text document index* operation is an operation on the output class, *document index.*

The *check for document matches* process produces the output values *document name* and *document records list* from several input values: *search vector, content query,* and *document index.* The content query is the most centrally located object in this subnetwork of the object model. The *check for document matches* operation will be placed with the *content query* object. *Content query* is a new object that must be included in the object model. *Document records list* is also a new object class that should be part of our model. However, *document records list* is not relevant to the analysis, but is important to the implementation, i.e., it may be used to locate specific sections of the document that have matches with the content query. We'll note in our design folder that *document records list* should be an object class and is used internally by the program. Later when we begin to work on design, we'll resurrect and use this information.

The *build document name list* process takes the *document name* and *document records list* input values and creates a *document name list. Document name list* is also a new object that must be included in the object model. The *search engine* object class performs the *find* operation and then constructs the *document name list.* The *build document name list* process is assigned to the *search engine* object class.

The *check for document reference information matches* process uses several input data flows, *queries, document reference information,* and *document index,* and produces a *document name* as the output flow. This operation primarily extracts data values from the *document reference information* input flow and compares these values with queries. *Document reference information* is the target object for this operation, and must be identified as a new object in the object model.

In summary, the operations and their respective object classes that have been identified from the functional model are as follows:

Operation	Object Class
file document	text document
find document	search engine
create text document index	document index
build search vector	search engine
check for document matches	content query
check for document reference information matches	document reference information
hash document record	hash engine
build document name list	search engine

Content query, search vector, document name list, and *document reference information* are new object classes that are added to the object model. The independent existence of these entities is important enough to warrant them being object classes rather than attributes. *Search engine* and *hash engine* are also added as new object classes to the object model.

These object classes have the following associations with other object classes in the model:

- ❑ search engine uses a content query
- ❑ search engine produces a search vector
- ❑ search engine produces a document name list
- ❑ search engine uses document reference information
- ❑ search vector *utilizes a* document index
- ❑ document reference information *describes* a text document

The association between *filing directory* and *user interface* object classes goes away, and a new association is added between the *search engine* and the *user interface* object classes. Author, keyword, and abstract are all parts of document reference information. This represents an aggregation relationship, which is a special form of association. The *document reference information* object represents a collection of author(s), keyword(s), and zero, or one, abstract.

Key operations, objects, and associations discovered from the functional model are shown in the revised class diagram of Figure 5.3.

5.1.1.2 Identifying Key Operations from the Object Model

Operations from the object model are related to reading and writing attributes and association links and are implied by the presence of an attribute. These operations are trivial and do not add much value to being able to explain the model to users or customers. Rumbaugh et al. (1991) recommends leaving these operations out of the object model during analysis since they are implied by the presence of an attribute.

5.1.1.3 Adding Key Operations from the Dynamic Model to the Object Model

Activities and actions in the dynamic model that require significant computation should be modeled as operations on object classes. A quick scan of the statecharts from Chapter 3 reveals that the only significant actions/activities are *file document* and *look for document(s)*. Also, events in the dynamic model may be represented as operations on objects. The event flow diagram, which is an overall diagram for all of the event traces in the system, is a good source for identifying events between objects. All of the following events and their respective objects come from the electronic filing event flow diagram:

Event	Object
process filing request	text document
find document(s)	filing directory
delete document index	filing directory

The *find document(s)* operation is now associated with the *search engine* object class. The event flow diagram will be updated to reflect this change. The *find* operation is the same thing as *find document(s)* or *looking for document(s)*.

The *process filing request* event and the *file document* activity both relate to the *file* operation. *Delete document index* is a new operation, which operates on the filing directory. The *delete document index* operation belongs to the *filing directory* object.

Many other events are identified in the event flow diagram and belong to the user interface class. We will not identify all of these events, which correspond to operations on object classes, at this time because they do not help us to increase our understanding of the problem domain. The design and specification of the user interface will be discussed in Chapter 6.

Several other operations are suggested by the dynamic model: *view document* and *print text document*. The functional model was not developed for either of these two potential operations because they are trivial. *Print text document* is shown as an activity for a state that is not decomposed into a sub-diagram. *View document* is shown as an event in the statechart. *View document* and *print text document* operate on the target object *text document*.

In summary, the operations and their respective objects that have been identified from the dynamic model, and included in the object model of Figure 5.3, are:

Operation	Object
view document	text document
print text document	text document
delete document index	filing directory

Print text document and *delete document index* will be shortened to *print document* and *delete index*, respectively, to conveniently fit in the object model diagram.

5.1.2 Checking for Completeness and Consistency

The revised class diagram shown in Figure 5.3 includes key operations and any new objects discovered while reviewing the models for key operations. The next step in iterating the analysis is to review all three models and check for completeness and consistency. The steps in this process are as follows:

1. Check the object model for any missing and unnecessary classes and associations. Also look for incorrect placement of associations and attributes.

2. Check the dynamic model for any missing and unnecessary key operations.

3. Check the functional model for any missing and unnecessary key operations. Also examine the key operations for missing target classes that might come from data stores or data flows.

4. Review the problem statement for objects, associations, or attributes that may have been missed during previous iterations.

5. Test the object model using previously developed scenarios.

6. Trace access paths through the object model by asking questions to determine if the model can answer all of situations you would expect it to. Use previously developed questions/statements and develop new questions/statements to test the revised object model.

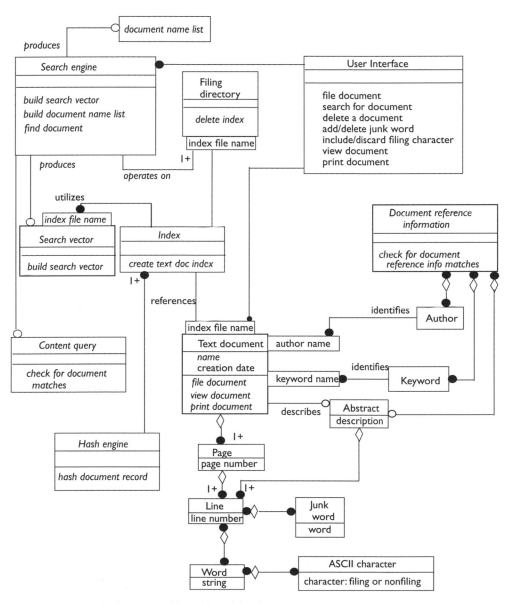

Figure 5.3. Revision 2 of Electronic Filing Object Model.

The idea here is to take another pass through the analysis. Most applications cannot be developed in a strict linear fashion because of the interactions between different parts of a program. All system requirements are generally not known and understood at the beginning of a project (Jacobson et al., 1992). Our knowledge of the electronic filing application has grown progressively as the work has progressed, as is typical for most application development. Now it is time to go back and review our analysis work again. There may be inconsistencies and imbalances within and across the object, dynamic, and functional models. For example, there may be objects with unrelated attributes or operations, associations or objects that now seem extraneous but initially seemed useful; data flows that were initially modeled as attributes but whose independent existence as an entity is now important; actions or activities that were passed over in the state diagram and not identified as operations; input events entering the system that pass from object to object that do not match the scenarios, etc.

Figure 5.4 shows where we are in the process (note that the current step is highlighted).

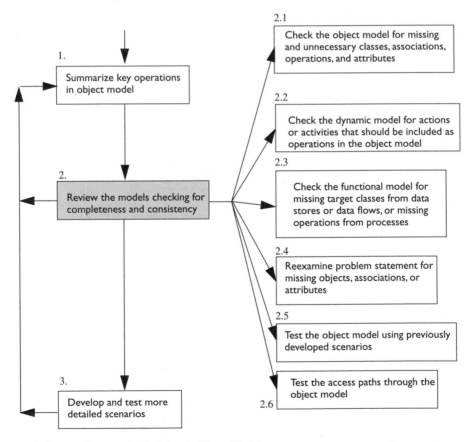

Figure 5.4. Process Diagram for Refining the Three Models.

5.1.2.1 Checking the Object Model—Step 1

The first step is to check the object model for any missing or unnecessary classes and associations. We will also look for incorrect placement of associations and attributes. Our approach will be to systematically examine each object, determining its attributes, operations, and associations. We will also use the data dictionary to see if objects and attributes have been appropriately represented in the object model.

Search Vector The *search vector* object currently has no attributes. Our data dictionary shows that a *search vector* is a string of bits. During the analysis phase of development we are not concerned with how attributes are physically represented, so we will just show a *vector* as an attribute of *search vector* and will not specify its representation at this time. *Build search vector* is a key operation for this object. A *search engine* produces one *search vector*; however, a *search vector* may be produced by one or more *search engines*.

Search Engine The *search engine* class was recently added to the object model. The *search engine* class collects the high-level search functions together in one place. The *search engine* maintains no state information about itself but assists in the execution of a complex task, i.e., conducting a search. Budd (1991) has developed the following category of classes (which is not complete): (1) data managers, data, or state classes, (2) data sinks or data sources, (3) view or observer classes, and (4) facilitator or helper classes. The *search engine* could be considered a facilitator class. The operations of the search engine operate on the *content query, search vector, filing directory,* and *document name list* object classes.

Hash Engine The *hash engine* class was recently added to the object model. The *hash engine* class collects the high-level hash functions together in one place. The *hash engine* class, like the search engine, maintains no state information about itself but assists in the execution of a complex task, i.e., it creates an index of a document and an address that will later be used to pinpoint the location of a word and/or phrase in a document.

Document Name List The *document name list* class should have an attribute that is a *name list*. The *name list* is generated as the result of a search and represents the documents that were found that satisfy the search criteria.

User Interface The design of the application interface is discussed in the next chapter. We'll postpone the discussion of the associations between the user interface class and the rest of the model until then. As mentioned in Chapter 3, the intent here is *not* to trivialize the importance of the user interface. The specific look and feel of the user/application interface can proceed in parallel with the remaining analysis of the domain model. A domain model is a class diagram developed for the electronic filing domain, which defines the fundamental information computed and maintained by the application, independent of the application interface (Rumbaugh, 1993b). The fundamental core of the application will be written as operations on the domain objects (which make up the domain model).

Content Query   The *content query* object currently has no attributes. The data dictionary shows that a *content query* is a collection of *phrase(s)* and *query operator(s)*, and a *phrase* is a collection of *word(s)*. A *word* is a collection of one or more ASCII *character(s)*. An *ASCII character* has an attribute *character*, which is of the type *filing* or *nonfiling character*. A collection type of relationship is shown as aggregation in the object model. A *phrase* object is added to the object model. A *query operator* object is also added to the object model.

Text Document, Page, Line   A *text document* is a collection of one or more *page(s)*. A *page* is a collection of one or more *line(s)*. And a *line* is a collection of zero or more *word(s)*. *Name* and *creation date* are the attributes of the *text document* object. *Name* is changed to *document name* because it is more meaningful. A directory name will also be needed to locate and read the document. *Directory name* is added as an attribute of text document. *File document*, *view document*, and *print document* are the key operations for the *text document* object.

Word, Junk Word, ASCII Character   A *word* is shown as a collection of *ASCII characters*. However, a *word* would be better represented in the context of this problem as either a *junk word* or a *nonjunk word*. A *nonjunk word* is a collection of *ASCII characters*. An *ASCII character* is either a *filing character* or a *nonfiling character*. We don't care about the composition of a *junk word*. A *junk word* is skipped over and not processed by the system.

Index   An *index* object refers to a *text document*. An *index* has one key operation—*create text document index*.

Filing Directory   A *filing directory* object has many indexes. *Filing directory* and *index* are object classes, and *index file name* is the qualifier (i.e., a special attribute). A *filing directory* plus an *index name* yield an *index*. Qualification reduces the *filing directory* to *index* association from one-to-many to one-to-one. The *filing directory* object has two key operations—*find documents* and *delete index*. *Directory name* is also identified as an attribute or property of the *filing directory* object. The name of the association between *filing directory* and *index* is *filing directory plus index name yield an index*.

Document Reference Information, Author, Keyword, Abstract   A *document reference information* object consists of zero or more *author* objects, zero or more *keyword* objects, and zero or one *abstract*. The *document reference information* object has an aggregate relationship with the *author, keyword,* and *abstract* objects. Notice that the parts (*author, keyword, abstract*) of this aggregate, *document reference information*, may appear in multiple aggregates. A *document reference information* object describes one or more *text document(s)*. A key operation for this object is to *check for document reference information matches*. The associations among *author, keyword, abstract,* and *text document* are extraneous and are therefore removed from the object model.

Many objects and associations that seemed right at first now feel awkward and don't seem to fit in. Our understanding of the problem domain from an object-oriented perspective has increased, and this has necessitated a restructuring of our model. We have also discovered some new attributes based on our increasing knowledge of the application domain. A revised class diagram is shown in Figure 5.5.

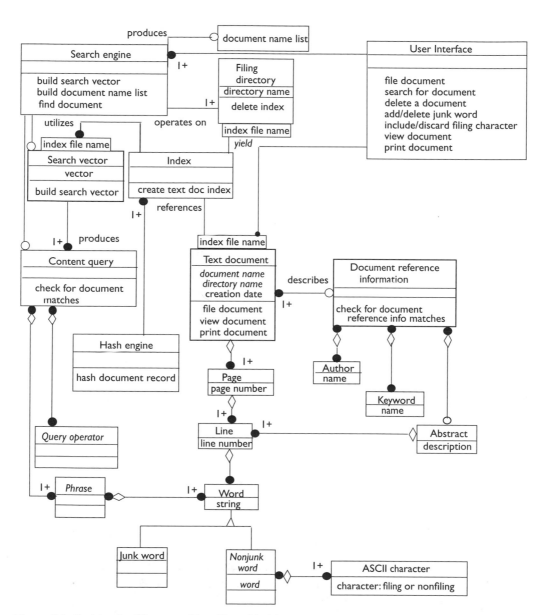

Figure 5.5. Revision 3 of Electronic Filing Object Model.

The object classes, attributes, and associations that are added to the object model are:

Object class	Attribute	Association
		content query is a collection of phrases
query operator		content query is a collection of query operators
phrase		phrase is a collection of words
		directory name
		document reference information describes text document

The following associations were removed from the object model: *author identifies text document, keyword identifies text document,* and *abstract describes text document.*

5.1.2.2 Checking the Dynamic Model—Step 2

We previously constructed a dynamic model for the user interface class. However, only the key operations, represented by various scenarios, from the user interface, were specified in the object model. A scan of each state diagram reveals that no missing or unnecessary key operations exist. Dynamic models were developed for several operations/functions that are included in the user interface, but not all of the functions/operations of the user interface are considered key to understanding the intent of the application. During the design of the user interface in Chapter 6, additional operations may surface.

5.1.2.3 Checking the Functional Model—Step 3

At this point we are checking the functional model for any missing or unnecessary key operations. We are also examining the key operations for any missing target classes that might come from data stores or data flows. The first two levels of the leveled set of data flow diagrams were previously examined for key operations. The process that we will follow now is to examine the same two levels of data flow diagrams for any missing or unnecessary key operations along with any missing target classes that might come from data stores or data flows.

Top-Level Data Flow Diagram The top-level data flow diagram for the EFP shows the following data flows:

- ❏ file
- ❏ document reference information, document file name, document directory name
- ❏ document index
- ❏ search criteria
- ❏ document name list

Text document is an alias for *file,* and *index* is an alias for *document index.* This should be reflected in the data dictionary, but it is not. The entries in the data dictionary for *file* and *document index* will be changed to include aliases for *text document* and *index,* respectively.

Dataflow Name:	document index
Aliases:	index

| Composition: | An index of all of the words in a document text file. |
| Notes: | The document index facilitates rapid retrieval of any nonjunk word in the content of the document. The document index is a file. |

Dataflow Name:	file
Aliases:	text document
Composition:	Program or data
Notes:	Files organize information used by a computer. A program or data is stored as a file on disk.

Text document and *index* are both identified as objects in the object model. *Document reference information* is also an object in the object model. *Document file name* and *document directory name* should be *document name* and *directory name* attributes for the *text document* and *filing directory* objects, respectively. Looking at the data dictionary, we see that *document name* and *directory name* are not aliases of *document file name* and *document directory name*, respectively. The data dictionary entries are updated to reflect these changes.

Dataflow Name:	document directory name
Aliases:	directory name
Composition:	$_1\{$alphanumeric characters$\}^n$
Notes:	A string of ASCII characters representing the name of a directory for the location of a document. The maximum number of characters in the name, n, is dependent upon the operating software platform.

Dataflow Name:	document file name
Aliases:	document name
Composition:	$_1\{$alphanumeric characters$\}^n$
Notes:	A string of ASCII characters representing the name of a file that is a document. The maximum number of characters in the name, n, is dependent upon the operating software platform.

Remember that data flows may represent either pure data values or normal objects. We will represent pure data values as attributes in the object model.

Document name list is an aggregate data store in our functional model or a passive object in our object model. It stores data for later access by the view, print, and successive search operations. Using the OMT criteria for discarding unnecessary and incorrect classes, we see that *document name list* is not a redundant class, an irrelevant class, a vague class, an attribute, an operation, or a role. *Document name list* may be an implementation construct for most applications, but it is a legitimate object class for this problem domain because it is a term that is commonly used in electronic filing, as noted in Chapter 1.

The association *document name list specifies one or more text documents* should also be added to the object model. A *document name list names one or more text documents*. Using the OMT criteria for discarding unnecessary and incorrect associations, we can see that these associations are not associations between eliminated classes, irrelevant or implementation associations, actions, ternary associations, or derived associations. These associations are added to the revised class diagram shown in Figure 5.6.

Also, there is one data store in the top-level data flow diagram—*filing directory. Filing directory* is already shown as an object in the object model.

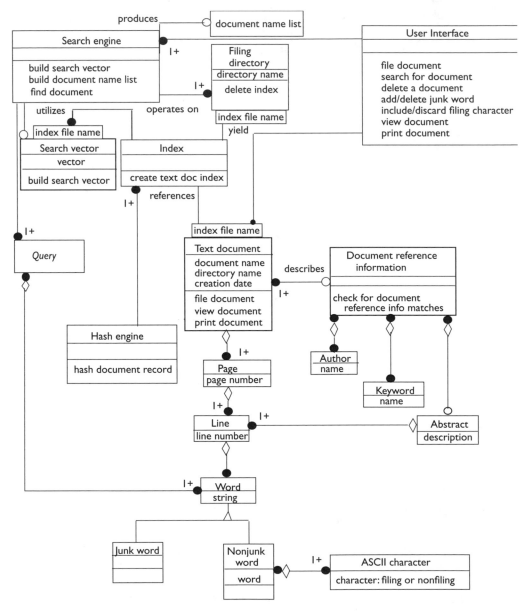

Figure 5.6. Object Model—Revision 4.

File Document DFD The File Document Data Flow Diagram has the following data flows:

- ❏ document directory name
- ❏ document file name
- ❏ document path
- ❏ document reference information
- ❏ text document type
- ❏ document index

We have already addressed the *document file name, document directory name, document reference information,* and *document index* data flows. *Document path* is a derived attribute (i.e., *document path* is derived from *document directory name* and *document file name*) and therefore is not shown in the object model. Rumbaugh recommends distinguishing between base attributes and derived attributes. Derived attributes should be shown with a "/" before the attribute name, if they are shown at all. As noted in Rumbaugh et al. (1991), derived attributes may be omitted from the object model to avoid overspecifying the state of an object. Computing a derived attribute does not change the state of the object.

Text document type is a data value and is a property of *text document.* Therefore, *text document type* may be shown as an attribute of text document. However, we will use the OMT criteria for discarding unnecessary and incorrect attributes to ensure that this is a valid attribute. *Text document type* is not an object, a qualifier, a name, an identifier, a link attribute, an internal value, or a discordant attribute. However, text document type is a minor attribute, which will not affect most operations—it is only necessary if we decide to process documents that are not in an ASCII format. Therefore, we will consider *text document type* to be fine detail and discard it, regarding it as an unnecessary attribute.

Find Document DFD The Find Document DFD has the following data flows:

- ❏ content query
- ❏ document index
- ❏ search vector
- ❏ document reference information
- ❏ abstract, keyword, and author queries and logical query operators
- ❏ document name
- ❏ document records list
- ❏ document name list

We have already addressed the *document reference information* and *document index* data flows. *Document name* is the same thing as *document file name* and is already represented as an attribute of *text document.*

Content query and *search vector* are also already shown as objects in the object model. *Query operator* is an alias for *logical query operator* and is also already shown in the object model.

Abstract query, keyword query, and *author query* are not currently shown in the object model. These entities are significant in their own right, and their independent existence is important. They will be represented as objects in the object model. We previously posed a number of queries to the application to ensure that the necessary access paths existed in the object model to answer these questions/queries (see Chapter 2 for examples). *Abstract query, keyword query, content query,* and *author query* are also defined in the data dictionary.

A *keyword query* is made up of *keyword(s)* and *query operator(s).* The data dictionary shows a *keyword* as consisting of alphanumeric characters. Actually a *keyword* can be a *word* or *phrase.* The data dictionary will be changed to show *keyword* as a *word* or *phrase.* *Author query* is made up of *author name* and *query operators.* An *author name* is listed in the data dictionary as composed of the name of a person associated with a document. The name of a author can actually be a *word* or *phrase.* The data dictionary will be changed to show *author* as a *word* or *phrase.*

Dataflow Name:	keyword
Composition:	word | phrase
Notes:	A keyword is a word that helps the user to uniquely identify a document. This entry is carried over from the initial data dictionary described in Chapter 2.

Dataflow Name:	author
Aliases:	author name
Composition:	word | phrase
Notes:	This entry is carried over from the initial data dictionary described in Chapter 2.

Abstract query, keyword query, and *author query* objects all have the same association with *document name list* as does the *content query* object. *Abstract, keyword, author,* and *content queries* all are made up of words or of phrases and query operators. Classes with similar attributes, associations, or operations can be organized to generalize their common aspects into a superclass using inheritance. We will create a superclass called *query. Abstract query, keyword query, content query,* and *author query* are all now subclasses of *query. Query* has an association with *document name list*—query *results in* a document name list.

At this point, the object model will no longer fit on one sheet of paper. One way of dealing with this is to group together a set of classes that captures some logical subset of the entire model into a module. The composite module itself is then shown in the main object model, and is then also expanded on a separate sheet. Here are several guidelines to follow in grouping classes into modules:

❑ When you are trying to decide what should be in a module, pick a set of classes, associations, generalizations, etc. that capture some logical subset of the object model.

❑ Try to minimize the number of bridge classes (i.e., the number of classes that connect the module with other parts of the object network).

❑ Group together in the same module classes that are closely connected by associations. A module should be functionally cohesive; its internal elements should be closely related to one another.

One logical subset of the object model is the classes that are logically related to a query. We will group together the classes that are logically related to a query into a *Query* Module. The *Query* Module has multiple classes that connect it to the rest of the object network. These classes form a bridge between the main object module and the *Query* Module and are therefore known as bridge classes. The objective is to minimize the number of bridge classes that connect modules or sheets. A module is the lowest-level subsystem in your application. (Subsystems will be discussed during systems design.)

The *Query* Module, shown on a separate sheet, shows all of the classes, associations, generalizations, etc. that comprise it, in addition to the bridge classes. A revised class diagram is shown in Figure 5.6. The *Query* Module is shown in Figure 5.7.

5.1.2.4 Reviewing the Problem Statement—Step 4

The next step in reviewing the models and checking for completeness and consistency is to reexamine the problem statement for objects, associations, or attributes that may have been missed during previous iterations. The initial problem statement is repeated here for convenience.

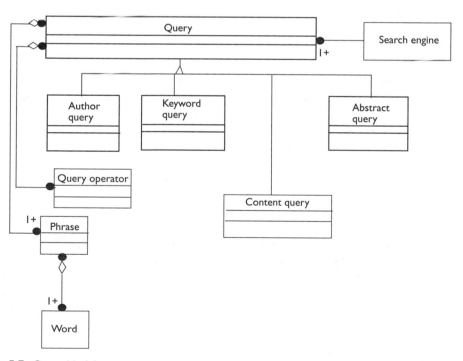

Figure 5.7. Query Module.

Initial Problem Statement

An electronic filing program (EFP) can be used to store and retrieve text documents. Any document created by a word processor, editor, or other means may be stored in the electronic filing system. Documents may be filed along with keywords, authors, and/or a document description or abstract describing the document. Documents filed in the system may also be removed or deleted.

Documents stored using the EFP are indexed to enable rapid retrieval. Documents are retrievable according to convenient schemes not found in conventional classifications; e.g., users may retrieve or locate documents based on their content, description, author(s), or user-defined keywords. Therefore, the document description, authors, keywords, and/or the actual text document itself may be searched.

A user may specify search criteria, which results in a number of documents being found that meet the specified search criteria. The user may then continue to specify additional search criteria, successively narrowing down the search until the required documents are found. Documents found that meet the user's search criteria may then be viewed or printed.

The user is provided with the capability of specifying any extraneous or "junk" words, which if found in the content of the document will not be searched or indexed—for example, and, or, not, the, if. The user can also specify which alphanumeric characters will be indexed and searchable (the filing character set), thereby limiting the search and index to only portions of a document(s).

Checking for Objects After reviewing the problem statement for potential objects and then discarding unnecessary and incorrect objects according to the OMT criteria, the following object classes remained: *text document, index, author, abstract, keyword, word, filing character, line, page, junk word.* A review of the problem statement reveals no potential object classes overlooked during the first pass in Chapter 2.

Checking for Associations After reviewing the problem statement for potential associations and then discarding, according to Rumbaugh's criteria, unnecessary and incorrect associations, the following associations remained: *index references words, document referenced by index, documents contain pages, pages contain lines, lines contain words, words contain alphanumeric characters, keyword identifies document, abstract describes document, text document identified by author, phrase contains words, line contains junk words, word contains alphanumeric character,* and *abstract contains lines.* Several new associations have become part of our object model as our level of understanding of the problem domain has increased. A review of the problem statement reveals no potential associations overlooked during the first pass (Chapter 2).

Checking for Attributes After reviewing the problem statement for potential attributes and then discarding unnecessary and incorrect attributes according to the OMT criteria, the following attributes remained: *document description, author name, index name, document name, date created, keyword name, string, character,* and *word.* These are all still attributes of objects in our current object model. The only attribute that is not obvious is *document description,* which has been renamed as *description* for the *abstract* object. Several new attributes have become part of our object model as our level of understanding of the problem domain has increased. A review of the problem statement reveals no potential attributes overlooked during the first pass.

Our initial object model is significantly different from our current object model. This necessitates a rewrite of our original problem statement to reflect corrections and understanding discovered during analysis. The original problem statement and subsequent problem statements, as well as other project deliverables—e.g., class diagrams, analysis document, design document, data dictionary, source code—should be placed under configuration management. A revised problem statement is subsequently stated.

Revised Problem Statement

An electronic filing program can be used to store and retrieve documents. Documents are first created by a word processor, editor, or other means. A document may then be filed along with document reference information. Document reference information contains keyword(s), author(s), and an abstract, which describe the text document. Document indexes, maintained in a filing directory, are created for documents filed in the system. The indexes then refer to the text documents that are filed in the system.

A text document may contain multiple pages, each page contains multiple lines, and each line contains multiple words. The words may be junk words (common vernacular not used by the program for filing or finding documents) or nonjunk words that are used by the electronic filing program. The words used by electronic filing may contain one or more ASCII characters. Each ASCII character may or may not be a character that is used in electronic filing.

Documents filed in the system may later be retrieved by using a query and conducting a search. A query is an author query, keyword query, abstract query, and/or content query. A query contains phrases separated by query operators. A search results in a document name list or search hit list. The user may select one of the documents in the document name list to view or print. Alternatively, the user may continue to specify additional queries or search criteria, successively narrowing down the search until the required documents are found.

The user is provided with the capability of specifying any extraneous or junk words, which if found in the content of the document will not be searched or indexed—for example, and, or, not, the, if. The user can also specify which alphanumeric characters will be indexed and searchable, thereby limiting the search and index to only portions of a document(s).

5.1.2.5 Testing the Object Model—Step 5

The next step in checking our models for completeness and consistency is to test the object model using previously developed scenarios. Our program has an interactive interface, which is dominated by the dynamic model. The dynamic model was produced by first preparing scenarios of typical interaction sequences between the system and one or more actors. Our scenarios depict dialogs between the program and the user, since the dynamic model and the user interface are essentially the same thing in this application.

An interactive interface has object classes in the object model that represent interaction elements. However, we have not yet specified objects for the object model that represent the user interface. The objects we have specified in the object model to date represent the internal structure of the problem domain and not the user interface. Therefore, the dynamic model or scenarios do not really "test" our object model. We will test the object model using detailed scenarios during object design, when all of the objects of the user interface will be specified in the model.

5.1.2.6 Testing Access Paths—Step 6

The next step is to test access paths through the object model to see if they still yield sensible results. The objective is to see if the object model can accommodate all of situations one would expect. As we did in Chapter 2, we are basically validating the model by picking one or more use cases/scenarios and tracing access paths through the object model to see if anything is missing.

Testing access paths allows us to "walk through" our model, making sure that the model accurately represents the problem and application domain. Not all of the details of the pseudocode for answering these questions at this level of abstraction will be shown at this point. Our goal is to demonstrate that the appropriate objects, associations, and operations completely represent the object model, and not to show the details of how each operation is implemented in the system.

The requests that we will ask of the object model are variations of the questions/statements from Chapter 2 in addition to some new requests. The requests that we will now pose to the object model are:

1. What are all of the documents indexed by the electronic filing program?

2. Given an author query, find all of the documents identified by the author query.

3. Given a word phrase or content query, find all of the documents identified by the word phrase in the content of a document.

4. Given an author query, abstract query, keyword query, and content query, find all of the documents identified by these queries. Next, show all occurrence of these queries in the document.

5. Given a date range, find all of the documents created within this date range.

6. File a document in the system with an author, keyword, and an abstract specified as document reference information.

1. **Problem:** What are all of the documents indexed by the electronic filing program?

   Solution: The name of each document index in the filing directory will be retrieved.

```
Filing_directory::retrieve_all_indexes () returns set of indexes
   index_names := create empty set;
   for each index_file_name in self
      add self.index_file_name to set index_names;
   end for each index_file_name
   return index_names;
```

The user interface currently has no provision for showing all of the documents that have been filed to date. In order to provide this capability, a new function would need to be added to *show all documents*. Also, this would require a new operation be added to the filing directory class *retrieve indexes*. We'll leave this as a future exercise for the reader.

2. Problem: Given an author query, find all of the documents identified by the author query.

Solution: Each author name between query operators in the *author query* will be compared against authors that are part of the document reference information for each indexed document in the filing directory. The specified logical operations will then be performed on the results of this search. If the query is satisfied, then the name of the text document is added to the set of documents that are returned as part of the query. The *check_for_author_match* operation is identified from the functional model and is assigned to the *author query* object because the *author query* object plays the lead role in the operation. A *check_for_abstract_match* and a *check_for_keyword_match* are assigned to the *abstract query* and *keyword query* classes, respectively, for the same reason. An attribute, *query*, will be assigned to the query class to represent the actual query entered by the user. The query attribute will be inherited by each of the author, keyword, content, and abstract query classes.

No mechanism for parsing a query currently exists in the object model. A *parse query* operation will be assigned to the query class. This operation may be inherited by each type of query.

```
Let dri = Document reference information.
User_interface::search_for_document ()
   author_query = the user entered query
   self.search_engine.find_documents (author_query) returns document name list
      create document_name_list := create empty set
      self.author_query.parse_query (author_query)
      for each index_file_name in self.filing_directory
         /* check each document filed in the system to see if its author
            component of document reference information matches the author
            query */
         if self.author_query.check_for_author_match (self.filing_directory.
         index.text_document.dri.authors) = TRUE then
            add self.filing_directory.index.text_document.document_name to
            document_name_list
         end if
      end for each index
   return document_name_list
```

3. Problem: Given a word phrase or content query, find all of the documents identified by the word phrase in the content of a document.

Solution: Each phrase between query operators in the *content query* will be searched for in the content of each indexed document in the filing directory. The specified logical operations will then be performed on the results of this search. If the query is satisfied, then the name of the text document is added to the set of documents that is returned as part of the query. The *check_for_document_matches* operation is identified from the functional model and is assigned to the *content query* object because the *content query* object plays the lead role in the operation.

```
Let dri = Document reference information.
User_interface::search_for_document ()
   content_query = the user entered query
```

```
self.search_engine.find_documents (content_query) returns document name list
   create document_name_list := create empty set
   self.content_query.parse_query (content_query)
   for each index_file_name in self.filing_directory
   /* check each document filed in the system to see if any of its content
      matches the content query */
      if self.content_query::check_for_document_matches
      (self.filing_directory.index.text_document) = TRUE then
         add self.filing_directory.index.text_document.document_name to
         document_name_list
      end if
   end for each index
return document_name_list
```

4. Problem: a. Given an author query, abstract query, keyword query, and content query, find all of the documents identified by these queries. b. Show all occurrences of these queries in the document.

Solution: a. The find_documents operation from the previous examples already satisfies each of these types of queries. We'll assume that a document name list contains the combined results of these queries. b. Each occurrence of a query match in a text document is displayed to the user. The document name list contains the name of every document found that matches the previously specified query. A document records list exists for every one of the found documents.

```
User_interface::view_document (document_name_list)
   self.text_document.view (document_name_list)
   for each document name in document_name_list
      for each record number in document_name_list.document records list
         display record of text document
      end for each record number
   end for each document name
   return
```

This query shows that a new association must be added to the model from the *user interface* class to the *document name list* class if the user is to be able to view document name list information.

5. Problem: Given a date range, find all of the documents created within this date range.

Solution: The name of each document filed into the system within the given date range will be retrieved. Each document filed in the system has a creation date. The filing directory is scanned for all indexed documents. Then the creation date of each text document associated with a document index is checked to see if it is within the specified date range. If so, then the document name is returned.

```
Filing_directory::find_dated_documents (date range) returns set of documents
   documents:= create empty set;
   for each index in self
   /* compare the creation date of each document with the given date range */
      if self.index.text_document.creation_date in date_range then
         add self.index.text_document.document_name to set documents
```

```
      end if
   end for each index
return documents
```

The user interface currently has no provision for finding all of the documents created within a date range. In order to provide this capability, a new function would need to be added to *find all documents by date range* to the user interface class. We'll leave this as a future exercise for the reader.

6. Problem: File a document in the system with an author, keyword, and an abstract specified as document reference information.

Solution: Documents are filed into the system through the user interface. The document reference information that is specified through the user interface and is used in filing the document will require an association between the *user interface* class and the *document reference information* class.

```
Let dri = Document reference information.
dri = user entered author, keyword, and abstract information
User_interface::file_document (document path, dri)
   self.text_document.file_document (document path, dri)
     self.index.create_text_doc_index (document path, dri);
     return
   return
```

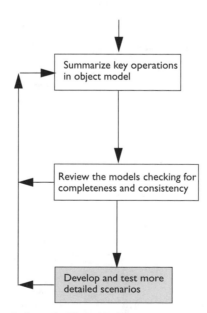

Figure 5.8. Process Diagram for Refining the Three Models.

5.1.2.7 Conclusions

Testing the access paths has revealed several new operations, an attribute, and associations. These are shown as processes in the functional model and should be included in the object model to completely

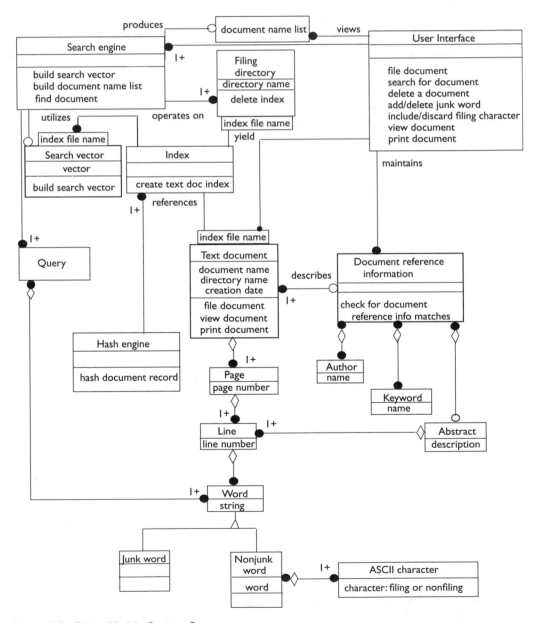

Figure 5.9. Object Model—Revision 5.

specify the problem and application domain. A revised class diagram including these changes is shown in Figure 5.9. A revised query module is shown in Figure 5.10.

The new operations are:

- ❑ check for abstract match
- ❑ check for keyword match
- ❑ check for author match
- ❑ check for document match
- ❑ parse query

The new associations are:

- ❑ user interface views document name list
- ❑ user interface maintains document reference information

The new attribute is *query*, and it is assigned to the *query* class.

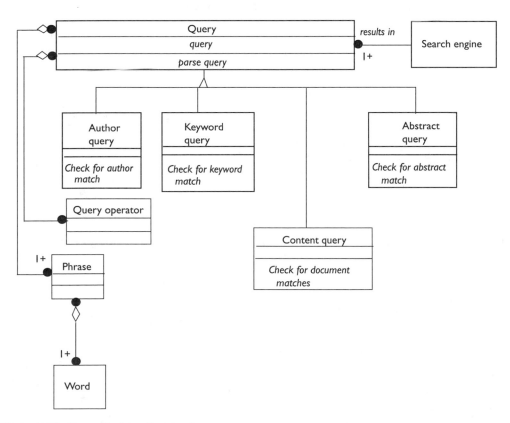

Figure 5.10. Query Module—Revision 1.

5.1.3 Developing and Testing More Detailed Scenarios

Another step that can be taken to verify the three models is to develop more detailed scenarios as variations on the basic scenarios, and then use these scenarios to verify the model.

Since the dynamic model involves mainly the user interface in our application, the main way of developing more detailed scenarios is to include exceptions related to the user interface. This would require specifying additional details about the user interface, which we will postpone for now.

Application objects are those objects that represent the user interface and other forms of control (Rumbaugh, 1993a). Application objects should be discovered during analysis and before the design of the system implementation. We will discover application objects during the design and specification of the application interface (not as part of the analysis of the domain model). Since the subject of designing and specifying the application interface is a major topic for this application, we'll postpone this discussion until Chapter 6. This may require us to verify, iterate, and refine the three models again.

5.2 SUMMARY OF PROCESS AND DELIVERABLES

In this chapter we have summarized key operations in the object model and iterated our analysis. These key operations were discovered during an examination of the dynamic and functional models. In the dynamic model, operations can come from events, actions, and activities. In the functional model, operations can come from functions/processes that have interesting computational structure.

The deliverables for summarizing key operations and iterating the analysis consist of updated

- ❑ data dictionary
- ❑ object model
- ❑ functional model
- ❑ dynamic model
- ❑ problem statement

The next step in the development of our program is to design and fully specify the application interface.

CHAPTER 6

Designing and Specifying
the Application Interface

Main Chapter Topics	Topic Questions/Explanations
application objects	99 what are application objects
interactive interface	100 what are the steps in designing an interactive interface
user interface design tools	101 what are the user interface design tools that will be used
main application user interface	102 what is the main application user interface
use cases	103 file a document use case
operations	126 combining models to obtain operations
object model	133 detailed user interface object model
analysis document	136 what is the analysis document

THE ELECTRONIC FILING application has an interactive interface, and interactive interfaces are dominated by the dynamic model. The dynamic model is used to define the protocol of the user interaction. The user interface is a major subsystem of the electronic filing program. The intent of this chapter is to design and specify the application interface (i.e., user interface subsystem) in terms of its classes, associations, attributes, and operations. Note that this is not the same as the design of the program itself. According to Rumbaugh (1993b), application objects should be discovered during analysis and before the design of the system implementation. The application interface defines the functionality of the electronic filing program itself and must be considered during analysis Rumbaugh (1993a). Figure 6.1 shows where we are in the analysis process— designing and specifying the application interface.

Application objects are objects that are visible to the outside users (Rumbaugh, 1993b). Application objects may be presentations, formats, controllers (user interfaces), devices, interfaces, or others. Domain objects represent the problem domain. The application objects are layered on top of the domain objects. Utility objects are the generic class library object classes that you buy from a vendor, e.g., set, bag, dictionary, string. Utility objects are used to implement programs.

The user should be involved in the design of the user interface (application objects) because it represents the user's conceptual view of the system. Also, the user must be satisfied with the

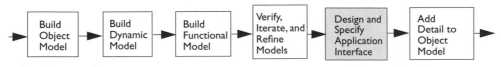

Figure 6.1. OMT Analysis Process.

"look and feel" of the application represented by the user interface. The user works only with the user interface portion of the program, so this is the part of the application that is frequently subject to change. Maintaining a loosely coupled interface between the application objects and the domain objects minimizes the degree of change that the domain objects will have to undergo as the user interface changes.

Up until now the user interface has been represented as a single subsystem, or course-grained object. However, our graphical user interface (GUI) will consist of many different classes from commercial off-the-shelf class libraries, e.g., Borland's Application Frameworks and Digitalk's Smalltalk/ V. This chapter will flesh out the design and specification of the application (user) interface.

A familiarity with windowing concepts is essential to understanding event-driven graphical user interfaces. A brief tutorial on windowing concepts and the use of two GUI tools to design the user interface is presented in Appendix B for interested readers.

6.1 DETAILED USER INTERFACE DYNAMIC MODEL

The dynamic model was developed around the user interface with minimal interactions with other classes. Now the detailed presentation formats of the user interface that support the general information flow between the application objects of the user interface subsystem and the domain objects will be specified. Additional details may also be added to the user interface to accommodate the limitations of the tools or class libraries we have chosen to use in our design and implementation. The existing scenarios, event traces, and statecharts or state diagrams may also be modified to reflect additional detail in the user interface. Our end product for the dynamic model will be detailed scenarios, event traces, event flow diagram, and statecharts or state diagrams. We will also have identified the application objects that comprise the application interface.

The following steps in designing the interactive interface are taken from Rumbaugh et al. (1991):

1. Isolate user interface objects from the objects that define the semantics of the application.

2. Use predefined windowing objects.

3. Use the dynamic model as the structure of the program.

4. Isolate physical events, such as taking input from a pop-up menu, from logical events (e.g., a graphical interface taking input).

5. Fully specify the application functions invoked by the user interface.

Our strategy all along has been to isolate the user interface objects from the objects that define the semantics of the application. The user interface has previously been represented as a subsystem with no definition of the internal objects that make up the subsystem. We are using predefined windowing objects from commercial off-the-shelf class libraries (Borland's Application Frameworks and Digitalk's Smalltalk/V) to design and implement the user interface. Our user interface is being designed and implemented as being event driven and as following the flow of control of the dynamic model.

During the development of the initial dynamic model, we separated physical events from logical events and specified only the information flow between the user and the application. Now we are at the stage where we will fully specify the application functions invoked by the user interface.

For each application function (use case) invoked by the user interface we must do the following:

1. Specify detailed presentation formats for the user interface function.

2. Update existing scenarios to include additional detail.

3. Update existing event traces to include additional detail.

4. Update existing statecharts to include additional detail.

6.1.1 Graphically Oriented User Interface Design Tools

A high-quality user interface design tool that generates readable and efficient code and enables the developer to provide input to the code generation process can be an efficient and productive way of developing a graphical user interface. This design tool should utilize a class library that encapsulates parts of the Windows Application Program Interface (API), insulating the programmer from the details of windows programming and saving programming time and effort. The alternative is to design the user interface by examining the class libraries and determining which classes are appropriate for various elements of the interface, and then to developing the necessary code.

We will use two GUI design tools for quickly designing menus for Windows applications: (1) Protogen, which generates code compatible with either ANSI C or Borland's ObjectWindows for C++, and (2) Window Builder, a GUI builder for Smalltalk/V and Win32.

After we have generated and tested the code for the user interface, we will examine the code and specify the classes and associations that are represented in the user interface. The classes and their associations will become the user interface subsystem of the object model for electronic filing. However, the first step in the design of a user interface is to lay out the entire GUI the way we wish to see it either on paper or with a GUI builder tool.

The main menu bar and its associated pull-down menus for electronic filing are shown in Figure 6.2. A menu item displayed with an ellipsis (…) indicates that a dialog box is attached to the

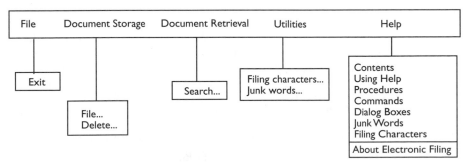

Figure 6.2. Electronic Filing Menu Bar and Pull-Down Menus.

menu item. An optional Help pull-down menu is also shown in Figure 6.2 for completeness. The help menu is not designed or implemented in this text, but is left to the reader as an exercise.

6.1.2 Main Application User Interface

The electronic filing application has five major use cases. Each use case represents a number of scenarios that may be invoked by a user when running the electronic filing application. The scenarios represent the invocation of the application functions. The user interface ties together all of these possible scenarios. The top-level statechart for the user interface is the same as that shown in Chapter 3.

The electronic filing use cases from Chapter 3 are now developed in more detail to include scenarios that have exception cases and details of the implementation of the user interface (e.g., dialog boxes, message boxes; *DB* is used to abbreviate *Dialog Box* in the statecharts for the user interface). Then the corresponding event traces and statecharts from Chapter 3, for each user interface operation, are also developed in more detail to reflect changes in the scenarios and "how" the event trace will be implemented. There may be new objects introduced during object design for the implementation environment that should also participate in an event trace. The purpose of each event trace is to describe the communication between different actors/objects and objects in our program.

The use cases from Chapter 3 are repeated here for convenience:

1. filing a document

2. searching for, or finding, a document(s)

3. deleting a document

4. changing the filing character set

5. changing the junk words

The process we will use to develop a more detailed dynamic model involves doing the following for each use case:

1. Specify detailed presentation formats for the user interface operation.

2. Review the normal scenario to see if events should be added, deleted, or modified based on the specific elements now contained in the dialog boxes associated with the scenario. Change events in the scenario accordingly.

3. Repeat step 2 for a scenario with exceptions. Add exceptions and change the scenario accordingly. Create new exception cases as needed to deal with new exception conditions.

4. Update existing event traces to include additional detail from the scenarios.

5. Update existing statecharts or state diagrams to include additional detail from the event traces.

This process will now be applied to each use case. Each use case represents the dialog for an application function.

Some sequence of steps is or may be common in several scenarios. These common steps will be grouped and noted for each scenario to promote reuse and to minimize redundancy.

> **Important:** The normal and exception scenarios in the remainder of this chapter represent some variations of user input and system response. Many other variations are possible! Modern user interfaces allow flexible input. The intent here is only to illustrate some possible variations of user input that bring out all of the graphical elements of the user interface for a particular scenario. The rigid interaction sequences subsequently depicted in scenarios and event traces only represent one or two possibilities.

6.1.2.1 File a Document Operation

Detailed Presentation Formats The *file a document* operation utilizes the following dialog boxes from the user interface:

- ❑ File a Document
- ❑ Document Reference Information
- ❑ Filing in Progress
- ❑ Invalid Filing Characters Error Message

The dialog box for *Filing a Document* is shown in Figure 6.3. Figure 6.4 shows the dialog box for specifying *Document Reference Information* when filing a document. A detailed scenario for filing a document (see Scenario 2) requires a "filing in progress" message to be displayed after the user has requested the filing of the document. This message will demonstrate a visible sign of filing progress by showing a "percent filing complete" as part of the message. The message box that will be displayed to the user while the document is being filed is shown in Figure 6.5.

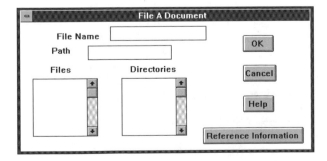

Figure 6.3. File a Document Dialog Box.

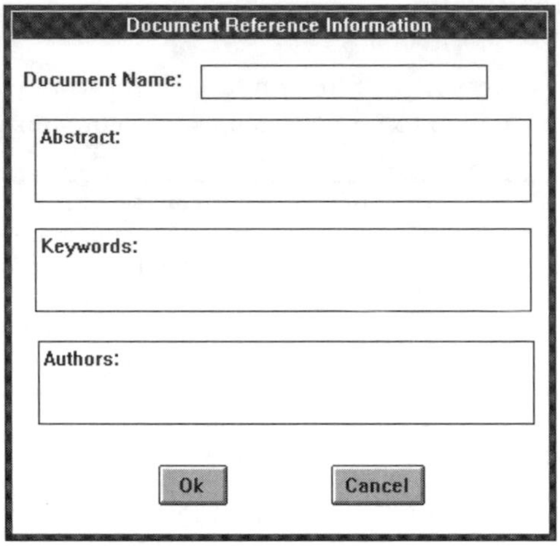

Figure 6.4. Document Reference Information Dialog Box.

Scenarios The sequence of events, or steps, that is common to both normal and exceptions scenarios is shown in Scenario 1. This setup sequence of events precedes both the detailed filing scenario and detailed filing scenario with exceptions.

A detailed filing scenario is depicted in Scenario 2. Note the difference in detail between this scenario and the normal filing scenario of Chapter 3. Chapter 3 scenarios address general information flow, whereas the scenarios presented here represent the specific objects that will be part of the user interface.

Scenario 1. Setup Sequence of Events Preceding All Filing Scenarios.

> The user selects the Document Storage menu-bar item from the menu bar.
> A pop-up menu for Document Storage appears.
> The user selects the file item from the pop-up menu.
> The File a Document dialog box is displayed.
> The user selects a directory from the scrolling list of directories.
> The directory name is displayed in the path edit control box.
> The user selects a document file from the scrolling list of files.
> The document file name is displayed in the path and file name edit control boxes.

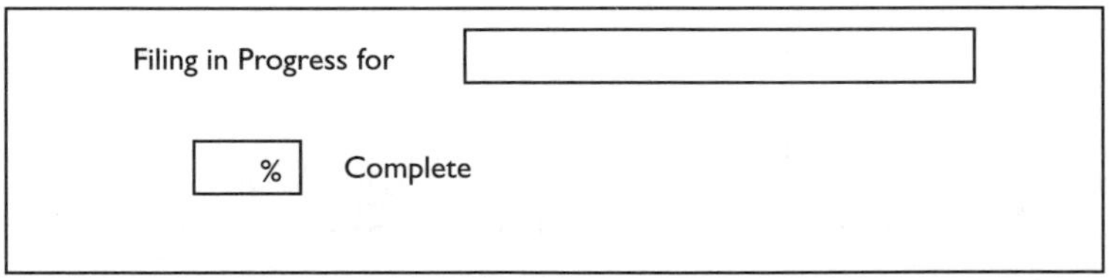

Figure 6.5. Filing in Progress Message Box.

The user selects the Reference Information push button in the dialog box.
A Document Reference Information dialog box is displayed.
The document name is displayed inside of the document name edit box.

Scenario 2. Detailed Filing Scenario.

The user enters a description of the document in the edit field for the abstract.
The user enters keywords for the document in the edit field for the keywords.
The user enters authors for the document in the edit field for the authors.
The user selects the OK push button in the Document Reference Information dialog box.
A filing in progress message box is displayed while the document is being indexed.
The filing in progress message box is cleared from the screen when the indexing of the document
   is completed.
The Document Reference Information and File a Document dialog boxes are cleared from the screen.
The main application window is redisplayed.

Scenario 3. Detailed Filing Scenario with Exceptions, for a Document.

The user enters keywords, consisting of all invalid filing characters, for the document in the edit field for the
   keywords.
The user selects the OK button in the Document Reference Information dialog box.
The EFP displays an error message and asks the user to reenter the keywords or change the filing character set.
The user selects the OK button in the error message box.
The error message box is cleared from the screen.
The keywords are cleared from the Document Reference Information dialog box.
The user selects the Cancel button in the Document Reference Information dialog box.
The Document Reference Information and File a Document dialog boxes are cleared from the screen.
The main application window is redisplayed.

A detailed scenario for filing a document, with exceptions, is shown in Scenario 3. This scenario requires an error message to be displayed if the user enters invalid filing characters for the abstract, authors, or keywords. The error message dialog box requires the user to acknowledge the error by selecting the OK push button before continuing with the program. The error message box that may be displayed to the user is shown in Figure 6.6.

Event Trace A detailed event trace for filing a document is shown in Figure 6.7. The main window, file dialog box, and document reference information dialog box objects represent the user interface subsystem. The "create" event in this diagram denotes the creation of an object. The file dialog box object is created and opened by the main window object. The document reference information object is created and opened by the file dialog box object. Finally, the text document object is created and opened by the document reference information object.

Invalid Filing Characters were specified in your data entry.

Please reenter the data or cancel your operation.

OK

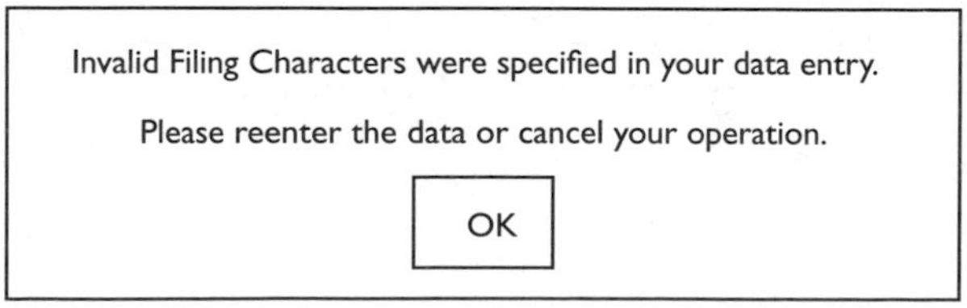

Figure 6.6. Invalid Filling Characters Error Message Box.

Statechart A revised *File Document* statechart is shown in Figure 6.8. This statechart contains the following new states along with their corresponding events:

- ❏ the Path Error state containing the *do: display error message box* activity
- ❏ the *Cancel* state with the activity *do: display cancel message box*

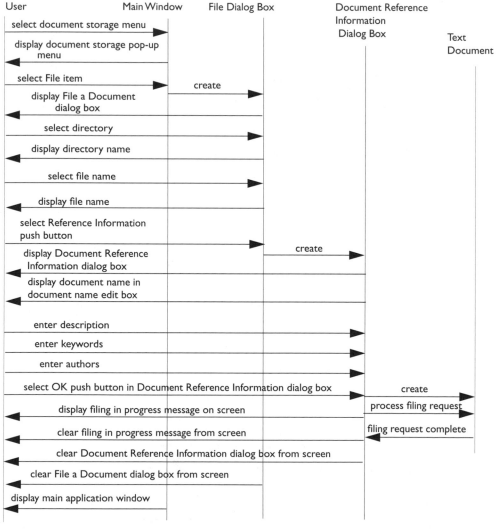

Figure 6.7. Detailed Filing Event Trace.

When either of these activities is performed, message boxes will be displayed that require a simple acknowledgment by the user, i.e., select the OK push button. Several event names have been

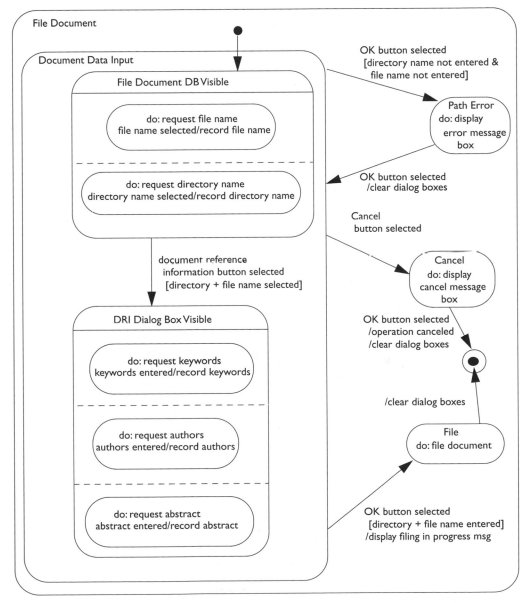

Figure 6.8. *File Document and DRI Dialog Box Class Statecharts.*

changed to indicate when a user selects various dialog-box push buttons. Also, some state names have been changed to reflect the use of implementation artifacts.

6.1.2.2 Delete Operation

Detailed Presentation Formats The *delete a document* operation utilizes the following dialog boxes from the user interface:

❑ Delete a Document
❑ Delete Error Message

The *Delete a Document* dialog box is shown in Figure 6.9. Only the directories that contain index files and the index file names themselves will be shown in the scrolling list boxes within the dialog box. This also allows the user to see all of the documents that were filed in the electronic filing system; i.e., all of the documents that were filed in the system must have an index file. The user may select and delete a document or just survey the document indexes and then cancel the operation. The document name is displayed in the file name edit control box. The path edit control box displays the location of a file within the directory tree.

Scenario 4. Setup Sequence of Events Preceding All Delete Scenarios.

The user selects the Document Storage menu-bar item from the menu bar.
A pop-up menu for Document Storage appears.
The user selects the Delete item from the pop-up menu.
The Delete a Document dialog box is displayed.

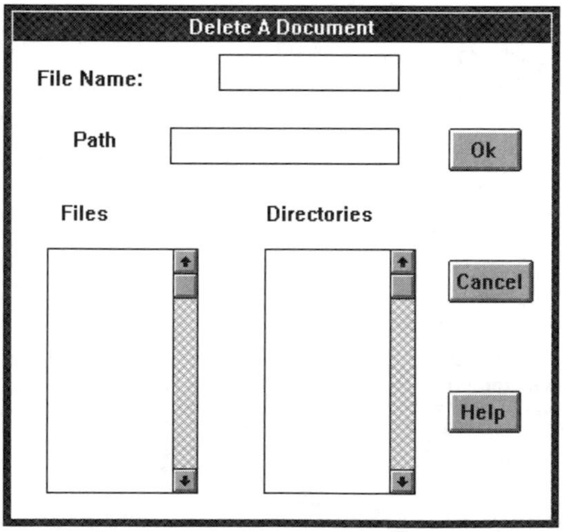

Figure 6.9. Delete a Document Dialog Box.

Scenario 5. Delete Scenario.

> The user selects a directory from the scrolling list of directories.
> The directory name is displayed in the path edit control box.
> The user selects a document file from the scrolling list of files.
> The document file name is displayed in the file name edit control boxes.
> The user selects the OK push button in the dialog box.
> The document index is deleted.
> The Delete a Document dialog box is cleared from the screen.
> The main application window is redisplayed.

Scenarios The sequence of events, or steps, that are common to both normal and exceptional delete scenarios is shown in Scenario 4. This setup sequence of events precedes both the detailed delete scenario and detailed delete scenario (with exceptions).

A detailed scenario for deleting a document is shown in Scenario 5, and a detailed scenario for deleting a document, with exceptions, is shown in Scenario 6. This scenario requires an error message to be displayed if the user selects the OK push button before specifying a directory and file. The delete error message dialog box (see Figure 6.10) requires the user to acknowledge the error by selecting the OK push button before continuing with the program.

Scenario 6. Delete Scenario with Exceptions.

> The user selects the OK push button in the dialog box.
> Delete error message box is displayed showing error message and asking user to specify
> > directory and file name.
> The user selects the OK push button in the delete error message box.
> The delete error message box is cleared from the screen.
> The user selects the cancel button in the dialog box.
> The Delete a Document dialog box is cleared from the screen.
> The main application window is redisplayed.

Event Trace A detailed event trace for deleting a document is shown in Figure 6.11. The main window and the delete dialog box objects represent the user interface subsystem. The delete dialog box object is created and opened by the main window object. The filing directory object is created when the application is first started and is destroyed at the completion of the application.

Statechart A revised *Delete Document* statechart is shown in Figure 6.12. This statechart contains the following new states along with their corresponding events:

❑ the *Path Error* state containing the *do: display error message box* activity

❑ the *Cancel* state with the activity *do: display cancel message box*

> A file must be selected before attempting to delete a document.
>
> Please select a document or cancel your operation.
>
> OK

Figure 6.10. Delete Error Message Box.

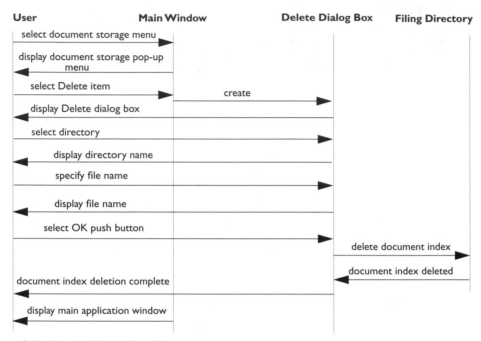

Figure 6.11. Detailed Delete Event Trace.

When either of these activities is performed, message boxes will be displayed that require a simple acknowledgment by the user; i.e., select the OK push button. Also, several event names have been changed to indicate when a user selects various dialog box push buttons.

A new exception case has been included in the statechart that is not shown in the event trace or in the scenario with exceptions. The exception case is that the dialog box may not display the correct document indexes and directories. This is because the user may switch windows and manipulate files so that the scrolling lists of file and directory names in the dialog box are no longer valid. Therefore, an error may occur because the user has selected a directory and file that no longer exists, unbeknownst to the program. This results in a *bad file* event causing a transition to the *File Unavailable* state. The *invalid file message box* in Figure 6.13 is displayed and the user is asked to respond by selecting the OK push button. The event *OK button selected* transfers the user interface back to the *Path Input* state.

6.1.2.3 Search Operation

Detailed Presentation Formats The *search* operation utilizes the following dialog boxes from the user interface:

❑ Search for a Document

❑ Search Results

❑ Search Error Message Box

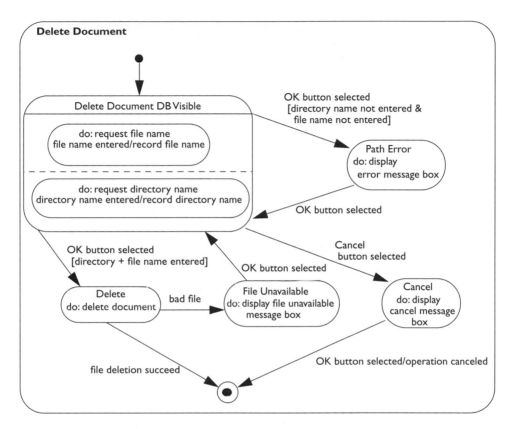

Figure 6.12. *Delete Document* Dialog Box Class Statechart.

The dialog box for searching for a document is shown in Figure 6.14. Here the user enters specific search criteria for locating one or more documents. Logical operators (i.e., AND and OR) may be used between words or phrases within a search query category (i.e., content, abstract, keyword, or author searches). The search query categories are also connected via logical operators. The logical connecting operators default to AND. A tab or enter key moves the cursor across fields in the search dialog box.

Figure 6.13. Invalid File Message Box.

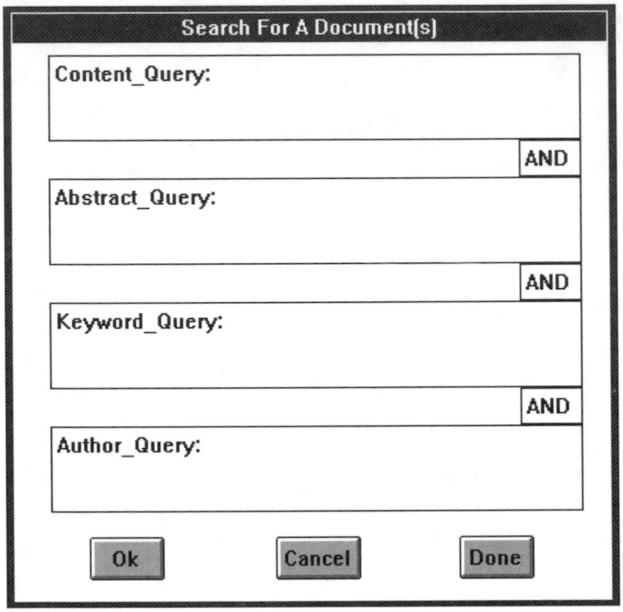

Figure 6.14. Search Dialog Box.

A search error message box (see Figure 6.18) is displayed if the user selects the OK push button before entering any search criteria. The search results are presented to the user via a search

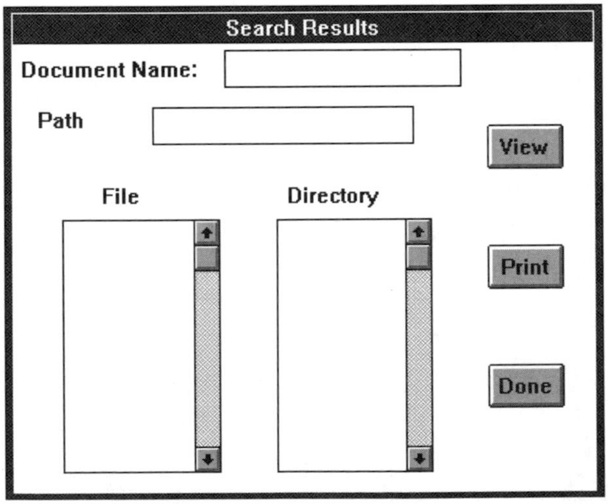

Figure 6.15. Search Results Dialog Box.

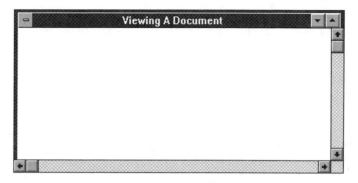

Figure 6.16. Viewing a Document Window.

results dialog box shown in Figure 6.15. The search results are displayed as a scrolling list of document names and directory names that were found which meet the search criteria. The user may then select one of those documents to view or print and then select the view or print push buttons. If the user selects a document to view, the document will appear in a new window, enabling the user to scroll through the document and examine its contents. The locations of the hits (i.e., places in the document where the search criteria were found) in the document may be highlighted. Highlighting the hits is left as an exercise to the reader. The view operation utilizes the *Viewing a Document* window shown in Figure 6.16. The print operation utilizes the *Print a Document* dialog box shown in Figure 6.17.

Scenarios The sequence of events, or steps, that is common to both normal-search and exceptions-search scenarios is shown in Scenario 7. This setup sequence of events precedes both the detailed search scenario and the detailed search scenario with exceptions.

A detailed scenario for searching for a document is shown in Scenario 8. This also includes the scenario for viewing a document, since the only documents that may be viewed or printed are those that have been retrieved as the result of a search. This scenario assumes that the user is not

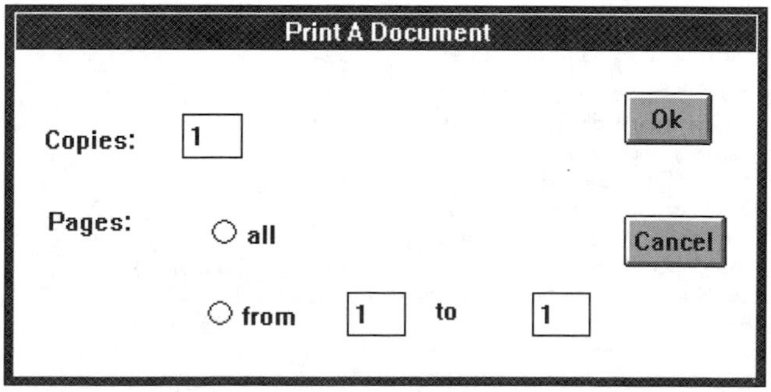

Figure 6.17. Print a Document Dialog Box.

changing the logical operators that connect the query categories. A scenario that requires multiple searches to find a document is simply a repetition of a single search and will not be shown.

Scenario 7. Setup Sequence of Events Preceding All Search Scenarios.

>   The user selects the Document Retrieval menu-bar item from the menu bar.
>   A pop-up menu for Document Retrieval appears.
>   The user selects the Search item from the pop-up menu.
>   The Search for a Document(s) dialog box is displayed.

Scenario 8. Search Scenario Including View.

>   The user enters a query in the content query edit field.
>   The user tabs over to the content query logical operator and changes it from AND to OR.
>   The user tabs over to the abstract query edit field.
>   The user enters a query in the abstract query edit field.
>   The user tabs over to the keyword query edit field.
>   The user enters one or more keywords and logical operators in the keyword edit field.
>   The user tabs over to the author query edit field.
>   The user enters one or more authors in the author query edit field.
>   The user selects the OK button in the Search for a Document(s) dialog box.
>   Search Results dialog box is displayed, showing the names of several documents found meeting the search criteria.
>   The user selects a directory from the scrolling list of directories.
>   The directory name is displayed in the path edit control box.
>   The user selects a document file from the scrolling list of files.
>   The document file name is displayed in the document name edit control box.
>   The user selects the view push button in the dialog box.
>   The viewing a document window appears within the main application window with the selected document being displayed.
>   The user selects the down arrow in the vertical scroll bar.
>   The document is scrolled upwards.
>   The user selects the system menu box in the left corner of the viewing a document window.
>   The system menu is displayed.
>   The user selects the close item from the system menu box.
>   The viewing a document window is cleared from the screen.
>   The user selects the done push button from the search results dialog box.
>   The search results dialog box is cleared from the screen.
>   The user selects the done push button from the search for a document dialog box.
>   The search for a document dialog box is cleared from the screen.
>   The main application window is redisplayed.

Scenario 9. Search Scenario with Exceptions.

>   The user selects the OK button in the Search for a Document(s) dialog box.
>   A search error message box is displayed showing an error message and asking the user to enter content, abstract, keyword, or author information as a query.
>   The user selects the OK push button in the search error message box.
>   The search error message box is cleared from the screen.
>   The Search for Documents dialog box is redisplayed.
>   The user selects the Cancel button in the Search for Document(s) dialog box.
>   The Search for Document(s) dialog box is cleared from the screen.
>   The main application window is redisplayed.

A detailed scenario for a document search, with exceptions, is shown in Scenario 9. This scenario requires an error message to be displayed if the user selects the OK push button before entering any

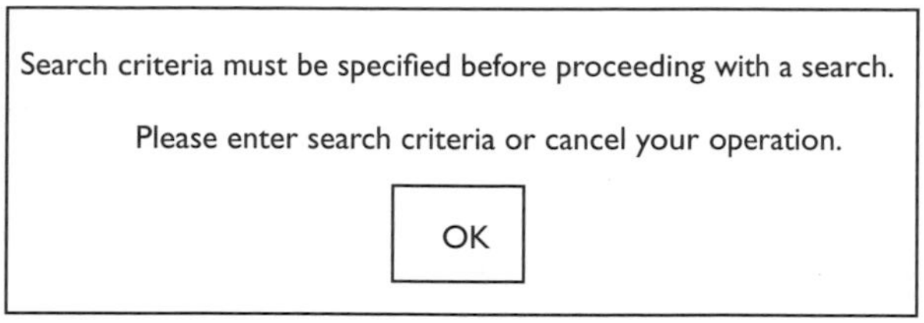

```
Search criteria must be specified before proceeding with a search.

Please enter search criteria or cancel your operation.

┌──────┐
│  OK  │
└──────┘
```

Figure 6.18. Search Error Message Box.

search criteria. The search error message dialog box (see Fig. 6.18) requires the user to acknowledge the error by selecting the OK push button before continuing with the program.

A detailed scenario for searching for a document, including print, is shown in Scenario 10. No meaningful exception conditions exist for the print function.

Event Trace The event trace for a normal search scenario, including print and view operations, is shown in Figures 6.19 and 6.20, respectively. Several details have been left out of the event trace because of its size (e.g., display pop-up system menu and clear system menu, search, and search results dialog boxes from screen). Notice that the Search dialog box, Search results dialog box, and View a Document window are objects that are created and destroyed during the course of the application. Also, a document is printed when the user selects OK in the Print dialog box.

Scenario 10. Search Scenario Including Print.

The user enters a query in the content query edit field.
The user tabs over to the content query logical operator and changes it from AND to OR.
The user tabs over to the abstract query edit field.
The user enters a query in the abstract query edit field.
The user tabs over to the keyword query edit field.
The user enters one or more keywords and logical operators in the keyword edit field.
The user tabs over to the author query edit field.
The user enters one or more authors in the author query edit field.
The user selects the OK button in the Search for a Document(s) dialog box.
The Search Results dialog box is displayed, showing the names of several documents found
    that meet the search criteria.
The user selects a directory from the scrolling list of directories.
The directory name is displayed in the Path edit control box.
The user selects a document file from the scrolling list of files.
The document file name is displayed in the document name edit control box.
The user selects the print push button in the dialog box.
The Print dialog box is displayed.
The user specifies the number of document copies.
The user selects the all radio button.
The radio button is highlighted.
The user selects the OK button in the Print dialog box.
The document is printed.
The Print dialog box is cleared from the screen.
The user selects the done push button from the Search Results dialog box.
The Search Results dialog box is cleared from the screen.
The user selects the done push button from the Search for a Document dialog box.
The Search for a Document dialog box is cleared from the screen.
The main application window is redisplayed.

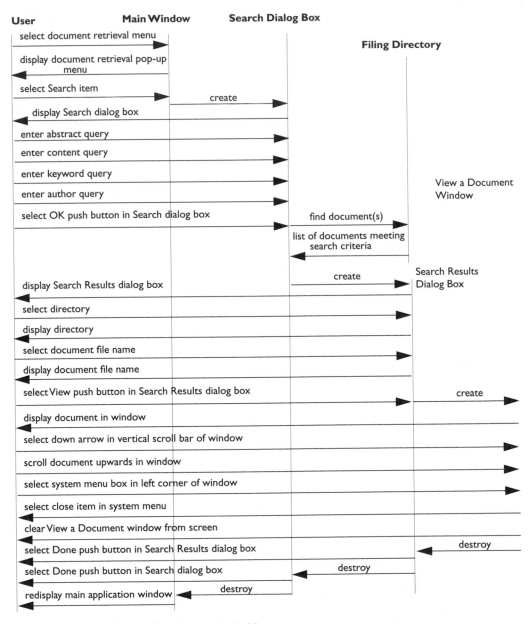

Figure 6.19. Detailed Search Event Trace Including View.

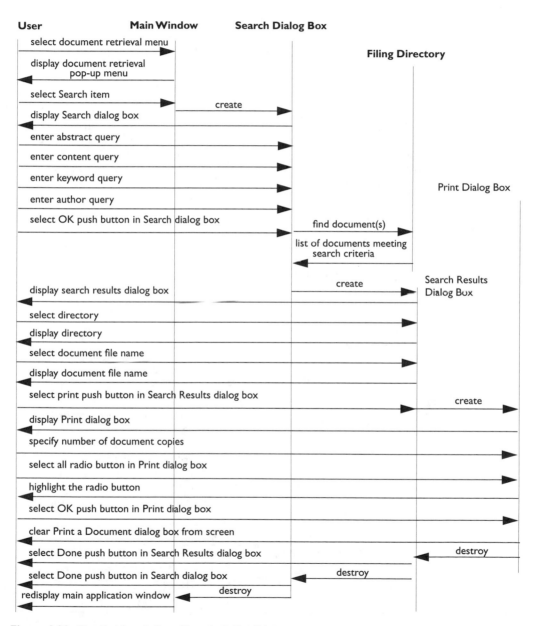

Figure 6.20. Detailed Search Event Trace Including Print.

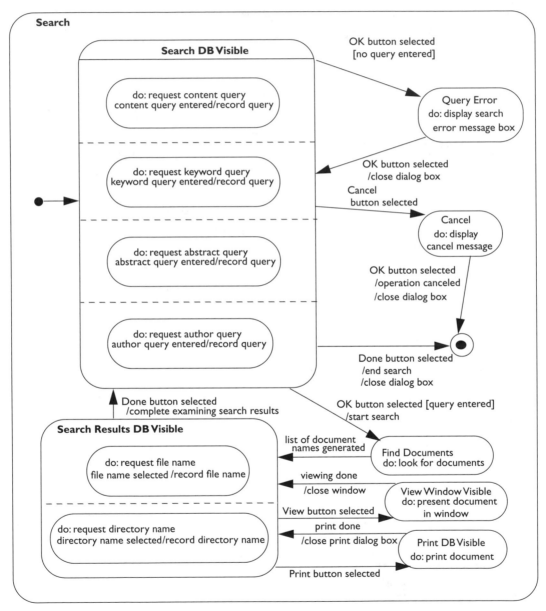

Figure 6.21. *Search and Search Results Dialog Box Classes Statecharts.*

Statechart The statechart for the search dialog box, including both view and print activities, is shown in Figure 6.21. The search results may either be viewed or printed by the user. The *look for documents* activity of the *Find Documents* substate in Figure 6.21 is the basic search for documents. This statechart contains the same information as the Search statechart of Chapter 3 in addition to information specific to how the user interface will work.

6.1.2.4 Filing Character Set Change Operation

Detailed Presentation Formats The *filing character set change* operation utilizes the following dialog boxes from the user interface:

❑ Filing Character Set
❑ Are You Sure

The *Filing Character Set* dialog box is shown in Figure 6.22. The scrolling list box displays all of the possible ASCII character that may be part of the filing character set. Characters that were once discarded from the filing set may again be selected and included in the filing set. An *Are You Sure* message box is used to verify that a user wants to cancel an include or discard operation.

Scenario 11. Setup Sequence of Events Preceding All Filing Character Scenarios.

The user selects the Utilities menu-bar item from the menu bar.
A pop-up menu for Utilities appears.
The user selects the Filing Characters item from the pop-up menu.
The Filing Character Set dialog box is displayed.
The user selects a character in the scrolling list.
The character is highlighted.
The user selects the Discard push button in the dialog box.
The selected character is redisplayed in gray.

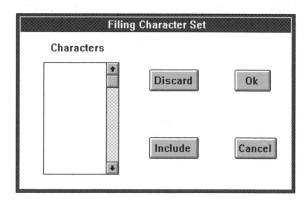

Figure 6.22. Filing Character Dialog Box.

Scenario 12. Filing Character Set Scenario.

> The user selects the OK push button in the Character Set dialog box.
> The Character Set dialog box is cleared from the screen.
> The main application window is redisplayed.

The sequence of events, or steps, that are common to both normal and exceptional filing character set scenarios are shown in Scenario 11. This setup sequence of events precedes both the detailed filing character set scenario and detailed filing character set scenario with exceptions.

A detailed scenario for discarding or including a character in the filing character set is shown in Scenario 12. This allows the user to scroll through the list box and see all of the characters that are included in/or excluded from the current filing character set.

Characters that are included in the current filing character set are shown in black, while characters that have been discarded from the filing character set will be shown in gray. This implementation of this color scheme will be left as an exercise to the reader.

Scenario 13. Filing Character Set Scenario with Exceptions.

> The user selects the Cancel push button in the Character Set dialog box.
> A message box asking Are You Sure is displayed.
> The user selects the Yes push button.
> The Are You Sure message box is cleared from the screen.
> The Filing Character Set dialog box is cleared from the screen.
> The main application window is redisplayed.

A detailed scenario for discarding or including a character in the filing character set, with exceptions, is shown in Scenario 13. If a user decides to cancel this operation after discarding or including a character in the filing character set, an *Are You Sure* message box (see Figure 6.23) is displayed on the screen. The user may then cancel the cancel operation, or select the Yes push button and complete the cancel operation.

Event Trace A detailed event trace for changing the filing character set is shown in Figure 6.24. The program retains a global set of filing characters, and each filed document retains its own local set of filing characters. The global set is used when filing a document, and the local set is used when searching for a document. The filing character set object is created and destroyed during the course of the application. The filing character set object is created when the program is first started and exists until the application is terminated by the user.

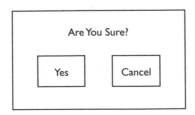

Figure 6.23. Are You Sure Message Box.

Statechart The statechart for changing the filing character set is shown in Figure 6.25. Note the use of several conditions associated with events. These conditions are used as guards on transitions. For example, the *select discard push button* event is only allowed if *a character is selected. Character selected* is the guard on the transition. The *Are You Sure* message box is referred to as the *cancel message box.*

6.1.2.5 Junk Word Set Change Operation

Detailed Presentation Formats The *junk word set change* operation utilizes the following dialog boxes from the user interface:

- ❑ Junk Words
- ❑ Are You Sure

The Junk Words dialog box is shown in Figure 6.26. The scrolling list box displays all of the junk words that are part of the junk word set. Junk words may be added to or deleted from the current set. An Are You Sure message box is used to verify that a user wants to cancel an add or delete operation. The Are You Sure message box is referred to as the *cancel message box.* The electronic filing program comes with a basic set of junk words that it always retains, whether or not a user deletes one or more of the basic junk words.

Junk words that are included in the current set are shown in black, while junk words that have been deleted from the program's basic junk words set will be shown in gray (left as an exercise for the reader). Junk words that a user adds to the program are not shown in the scrolling list after they have been deleted.

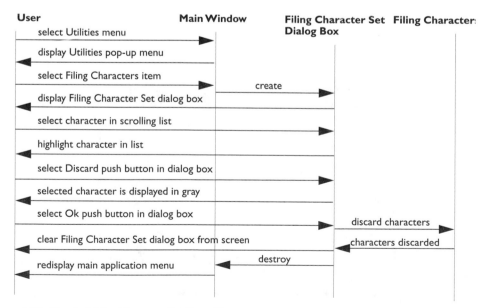

Figure 6.24. Detailed Filing Character Set Event Trace.

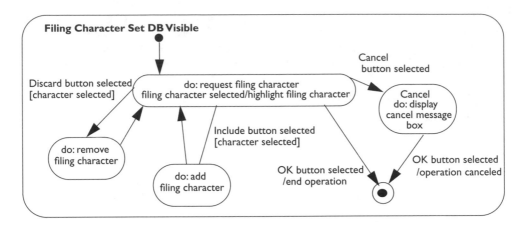

Figure 6.25. *Filing Character Set* Dialog Box Class Statechart.

Scenarios The sequence of events, or steps, that are common to both normal and exceptions junk word scenarios are shown in Scenario 14. This setup sequence of events precedes both the detailed junk word scenario and detailed junk word scenario with exceptions.

A detailed scenario for adding or deleting a junk word from the set of junk words specified for the electronic filing program is shown in Scenario 15.

Scenario 14. Setup Sequence of Events Preceding All Junk Word Scenarios.

> The user selects the Utilities menu-bar item from the menu bar.
> A pop-up menu for Utilities appears.

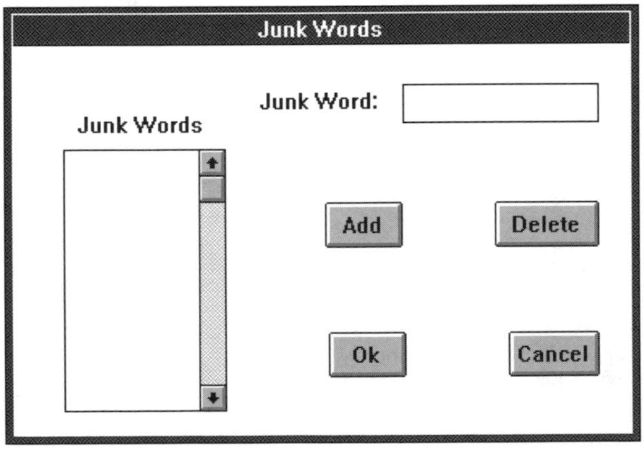

Figure 6.26. Junk Words Dialog Box.

The user selects the junk words item from the pop-up menu.
The Junk Words dialog box is displayed.
The user selects the down arrow in the scroll bar for junk words.
The junk word display is scrolled upward.
The user enters a junk word into the junk word edit box.
The user selects the Add push button.
The word is added to the list of junk words in the scrolling list.

Scenario 15. Junk Words Scenario.

The user selects the OK push button in the Junk Words dialog box.
The Junk Words dialog box is cleared from the screen.
The main application window is redisplayed.

Scenario 16. Junk Words Scenario with Exceptions.

The user selects the Cancel push button in the junk words dialog box.
A message box asking Are You Sure is displayed.
The user selects the Yes push button in the message box.
The Are You Sure message box is cleared from the screen.
The Junk Words dialog box is cleared from the screen.
The main application window is redisplayed.

A detailed scenario, with exceptions, for adding or deleting a junk word from the set of junk words is shown in Scenario 16. If a user decides to cancel this operation after adding or deleting a junk word, an Are You Sure message box (see Figure 6.23) is displayed on the screen. The user may then cancel the cancel operation or select the Yes push button and complete the cancel operation.

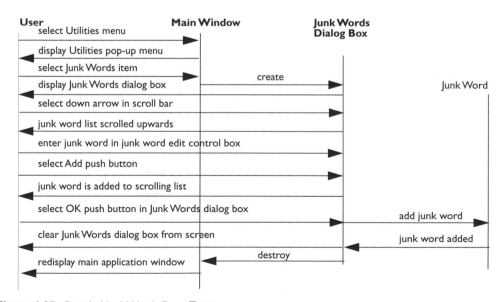

Figure 6.27. Detailed Junk Words Event Trace.

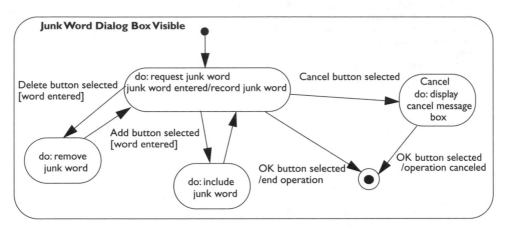

Figure 6.28. *Junk Word* Dialog Box Class Statechart.

Event Trace A detailed event trace for changing the junk word set is shown in Figure 6.27. The program retains a global set of junk words, and each filed document retains its own local set of junk words. The global set is used when filing a document, and the local set is used when searching for a document. The junk words object (dialog box) is created and destroyed during the course of the application. The junk word object is created when the program is first executed and exists until the application is terminated by the user.

Statechart The statechart for changing the junk word set is shown in Figure 6.28. Note the use of several conditions associated with events, similar to the filing character statechart.

6.2 DETAILED USER INTERFACE OBJECT MODEL

The graphical user interface (GUI) for electronic filing is developed using the Window Builder and ProtoGen tools. The design of the user interface is heavily dependent upon the user interface objects of the Borland C++ and Digitalk Smalltalk/V class libraries. All of the objects of the user interface are defined as instances of existing classes whose methods may be inherited. Without such class libraries of reusable and extensible graphical objects, user interface programming would be much more difficult and time consuming. A discussion of the Borland C++ and Digitalk Smalltalk/V classes that make up the user interface dialog boxes appears in Appendix L for readers interested in that level of detail.

Application object classes are object classes that are visible to the outside users (Rumbaugh, 1993a), i.e., user interface object classes. Domain objects represent the problem domain. Utility objects are the generic class library object classes that you buy from a vendor, e.g., set, bag, dictionary, string. Utility objects are used to implement programs. The user interface subsystem module

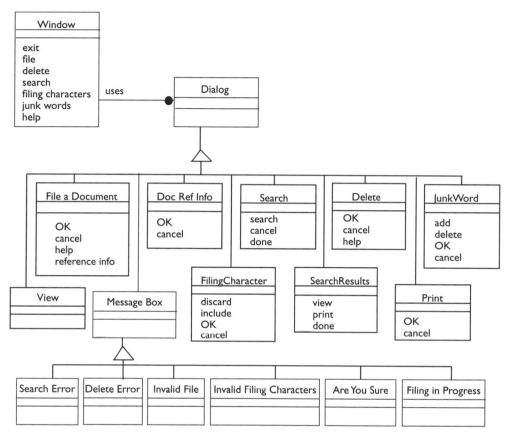

Figure 6.29. User Interface Class Diagram.

that will be part of the OMT object model is shown in Figure 6.29. This figure depicts only the application object classes. The relationships between some of the application object classes and the domain object classes is shown in Figure 6.30.

The user should be involved in the design of the user interface (application objects), because this interface represents the user's conceptual view of the system. Also, the user must be satisfied with the "look and feel" of the application represented by the user interface. The user works only with the user interface portion of the program, so that this is the part of the application that is subject to the most change. Maintaining a loosely coupled interface between the application objects and the domain objects minimizes the degree of change that the domain objects will have to undergo as the user interface changes and also allows the domain objects to be reused with many different types of user interfaces.

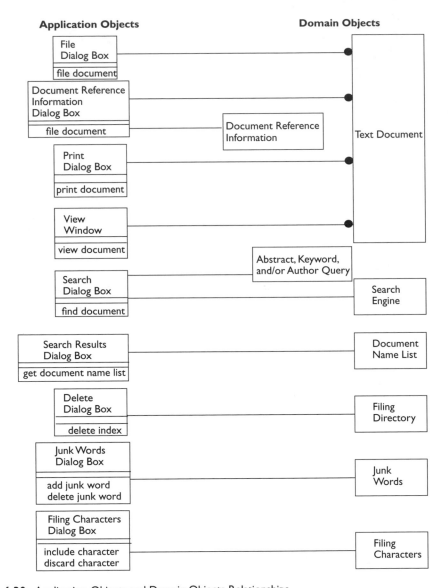

Figure 6.30. Application Objects and Domain Objects Relationships.

6.3 COMBINING THE THREE MODELS TO OBTAIN OPERATIONS ON CLASSES

Now that the application object classes have been identified, we'll go back and examine the dynamic and functional models to obtain operations on classes and then incorporate these additions

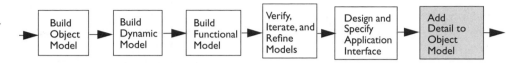

Figure 6.31. OMT Analysis Process.

into the object model, i.e., add detail to the object model. This needs to be done prior to system design so that the system architecture can cleanly separate the structure of our program/system. Figure 6.31 shows where we are in the analysis process.

The actions/activities of the dynamic model and the processes of the functional model may be made operations/methods of the classes in our object model. The design of the electronic filing program, or any other application, will be built around the object model. Our implementation will later be based on the objects and their properties, behavior, and relationships shown in the object model.

The process that will be used to combine the three models and to identify operations for each object is, for each major function of the user interface:

1. Proceeding from the highest to the lowest leveled set of data flow diagrams, determine the target object for each process in the data flow diagram. Then attach the process, or suboperation, to a specific class in the object model.

2. Follow the flow of control of the state diagram in the dynamic model. Map actions and activities of the state diagram into operations attached to classes in the object model.

6.3.1 Obtaining Operations from the Functional Model

The functional model (FM) has the following relationships with the object model (OM) and the dynamic model (DM):

❏ Functions/processes in the FM correspond to operations/methods in the OM; e.g., functional primitives in the FM may correspond to operations on basic objects in the OM, while higher-level functions in the FM may correspond to more complicated objects in the OM.

❏ Data flows may represent values in the OM or normal objects. A data flow that is input to a process may be the target object for that process, while other input data flows may be input parameters.

❏ Data stores in the FM may be objects in the OM or attributes of objects. Data flows into or out of a data store correspond to an operation on that object in the OM.

The process that will be used to obtain operations from the functional model, based on these relationships, is to pick out each process in the functional model, progressing from the high-level to low-level data flow diagrams, and then to determine the target object with which this process should be placed.

Two key operations—*file document* and *find document(s)*—were previously identified in the functional model and then added to the object model. However, these are high level operations, and many middle- and lower-level operations, or functional primitives, are needed to support them. These middle- and lower-level operations will now be chosen from the functional model and assigned to objects.

A process hierarchy diagram, shown in Figure 6.32, shows the supporting operations that the *file document* process requires. The diagram is based on the data flow diagram for the file document process and reflects three levels of decomposition of the *file document* process; e.g., the *file document process* is composed of the *validate document path* and *create text document index* processes; the *hash document record* is composed of the *hash the word* and *build hash record* processes.

A process hierarchy diagram for the *find document(s)* process is shown in Figure 6.33. This diagram shows three levels of decomposition.

Now that we have identified the processes in the functional model that show objects related by function, the next step is to identify the target objects for these operations (i.e., what objects do these processes/operations belong to). The following guidelines from Rumbaugh et al. (1991) will be used to determine the target object of a suboperation:

1. If a process extracts a value from an input flow, then the input flow is the target.

2. If a process has an input flow and an output flow of the same type and the output value is substantially an updated version of the input flow, then the input/output flow is the target.

3. If a process constructs an output value from several input flows, then the operation is a class operation (constructor) on the output class.

4. If a process has an input from or an output to a data store or an actor, then the data store or actor is a target of the process. (In some cases, such a process must be broken into two operations, one for the actor or data store and one for a flow value.)

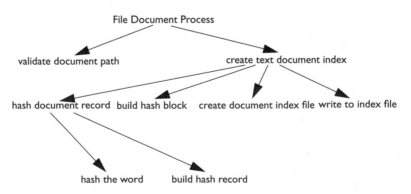

Figure 6.32. *File* Process Hierarchy Diagram.

6.3.1.1 Converting the File Document Process into Operations Attached to Classes

The *file* operation is assigned to the text document object.

Validate document type *Validate document type* has an input from a data store, namely, the user's directory. However, the user's directory has not been defined as an object because it does not have real meaning for this application. No significant state or behavior is associated with it. This is an internal operation of the text document object, which operates on attributes of both the object and the text document itself.

Create text document index This is a high-level process that has an input from a data store and an output to a data store. A text document is an input to this process. The text document is read from the user's directory. Text document type, document path, and document reference information are parameters of this operation. A document index is the output of this process. This process constructs a document *index* object and then calls upon the index object to create the document index file from the text document. This operation is currently called *create text doc index*.

Hash document record The *hash document record* process operates on a record that is part of the text document. This process creates a *hash record* object and is already assigned to the *hash engine* object class. *Hash record* is a new object class that should be included in the object model.

Build hash block *Build hash block* builds a hash block out of hashed records. It is a constructor of a hash block. *Hash block* is a new object class that should be included in the object model. An

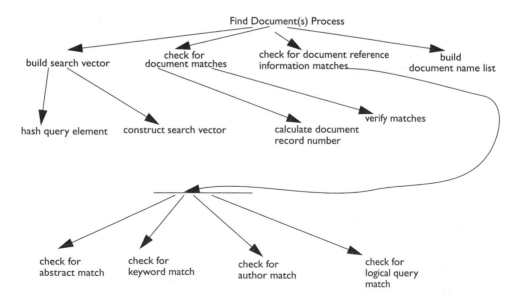

Figure 6.33. *Find* Process Hierarchy Diagram.

index is composed of one or more hash blocks, and a hash block contains one or more hash records. Note that at this late stage of analysis we are beginning to move toward the design phase, specifying how the hashing process will work. There is no absolute line between analysis and design, and the *hash block* and *hash record* object classes are necessary to fully describe the functions of the application interface.

Create document index file The target object is implicit—this process is an internal operation of the *index* class.

Write to index file A document index is the same class of object for both input and output. Document index is the target object.

Hash the word The target object is implicit—*hash the word* is an internal operation of the hash engine object.

Build hash record *Build hash record* hashes a word and includes it as part of a hash record. This process is an operation of the *hash record* class.

6.3.1.2 Converting the Find Document Process into Operations Attached to Classes

The *find* operation is currently assigned to the *filing directory* object class. The target object for suboperations, or processes, is easier to determine for some processes than it is for others. Several of the processes for the find operation involve extracting values from an input flow, and for these, it is easy to identify the target object. The target object for other processes may not be so obvious and may require the creation of new objects, as we saw in the previous discussion for filing a document. This is because some operations may not seem to fit right into the existing object model.

Build search vector *Build search vector* is a top-level process that is implemented by several low-level processes. *Build search vector* takes a content query and builds a search vector. "Build search vector" is an operation of the *search engine* object.

Check for document matches The *check for document matches* process is a high-level process with several inputs and outputs. The *search engine* is the target object because it is the most centrally located in this subnetwork of the object model. This is a high-level operation that is a client of other classes which supply internal operations to perform this process.

Check for document reference information matches This process extracts an input flow from the document reference information and compares this data with query data. The input flow, *document reference information*, is the target object.

Build document name list The *build document name list* process has one input, document name, and one output flow, document name list, of the same type. The search engine is the target object because it is the most centrally located in this subnetwork of the object model. This is a high-level operation that is a client of other classes that supply internal operations to perform this process.

Hash query element The *hash query element* takes a query element and produces a hashed query element. The input and output flows are essentially of the same type. This process is an internal operation of the *hash engine* class.

Construct search vector The *construct search vector* process constructs an output value, search vector, from several input flows, hashed query elements and logical query elements. *Construct search vector* is a class operation, or constructor, on the output class search vector. We'll postpone showing constructors in our models until we develop an implementation model.

Calculate document record number *Calculate document record number* extracts values from an input flow, search vector. It then uses these values to read a document index and to calculate record numbers. The input flow, *search vector*, is the target object class.

Verify matches The *verify matches* process has several input data flows, namely, text document record and content query, and several output data flows, namely, document name and document records list. The *search engine* is the target object class because it is the most centrally located in this subnetwork of the object model.

Check for abstract match This process extracts values from several input flows, namely, the text document abstract and the abstract query elements. Values from these two data flows are then compared, resulting in a true or false indicator. This operation is assigned to the *abstract query* class because it plays the lead role in the operation.

Check for keyword match This process extracts values from several input flows, namely, the text document keywords and the keyword query elements. Values from these two data flows are then compared, resulting in a true or false indicator. This operation is assigned to the *keyword query* class because it plays the lead role in the operation.

Check for author match This process extracts values from several input flows, namely, the text document authors and the author query elements. Values from these two data flows are then compared, resulting in a true or false indicator. This operation is assigned to the *author query* class because it plays the lead role in the operation.

Check for logical query match This process extracts values from several input flows, namely, the match indicators, the text document authors, and the author query elements. A logical operation is then performed on the match indicators and logical query operators, with either a document name or no-document name resulting. A document index is also input to this process. The *search engine* is the target object because it is the most centrally located in this subnetwork of the object model.

6.3.2 Obtaining Operations from the Dynamic Model

During analysis the actions and activities of the statecharts that had interesting computational structure were defined as *key* operations and summarized in the object model. Events that correspond to operations on objects were not explicitly listed in the object model. According to Rumbaugh et al. (1991), we should represent events merely as labels on state transitions during analysis and not include them as operations in the object model.

Now we will go back and examine the statecharts for each use case and identify other operations to include in the object model. Actions and activities may be assigned to classes as operations. An operation may be associated with each event received by an object. Some of the events may be handled by event handlers that are part of the component library and may not require the definition of explicit methods in our object model.

Many events, activities, and actions become operations in the object model. The mapping of event, activity, and action names from the statecharts to operations in the object model is summarized in Appendix C. Shorter names are used for operations to save space in the object model and to more closely represent the syntax rules for computer languages. A new user interface class diagram incorporating these changes is shown in Figure 6.34.

Figure 6.2 shows a diagram of the main menu and pull-down menus for the electronic filing user interface. GUI tools were used to construct the main menu and the pull-down menus. Building a dynamic model of the main menu and pull-down menus is negated by the use of these GUI tools.

The following actions and activities still need to be assigned as operations attached to classes:

- ❑ *start search*
- ❑ *look for documents*

The *start search* action will create a *Search Engine* object. This does not create a new operation. The *start search* action will be a part of the operation that handles the *OK button selected* event. A *find documents* message will then be sent to the *Search Engine* object. This is an event sent by the *search dialog box* object to the *search engine* object. The event triggers an action by the *search engine* object, and a second event from the *search engine* object returns a result or indication of completion of that action. This event pair is mapped into an operation that performs the action and returns control. The operation is called *find document*. The *search engine* object class provides the *find document* service, and the *search dialog box* object is the client requesting this service.

6.3.3 The Detailed Object Model

Now that we have combined operations from the functional and dynamic models into the object model, we'll make another check of the object model, reviewing the model for completeness and consistency. We'll check the object model for any missing and unnecessary classes and associations, and for incorrect placement of associations and attributes. We will also use the data dictionary to see if objects and attributes have been appropriately represented in the object model. An examination of the user interface class was postponed from Chapter 5 until Chapter 6. Now we'll examine the user interface class.

User Interface Upon examining the basic operations of this class, it is apparent that some associations are missing. It is a sign of missing associations when the object model does not possess access paths for operations. Several access paths for user interface operations appear to be missing from our model. These associations are:

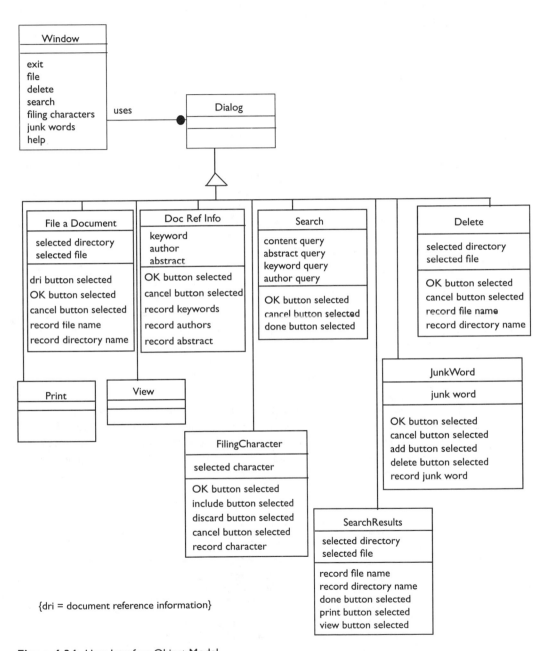

Figure 6.34. User Interface Object Model.

❑ *user interface uses filing directory* to delete a document

❑ *user interface uses junk word* to add/delete a junk word

❑ *user interface uses filing character* to include/discard a filing character

Filing character must be made a class. The filing character must have operations to include/discard a filing character on which the electronic filing program operates. Also, the *hash engine* will need to check for filing characters when hashing. *Hash engine* and *user interface* are the only classes that must deal with both the *filing character* and *junk word* classes. Based on our knowledge of the application domain, we know that junk words are not included in a document index and must therefore be skipped over by the *hash engine*. Here again the object model is missing access paths for operations. The other associations that relate the *hash engine* to the *filing character* and *junk word* classes, and which must be included in the object model, are:

❑ *hash engine skips all junk words*

❑ *hash engine checks all filing characters*

Author, keyword, and *abstract* classes have been made attributes of the *document reference information* (DRI) object class. These classes are unnecessary because they lack attributes and/or operations. The only potential attributes were the author names, the keyword names, and the abstract description. And the only potential operations were the reading and writing of author, keyword, and abstract elements. The page, line, word, nonjunk word, nonfiling character, and ASCII character are eliminated as classes for the same reason. All of the associations between eliminated classes are removed from the object model.

All of the junk words for the electronic filing program are stored in a junk word file. The junk word class is renamed *junk words* because this is more representative of the information maintained in the junk words file represented by this class. The junk word class must have operations to *add junk word* and to *delete junk word*. No other object class accesses the *junk words* file.

All of the filing characters for the electronic filing program are also stored in a file—the filing characters file. The *filing character* class is renamed *filing characters* because this is more representative of the information maintained in the *filing character* file represented by this class. The *filing character* class must have operations to *include filing character* and to *discard filing character*. No other object class accesses the *filing character* file.

Some classes have also been eliminated from the Query Module. Phrase and query operator also lack state and behavior and are therefore removed from the model.

The object classes, attributes, and associations that are added to the object model are:

Object class	Attribute	Association
		user interface uses filing directory
		user interface uses junk word
		user interface uses filing character
filing character		
		hash engine skips all junk words
		hash engine checks all filing characters

A revised class diagram incorporating these additions is shown in Figures 6.35 and 6.36. Note that the user interface class is now a separate module (see Figure 6.29). Figure 6.30 shows the application-objects-to-domain-objects relationships. All of the relationships between domain classes and the user interface class were removed from the object model due to lack of space.

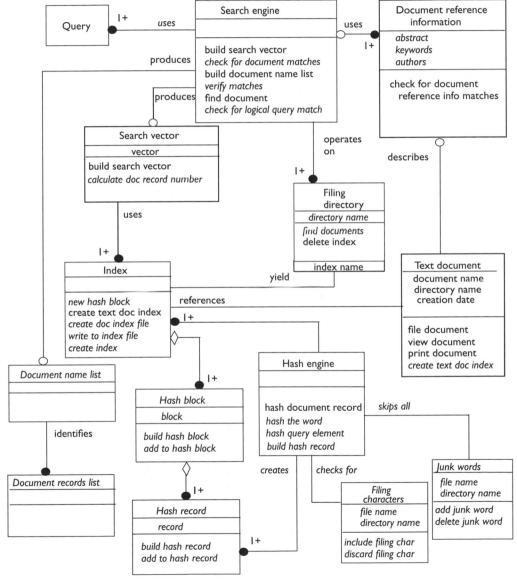

Figure 6.35. Object Model—Revision 6.

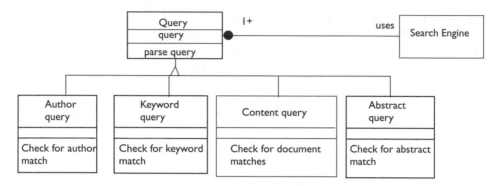

Figure 6.36. Query Module—Revision 2.

6.4 USER INTERFACE IMPLEMENTATION

The use of a graphically oriented user interface design tool, such as Window Builder or ProtoGen, may save a software developer time in developing a user interface. However, several additional steps must be taken before the user interface is functioning and can be used to test-drive the application; e.g., comments should be added to the user interface to document the various objects of the user interface; code must be added to the radio and push button controls so that they return control to other elements of the user interface; code must be developed for the edit and list box controls so that they are functional. The completed user interface will then serve as the test driver for all of the use case scenarios.

At this point the user interface code should be flushed out further so that the user can test-drive the application to see if this is what he or she has in mind. There is less rework involved if the user interface code changes now before it is hooked up to the domain objects, rather than later. At this point we have added a minimal amount of code to the user interface necessary to exercise its basic functionality and drive our scenarios.

6.5 THE ANALYSIS DOCUMENT

The needs of the object, dynamic, and functional models depend on the needs of the application. Our application has an interactive interface, which is dominated by the dynamic model, but the dynamic model is trivial for the electronic filing application. The object model is also fairly simple. However, two functions in our application have interesting computational structure: (1) *file* a document and (2) *find/search* for a document(s). The functional model for electronic filing is interesting due to these two computations within the program.

Our object model describes both the structure of objects in our program and their relationships. The three models together provide a static and dynamic view of our program as well as the information flow within the program.

The analysis document consists of the:

1. problem statement

2. object model (class diagrams, object diagrams, data dictionary)

3. dynamic model (state diagrams or statecharts, event flow diagram for electronic filing, scenarios, user interface formats)

4. functional model (context diagram, data dictionary, data flow diagrams, constraints, and descriptions of atomic processes)

The problem statement is the newly revised problem statement based on the latest revision of the object model. The latest class diagram is included in the object model. The data dictionary is a merging of the data dictionary from Chapter 4 and Chapter 2. Several elements have been deleted (i.e., line and page) due to changes in the object model.

The analysis document represents a model of what the system is supposed to do. The model can be used as a basis for eliciting requirements and as a basis for design. The analysis model can be designed and implemented in a variety of different ways. The analysis document, shown in Appendix D, is the first part of the OMT specification developed for electronic filing.

6.6 SUMMARY OF PROCESS AND DELIVERABLES

The objective of this chapter was to fully specify the details of the application interface (i.e., the user interface subsystem and its classes, associations, attributes, and operations). The process for doing this involved examining each use case (which centers around an application function) and:

- ❏ specifying detailed presentation formats for each user interface function (use case)
- ❏ refining normal and exception scenarios to include additional detail
- ❏ refining event traces to include additional detail
- ❏ refining statecharts to include additional detail

The deliverables for the detailed user interface consist of:

- ❏ presentation formats of the user interface, i.e., all windows and dialog boxes
- ❏ an updated dynamic model, including updated scenarios, event traces, event flow diagram, and statecharts
- ❏ an updated object model

The next step in development is system design—choosing the high-level structure for our system.

System Design

IN THE PREVIOUS chapters on analysis, we focused on what needs to be done. We developed models of the problem and application domain. During system design, decisions will be made at a high level about how the problem will be solved (i.e., policy decisions). The basic approach to solving the problem will be selected. Figure 7.1 shows where we are in the OMT process.

Strategic implementation decisions made during system design include: what component libraries (application oriented and generic), databases, networking mechanisms, windowing systems will be used, and how will we use them; what will our error handling consist of, and how will we do it; how will tasks communicate; how will tasks be allocated to processors; what is our design philosophy; what is the target environment for the application; will the application need to run on multiple platforms (if so it must be designed to have system dependencies encapsulated as much as possible); what programming language will be used to implement the design; and how will we deal with performance or memory constraints. The system design stage of the development process may alter the structure of our object model and bring new objects, associations, operations, and attributes to light.

The decisions that we will address during system design are:

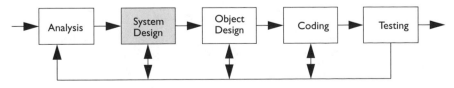

Figure 7.1. OMT Process and Testing.

1. Organizing the system into subsystems

2. Identifying concurrency

3. Allocating subsystems to processors and tasks

4. Choosing the strategy for implementing data stores

These decisions determine the architecture of the system. The architecture forms the basis for all future design decisions. The structure of the basic architecture for the system as well as high-level strategy decisions will be captured in a system design document.

System design for the electronic filing application is extremely trivial. The scale of the problem is small; therefore so is the number and size of the subsystems. However, the application can be logically divided into a number of small subsystems, providing a coherent way of looking at various aspects of the problem.

7.1 ORGANIZING THE SYSTEM INTO SUBSYSTEMS

The first step in systems design is to divide the system into a small number of components referred to as subsystems. This is an appropriate step to take at this point in time for small programs or systems. However, for large applications, the division of a system into subsystems would occur much earlier in the development cycle (i.e, during analysis) to facilitate the distribution of the development work. For large systems it is useful to construct high-level models first to guide decomposition into subsystems. The subsystems should be cohesive and coherent.

A subsystem is an interrelated collection of classes, associations, and operations. Each subsystem should be viewed as a black box with a well-defined interface with the rest of the system but without details on how the subsystem is implemented internally. This allows subsystems to be designed independently without affecting the rest of the system. Not all objects that are part of a model may fit neatly into a subsystem. Some objects may appear in our architectural model that are placed outside of all subsystems.

Subsystems can themselves be divided into subsystems of their own. Large systems are typically divided into a small number of subsystems, which in turn are decomposed into smaller subsystems of their own. The OMT refers to the lowest-level subsystem in a system as a *module.*

Several heuristics can be applied to determine if a group of classes and their relationships form a subsystem:

1. Do some group of classes share a common property? (e.g., similar functionality, the same physical location, operation on the same hardware, operation on the same conceptual entity, etc.) (Rumbaugh et al., 1991)

2. Try naming a group of classes and their purpose (Wirfs-Brock et al., 1991). A name specifies some role that these classes fulfill in the system. Each class must fulfill the goals of the subsystem. The classes within a subsystem should be highly cohesive.

3. Does a group of classes provide the same type of service? (e.g., I/O processing, mathematical computations, file management, searching or sorting techniques, user-interface processing, etc.) (Rumbaugh et al., 1991)

4. Are the classes strongly coupled? Are most of the interactions among a group of classes (i.e., within a possible subsystem), or do they cross subsystem boundaries? Most interactions should be among classes within a subsystem.

In addition, Jacobson et al. (1992) provide several criteria to determine if objects are strongly functionally related:

1. Will changes in one object lead to changes in the other object?

2. Do they communicate with the same actor?

3. Are both of them dependent on a third object, such as an interface object or an entity object?

4. Does one object perform several operations on the other?

7.1.1 Identifying Subsystems from the Object Model

We will identify subsystems from the object model and use the heuristics previously identified to determine if a group of classes and its relationships form a subsystem. Electronic filing has an interactive interface, which is dominated by the dynamic model. The interactive interface consists of many application interface objects, defined in Chapter 6. These object classes share a common property and provide the same type of service—they are all application interface object classes. The *user interface,* or *application interface,* is a part of the system that should be represented as a subsystem.

We previously identified a query module as a subsystem of our system. The query module represents a group of classes and their associations and operations, which also share a common property. They all are functionally related to representing and processing queries—this is their purpose. Also, there is minimal coupling between this subsystem and the rest of the system—through the *search engine* object class.

Another group of classes that share common properties and serve the same purpose are the *document name list* and *document records list* classes. The purpose of these classes is to represent the search results from a search operation, where a user has specified some query and is trying to find one or more documents. These objects will be grouped to form a subsystem known as a *search results module* in the object model. They represent a self-contained piece of functionality. The *search engine* and the *search results dialog box* are the only classes that access this subsystem.

The object model shows another group of classes that share common properties. The *text document, index,* and *document reference information* object classes all operate on the same conceptual entity—a document and the information representing a text document that has been provided by a user. Their purpose is to represent a document and the processing of that document. These objects will be grouped to form a subsystem known as a *document module* in the object model.

The *hash engine, filing character, junk word, hash block*, and *hash record* classes also share common properties. They are all associated with the hashing operation. Each class fulfills the goals of the subsystem—creating an indexed representation of a text document. We'll call this subsystem the hashing subsystem.

The *search engine* and *search vecto*r classes along with the query and search-result subsystems also form a subsystem. These subsystems and classes all share a common property—they all work together to perform a search when requested by the user. The interactions of the query subsystem are strongly coupled to the *search engine* class. The query subsystem has interactions only with the *search engine* class. We'll call this new subsystem the search subsystem.

The electronic filing program is a small application and therefore has only a few subsystems. These subsystems, with the exception of the search subsystem, are represented as modules because they are not part of other subsystems, but are the lowest-level subsystems in the system. To summarize, the subsystems of the electronic filing program are

- ❑ user interface
- ❑ document
- ❑ query
- ❑ search results

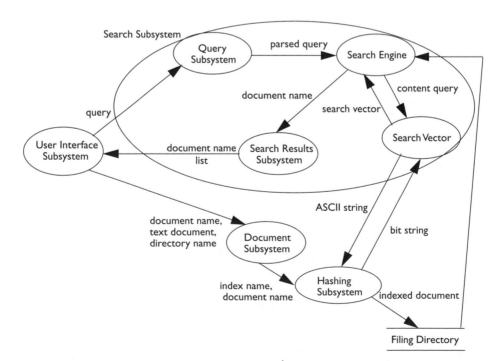

Figure 7.2. Information Flow Among Subsystems.

❑ hashing

❑ search

According to Rumbaugh et al. (1991), a system should be divided into a small number of sub-systems—probably fewer than 20. We have identified 6 subsystems within electronic filing—well within this guideline. The number of subsystems depends on the problem domain. However, the number of subsystems at each level of abstraction should be appropriate, i.e., probably also fewer than 20.

The information flow among subsystems is shown in the data flow diagram of Figure 7.2. During object design when the interactions among and within subsystems are fully defined, we will work at simplifying the interactions among subsystems, if necessary.

7.1.2 Layers and Partitions

Systems can be organized as a sequence of horizontal layers and/or vertical partitions. In a layered system, a layer provides a set of services through a well-defined interface to the layer above it. Each layer can correspond to a set of objects. The top layer of a system is generally the application itself, while the bottom layer represents the hardware and software platform. Intermediate layers provide logical groupings of objects based on functionality. A software application that has a requirement to be portable and run on several hardware platforms will need at least one layer of abstraction between the application and the hardware/software platform to isolate system dependencies.

Various combinations of layers and partitions are possible, with a partition consisting of several layers or a layer consisting of several partitions. Each layer or partition effectively represents a subsystem. Partitions are used to vertically divide a system into subsystems that are loosely coupled. Each subsystem provides a set of well-defined interfaces and services. However, the vertically partitioned subsystems may or may not know about each other.

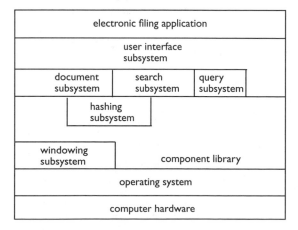

Figure 7.3. Subsystem Block Diagram of Electronic Filing.

Figure 7.3 shows a subsystem block diagram of the electronic filing program representing various types of subsystems in layers and partitions. Several of the electronic filing classes that are not part of a subsystem are omitted from this diagram. The computer hardware and the electronic filing application represent the bottom and top layers of our system, respectively. The operating system is part of our computer platform. Our application has a user interface subsystem that uses the services of several application modules/subsystems: document subsystem, query subsystem, and search results subsystem. The user interface subsystem also interfaces with a component library to provide its functionality. The component library interfaces with both a windowing subsystem, such as Microsoft Windows or Motif or Presentation Manager, and the computer operating system.

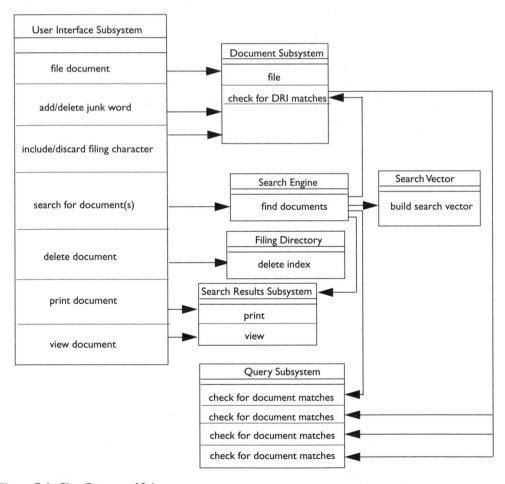

Figure 7.4. Class Diagram of Subsystems.

The component library will be a commercial off-the-shelf class library that will provide windowing functionality and will include a basic, generic object library. If a high-level class library for this commercial application were available, this library would also be included as part of our architecture. Unfortunately, the components industry is still in its infancy and not many high-level application class libraries are available in the marketplace.

Figure 7.4 shows the relationships among the systems subsystems and classes along with their public operations. This diagram is not part of the OMT notation. Public operations/methods that are used by other operations are shown in the figure, with no regard to sequence. Also, the supplier of a method/operation that a client operation of some subsystem/class uses is also listed in the Figure 7.4. Additional subsystem and object class dependencies will surface during object design when the remaining public and private operations are fully specified in the object model.

The OMT approach places less emphasis on identifying operations during *analysis* than do other object-oriented approaches. Therefore, not many operations have been identified in the object model at this point. The maximum number of associations that a class/subsystem has with another class/subsystem is three. The maximum number of requests supported by a subsystem (i.e., the *document* subsystem) is five. Also, the maximum number of classes/subsystems called upon by another subsystem to implement an operation is three (i.e., the *find* operation of the filing directory class). These numbers are not unreasonable and indicate that the patterns of interaction among classes and subsystems is simple and maintainable. The issue of simplifying interactions among subsystems and classes will be revisited again during object design when many more objects, associations, operations, and attributes will be identified in the models.

7.2 IDENTIFYING CONCURRENCY

The next step in system design is to identify concurrency in our system using the dynamic model as a guide. Objects that are mutually exclusive can be packaged together on a single thread of control (i.e., in a task). Objects that must be active concurrently form their own tasks.

To identify concurrency one must examine the dynamic model for objects that can receive events at the same time without interacting. If the events are synchronized, then the objects can be packaged together into a single task. If the events are unsynchronized, then the objects cannot have the same thread of control.

The dynamic model for our program mainly involves the user interface. We choose to use an event-driven system for the user interface. Event-driven systems are more modular than procedure-driven systems and are also well suited to graphical user interfaces. Several parts of the user interface are concurrent, i.e., selecting directory and file names, entering query information. However, we will specify that the programming environment for our event-driven user interface will provide a dispatcher or monitor that will handle events.

The following could be concurrent activities:

❑ the event-driven user interface—root of main program
❑ printing of a document—create a print operation object

❑ viewing of a document—create a view document window object

❑ document subsystem associated with the filing of a document

❑ hashing subsystem associated with both the filing and retrieval of a document

❑ filing directory object and search subsystem associated with the finding and deleting of a document(s)

7.3 ALLOCATING SUBSYSTEMS TO PROCESSORS AND TASKS

Process diagrams as shown in Booch (1994) are used to show the allocation of processes/concurrent activities/tasks to processors in the physical design of a system. The three-dimensional box in Figure 7.5 denotes a processor. The root of a main program and active objects are listed under each processor box with which they are associated.

The electronic filing application could be designed to operate on multiple processors or on a single processor. The single processor could simulate logical concurrency with separate threads of control being known as *tasks* or *daemons*. Many different possible allocations of subsystems to processors and tasks are possible. Some of these possibilities are subsequently discussed.

In Figure 7.5 a local area network (LAN) ties all computers together for shared E-mail, office automation, directory, computational, and printing services. The LAN requires basic communication hardware and software, such as Ethernet, in order for these computers to communicate with each other. The electronic filing client and server also require an application level protocol in order to share information and perform the functions of an electronic filing system. The event-driven user interface, objects necessary for the viewing of a document, and the application protocol exist on the client machine running as independent tasks. The print server

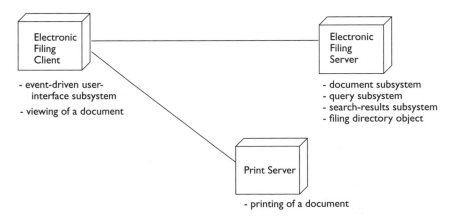

Figure 7.5. Electronic Filing Client-Server Process Diagram.

- user-interface subsystem
- document subsystem
- query subsystem
- search-results subsystem
- printing of a document
- viewing of a document
- filing directory object

Figure 7.6. Electronic Filing with Multiple Tasks Process Diagram.

provides the ability to print a document. The electronic filing server has the document, query, and search–results subsystems and filing directory object running as independent tasks. The advantage of this approach is the higher performance that is achievable using multiple processors and multiple tasks.

Figure 7.6 combines the client and server subsystems and objects on one processor. The respective subsystems and objects each run as independent tasks. In this configuration, an application-level protocol is still necessary in order to share information and perform the functions of an electronic filing system. The disadvantage of this approach is that the overall throughput for filing and retrieving documents will be less than the multiple processor approach under heavy load.

In Figure 7.7 all subsystems and objects for the electronic filing application are packaged together into a single task running on a single processor. This configuration provides the simplest implementation but will not perform as well as the previously discussed configurations under heavy or moderate loads.

The configurations depicted in Figure 7.5 and Figure 7.6 require the use of a multitasking operating system for each processor. Figure 7.7 does not require the use of a multitasking operating system. We will assume that this application is being developed for Microsoft Windows and that it will run as a single task. Therefore we will opt for the configuration shown in Figure 7.7. However, various multitasking operating systems (OS2, Windows NT, a number of different Unix systems) could be used on a PC to support the configuration shown in Figure 7.6.

- all electronic filing subsystems and objects

Figure 7.7. Electronic Filing with Single Task Process Diagram.

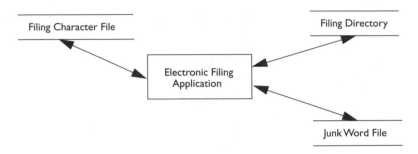

Figure 7.8. Data Stores for Electronic Filing.

7.4 CHOOSING THE STRATEGY FOR IMPLEMENTING DATA STORES

According to Rumbaugh et al. (1991), "a data store is a passive object within a data flow diagram that stores data for later access. Unlike an actor, a data store does not generate any operations on its own but merely responds to requests to store and access data." Data stores could be implemented as databases, files, or memory data structures.

The functional model is the place to look for data stores that may not yet have been identified. Several possible data stores are shown in the data flow diagrams for the functional model: junk word file, filing character file, user's directory, and filing directory. Junk word, filing character, and filing directory are already represented as objects in the electronic filing object model. *Junk word* and *filing character* interface to the junk word file and filing characters file, respectively. The *filing directory* object maintains a list of the index files in memory that are part of the filing directory.

The user directory has little behavior and state associated with it. We choose to access files in the user directory through file and directory names. The user directory is generated prior to invoking the electronic filing program; i.e, the electronic filing program does not store data in the user's directory—any text documents accessed already exist in the user's directory.

The data stores for electronic filing are shown in Figure 7.8. Objects have already been identified to represent the filing characters, junk words, and filing directory. Access to these data stores is managed through the identified objects.

7.5 HIGH-LEVEL STRATEGIC DECISIONS

The following summarizes the high-level strategy decisions for the development of our electronic filing program:

❏ The user interface will be an event-driven graphical user interface.

❏ Standard files and directories along with the indexing techniques specified in Knuth (1973) will be used for index and retrieval of text.

❑ Component libraries in C++ and Smalltalk will insulate us from the details of the application programming interface of the windowing environment for our platform(s).

❑ This application, being developed for a PC Microsoft Windows environment, will run on a single processor and as a single task, negating the requirement to allocate subsystems to processors and tasks.

7.6 SUMMARY OF PROCESS AND DELIVERABLES

In this chapter we have developed a basic approach to solving the problem. This is our first attempt at making decisions on *how* the problem will be solved, as opposed to defining *what* the problem is, as we did during analysis. We applied the steps identified by the OMT that made sense for the scale of our application. These steps included the following:

❑ specifying high-level strategy decisions

❑ organizing the system into subsystems

❑ identifying concurrency inherent in the problem

❑ allocating subsystems to processors and tasks

❑ choosing an approach for management of data stores

The deliverables for developing the system design consist of the following:

❑ a data flow diagram showing the information flow among subsystems

❑ a list of the high-level strategy decisions

❑ a list and description of the subsystems that are part of the system

❑ a subsystem block diagram showing the layers and partitions of the system

❑ a class diagram of subsystems

❑ a list of potential concurrent tasks and their object representations

❑ one or more process diagrams showing possible allocations of subsystems to processors and tasks and the recommended approach

❑ a diagram of the data stores represented as objects

The system design document consists of all of these deliverables. The system design document represents the basic approach to solving the problem The entire system design document is shown in Appendix E.

The next step in the development of our program or application is object design. We will fully identify the remaining objects necessary to implement the system.

Object Design

OBJECT DESIGN IS concerned with fully specifying the existing and remaining classes, associations, attributes, and operations necessary for implementing a solution to the problem. Algorithms and data structures are fully defined along with any internal objects needed for implementation. In essence, all of the details for fully specifying how the problem will be solved are specified during object design. Later, during our implementation, many of the design decisions will be translated into code using two different languages: Smalltalk/V and C++. However, some of the design decisions we have made will be left for the reader to implement.

All of the classes defined during analysis and the subsystems defined during systems design will be carried forward to object design. At this stage of development we are just refining our models and adding detail. Figure 8.1 shows where we are in the OMT process.

The high-level design of the user interface has already been completed. We have already combined the three models to identify operations for each class prior to systems design so that the system architecture would cleanly separate the structure of our program/system. The process that we will use in the detailed object design of all of our application consists of the following steps (Rumbaugh et al., 1991):

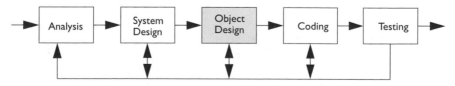

Figure 8.1. OMT Process and Testing.

1. Flush out algorithms to implement operations

2. Determine object representation

3. Implement control for external interactions

4. Adjust class structure to increase inheritance

5. Design associations

6. Optimize access paths for data

7. Package classes and associations into modules

The results of object design will be captured in an object design document at the completion of this process. This document should be saved in electronic form for possible reuse in future designs in the same and similar problem domains. Reusing class libraries during coding is not enough. Reuse must be practiced at all stages of the object-oriented software development life cycle to fully realize the benefits of object-oriented technology.

Commercial off-the-shelf class libraries will be used to design the program. As noted in the previous chapter, this program is being designed to run on a PC under Microsoft Windows. If our intentions were to make this program as portable as possible so that it would run on multiple platforms, we would choose class libraries that support multiple platforms and require minimal or no changes in the class interfaces.

The class libraries that are part of Borland's Application Frameworks and Digitalk's Smalltalk/ V will be used to design and implement the program with two different object-oriented programming languages, C++ and Smalltalk, respectively. If any high-level class libraries were available for this application, those libraries would also be used during the design.

8.1 THE DETAILED OBJECT MODEL

The design of a program is built around the object model. Our implementation will later be based on the object classes and their properties, behavior, and relationships shown in the object model. The form and content of the object model differs for the different stages of the object-oriented development cycle (Rumbaugh, 1994c). Rumbaugh also states that you normally would not keep separate object models for design and implementation unless you were going to port to different languages. However, since we plan on providing an implementation of the electronic filing program in both the Smalltalk/V and C++ languages, we will maintain separate object models for design and implementation. A design model that appears in this chapter is independent of the programming language. In Chapter 9, two implementation models will be presented, one for each programming language for which we are specializing the design.

As we move from analysis to design to implementation, the object model will continue to expand and fill out with more elements (classes, attributes, operations, associations). During object design we'll exclude the identification of junk and buck-passer methods, which don't do much for the main logic of the application but are still necessary, until implementation time. Junk methods are methods such as constructors, destructors, attribute accessors, initializers, and association maintainers. Buck-passer methods transfer control between two objects that are not directly accessible to one another.

8.2 FLUSHING OUT ALGORITHMS TO IMPLEMENT OPERATIONS

At this point we are ready to flush out the algorithms to implement operations. The procedure that we will follow consists of the following steps:

1. Show the hierarchy of messages/methods for all user interface functions/use cases and their corresponding scenarios. [This information will be depicted in a message hierarchy diagram (not part of the OMT notation). The message hierarchy diagram was presented in Norton and Yao (1992) as a hierarchy of functions diagram.] Additionally, pseudocode will be included in this diagram to show how the operation should work. This will help us to sort out what is actually happening.

2. Specify the algorithm for each method and the type of data structure necessary for each algorithm (i.e., generic container classes such as arrays, lists, stacks, etc.).

3. Define any new internal classes, attributes, and operations that may be necessary to implement the algorithms, and ensure that the operations are assigned to the appropriate target objects.

4. Draw an event trace diagram for each scenario. This is equivalent to an object interaction diagram (Rumbaugh, 1994b) and shows the list of interactions ordered in time. Both calls and returns are shown as separate control flows.

The message/method hierarchy diagrams are built using the previously constructed event traces, which show the interactions among objects. The data flow diagrams from the functional model are used to trace the data flow through the system and to determine which objects send messages to other objects. The pseudocode developed for each process in Chapter 4 is also examined to determine the message flow among objects. All data flows along control paths, so both data flow diagrams, which show data flow, and event traces, which show control flow, are important in depicting how the objects in a system work together.

For the Borland C++ implementation, the *TMainWindow* class initiates each of these scenarios since the operations are driven by the user interface; i.e., the creation of the first dialog box in each of these scenarios is initiated through some code that is part of the *TMainWindow* object. The *Efiling* class in Smalltalk creates or opens the main application menu and initiates the invocation of event handlers based on selections of items in the pull-down menus. So the *Efiling* class initiates the scenarios in the Smalltalk implementation.

As the program development moves closer to implementation, the algorithms, data structures, and methods take on more of an object-oriented flavor. The object model will also contain many more elements, operations and attributes than the preceding analysis object models. We will use an object-oriented pseudocode, as discussed in Blaha (1994), to describe the algorithms for each method. The syntax for sending a message is as follows: receiver object.method.argument. A data structure will be identified as follows: data structure: type of data structure. Method names will begin with a lowercase letter. A data structure will begin with an uppercase letter.

8.2.1 File Operation

The message hierarchy diagram for the *file* operation is shown in Figure 8.2. This diagram describes the single execution scenario of filing a document with document reference information. An execution scenario for filing a document with no document reference information is the same as in Figure 8.2, except with all pseudocode referring to the DRIDB and document reference information removed from the message hierarchy diagram. The following abbreviations are used in the message hierarchy diagram: File_Dialog_Box = FDB, Text_Document = TD, Document_Reference_Information_Dialog_Box = DRIDB.

Note that in the File Operation Message Hierarchy Diagram, the receiver object.method (arguments) syntax is used. This same syntax will be used to describe the algorithms for each method.

A new File dialog box object is created by the *TMainWindow* object (C++ Application Frameworks implementation) and the *Efiling* object (Smalltalk implementation) when the user selects the File item from the Document Storage pop-up menu. The user then selects the directory and file

```
user selects File item
   new FDB()
   user selects directory and file
   FDB.referenceInformation()
         new DRIDB ()
         user enters document reference information
         DRIDB.ok()
           new TD()
           TD.fileDoc ()
              new Index()
              Index.createDocIndex ()
              Filing.addIndexFile ()
              Index.createIndex ()
              Index.buildIndexFileHeader()
              new HashEngine()
              HE.buildHashBlock()
                 HE.hashDocRec ()
                    HE.hashTheWord ()
                       HE.hash1stChar ()
                       HE.hash2ndChar ()
                       HE.hash3rdChar ()
                       HE.hashOtherChar ()
      clear DRI dialog box from screen
   clear File dialog box from screen
display main application window
```

Figure 8.2. File Operation Message Hierarchy Diagram with Document Reference Information.

name of the document to be filed into the system. When the user selects the Reference Information-tion push-button in the File dialog box, a document reference information (DRI) dialog box object is created by the File dialog box object. The DRI dialog box then displays itself and awaits user input. When the user has completed entering DRI information and has selected the OK push-button, a text document object is created by the DRI dialog box object. The DRI dialog box then sends a message, *fileDoc*, to the TextDocument object, which is responsible for filing the document in the system.

The TextDocument object then invokes the *fileDoc* method, which calls methods in the Text-Document object to fulfill its responsibilities. The TextDocument *fileDoc* method creates an Index object and then sends a message to the Index object, invoking the *createDocIndex* method. The *createDocIndex* method calls the *createIndex* method in the Index object. The *createIndex* method then invokes the *buildIndexFileHeader* method. Next, the *createIndex* method creates a new *HashEngine* object and sends a message to the *HashEngine* object, invoking the *buildHashBlock* method.

The *buildHashBlock* method creates hash blocks for the text document and outputs them to the text document index file. Hashed blocks are built from hashed records, which in turn are built from text document ASCII records. This process continues until all of the text document records have been processed by the *buildHashBlock* method. A record is just some predetermined number of characters in a file.

The *buildHashBlock* method first clears the hash block and then retrieves document records from the text document file using a *DocumentFileStream* object. A *hashDocumentRecord* message is next sent to the hash engine object, which creates a hashed record by calling the *hashTheWord* internal method. The *hashTheWord* method uses the internal methods *hash1stChar*, *hash2ndChar*, *hash3rdChar*, and *hashOtherChar* to index all of the characters in the word. The *buildHashBlock* method continues this process until the hash block is full or all of the document records have been processed. When the hash block is full, the hash block is cleared and the *buildHashBlock* method continues processing text document records.

After the hash block has been processed, the *buildHashBlock* method sends a message to the *IndexFileStream* object to write the hash block to disk. The *IndexFileStream* object is used for all output to the text document index file.

The hashing or indexing of a document text file is a nontrivial operation. Appendix F contains the pseudocode for implementing this algorithm, specifies the data structures necessary for the algorithm, and defines any new internal classes and operations needed to hold intermediate results. The rest of the code that is needed to implement the file operation is fairly straightforward and will not be specified in the pseudocode. The *buildHashBlock* method from the *HashEngine* object implements the basic hashing algorithm, which is taken from Knuth (1973).

A data dictionary entry that will be added for the index file is as follows:

File or Database Name:	Index file
Composition:	hash block word vector size + total block count + total record count + filing characters + junk words + random number table + $_1${hashed block}^{n}
Organization:	Blocks are sequential.
Notes:	Each block contains up to 512 data records that have been hashed.

An event trace diagram for a file operation is shown in Figure 8.3. This type of diagram depicts the objects that are created and destroyed and the messages that are sent between various objects. Event trace diagrams are very useful for implementing and testing scenarios. These diagrams show only some of the messages that are sent between objects. However, some of the messages that are sent from an object to itself (internal operations) are also included in these diagrams. Return message flows are shown only when a message returns an object other than itself.

Like the message hierarchy diagram, the event trace describes a single execution scenario. This scenario includes the filing of document reference information, i.e., author, abstract, and/ keyword information. The message hierarchy diagram shows the procedural flow of control clearly. In the event trace diagram the timing is more apparent. Both views are useful and help to bring out different aspects of the information. The event trace and message hierarchy represent only one possible scenario for the file document use case.

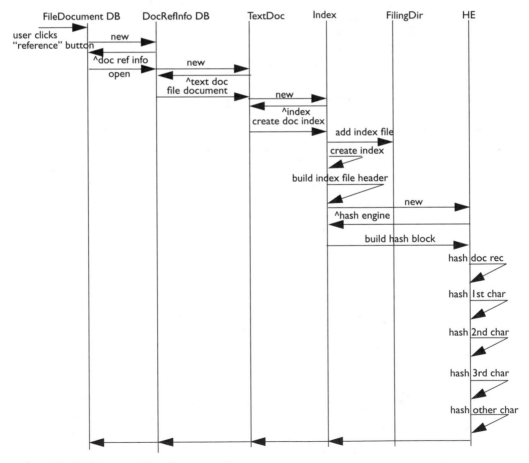

Figure 8.3. File Document Event Trace.

Another important diagram announced as a major extension to the OMT for design purposes is the object interaction diagram (Rumbaugh, 1994b). This diagram is intended to show the flow of control and data through and among objects in an application or system. The interaction diagram is used to describe procedural behavior during design. Note that this interaction diagram is not the same as those from other authors. The interaction diagrams depicted in Booch (1994) and Jacobson et al. (1992) are event traces in OMT notation. In Rumbaugh (1994) it was noted that the object interaction diagram is equivalent to the event trace diagram described in Rumbaugh et al. (1991). However, the timing of interactions is more apparent in the event trace diagrams.

Object interaction diagrams (OID), as well as other diagrams and notations, can be applied at different levels of abstraction. The OID is an instance diagram with some additional notation; i.e., control flows are shown as message labels with an arrow on the label showing the direction of control flow. (Remember that an instance diagram shows how a set of objects relate to one another.) The label may show the message name along with any parameters that are passed. The messages

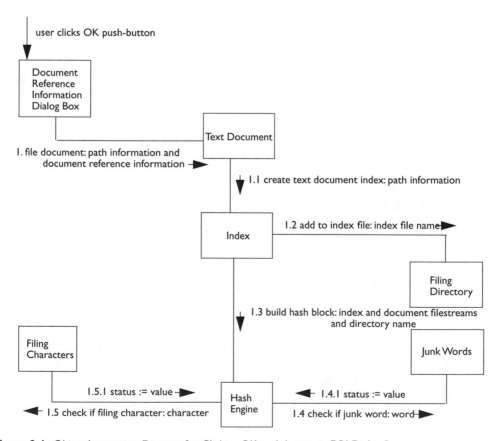

Figure 8.4. Object Interaction Diagram for Clicking OK push-button in DRI Dialog Box.

are numbered using a Dewey Decimal kind of notation. Note that these numbers show the sequence of nested operations. Return values are also shown in the OID as labels. Return values are indicated by assignment statements.

The object interaction diagram shown in Figure 8.4 shows the flow of control and data at a high level for a filing scenario. When a user selects the OK button in the document reference information dialog box object, a *file document* message with path information and document reference information is sent to the *TextDocument* object. File document is the main operation for this scenario. A number of suboperations (1.1 through 1.5) are executed to carry out the *file document* operation. The *TextDocument* object sends a *create text document index* message with path information as a parameter to the *Index* object. The *Index* object sends an *add to index file* message with an index file name as a parameter to the *FilingDirectory* object, followed by sending a *build hash block* message and some parameters to the *HashEngine* object. The OID also shows that the *HashEngine* object sends a *check if junk word* message with a word as a parameter to the *JunkWords* object. Note that the *check if junk word* method returns a value. The result of calling the *check if junk word* method on the *JunkWords* object is the value that we call *status*. The *HashEngine* object also sends a *check if filing character* message to the *FilingCharacters* object and a value is returned which we also call *status*.

8.2.2 Search Operation

The message hierarchy diagram for the *search* operation is shown in Figure 8.5. Some of the details have been abstracted out to focus on the essentials and to fit within a single diagram. The following abbreviations are used in this figure:

```
Search_Dialog_Box = SDB
Text_Document = TD
Search_Results_Dialog_Box = SRDB
Document_Reference_Information_Dialog_Box = DRIDB
Search_Engine = SE
```

A new Search dialog box is created when the user selects the Search item from the Document Retrieval pop-up menu. The user then enters the content, abstract, keyword, and/or author queries with the connecting logical operators. When the user selects the OK push-button in the Search dialog box a *SearchEngine* object is created. A *findDocument* message is then sent to the *SearchEngine* object to locate the documents meeting the specified search criteria entered by the user.

The *findDocument* method of the *SearchEngine* object creates a new *SearchVector* object. It then sends a message to the *SearchVector* object to build the actual search vector, invoking the *buildSearchVector* method. The *buildSearchVector* method sends a *parseQuery* message to the *ContentQuery* object to parse the query. Next, a *hashQueryElement* message is sent to the *HashEngine* object to hash the query element. The *buildSearchVector* method now calls the *constructVector* method to create the actual search vector with this hashing information.

Now that the search vector has been built to do a content search, the next thing to do is to read specific records of each document using the search vector and then to verify the matches. The *findDocument* method of the *SearchEngine* object now invokes the *checkForDocumentMatches* method. The *checkForDocumentMatches* method processes each document index file to see if any matches actually exist within the document(s).

The *checkForDocumentMatches* method sends a *calculateDocRecNumbers* message to the *SearchVector* object to retrieve document record numbers to read. The *checkForDocumentMatches* method next sends a *verifyMatches* message to the *SearchEngine* object to verify that a match exists within these records of the document. This process is repeated for each and every document index file in the system. The *verifyMatches* method removes any record numbers from the document record list for which there is no match. The *checkForDocumentMatches* method checks to see if this list is not empty. If the document record list is not empty, the document record list is associated with the document name in the document name list and the document name remains in the document name list.

Next, the *findDocument* method of the *SearchEngine* object invokes the *checkForDRIMatches* method. This method first parses all queries. Then for each and every *DocumentReferenceInformation* object it sends a *checkForAbstractMatch* message to the *AbstractQuery* object. A *checkForAuthorMatch* message is sent to the *AuthorQuery* element in the same fashion. A *checkForKeywordMatch* message is also sent to the *KeywordQuery* element in a similar fashion. Finally, a *checkForLogicalQueryMatch* message is sent to the *SearchEngine* object. A result indicating whether or not a DRI match occurred is returned to the *checkForDRIMatches* method. The *checkForDRIMatches* method now cre-

```
user selects Search item
   new SDB ()
   SDB.ok ()
     new Search Engine
     SE.findDocument()
       new SearchVector
       SV.buildSearchVector ()
         CQ.parseQuery ()
         HE.hashQueryElement ()
       SV.constructVector ()
       SE.checkForDocumentMatches ()
         DO
         SE.calculateDocRecNumbers ()
         SE.verifyMatches ()
         DocumentNameList. put records list ()
         UNTIL all document index files processed
       SE.checkForDRIMatches ()
         parse all queries
           FOR each document reference information object
         ABSQ.checkForAbstractMatch ()
         AUTQ.checkForAuthorMatch ()
         KEYQ.checkForKeywordMatch ()
         SE.checkForLogicalQueryMatch ()
           DocumentNameList.add document name
         ENDFOR
       new SRDB()
       SRDB.view ()
       new ViewDB ()
       clear SRDB from screen
   clear SDB from screen
display main application window
```

Figure 8.5. Search Operation Hierarchy.

ates a document name list (DNL) if none exists, a document records list if necessary, and then adds the document name to the DNL.

The search operation has now been completed, and what remains is to present the results to the user. A Search Results dialog box is created by the *SearchEngine* object and displayed on the screen. The user may now select either the print or view push-button within the dialog box. The Search Results dialog box is cleared from the screen when the user selects the Done push-button. The Search dialog box still remains on the screen. The user may conduct another search at this point or select the Done push-button and terminate the search process—clearing the Search dialog box from the screen.

An event trace diagram for the search operation is shown in Figure 8.6. This search is of the content of the document only, i.e., no search of abstract, author, or keyword information. This

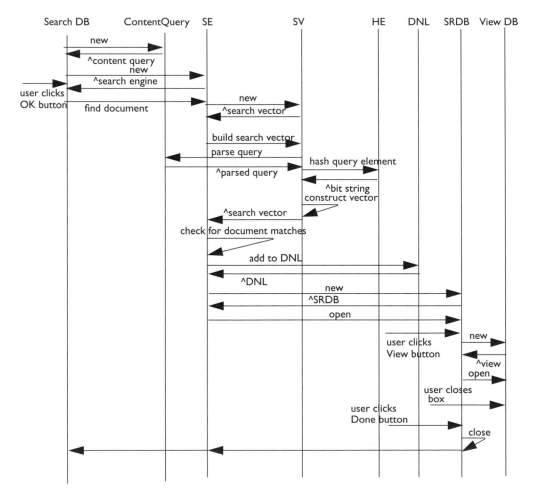

Figure 8.6. Search for Document(s) Event Trace.

represents only one possible scenario for the search use case. Some details have been abstracted out due to lack of space in the diagram.

An object interaction diagram for the search operation is shown in Figure 8.7. When a user selects the OK push-button in the search dialog box object, a *find document* message with the user-entered queries is sent to the *SearchEngine* object. *Find document* is the main operation for this scenario. A number of suboperations (1.1 through 1.11) are executed to carry out the *find document* operation. The reader may trace through the execution of message-sending in this diagram using the same technique used for the object interaction diagram for the *file operation*.

Searching and retrieving one or more documents based on an index method that uses hashing is a nontrivial operation. Appendix F contains the pseudocode for implementing this algorithm, specifies the data structures necessary for the algorithm, and defines any new internal classes and operations needed to hold intermediate results. The rest of the code that is needed to implement the search operation is fairly straightforward and will not be specified in the pseudocode.

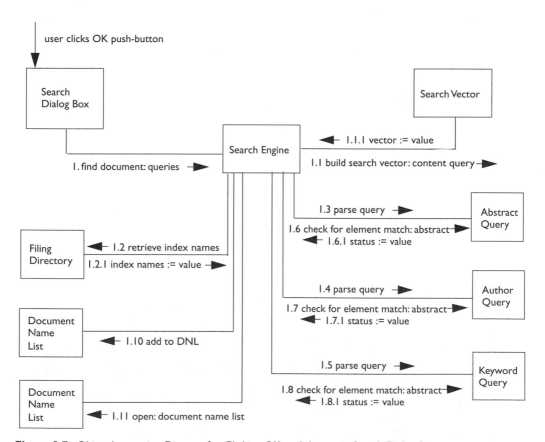

Figure 8.7. Object Interaction Diagram for Clicking OK push-button in Search Dialog Box.

```
user selects Delete item
   new DDB ()
      display filing directories
      display filing directory files
      DDB.ok ()
         FD.delete index
   clear DDB from screen
display main application window
```

Figure 8.8. Delete Operation Hierarchy.

8.2.3 Delete Operation

The message hierarchy diagram for the delete operation is shown in Figure 8.8. The following abbreviations are used in this figure:

```
Delete Dialog Box = DDB
Filing Directory = FD
```

A new Delete dialog box is created when the user selects the Delete item from the Document Storage pop-up menu. The Delete dialog box event handlers for the file list box and the directories list box retrieve the list of files for the current filing directory and the list of filing directories, respectively. This information is then displayed in the scrolling list boxes of the delete dialog box. When the user selects the OK push-button in the Delete dialog box, the selected index file is deleted from the specified directory. The deletion is accomplished by sending a *deleteIndex* message to the *FilingDirectory* object. The Delete dialog box is then cleared from the screen and the main application window is redisplayed.

8.2.4 Filing Character Operation

The message hierarchy diagram for the filing character operation is shown in Figure 8.9. The following abbreviations are used in this description:

```
Filing_Characters = FC
Filing_Characters_Dialog_Box = FCDB
```

Note that curly brackets, {}, are used to mark off several alternative blocks of code. Each block of code is separated by an OR statement. A specific block of code is executed depending upon the event that is received by the program.

A new Filing Characters dialog box is created when the user selects the Filing Characters item from the Utilities pop-up menu. The Filing Characters dialog box sends the *getIncludedCharacters* and *getDiscardedCharacters* messages to the *FilingCharacter* object. These messages return the included and discarded filing characters, which are then displayed in black and grey, respectively, in the scrolling list box of the Filing Characters dialog box. The *displayCharacters* method from the Filing Characters dialog box object is invoked to display these characters.

The user may now select a character and then either discard it or include it in the filing character set by selecting the Discard or Include push-button. The *addToIncludeList* or *addToDiscardList* methods are invoked to carry out these operations. These methods add characters to temporary include/discard lists.

```
user selects Filing Character item
  new FCDB ()
    FC.getIncludedCharacters ()
    FC.getDiscardedCharacters()
    FCDB.displayCharacters ()
    {FCDB.discard ()
      FC.addToDiscardList ()
  OR
    FCDB.include ()
      FC.addToIncludeList ()}
    DDB.Ok ()
      {FC.setDiscardChars()
  OR
      FC.setIncludeChars()}
  clear FCDB from screen
display main application window
```

Figure 8.9. Filing Character Operation Hierarchy.

When the user selects the OK push-button in the Filing Characters dialog box, the characters in the temporary include/discard lists are moved to the permanent set of include/discard characters by invoking the *setDiscardChar* and *setIncludeChar* methods. These changes are also written to the filing characters file. The Filing Characters dialog box is then cleared from the screen.

8.2.5 Junk Words Operation

The message hierarchy diagram for the junk words operation is shown in Figure 8.10. The following abbreviations are used in this description:

```
Junk_Words = JW
Junk_Words_Dialog_Box = JWDB
```

Note that curly brackets, {}, are used to mark off several alternative blocks of code, in the same manner as in the Filing Characters operation.

```
user selects Junk Word item
  new JWDB ()
    JW.getCurrentJunkWords ()
    JW.getDeletedJunkWords()
    JWDB.displayWords ()
    {JWDB.delete ()
      JW.deleteWord ()
  OR
    JWDB.add ()
      JW.addWord ()}
    JWDB.ok ()
      {JW.setDeletedWords()
  OR
      JW.setAddedWords()}
  clear JWDB from screen
display main application window
```

Figure 8.10. Junk Words Operation Hierarchy.

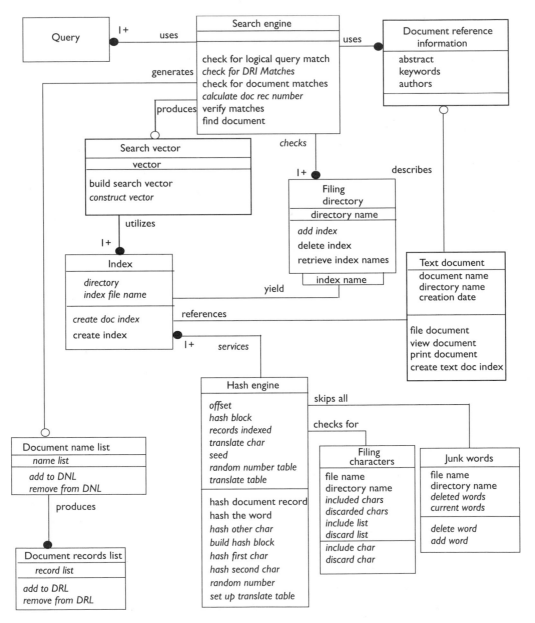

Figure 8.11. Class Diagram—Revision 7.

A new Junk Words dialog box is created when the user selects the Junk Words item from the Utilities pop-up menu. The Junk Words dialog box sends the *getCurrentJunkWords* and *getDeleted-JunkWords* messages to the Junk Words object. These messages return the current and deleted junk words, which are then displayed in black and grey, respectively, in the scrolling list box of the Junk Words dialog box. The *displayWords* method from the Junk Words dialog box object is invoked to display these words.

The user may now select a word and then either add it *or* delete it in the junk words set by selecting the Add *or* Delete push-button. The *addToCurrentList* or *addToDeleteList* methods are invoked to carry out these operations. These methods add words to temporary add/delete lists. The user may alternatively enter a junk word in the edit box, and the word will either be added to deleted from the junk word set depending upon the option selected by the user.

When the user selects the OK push-button in the Junk Words dialog box, the words in the temporary add/delete lists are moved to the permanent set of added/deleted words by invoking the *setAddedWord* and *setDeleteWord* methods. These changes are also written to the junk words file. The Junk Words dialog box is then cleared from the screen.

A revised class diagram incorporating all of the changes previously noted is shown in Figures 8.11 and 8.12. Note that new attributes have been discovered while flushing out the algorithms, and some operations may have been added, eliminated, or moved to other classes. The Document Reference Information class is a data manager type of class; i.e., its principal responsibility is to maintain data. During design we have elected not to show operations that provide access to attributes. As we move further into implementation, these types of operations will be shown in the implementation model.

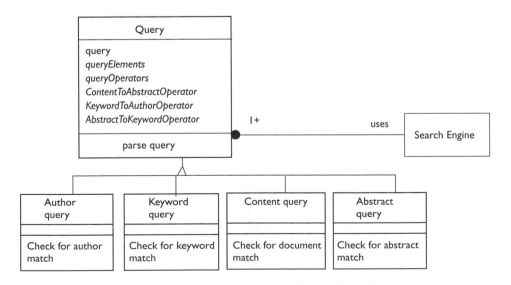

Figure 8.12. Query Module—Revision 3.

8.3 REPRESENTING OBJECTS

Figure 8.13 shows where we are in the design process (see the highlighted section). Object representation means choosing how to implement objects. This is dependent upon the language and class library that is used during the implementation. In Smalltalk/V each object class will either be self-standing (i.e., a subclass of the root object in the class hierarchy—*Object*) or a subclass of another class in the class library other than *Object*. All classes are contained in a single large inheritance structure in Smalltalk. In C++, an object may either be self standing, a subclass of another class in the class library other than *Object*, or stand alone (a class that does not inherit from any class in the class library). Classes that are not related may be made entirely distinct in C++, resulting in multiple inheritance trees. In this case there is no functionality or behavior that is common to all classes; i.e., C++ allows a forest of multiple inheritance trees, whereas Smalltalk allows only one inheritance tree.

When examining class libraries to determine what class to subdivide, the designer should look for an existing class that (1) implements most of the behavior needed by the new class, and (2) represents the type of object from a data standpoint (e.g., does the object represent a list, string, queue, bag, dialog box, window, file, directory, etc.), i.e., is a similar type of class. The more familiar you are with a class library, the more quickly you will make these decisions. This is a task of enormous magnitude. Some object-oriented proponents claim that it takes a programmer about one day to become familiar with a class (Graham, 1991). There are approximately 200 classes in the Smalltalk/V encyclopedia of classes. However, the average application will utilize only a handful of these classes. Nevertheless, the more familiar you are with the class library, the better the decisions you will make concerning object representation.

Knowing when to use the *is-a* (inheritance) versus *has-a* (aggregation) relationship to represent a class is not necessarily straightforward. It is generally easier and quicker to use inheritance, which is probably why most programmers choose inheritance. However, if class *A* subclasses from class *B*,

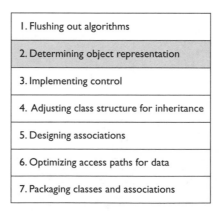

Figure 8.13. Determining Object Representation in the Design Process.

class *A* may inherit many methods that provide unwanted behavior for the user of class *A*. The use of some of these unwanted methods may cause class *A* to behave unexpectedly. Budd (1991) provides a more comprehensive discussion on the advantages and disadvantages of using the *is-a* relationship versus the *has-a* relationship. Another option when you are considering the use of inheritance is that if a class represents only some of the behavior and state that you are looking for, then you may be better off copying the code in which you are interested and placing your class at another location in the class hierarchy.

The object classes for our application and their representations using the Smalltalk/V for Windows Encyclopedia of Classes and Borland C++ with Application Frameworks are discussed later.

8.3.1 Smalltalk Object Representations

The complete Smalltalk/V class hierarchy is shown alphabetically in the *Smalltalk/V for Windows Tutorial and Programming Handbook* (Digitalk 1992b). The *Smalltalk/V for Windows Encyclopedia of Classes Handbook* (Digitalk 1992a) describes all of the public methods and their classes available to developers. We will systematically examine each object class for electronic filing and make a determination as to what class in the Smalltalk/V class library to divide into subclasses.

SearchEngine The *SearchEngine* class collects the high-level search functions together in one place. An instance of the *SearchEngine* class acts as an agent responsible for carrying out the search algorithm. No existing class in the class library is similar to the *SearchEngine* class. The *SearchEngine* class will be a subclass of class *Object* (i.e., self-standing).

HashEngine The *HashEngine* class collects the indexing functions together in one place. An instance of the *HashEngine* class acts as an agent responsible for carrying out the indexing algorithm. No existing class in the class library is similar to the *HashEngine* class. The *HashEngine* class will be a subclass of class *Object* (i.e., self-standing).

DocRefInfo Document reference information may be entered by a user when filing a document. Document reference information consists of an abstract/description, author(s), and/or keyword(s) associated with the document. There are no classes similar to the *DocRefInfo* class in the class library. The *DocRefInfo* class will be a subclass of class *Object* (i.e., self-standing).

SearchVector A search vector is used during the search of the content of a document(s). A search vector is used to determine those records of the document index that should be read. The document index is then read to determine those data records of the document file that are to be read. Specific records of the document file are then read to determine if there is a match between the content query and the content of a document. The behavior and state information of the Search-Vector class is unique to the application and will also be a subclass of class *Object*.

TextDocument The *TextDocument* class represents a document that is filed by the electronic filing program. The *File* class contains the behavior necessary for opening, closing, reading, and writing data from/to a file. However, the operations of the *TextDocument* class are at a higher level of abstraction than the *File* class. The *TextDocument* class will be a subclass of class *Object*.

FilingDirectory A FilingDirectory object represents all of the document index files, keeping track of all of the names of the documents that have been indexed by the program. The *Directory* class contains only the behavior necessary to get the directory name. The *File* class provides sequential or random access to a file. Since a *FilingDirectory* represents a collection of files, a *Collection* type of class is more in order. An *OrderedCollection* can be used like a dynamic array, stack, or queue and allows elements to be dynamically added or removed from the collection. However, an *OrderedCollection* has about 25 instance methods, and most of this behavior is inappropriate for our needs.

A more appropriate way of representing a filing directory would be to make *FilingDirectory* a subclass of class *Object* and an *OrderedCollection* of file names an attribute of the *FilingDirectory* class. Only meaningful operations should be delegated to the *OrderedCollection* object. Additional behavior beyond that provided by the *OrderedCollection* class will be included in the *FilingDirectory* class.

JunkWords Junk words are extraneous words, which, if found in the content of a document, are not indexed and are not retrievable via a search operation using a content query; e.g., junk words are words such as: and, the, we, him, then, that, from. The junk words in the electronic filing system represent a group, or collection of objects (words). These objects or junk words need to be presented to the user in some sort of order. The class library has a *SortedCollection* class that seems appropriate to represent this structure. However, most of the behavior of the *SortedCollection* class is unnecessary for junk words.

A more appropriate way of representing junk words would be to make *JunkWords* a subclass of class *Object* and a *SortedCollection* of junk words an attribute of the *JunkWords* class. Only meaningful operations should be delegated to the *SortedCollection* object. Junk words can be added or removed from the collection of junk words, and the collection will still remain in sorted order. Application-specific behavior in addition to the *add* and *remove* operations of the *SortedCollection* class will need to be included in the *JunkWords* class.

FilingCharacters Filing characters are ASCII characters that allow the user to restrict the indexing and retrieval operations to only certain characters. The filing characters in the electronic filing system represent a group, or collection of objects (characters). These objects or filing characters need to be presented to the user in some sort of order (e.g., alphabetical). The *SortedCollection* class in the Smalltalk/V class library seems appropriate to represent this structure. However, most of the behavior of the *SortedCollection* class is unnecessary for filing characters.

A more appropriate way of representing filing characters would be to make *FilingCharacters* a subclass of class *Object* and a *SortedCollection* of filing characters an attribute of the *FilingCharacters* class. Only meaningful operations should be delegated to the *SortedCollection* object. Objects can be added or removed from the collection and the collection will still remain in sorted order. Application-specific behavior in addition to the *add* and *remove* operations of the *SortedCollection* class will need to be included in the *FilingCharacters* class.

DocumentNameList The electronic filing program presents the user with a list of file names (documents) that satisfy the search request—commonly known as a *search hit list* or *document name list*. A document name list in the electronic filing system represents a group, or collection of objects (document names). The *OrderedCollection* class in the Smalltalk/V class library seems appropriate for this purpose. However, most of the behavior of the *OrderedCollection* class is unnecessary for the *DocumentNameList*.

A more appropriate way of representing a document name list would be to make *Document-NameList* a subclass of class *Object* and an *OrderedCollection* of document names an attribute of the *DocumentNameList* class. Only meaningful operations should be delegated to the *OrderedCollection* object. Application-specific behavior beyond that provided by the *OrderedCollection* class will need to be included in the *DocumentNameList* class.

DocumentRecordsList A document records list is a list of record numbers where a word or phrase specified in a search query has been found in the content of a document: so a document records list in the electronic filing system represents a group, or collection of document record numbers. The *OrderedCollection* class in the Smalltalk/V class library again seems appropriate for this purpose. However, most of the behavior of the *OrderedCollection* class is unnecessary for the *DocumentRecordsList*.

A more appropriate way of representing a document records list would be to make *Document-RecordsList* a subclass of class *Object* and an *OrderedCollection* of document records an attribute of the *DocumentRecordsList* class. Only meaningful operations should be delegated to the *OrderedCollection* object. Application-specific behavior beyond that provided by the *OrderedCollection* class will need to be included in the *DocumentRecordsList* class.

Index An index represents an indexed document file, so an index is a type of file. The *File* class conceptually represents a file and contains the behavior necessary for opening, closing, reading, and writing data from/to a file. However, the operations of the *Index* class are at a higher level of abstraction than is the *File* class; i.e., an *Index* object does not do low-level I/O operations. The *Index* class will be a subclass of class *Object*.

Query A query represents words and/or phrases that may be separated by logical operators (e.g., AND or OR). A query class is an abstract class for all of the query-type classes. It provides some of the behavior common to all query classes, such as parsing the query, getting the query elements, and getting the logical operators. This class will be a subclass of class *Object*—no other classes in the Smalltalk/V class library seem appropriate for this purpose.

AuthorQuery An author query comprises one or more author names separated by logical operators. *AuthorQuery* is one type of query and is made a subclass of class *Query*. *AuthorQuery* also has some unique behavior.

KeywordQuery A keyword query comprises one or more keywords separated by logical operators. *KeywordQuery* is one type of query and is made a subclass of class *Query*. *KeywordQuery* also has some unique behavior.

ContentQuery A content query comprises one or more words or phrases separated by logical operators. *ContentQuery* is one type of query and is made a subclass of class *Query*. *ContentQuery* also has some unique behavior.

AbstractQuery An abstract query comprises one or more words or phrases separated by logical operators. *AbstractQuery* is one type of query and is made a subclass of class *Query. AbstractQuery* also has some unique behavior.

Notice that almost all of the classes in our application domain have been made subclasses of class *Object*, with the exception of the specialized query-type classes. Also, many of these classes used delegation rather than inheritance from another class in the class library, which provides only some of the behavior needed by our application class. Some of our application objects will catch an operation on **self** and send it to another object that is part of the application object.

8.3.2 C++ Representations

The complete ObjectWindows class hierarchy, and a description of all of the public methods and their classes available to developers is shown in the *Borland ObjectWindows for C++ Reference Guide* (Borland International, 1991). The Borland container class libraries (an enhanced version of the Object-based library supplied with version 2.0 and a brand new implementation based on templates) are described in the *Borland C++ 3.1 Programmer's Guide* (Borland, 1992). In addition to these class libraries, a large run-time library of C++ functions is available that may be utilized to implement the methods of application classes (see Borland *C++ 3.1 Library Reference Manual*).

Borland C++ with Application Frameworks provides the following class libraries: streamable classes, standard ObjectWindows classes, ObjectWindows miscellaneous components, and container class libraries (one is based on templates and the other is not). These classes do not provide the functionality needed by any of the electronic filing application classes. Therefore, all of the application classes for electronic filing are stand-alone classes in C++. However, many of the application classes will use the streamable classes and the container classes to provide their behavior and representation.

The following sections discuss how some electronic filing classes will choose to internally represent their data structures.

JunkWords, FilingCharacters HashTable, Bag, List, DoubleList, Deque, Queue, and BTree classes are all inappropriate to represent these collections. A *Set* is a collection that allows only one instance of any one object and seems the most suitable class of the Collection classes to represent these groupings of words and characters.

DocumentNameList A collection of unique document names is best represented by the *Set* class. The *Set* class provides behavior to add, remove, or retrieve objects in the container.

DocumentRecordsList Record numbers in the DocumentRecordsList should be unique. The Set class allows only one instance of any particular object in its collection.

Query A *Query* class is an abstract class for all of the query-type classes. It provides some of the behavior common to all query classes.

AuthorQuery The author names in the author query and the logical operators can inherit behavior from the *Query* class. The author names and the logical operators should always be processed on a first-in, first-out basis because the author query is parsed from left to right with the first author name and the logical operator to enter the queue.

KeywordQuery The keywords in the keyword query (and the related logical operators) can inherit behavior from the *Query* class. The keywords (and the logical operators) should always be processed on a first-in, first-out basis because the keyword query is parsed from left to right with the first keyword and the logical operator to enter the queue.

ContentQuery The words and phrases in the content query (and the related logical operators) can inherit behavior from the *Query* class. The words and phrases (and the logical operators) should always be processed on a first-in, first-out basis because the content query is parsed from left to right with the first word or phrase and the logical operator to enter the queue.

AbstractQuery The words and phrases in the abstract query (and the related logical operators) can inherit behavior from the *Query* class. The words and phrases (and the logical operators) should always be processed on a first-in, first-out basis because the abstract query is parsed from left to right with the first word or phrase and the logical operator to enter the queue.

Notice that, unlike Smalltalk/V, in C++ we can have multiple trees of classes, and, in fact, do in our application. We are not directly subclassing *Object* for any of our application classes.

8.4 IMPLEMENTING CONTROL

The user interface that we have implemented for electronic filing is event driven. The program is mostly in a state wherein it is waiting for the user to provide instructions on what to do next. The instructions come in the form of selecting and clicking items with the mouse and entering data on the keyboard.

As a result of the user providing instructions to the program in the form of events, specific actions are taken by the program. The actions taken in filing a document or searching for document(s) are procedure driven. Numerous methods/procedures are called to take specific action based on previous input provided by the user. The location within the program implicitly defines the program state, which varies through many levels of procedure/method calls.

No concurrent tasking is used within the program.

8.5 ADJUSTING THE DESIGN TO INCREASE INHERITANCE

At this stage of the design (see Fig. 8.14), we will examine the object model to determine if any classes and operations/methods can be rearranged to increase inheritance and abstract out any behavior that is common to a group of classes. Abstracting out behavior may result in the creation of a new common superclass or may just add to the methods and/or attributes of an existing superclass.

| 1. Flushing out algorithms |
| 2. Determining object representation |
| 3. Implementing control |
| 4. Adjusting class structure for inheritance |
| 5. Designing associations |
| 6. Optimizing access paths for data |
| 7. Packaging classes and associations |

Figure 8.14. Adjusting Class Structure in the Design Process.

One opportunity to increase inheritance by abstracting out behavior lies with the *Query* class. The *Query* class is a superclass of the *AuthorQuery, KeywordQuery, ContentQuery,* and *AbstractQuery* classes. The specialized query classes already inherit/share the method *parse query*. Parsing a query involves separating logical group of words or phrases (getting a query element) from logical operators (e.g., AND or OR). This is the same for any of these queries. Therefore, the general *parse query* method is included in the behavior of the *Query* class.

The Query Module of Figure 8.11 shows the operations *check for author match, check for keyword match,* and *check for abstract match* associated with the author, keyword, and abstract query classes, respectively. These operations all have common behavior. We will abstract this behavior into the *Query* class and rename the operation *check for element match.* The *check for document matches* operation in the *Content Query* class is a specialized operation that is central to the *Search Engine* class. This operation is eliminated from the *Content Query* class.

The behavior for accessing query elements (i.e., "getting a query element") may likewise be abstracted out of these classes and included in the behavior of the *Query* class. Abstracting out common behavior into a superclass allows us to share code and specify a protocol common to all subclasses.

8.6 DESIGNING ASSOCIATIONS

Now we'll look at each association and analyze how it is used, and then determine the technique for implementing the association. During implementation we will hide the details of our access methods/operations that traverse and update the association so that if the application changes later on and requires different associations, the changes required to the program will be localized.

The following is a list of all of the associations (indicated in *italics*) and the multiplicity (indicated in parentheses) between object classes. All of the listed associations are traversed in the forward direction only (i.e., the direction implied by the name), unless otherwise indicated.

Rumbaugh *et al.* (1991) point out that we could contemplate using a global strategy for implementing associations in the object model, or we could look at how each association is used in the object model and then make a particular decision for each association. We'll select a particular technique for each association depending on how it is used in the application.

***SearchEngine* uses *(one or more)* *Query*:** Although a *SearchEngine* may use one or more *Query* objects, it can use only one *ContentQuery*, one *AuthorQuery*, one *AbstractQuery*, and one *KeywordQuery* at a time. Attributes are used in the *SearchEngine* object to refer to each one of these types of *Query* objects.

***SearchEngine* uses *(zero or more)* *DocRefInfo*:** A global name, *DRIs*, will represent a *Set* of *DocRefInfo* objects. *DocRefInfo* objects can then be referenced anywhere in the application. Document reference information objects are used during both filing and searching operations.

***TextDocument* is described by *(zero or one)* *DocRefInfo*:** An attribute in the *TextDocument* object referring to the *DocRefInfo* object.

***SearchEngine* generates *(zero or one)* *DocumentNameList*:** An attribute in the *SearchEngine* object referring to the *DocumentNameList* object.

***DocumentNameList* identifies *(zero or more)* *DocumentRecordsList*:** An attribute in the *DocumentNameList* object is a *Dictionary* type of object. The *Dictionary* object uses index file names as the keys and *DocumentRecordsList* objects as the values.

***SearchEngine* produces *(zero or one)* *SearchVector*:** An attribute in the *SearchEngine* object referring to the *SearchVector* object.

***SearchVector* utilizes *(one or more)* *Index*:** An attribute in the *SearchVector* object referring to a *Set* of *Index* objects.

***SearchEngine* checks *(one or more)* *FilingDirectory*:** A FilingDirectory object will be common to several operations: delete, file, and search. We'll use a global name, *Filing*, to represent a *FilingDirectory* so that universal access can be provided. Also, for now we will restrict the program to have one *FilingDirectory*.

***FilingDirectory* plus index name yield an *Index*:** The *FilingDirectory* will only be used to maintain the names of index files. Therefor the association between *FilingDirectory* and *Index* classes can be removed. Index objects are created and used only during the filing of a document. *FilingDirectory* has an attribute, which is a *Collection* of index names.

***Index* references *(one)* *TextDocument*:** An attribute in the *Index* object referring to the *TextDocument* object.

***HashEngine* services *(one or more)* *Index*:** An attribute in the *HashEngine* object referring to a *Set* of *Index* objects.

HashEngine **skips all** *(one) JunkWords:* An attribute in the *HashEngine* object referring to the *JunkWords* object.

HashEngine **checks for** *(one) FilingCharacters:* An attribute in the *HashEngine* object referring to the *FilingCharacters* object.

8.7 OPTIMIZING THE DESIGN

As noted in Chapter 1, object-oriented development is both interactive and incremental. Many iterations of our design will be done before arriving at a satisfactory solution. Jacobson et al. (1992) recommend starting with the construction of your program early in the development cycle, i.e., at the same time that you start working on the analysis model. Our implementation actually started with the construction of the user interface subsystem in an earlier chapter. We will now continue with the construction of our program by developing a basic implementation for the objects (and their methods) shown in the latest version of the object model and integrating this implementation with the user interface subsystem already developed.

Continuing with the implementation at this point in the object-oriented development life cycle will serve several purposes. It will

1. identify areas of the design where redundant associations should be added for efficient access

2. identify areas of the design where algorithms should be optimized to improve efficiency

3. identify areas of the design where derived attributes should be saved to avoid recomputation

4. help us deal with potential problems early, before we begin to spend of our efforts on coding (There will undoubtedly be some areas of the program design that will not be as fully advanced as we thought they were. These will surface when we begin doing some implementation. This will give us an opportunity to flesh out these areas now before the design is fully implemented and a lot of rework becomes necessary.)

5. validate the design

The methods that we implement for our objects will not be fully developed at this time: Some of the method implementations may be stubs. The purpose of implementing these objects now is to help validate the design to see if any changes are necessary. From a project-management perspective, this also serves another purpose. It demonstrates to management that we are making progress; i.e., it may help the project to gain management support and continue to receive funding.

The implementation of the user interface object classes and other object classes has yielded several discoveries—a number of the associations need to be changed in the design. These changes are:

❑ An *Index* uses a *HashEngine*—not *HashEngine* services one or more *Index* objects.

❑ There is no association between *SearchVector* and *Index*.

❑ *TextDocument* creates *Index*, not *Index* references *TextDocument*.

8.8 DETAILED OBJECT DESIGN MODEL

The revised class diagram that incorporates the changes discussed in previous sections of this chapter is shown in Figures 8.15 and 8.16. Note that this model differs slightly from previous models. During analysis we treat all references between objects as bidirectional associations. However, during design we no longer want to make that assumption. Rumbaugh (1994b) uses an arrowhead on an association to indicate which way the association is implemented. Note that in our object model the associations are all implemented in one direction. An explanation of the object model follows.

The search engine uses a query to determine what criteria to use in finding documents for the user. A query may be an author query, keyword query, abstract query, or content query. An author query consists of author names separated by logical operators. A keyword query consists of one or more keywords separated by logical operators. An abstract query is one or more words or phrases separated by logical operators that might be found in some document abstract. A content query is also one or more words or phrases separated by logical operators that might be found in the content of a text document.

The search engine produces a search vector based on a content query. The search engine uses a document index to determine which document records might have words or phrases that match a word or phrase in a document record.

The search engine also operates on one filing directory, which has document indexes. The search engine uses document reference information, which describes a text document filed in the system. A text document creates only one index.

A document index contains one or more hash blocks. Each hash block contains one or more hash records.

A hash engine checks for filing characters when hashing a text document. A hash engine also checks for junk words when hashing a text document.

The user interface subsystem classes interface to several electronic filing domain classes. The file, document reference information, and print dialog boxes use a text document. The search dialog box uses the search engine. The search engine uses a search-results dialog box. The delete dialog box uses a filing directory. The filing-characters dialog box uses the filing-characters object class. The junk-words dialog box uses the junk-words object class. The filing-characters object and junk-words object represent the filing characters file and the junk words file, respectively.

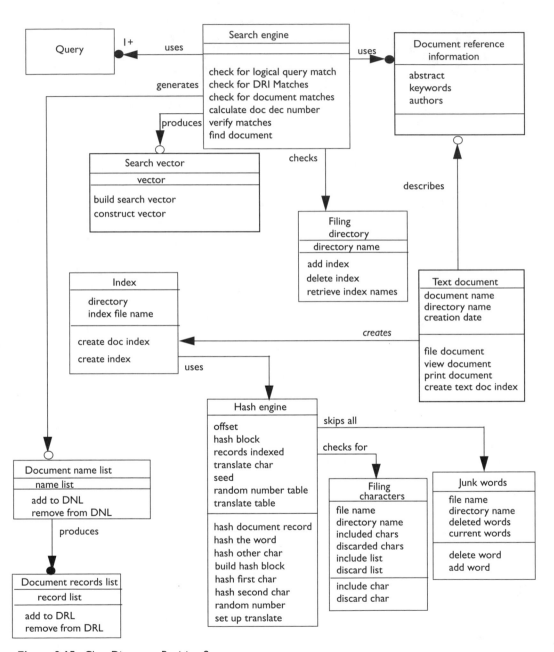

Figure 8.15. Class Diagram—Revision 8.

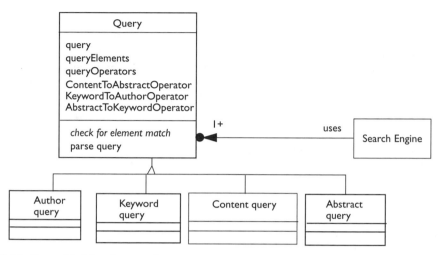

Figure 8.16. Query Module—Revision 4.

8.9 PHYSICALLY PACKAGING THE PROGRAM

Physical packaging of the program is concerned with

1. constructing physical modules

2. ensuring that classes, methods/operations, and modules are coherent

3. ensuring that the external interface of a class is the only part of the class that is made public (internal details of classes are hidden from outside view, i.e., information hiding is used)

8.9.1 Constructing Physical Modules

The construction of physical modules is language dependent. The physical packaging of the various elements of a program depends upon a language and its constructs.

The basic elements in Smalltalk are objects. The Smalltalk/V "image" comprises all of the objects, including both data and code. No physical modules can be developed in Smalltalk. However, configuration management tools are available to manage "groupwork," so that a team of software engineers can collectively and collaboratively work on a system implementation.

The Smalltalk application will require more time than the C++ application to produce a shippable, executable product. Basically, the development environment must be stripped from the Smalltalk environment, leaving the basic application and the Smalltalk classes necessary to support that application. Care must be taken in removing object classes that could or will be referenced in the runtime environment. Kirkpatrick (1994) discusses the issues involved in developing a commercial engineering application in Smalltalk.

C++ programs are generally organized as a set of header files and source files. The header files contain class declarations, types and names of external variables, structure definitions, constants, macros, etc. The class declaration lists the members (i.e., data and methods/operations) of the class. The class implementations are contained in the source files. The class implementation defines the methods for the class. One header file and one source file will be defined both for each subsystem in the electronic filing implementation and for each class that is not part of a subsystem.

8.9.2 Examining Subsystems and Classes for Coherence of Entities

We next review the design to examine for coherence of entities. This means that all of the entities in a subsystem, for example, should be an integral part of and essential to the performance of the subsystem's function. At the class level, all of the methods should be serving the main purpose of that class and not trying to serve many purposes. At the method level, the elements of a method should be tightly bound and related to one another. All of the elements of the method should be essential to the performance of the single function of the method.

To check for coherence of entities, we'll review each subsystem and then review each class within the subsystem. First we'll examine the purpose of the subsystem and then review if the subsystem performs this purpose or tries to perform many purposes. The examination of the subsystems and classes for coherence of entities can be found in Appendix G.

8.9.3 Ensuring That Only the External Interface of a Class Made Is Public

The next step is to ensure that the principles of information hiding have been applied to the design. Each class in the application has an interface part and an implementation part. The interface part describes how the class relates to the outside world. The implementation part describes how a specific interface function or responsibility is realized. In C++ the interface part may specify different access levels: public, protected, or private. Methods and attributes of a class may be either invisible or visible to the outside world in C++. In Smalltalk, all methods of a class are visible to the outside world, but attributes of the class are accessible only through the methods associated with the class. The interface parts of the application classes for Smalltalk/V and C++ are discussed later.

8.9.3.1 Smalltalk Design for Object Interfaces

In Smalltalk all methods are public by definition, and attributes are accessible only through these methods. Methods that are used internally within a class are typically regarded as "Private" and remain private only by programmers' agreement. The public methods (or interface part) of the implementation, for the application domain classes employed in electronic filing, are discussed in terms of the class name and the methods that are public by definition.

An example of the interface specification for the **DocumentNameList** class in Smalltalk is as follows:

DocumentNameList *Class Description*

Definition—The hierarchy for class **DocumentNameList** is **Object**. Objects of class **Document-NameList** represent lists of document names associated with a specific search request. The **DocumentNameList** class has 1 class method and 9 instance methods. It has no shared data or pool dictionaries.

Instance methods: addToDNL: anObject - Public. Add anObject to the documentNameList.

do: aBlock—Public. For each document name in the documentNameList, evaluate aBlock with a document name as the argument.

getRecordsList: indexFileName—Public. Answer with an **OrderedCollection** representing the list of record numbers for the *indexFileName*.

removeFromDNL—Public. Answer a **String** representing a document name removed from the head of the *documentNameList*.

size—Public. Answer an **Integer** which is the number of entries in the *documentNameList*.

includes: anObject—Public. Answer True if anObject is included in the DNL, else answer False.

putRecordsList: theRecordsListObject with: indexFileName—Public. Associate a **DocumentRecordsList** object with the indexFileName.

retrieveDocumentNames—Public. Answer with the documentNameList.

Class methods: new—Public. Create a new **DocumentNameList** object.

The public and private methods and the attributes associated with each class are presented and discussed in Chapter 9 and in Appendix M.

8.9.3.2 C++ Design for Object Interfaces

In C++ we distinguish between the interface and implementation files of a program. The interface files (usually given a ".h" extension) for electronic filing contain descriptions of the classes that are part of the same subsystem.

The members (member functions and instance variables or data members) of each class in the interface file are organized into sections, with each section having its own access level: public, protected, and private. A public access level means that this member is accessible to everyone. A protected access level is accessible to the member functions of this class and to any member functions that are part of a class derived from this one. Finally, a private access level means that only member functions of this class can access this member. Since users are mostly interested in the public access level, the public access level will be listed first within each class, followed by the protected access level for the interface specification.

An example of the interface specification for the **DocumentNameList** class in C++ is as follows:

DocumentNameList *Class Description*

Definition—**DocumentNameList** is a stand-alone class that is not part of the existing class hierarchy. Objects of class **DocumentNameList** represent lists of document names associated with a specific search request.

Public: Class **DocumentNameList** has nine member functions.

DocNameL ()—*DocNameL* is a constructor for the *DocNameL* class.

~DocNameL ()—*~DocNameL* is a destructor for the *DocNameL* class.

addToDNL (documentName)—Add a documentName to the docNameList.

getRecordsList (documentName)—Answer with a **Set** representing the list of record numbers for the documentName.

size ()—Answer an **Integer** which is the number of entries in the *documentNameList*.

removeFromDNL (documentName)—Answer a **String** representing a document name removed from the head of the *documentNameList*.

includes (documentName)—Answer True if documentName is included in the DNL, else answer False.

putRecordsList (docRecListObj, indexName)—Associate a **DocumentRecordsList** object with the *indexName*.

retrieveDocumentNames ()—Answer with the *documentNameList*.

The class protocols for the interface files are presented in Chapter 9 and in Appendix M, including a discussion of all of the C++ member functions (public, private, and protected) and the attributes associated with each class.

8.10 THE DESIGN DOCUMENT

The design document consists of the detailed object, functional, and dynamic models. Our functional and dynamic models remain the same as those shown in previous chapters. However, the object model has undergone considerable revision. Operations have been added to the object model and associations between objects have changed based on what we have learned during our design and implementation so far.

The design document shown in Appendix H consists of the following:

- ❑ detailed object model (class diagrams)
- ❑ algorithms for the File, Search, Delete, Filing Characters, and Junk Words operations
- ❑ object representations for Smalltalk and C++ languages
- ❑ physical packaging information
- ❑ revised data dictionary
- ❑ association implementations

The design phase of the electronic filing system application has taken the analysis document and added implementation details and refinements. The object design phase has defined the classes, their methods and attributes, and the association among classes and implementations of them. This has helped to validate and refine the current design and to test the implementation to date. The skeleton of the program is implemented and is working at this point. In the next chapter we will define the full internal implementation of each of the classes in the system.

8.11 SUMMARY OF PROCESS AND DELIVERABLES

In this chapter we have fully specified the existing and remaining classes, associations, attributes, and operations necessary for implementing a solution to the problem.

- ❑ The first step was flushing out algorithms to implement operations based on scenarios for each use case. Message hierarchy diagrams were developed to show the procedural behavior during design, and event traces were also developed to show the interaction between objects and the timing of events and messages.
- ❑ Next, we decided how each object would be represented, i.e., how to implement each object. This is dependent upon the language and class library used during the implementation. Both Smalltalk/V and C++ representations were chosen.
- ❑ The next step was looking at each association and analyzing how it was used and then determining the technique for implementing the association.
- ❑ The next step was optimizing the design.
- ❑ In the last step we determined the packaging of our program. In Smalltalk/V we have an image. In C++ we have both header and implementation files. We will package our subsystems together in an implementation file and a header file.

The deliverables for object design consist of an updated

- ❑ data dictionary
- ❑ object model
- ❑ message hierarchy diagrams

❑ event traces

❑ functional model (if still necessary)

❑ dynamic model (if still necessary)

The next step in the development of our electronic filing application is to complete the implementation of the program. This involves changing the contents of the object model to observe the syntax and restrictions of the programming language(s) and then completing the coding and testing of the program. We'll also look at using some object interaction diagrams as depicted in Rumbaugh (1994b).

Deciding on Implementations for Objects

Dᴜʀɪɴɢ ᴛʜᴇ ɪᴍᴘʟᴇᴍᴇɴᴛᴀᴛɪᴏɴ of the electronic filing application, we will continue to identify C++ and Smalltalk representations of our design. We will also continue to code our application at this time, filling in more of the detail. Both the design representation and the coding of many of the objects at the lower levels of abstraction in our application will occur at the same time. Figure 9.1 shows where we are in the OMT process.

Some of our goals during the implementation of this program are to

1. maximize code reuse

2. maximize our productivity

3. maximize the extensibility and maintainability of our program

During the remaining implementation of the electronic filing application, we will place a higher priority on reviewing existing code to identify opportunities for reuse rather than on writing new code. This will not only improve our productivity but will increase the reliability of our code because we will employ existing methods that have been previously used and tested. The approach that we

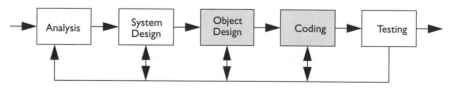

Figure 9.1. OMT Process and Testing..

will take is to look for classes that have behavior similar to what we need and then use either inheritance or composition to reuse this code—whichever is more appropriate for the situation.

In this chapter we will also develop the final detailed models (implementation models) before fully implementing the electronic filing program. Actually, we continue to develop the implementation model while we are writing code—although much of the model is developed prior to writing most of the code.

Before jumping into the Smalltalk/V and C++ implementations, we will discuss object-oriented programming style guidelines. These guidelines will be used to evaluate the "goodness" of our code and to point out where improvements are still necessary.

9.1 OBJECT-ORIENTED PROGRAMMING STYLE GUIDELINES

Many object-oriented programming style guidelines also apply to non–object-oriented programs. The guidelines presented here, borrowed from Rumbaugh et al. (1991), fall under the categories of reusability, use of inheritance, extensibility, and robustness.

9.1.1 Reusability

Reusing code to develop a new application has several advantages: the program is easier to maintain and understand because there is less code, and the program may be developed more quickly because the implementors are familiar with the code that is being reused and don't have to write new code instead. The following style rules for reusability apply both to the sharing of new code that has been written for some new application and to the reuse of code developed for previous applications:

1. Keep methods coherent: A coherent method should perform one function.

2. Keep methods small: A method should not exceed 100 lines of code or 1–2 pages.

3. Keep methods consistent: Make sure that similar methods use the same attributes, names, return values, etc.

4. Separate policy from implementation: The decision-making modules should be separate from the modules that implement the algorithms.

5. Provide uniform coverage: Cover all combinations of retrieving, storing, or processing data.

6. Broaden the method as much as possible: Generalize the method by adding additional code so that it may be applicable to more than one situation.

7. Avoid global information: Minimize the use of global objects so that methods can be used in more than one context.

8. Avoid modes: Avoid the development of methods that change their behavior depending on the context.

9.1.2 Use of Inheritance

Sometimes programmers misuse inheritance by using the *is-a* relationship when only a single method (or a few methods) of the superclass is applicable to the class inheriting its behavior. When methods on different classes are not similar enough to represent with a single inherited method, the following techniques should be used to foster inheritance:

1. Subroutines: Factor out the code that is common to each method and assign this common code to a superclass.

2. Factoring: Factor out the code that differs between two methods of different classes and make the remaining code a shared method between classes.

3. Delegation: Capture an operation on one object and invoke a method on another object that is related to the original object.

4. Encapsulate external code: Sometimes you may want to reuse code that has been developed for an application that had different interfacing conventions, that is part of a legacy system that is being reengineering using object-oriented techniques, or that is from another application that is likely to change in the future. An easy way to preserve your interface to this code is to encapsulate its behavior within a method of a class, rather than to make direct calls to it.

9.1.3 Extensibility

Software changes over time in ways that programmers are not always enable to envision. Here are some principles you may apply to enhance extensibility:

1. Encapsulate classes: The internals of a class should be accessible only through its methods.

2. Hide data structures: Data structures that are internal to a class should remain so.

3. Avoid traversing multiple links or methods: Methods should not traverse links to a neighbor and then traverse the neighbors links to other neighbors. Always invoke a neighbors method to access data in a more distant class.

4. Avoid case statements on object type: Do not circumvent methods by selecting behavior based on object type.

5. Distinguish public and private operations: Public operations define the interface part of the class; private operations define the implementation part of the class (i.e., how the operations are achieved by the class).

9.1.4 Robustness

A program that is robust continues to function under abnormal conditions, i.e., it receives improper parameters, encounters numerous error conditions, etc. Here are guidelines for robustness:

1. Protect against errors: Methods should protect themselves against application/user errors, system errors, and programming bugs.

2. Optimize after the program is running: First get the program working, then measure its performance and determine where optimization would be beneficial.

3. Validate arguments: Public methods should validate the arguments of their methods to ensure that users aren't violating restrictions on arguments.

4. Avoid predefined limits: Use dynamic memory allocaiton rather than static memory allocation since it is difficult to predict the amount of resources needed for an application.

5. Instrument the program for debugging and for performance monitoring: If necessary, add code to your program to gather statistics on performance and to aid in the debugging.

9.2 IMPLEMENTATION MODELS

During implementation we'll use the notation specified in Rumbaugh (1994c), which further specifies the implementation and complements the design model in Chapter 8. A summary of that notation is as follows:

❑ Comments are enclosed in braces: {Here is a comment}.

❑ Class attributes or methods have a "$" prefixed to the attribute name.

❑ Public, private, and protected access is indicated by prefixing "+," "-," and "#" symbols to the attribute or operation names, respectively. Class methods are additionally prefixed by a "$" symbol.

❑ An arrowhead will be used on an association to indicate that the association is implemented in the direction of the arrow (this convention was also used in the design model).

In addition, each implementation model must observe the syntactic rules for the target language as well. For example, class names in Smalltalk/V will begin with a capital letter by convention, and for C++ no embedded spaces may exist in names.

As we move from design to implementation, we see a big increase in the number of methods in the model. Many of these methods are what Rumbaugh (1994c) refers to as junk, utility, and/ or buck-passer methods. Our new object models incorporating this additional notation will be referred to as implementation models.

Note that the data links, or relationships between pairs of objects, can be implemented as:

❑ pointers to other objects

❑ parameters to an operation, or local variables within an operation

❑ something global (i.e., known to all objects)

All of these methods will be used in building the code for our application.

> **Note:** Only a few of the classes for the C++ and Smalltalk implementations of electronic filing are discussed in this chapter. The interested reader may refer to Appendix M for a further discussion of additional classes in the C++ and Smalltalk implementations.

Throughout the course of design we made some decisions to restrict the implementation of our program. In this chapter we would also like to restrict our implementation in several different ways in the interests of time. These implementations are left to the reader as an exercise. The restrictions can be summarized as follows:

- ❑ Searching will not be based on the creation date of a document. This eliminates the creation date attribute in the TextDocument class.

- ❑ Only one filing directory will be supported. All filed documents will be placed in this directory.

- ❑ Help menus and functions will not be implemented.

- ❑ The junk words operation will not retain nor display junk words that have been deleted in the scrolling list box. Once a junk word has been deleted, the only way for a user to include the word again is to explicitly add the word to the junk word list.

- ❑ The same restriction exists for filing characters as for junk words, except that we are talking about a filing character rather than a junk word.

- ❑ Neither Smalltalk nor C++ implementation is fully complete. The Smalltalk implementation is more complete than the C++ implementation. This is because it takes much more time and work to program in an object-oriented fashion using C++.

- ❑ The Smalltalk and C++ code produced through the writing of this text is NOT production code. The main focus of this book is the OMT, and not object-oriented programming. Much more work needs to be done to make both the Smalltalk and C++ codes production code, e.g., complete the implementation, add more error handling, and conduct more testing.

9.3 SMALLTALK IMPLEMENTATION

The Smalltalk/V implementation for electronic filing will be discussed on a subsystem basis. Classes that are not part of a subsystem will be discussed individually following the subsystem discussions. Each class will be discussed in terms of the fundamental elements of a class description protocol. A class description protocol is described by properties, features, and methods that describe any instantiation of that class.

Note that all methods in Smalltalk are *public* by definition. However, our methods in the electronic filing program are commented as either *public* or *private*. The methods commented as *public* should be accessible to other objects. The methods commented as *private* should not be used by other objects. Callback methods are also noted in the method description. Any methods commented as being *private* remain *private* only if the programmer respects and preserves the privacy.

We will reuse code to the maximum practical extent. As with the C++ implementation of the electronic filing program, the developer relies heavily on a class library to scavenge for reusable code. Code is reused either (1) through inheritance by creating subclasses of existing classes and overriding some of its methods, (2) by composition, or (3) by copying and pasting methods from an existing class to your new class that is not part of the same hierarchy.

The following format will be used to discuss each class:

❑ Definition: Identify the location of the class in the Smalltalk class hierarchy. Also identify the elements of the class such as private data (instance variables), shared data (class variables), pool dictionaries, and number of instance and class methods. Private and shared data names will be shown in **bold**, while instance and class method names will be shown in *italics*.

❑ Private data: A description of each instance-variable type.

❑ Shared data: A description of each class-variable type.

❑ Pool dictionaries: A description of each pool dictionary–variable type.

❑ Instance methods: A description of each instance method and what it does.

❑ Class methods: A description of each instance method and what it does.

❑ Inherited protocol: A description of any protocol inherited by an application class

❑ Discussion on programming style: If programming style improvements are suggested.

❑ Design versus implementation differences (the implementation model will be compared against the design object model shown in the previous chapter).

Full code listings for each class within a subsystem for the current implementation are shown in Appendix I. Some class and instance methods have been deleted or renamed. The deleted methods were not needed, and some methods were renamed to more accurately reflect what they actually do. The following discussions about the Smalltalk implementation are based on the code in Appendix I.

9.3.1 User Interface Subsystem

The structure and operation of the user interface for the electronic filing program centers around user-generated events; e.g., mouse clicks and keystrokes. This is true for both the Smalltalk and C++ implementations. Whenever a push-button is selected or data characters are entered, an event is generated. Whenever an event is generated, a message is sent to the current window or dialog box object. The message is defined by the name of the method to invoke that is part of the behavior of the current window or dialog box. This method is generally referred to as an *event method, event handler, message-response member function,* or *call-back* function. Many of the methods for the user interface classes are event handlers. Other methods may exist to support the event handlers.

At this point in our design, we'll pause and implement the user interface methods to increase our understanding of the design of the application. The main purpose in doing this is to gain new insights into the design that will become evident due to our increased understanding of the implementation.

The following steps must be taken next to completely fill out the user interface code for the Smalltalk implementation:

1. Add comments to the user interface code generated by Window Builder as deemed appropriate.

2. Add code to each dialog box class so that all of the radio buttons and push-buttons are functional and the dialog boxes are erased from the screen when they are supposed to be.

3. Include code to add items to the list boxes that are part of each dialog box. Code must also be added to get selections from a list box that have been chosen by the user.

4. Add code to retrieve and paste/insert text from and into an edit control box, respectively.

5. Declare and implement any additional objects from the Smalltalk class library necessary to complete the implementation of the user interface.

Steps 2 through 5 require flushing out the code for the event handlers, or callbacks, in Smalltalk. Code has already been added to the user interface to close each dialog box when the *OK* or *Done* push-button has been selected by the user. The remaining user interface code needs to be completed now.

The user interface subsystem classes were generated with the use of WindowBuilder. All callback or event handler stubs are also generated by WindowBuilder. Additional programming was necessary to close dialog boxes, fill the contents of a list box, write code to deal with text edit boxes and buttons, and add code to the callbacks or event handlers to perform the necessary event processing. The **FileADocument** user interface class will be discussed here as an example of a user interface class implementation. The implementation model for the user interface classes is shown in Figures 9.2 and 9.3. Note that this model has been divided into two figures owing to the lack of space on a single diagram. Also note that the print and view dialog boxes are not shown as part of this model. The print dialog box and the view dialog box will be implemented using the **PrintDialog** and **WindowDialog** classes, respectively, in the Smalltalk/V class library.

FileADocument *Class Description*

Definition—The hierarchy for class **FileADocument** is **Object-ViewManager-WindowDialog**. It has no shared data (class variables). Objects of class **FileADocument** represent the File a Document dialog box. The **FileADocument** class has 1 class method and 12 instance methods.

Private data—Class **FileADocument** has four instance variables.

selectedDirectory—An instance of **Directory** representing the current directory selected by the user from the Directories scrolling list box.

selectedFile—An instance of **String** representing the current file selected by the user from the Files scrolling list box.

directoryList—An instance of **OrderedCollection** representing the list of current directories in the Directories scrolling list box.

pathNameArray—An instance of **OrderedCollection** representing the list of path names for each of the directory names shown in the Directories scrolling list box.

Pool dictionaries:

ColorConstants—Associates color names to system color palette indices.

WBConstants—Constants used by the WindowBuilder tool.

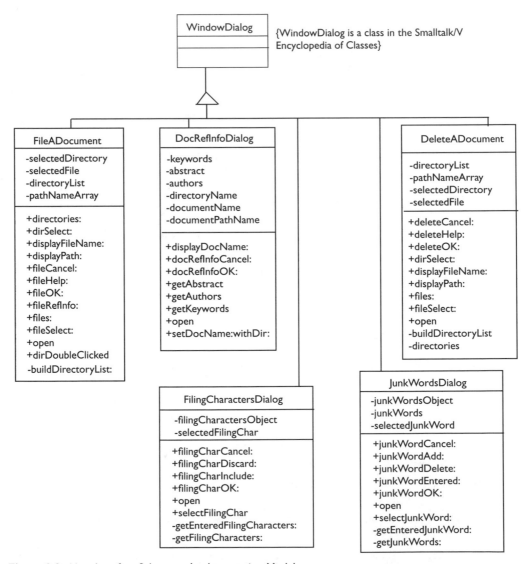

Figure 9.2. User Interface Subsystem Implementation Model.

Instance methods:

> *buildDirectoryList*—Private. Build an **OrderedCollection** of directory name strings for all directories on the disk. Precede names with spaces to indicate directory hierarchy.
>
> *directories: directoryListBox*—Callback for the #getContents event in an unnamed **ListBox**. Fill the directoryListBox pane with the list of directories for the selected device.

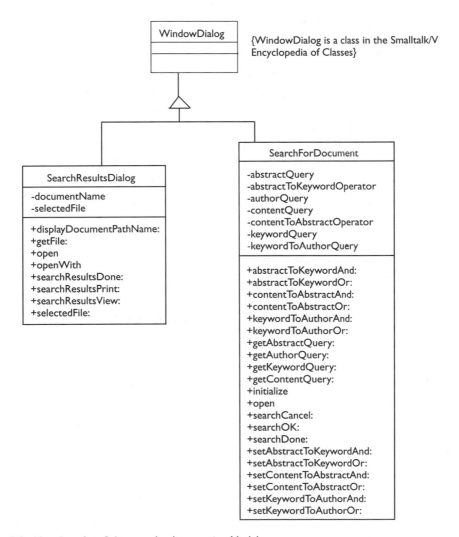

Figure 9.3. User Interface Subsystem Implementation Model.

dirSelect: aPane—Callback for the #select event in directoryListBox. Get the directory name selected by the user.

displayFileName: aPane—Callback for the #getContents event in the **EntryField** named 'file-NameEntryField.' Insert the file name in the **EntryField**.

displayPath: aPane—Callback for the #getContents event in the **EntryField** named 'pathEntry-Field.' Insert the path name in the **EntryField**.

fileCancel: aPane—Callback for the #clicked event in an unnamed **Button** (contents is 'Cancel'). Confirms if a user wants to cancel the operation.

fileHelp: aPane—Callback for the #clicked event in an unnamed **Button** (contents is 'Help'). Displays help information to the user.

fileOK: aPane—Callback for the #clicked event in an unnamed **Button** (contents is 'OK'). Add document name (selectedFile) to **Filing** dictionary. There is one directory for the electronic filing application, '**Filing**.' All text documents filed in the system have their names in the **Filing** dictionary.

fileRefInfo: aPane—Callback for the #clicked event in an unnamed **Button** (contents is 'Reference Information'). Add document name (selectedFile) to **Filing** dictionary.

files: aPane—Callback for the #getContents event in the **ListBox** named 'fileListBox.' Fill the **ListBox** with a sorted list of files for the selected directory.

fileSelect: aPane—Callback for the #select event in an unnamed **ListBox**.

open—Public. Create the **FileADocument** dialog box. Entirely generated by WindowBuilder.

dirDoubleClicked—Callback for the #doubleClickSelect event. A directory name was double-clicked. Get the directories subdirectories, if any.

Class methods:

wbCreated—This is generated by WindowBuilder and used by the **ViewManager** class.

The user interface classes are almost entirely generated by WindowBuilder. Many of the methods are *callbacks*. The *open* method in the **FileADocument** class is rather large, but it is cohesive. It builds the File a Document dialog box. WindowBuilder uses inheritance to build the dialog box, subclassing the **WindowDialog** class.

This class uses a global variable, *Filing*, which retains the filing directory name and an **Ordered-Collection** of files that have been indexed by the program. This allows the program to maintain a reference to all indexed documents. The use of global variables should be minimized in the implementation of any program.

The **FileADocument** class doesn't check against all user errors, such as ensuring that the user has selected a file/document that this program recognizes and is able to file. This code should be added to protect the program from trying to process invalid data and generating erroneous results.

Future implementations should drop the "get" from the method names to improve readability (Lorenz, 1993). For example, the *getKeywords* method of the **DocRefInfoDialog** class should be changed to *keywords*.

9.3.2 Miscellaneous Classes

The miscellaneous class that is not part of another subsystem is **FilingDirectory.**

FilingDirectory *Class Description*

Definition—The hierarchy for class *FilingDirectory* is *Object*. Objects of class *FilingDirectory* represent a directory and the index files used by the application in storing and retrieving document indexes. The *FilingDirectory* class has four instance methods and one class method. It has no shared data or pool dictionaries.

Private data—Class **FilingDirectory** has two instance variables.

directoryName—An instance of **String** representing the name of the filing directory.

files—An instance of **OrderedCollection** used to contain the names of the index files.

Instance methods:

addIndexFile: fileName—Public. Add a file name in the form of a **String** to *files.*

deleteIndexFile: indexName—Public. Deletes the specified index file from disk and removes the *indexName* from files.

initialize—Private. Set up **directoryName** and **files**.

retrieveIndexNames—Public. Answer **files**.

Class methods:

new—Public. Create a new **FilingDirectory** object.

*Protocol inherited from **Object** and used*—none.

An implementation model (a class diagram) showing the filing directory class, search subsystem, and other subsystems in the model is shown in Figure 9.4. The implementation model has many more elements, operations, and attributes than the object model (design model) from Chapter 8. Note that the implementation model has involved changing the contents of the object model to observe the syntax and restrictions of the programming language.

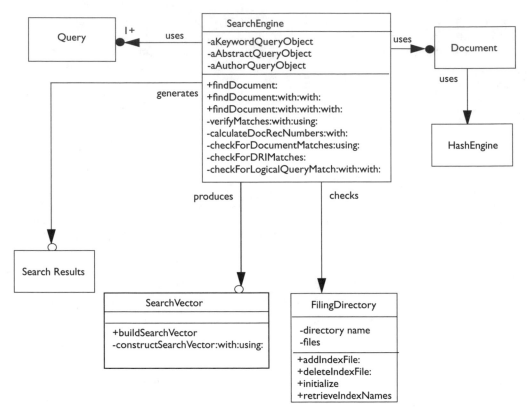

Figure 9.4. Implementation Object Model.

9.4 C++ IMPLEMENTATION

Some of the terms used throughout the text, such as methods and messages, are seldom used in languages such as C++. A "method" in C++ is a *member function,* and sending a message to an object is referred to as *invoking a member function.* Variables are referred to as *data members* in C++. The data members, member functions, and levels of information-hiding are specified within the C++ class body. This terminology will be used throughout the discussion of the C++ implementation.

Note that in C++, unlike Smalltalk, there are multiple levels of information hiding for the data members and member functions of each class—*public, protected,* and *private.* Only the member functions that provide the external interface to the class are declared as *public.* The data members and the member functions used internally by the class are typically declared as *private.* Any member functions or data members declared as protected are accessible only to derived classes and to the base class they are declared in.

As with the Smalltalk implementation, we will reuse code to the maximum practical extent. We will rely heavily upon the Borland C++ class libraries to scavenge for reusable code. These class libraries are for the streamable classes, Windows classes, and container classes. Additionally, we will make use of the Windows functions and the run-time library that are provided with our C++ environment.

Each class will be discussed in terms of the data members and member functions provided at each level of information hiding. The following format will be used to discuss each class:

- ❏ Definition: Identify the location of the class in the C++ class hierarchy. Also identify the elements of the class such as data members and member functions. Data member names will be shown in **bold**, while member function names will be shown in *italics*.

- ❏ Public: A description of each data member and each member function defined at this level of information hiding.

- ❏ Protected: A description of each data member and each member function defined at this level of information hiding.

- ❏ Private: A description of each data member and each member function defined at this level of information hiding.

- ❏ Data members: The data members specified at a specific level of information hiding.

- ❏ Member functions: The member functions specified at a specific level of information hiding.

- ❏ Inherited protocol: A description of any protocol inherited by an application class

- ❏ Discussion on programming style: If programming style improvements are suggested.

- ❏ Design versus implementation differences (the implementation model will be compared with the design object model shown in the previous chapter).

Full code listings for each class within a subsystem for the current implementation are shown in Appendix J. Some member functions have been deleted or renamed. The deleted member functions were not needed, and some member functions were renamed to more accurately reflect what they do.

The following discussions are based on the code in Appendix J. Each level of information hiding for a class is discussed only if there are data members or member functions defined for that level of access. Also, the constructors and destructors for each class will not be discussed unless they contribute such unique behavior to the program that they warrant discussion.

9.4.1 User Interface Subsystem

The following steps must be taken to completely fill out the user interface code for the C++ implementation:

1. Add comments to the user interface code (ef.cpp) generated by Protogen. The comments should note the various dialog boxes, push-buttons, etc.

2. Add code to the ef.cpp file so that all of the radio buttons and push-buttons are functional and that dialog boxes are erased from the screen when they are supposed to be.

3. Add code to add items to the list boxes that are part of each dialog box. Code must also be added to get selections from a list box that have been chosen by the user.

4. Add code to retrieve and paste/insert text from and into an edit control box, respectively.

5. Declare and implement any objects from the container class library necessary to implement the user interface.

Steps 1 and 2 have previously been completed and are reflected in the code. Note that for the C++ implementation, when the electronic filing program closes a window/dialog element, ObjectWindows will automatically delete the dialog object. Steps 3 through 5 need to be completed now.

    The user interface subsystem classes were generated with the use of ProtoGen. Some callback or event handler stubs are also generated by ProtoGen. Additional programming was necessary to close dialog boxes, fill the contents of a list box, write code to deal with text edit boxes and pushbuttons, and add code to the callbacks or event handlers to perform the necessary event processing. The **FileADocument** user interface class will be discussed here as an example of a user interface class implementation. Many of the names of member functions generated by ProtoGen were changed to make them more meaningful.

FileADocument *Class Description*

Definition—The TDIALOG_1Dlg class generated by ProtoGen has been renamed to **FileADocument**. The hierarchy for class **FileADocument** is **Object-TWindowsObject/TStreamable-TDialog**. Note that TDialog multiply inherits from both **TWindowsObject** and **TStreamable**. Objects of class **FileADocument** represent the File A Document dialog box. The **FileADocument** class has six data members and nine member functions.

Public:

Class **FileADocument** has six data members. Two of those data members are edit control boxes. Another two of those data members are list box elements.

    selectedDirectory—A character string representing the current directory selected by the user from the Directories scrolling list box.

    selectedFile—A character string representing the current file selected by the user from the Files scrolling list box.

Class **FileADocument** has nine member functions. This includes both a constructor and a destructor.

    handleFileListBoxMsg ()—Callback for any event associated with the file list box.

    handleDirListBoxMsg ()—Callback for any event associated with the directory list box.

    setUpWindow ()—Sets up the dialog box.

    refInfoPushButton ()—Callback for any event associated with the Reference Information **push** button.

helpPushButton ()—Callback for any event associated with the Help **push** button.

cancelPushButton ()—Callback for any event associated with the Cancel **push** button.

okPushButton ()—Callback for any event associated with the Ok **push** button.

The user interface classes are almost entirely generated by ProtoGen. (Note that ProtoGen places regeneration brackets in its output code. The developer can add code between these regeneration brackets and ProtoGen will not destroy that code—unless the developer deleted the basic entity associated with that code, such as a dialog box. This allows the developer to go back and forth between the GUI builder and the code for enhancing the maintenance process.)

Several of the member functions are *callbacks*. Many of the names generated by ProtoGen for user interface class names and member function names are not meaningful to the programmer. This is typical of user interface generation tools. These names have been manually changed to improve the clarity of the code and our understanding of the program. ProtoGen uses inheritance to build the dialog box, subclassing the **TDialog** class. All of the member functions are fairly small, i.e., less than one page of code.

The **FileADocument** class doesn't check against all user errors, such as checks to ensure that the user has selected a file/document that this program recognizes and is able to file. This code should be added to protect the program from trying to process invalid data and generating erroneous results.

The user interface code developed by the graphical user interface (GUI) builder tool for C++ is much more difficult to follow than is the code developed for the Smalltalk GUI. Callback or event handler names are some arbitrary combination of alphanumeric and numeric characters rather than meaningful names/labels. The Smalltalk GUI tool allows the developer to specify each event-handler name, while the C++ tool does not. Therefore, no implementation model was developed for the user interface subsystem.

9.4.2 Miscellaneous Classes

The miscellaneous class that is not part of another subsystem is **FilingDirectory.**

FilingDirectory *Class Description*

Definition—The hierarchy for class **FilingDirectory** is **Object**. Objects of class **FilingDirectory** represent a directory and the index files used by the application in storing and retrieving document indexes.

Public:

Class **FilingDirectory** has six public member functions, which include both a constructor and a destructor.

FileDir ()—FileDir is the constructor for the *FilingDirectory* class.

~FileDir ()—~FileDir is the destructor for the *FilingDirectory* class.

addIndexFile (fileName)—Add a file name to *files* in the form of a **String**.

deleteIndexFile (indexName)—Deletes the specified index file from disk and removes the *index-Name* from *files*.

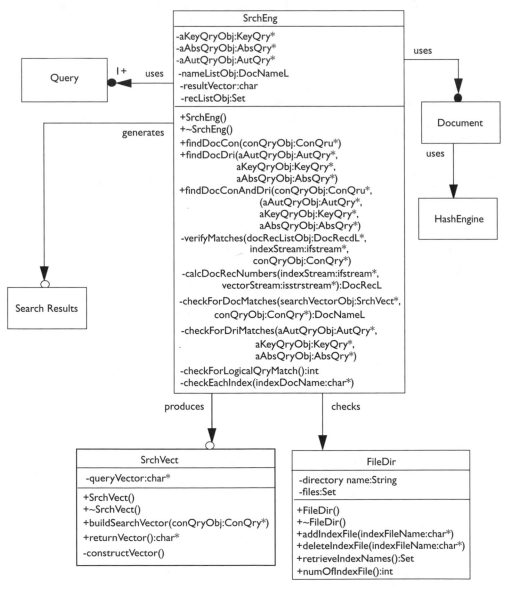

Figure 9.5. Implementation Object Model.

retrieveIndexNames ()—Answers with **files**.

numberOfIndexFiles ()—Answers with the number of index files.

Private:

Class **FilingDirectory** has two private data members.

directoryName—An instance of **String** representing the name of the filing directory.

files—An instance of **Set** used to contain the names of the index files.

An implementation model showing the filing directory class, search subsystem, and other subsystems in the model is shown in Figure 9.5.

9.5 TESTING THE ELECTRONIC FILING APPLICATION

The implementation and testing of this application actually began during the analysis stage. Much of the user interface subsystem was implemented first, top down, in skeleton form and then used as a driver for incrementally adding and testing other objects in the application, bottom up. The document subsystem (the portion that allowed the filing of the contents of a document only) was partially implemented and tested next. This was followed by the hashing subsystem. At this point documents could be indexed/filed using the electronic filing application.

The remaining part of the document subsystem that dealt with document reference information was implemented and tested next. Now documents with or without document reference information could be filed in the system.

The next item was to partially implement and test the query subsystem in order to implement some part of a query and to send a message to the search subsystem to find a document. The search subsystem was implemented and tested next. Now the application could find a document, but still could not present the search results to the user. Finally, the search results subsystem was implemented and tested, enabling the user to view the documents that were found as a result of the search.

Within each subsystem, the parts of the subsystem that were absolutely necessary to file and retrieve a document were implemented and tested first. For example, the adding of junk words to the system via the user interface was necessary right away so that the system could eliminate those junk words to narrow the indexing of each document. The deleting of junk words to the system via the user interface was not necessary at this point. The deletion capability was implemented and tested after the basic filing and searching capabilities were functional.

Implementation and testing were done in an incremental fashion on a subsystem-by-subsystem basis. The relationship among the subsystems is client-supplier or client-server. A client requests a service from a server subsystem, and the server subsystem provides the service and responds with a result. The services provided by the server objects are defined by their message interfaces. As server objects were added to a subsystem, they would be implemented initially as

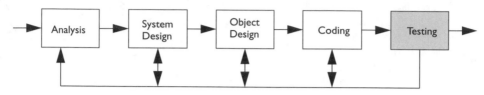

Figure 9.6. OMT Process and Testing.

stubs, providing some standard result to the client so that the client function could be implemented and tested. When the client was implemented and working, the server would then be implemented more fully and tested. The server object might then act as a client in requesting services of another object. The same type of implementation and test pattern would be repeated until all of the subsystem operations were completely implemented for the program.

Figure 9.6 shows where we are in the OMT process. An independent validation of the system might occur at this point. Test cases based on many variations of scenarios for the use cases might be generated and executed. Significant savings in labor hours may result from the use of automated testing tools, such as a test case generator (Poston, 1994).

9.6 SUMMARY OF PROCESS AND DELIVERABLES

In this chapter we have implemented the electronic filing program in two programming languages: C++ and Smalltalk/V. The implementation proceeded top down for the user interface and bottom up for much of the rest of the program. Our implementation process consisted of incrementally coding and testing closely related pieces of the program, continually adding more capability to the program as we proceeded with the implementation.

The deliverables for the implementation consist of:

❑ implementation models

❑ class descriptions

❑ object interaction diagrams (if necessary)

❑ completed code for programs in C++ and Smalltalk/V programming languages

The implementation models, class descriptions, and any detailed object interaction diagrams produced during this phase of development could be part of an implementation document. The implementation document might also describe hardware and software platform constraints for the application, measured performance of the program, limitations of the program, etc.

In the next, and final, chapter of this book, we will present the lessons learned during the analysis, design, and implementation of the electronic filing program using the OMT.

CHAPTER 10

Summary and Lessons Learned

THROUGHOUT THE DEVELOPMENT of the electronic filing application, I learned many lessons regarding object-oriented software development. The following includes not only a summary of these, but some general observations about the OMT and about object-oriented software development.

You should create an electronic folder or chapter in the OMT specification for each phase of the OODP. As you begin doing analysis, you may initially specify too much detail. As you iterate through your analysis you will recognize this and be able to abstract out that detail and capture it in the design part of your OMT specification. Similarly during design you may tend to specify too much material, which could be captured in the code section of your OMT specification.

Object-oriented software development requires much more iteration than does software development using traditional techniques such as structured analysis and design. The multimodel nature of the OMT promotes additional iteration. However, I think that the amount of iteration in your software development process is a function of things such as your knowledge of the problem domain, your knowledge of the reusable elements (analysis and design results, application frameworks, class libraries), the amount of experience you have in building the same or similar applications, etc.

The OMT is a little weak in the area of specifying how to do subsystem design. Some heuristics borrowed from other authors (Wirfs-Brock et al., 1990; Jacobson et al., 1992) were presented in this text to add value to the OMT approach.

Many, if not most, operations are not discovered until the object design phase using the OMT approach. This may cause several iterations of the object model to occur before a realistic representation of a solution to the problem has been discovered by the developer.

Class libraries take a long time to learn. The spin-up time can be significant. The programs you write at the outset may not fully capitalize on the capabilities of the class library. Your productivity will improve significantly as you become familiar with the class library. Productivity improvements of as much as 1400% with object technology (compared to traditional techniques) have been documented in the literature (Taylor, 1992).

A GUI tool for C++ may generate the user interface code and place all of it in one large file. For a user interface with many dialog boxes and windows, this file may become unmanageable. The object engineer needs to work with this file to break it up into manageable chunks, based on subsystems and classes, so that it is easier to work with.

CASE tools that support the OMT and each of its models can save a developer many hours of work.

Inheritance is important in the design of your application but its importance is overstressed in general. Very little of this application was based on inheritance—except in Smalltalk, where there is only one tree and everything inherits from *Object*.

Design and code walkthroughs are just as important when applying OOT as when employing traditional approaches to development. Walkthroughs of the design lead to changed associations among classes, to elimination of methods, to regrouping of classes into subsystems, etc. Walkthroughs of code lead to the addition or removal of data or methods, to changed and improved methods requiring less code, to changed associations between classes, and to regrouping of subsystems.

C++ class libraries lack functionality compared to Smalltalk class libraries. Much more work is required in C++ to accomplish the same thing in Smalltalk. The number of member functions per class in C++ is very small, typically six or fewer. In Smalltalk it is probably always six or MORE. You have to worry about much more detail in C++ at the programming language level than you do in Smalltalk. The C++ language generally expresses ideas at a lower level of abstraction than does the Smalltalk language. Some people consider C++ to be a system-programming language rather than an application-development language (Love, 1993).

The Borland C++ class library is more difficult to get your arms around because of the way its organization is presented to the user. The Digitalk Smalltalk class library is presented in a hierarchical fashion, where you can pick out a class to examine and then look through its attributes and methods. This organization makes it easier to understand and to grasp the inheritance structure (at least to me it does).

One problem that I have in moving back and forth between Smalltalk and C++ is that of dealing with language typing. While developing C++ code, I continually specify variables but forget to declare their type. This results in a lot of compilation errors, causing me to go back and recompile and relink my program.

Windows programming is much faster and easier in Smalltalk than in C++. The Window Builder tool in Smalltalk prompts the developer for the events and the corresponding event handlers/callbacks for the different components of the user interface. This greatly simplifies the building of GUIs in Smalltalk, saving the developer a lot of time. This also simplifies the maintenance, since meaningful names for event handlers can be specified by the developer.

Dealing with lots of files in C++ complicates the development effort and increases the probability of introducing errors and rework. For example, in C++ you have many different types of files, e.g., header, implementation, defines, externals, etc. In Smalltalk you just have an image and some application class files to share (if this is a multideveloper environment).

Before collecting process metrics, I should have specified various codes for the different activities that I wished to track (for example, TS for testing Smalltalk code, TC for testing C++ code, CU on coding the user interface, PU for prototyping the user interface, etc.). The codes and the times spent on the various activities should have been stored in a computer file. A program could have been easily written to tally up this data.

The event trace is an important tool to use during the building of your application. The event trace shows collaborations among object classes in a graphic format. Object interaction diagrams (OID) are a useful tool to describe the procedural behavior of your program. Message hierarchy diagrams are easier to develop than either event traces or OIDs and don't require a special drawing tool.

The biggest lesson learned: using object-oriented software development is a more natural way to develop programs than traditional techniques. Using Smalltalk and C++ (especially Smalltalk) gets you in the mode of always trying to reuse existing code before you write any new code. Reuse is the key both to productivity improvements and to high-quality programs. Both Smalltalk and C++ have their place in the world. The ideal case to me is to use Smalltalk for building as much of your application as is practical.

APPENDIX **A**

Data Flow Diagram Process Descriptions

A.1 DESCRIBING EACH FUNCTION

After the data flow diagrams have been developed and refined, the next step in the process in constructing the functional model is to develop descriptions for each *primitive* process/function in the DFD. A primitive process or function is a DFD process (or bubble) that cannot be further decomposed; i.e., it is a primitive. The number of process/function descriptions will be equal to the number of primitive processes (or bubbles) in the leveled DFD set that we previously completed. Each primitive process/function in the DFD will eventually be implemented as an operation on objects.

Each primitive function in our leveled set of DFD diagrams will have an entry in the data dictionary. The data dictionary entry for a functional primitive will have the following format:

    Function Name:
    Function Number:
    Function Description:

The function, or process, name is the name of the primitive process that we have already written inside of the bubble. The function description is a concise description of the functional primitive. The purpose of the function description is to indicate what a function must do logically, not how it must be implemented. We will describe each of our functional primitives as a procedural description in pseudocode. Each functional description will have the following format:

    Function Inputs:
    Function Outputs:
    File/Database:
    Function Transformation:
    Function Constraints:

Each function has inputs that are necessary to produce some output. The function transforms the inputs to some output. The function may need to read/write data from/to a file or database. The file/database component of the description for the function is optional, since most processes will not access a file or database. Additionally, there may be constraints that specify restrictions on functions; e.g., input values and output values must stay within certain values. All functional primitives for the *find documents* and *file document* processes are described in this appendix.

A.2 FILE DOCUMENT FUNCTIONAL PRIMITIVES

The functional primitives for the file document process are described in this section according to the previously specified format. Functional primitives are identified by looking at each and every process or bubble in the DFD to see if there is any further decomposition. If no further decomposition of a bubble is achievable, then it is a functional primitive.

Validate Document Type

Function Name:	validate document type
Function Description:	
Inputs:	document path
Outputs:	text document type
File/Database:	user's directory
Transformation:	open the file using the specified path
	check file type
	get document type
	return document type
Constraints:	document path must be valid, file must exist and be accessible, text document type must be supported by the system

Hash the Word

Function Name:	hash the word
Function Description:	
Inputs:	word
Outputs:	hashed word
File/Database:	filing character set
Transformation:	hash each character
	add each hashed character to hashed word
	return hashed word
Constraints:	a character is a filing character

Build Hash Record

The *build hash record* process adds the hashed word to the hashed record.

Function Name:	build hash record
Function Description:	
Inputs:	hashed word
Outputs:	hashed record
Transformation:	get hash record

OR hashed word to hashed record
return hashed record

Build Hash Block

The *build hash block* process adds a hashed record to part of a hashed block. A document index file may consist of a number of hashed blocks, depending on the size of the text document.

Function Name:	build hash block
Function Description:	
Inputs:	hashed record
Outputs:	hashed block
Transformation:	create a hash block if the hash block is full
	add hashed record to the block
	return hashed block

Create Document Index File

Function Name:	create document index file
Function Description:	
Inputs:	document file name
Outputs:	document index file name
File/Database:	filing directory
Transformation:	document index file name = index file extension name concatenated to document file name
	create file in filing directory using document index file name
	return document index file name
Constraints:	sufficient space exists for creating new files of the required size

Write To Index File

The filing directory is the interface between the *file* and *find* processes. The *write to index file* process outputs all of the document index and other relevant information to the document index file in the filing directory.

Function Name:	write to index file
Function Description:	
Inputs:	document index file name, hashed block, document reference information, text document type
Outputs:	document index
File/Database:	filing directory
Transformation:	format document reference information for output to filing directory
	output document reference information to filing directory
	output document index to document index file
	output text document type to document index file

A.3 FIND DOCUMENT'S FUNCTIONAL PRIMITIVES

The functional primitives for the *find document* process are described in this section. These primitives are identified by looking at each and every bubble that is part of the *find document* process at

each level of DFD to see if there is a further decomposition. If no further decomposition of a
bubble is achievable, then it is a functional primitive.

Hash Query Element

The *hash query element* function is part of the *build search vector* process (see Figure 5.7). It
represents another functional primitive in this DFD. The filing character set file is accessed
internally to this process.

Function Name: hash query element
Function Description:
    Inputs: query element
    Outputs: hashed query element
    File/Database: filing character set
    Transformation: hash each character in the word
                           add hashed characters to hashed query element

Construct Search Vector

The *construct search vector* process is the last subprocess of the higher-level process *build search
vector*.

Function Name: construct search vector
Function Description:
    Inputs: hashed query element, logical operator
    Outputs: search vector
    Transformation: **IF** logical operator = **AND THEN**
                               search vector = search vector **AND** hashed query element
                           ELSE
                               search vector = search vector **OR** hashed query element
                           ENDIF
                           return search vector

Calculate Document Record Number

Function Name: calculate document record number
Function Description:
    Inputs: search vector, document index
    Outputs: record numbers, document path
    Transformation: read document path from document index file
                           read the relative document index record for each search vector bit
                           convert each document record bit number to record number
                           add record number to record numbers
                           return record numbers, document path

Verify Matches

The *verify matches* process verifies that the record numbers produced by the hashing algorithm actually represent query matches in a document.

Function Name: verify matches
Function Description:
    Inputs: record numbers, document path, content query

Outputs:	document name, document record list
File/Database:	user's directory
Transformation:	use each record number to read the text document record
	add record number to document records list for each content query found
	return document name, document records list

Check for Abstract Match

The *check for abstract match* process (see Figure 4.10) checks to see if each phrase in the abstract query is actually part of a document abstract and then performs the logical ANDing or ORing for each possible match. The output of this process is that either the abstract search query was found (TRUE) or it was not found (FALSE).

Function Name:	check for abstract match
Function Description:	
Inputs:	abstract, phrase, query operator
Outputs:	abstract match indicator
Transformation:	all phrases in the abstract query are checked to see if they exist in the abstract
	the logical operations specified in the abstract query are then performed on these results
	a true or false indication of the success of the match is the result (abstract match indicator)
Constraints:	abstract match indicator is either true or false

Check for Keyword Match

The *check for keyword match* process (see Figure 4.10) checks to see if each keyword in the keyword query is actually part of the keywords specified for a document and then performs the logical ANDing or ORing for each possible match. The output of this process is that either the keyword search query was found (TRUE) or it was not found (FALSE).

Function Name:	check for keyword match
Function Description:	
Inputs:	keyword, query operator, keywords
Outputs:	keyword match indicator
Transformation:	all keywords in the keyword query are checked to see if they exist in the keywords previously specified for a document
	the logical operations specified in the keyword query are then performed on these results
	a true or false indication of the success of the match is the result (keyword match indicator)
Constraints:	keyword match indicator is either true or false

Check for Author Match

The *check for author match* process (see Figure 4.10) checks to see if each author in the author query is actually part of the list of authors specified for a document, and then performs the logical ANDing or ORing for each possible match. The output of this process is that either the author search query was found (TRUE) or it was not found (FALSE).

Function Name:	check for author match

Function Description:
  Inputs: author, query operator, authors
  Outputs: author match indicator
  Transformation: all authors in the author query are checked to see if they exist in the authors
          previously specified for a document
         the logical operations specified in the author query are then performed on
          these results
         a true or false indication of the success of the match is the result (author
          match indicator)
  Constraints: author match indicator is either true or false

Check for Logical Query Match

The *check for logical query match* process (see Figure 4.10) is the last subprocess of the *check for document reference information matches* process. This process performs logical operations against the results of the *abstract, keyword,* and *author query* matches.

Function Name: check for logical query match
Function Description:
  Inputs: abstract match indicator, keyword match indicator, author match indicator,
         logical query operator, document index
  Outputs: document name
  Transformation: query match indicator = abstract, keyword, and author match indicators
         applied against the logical operators
         document name retrieved from the document index

Build Document Name List

The *build document name list* process is a subprocess of the *find document* process of Figure 4.7. The purpose of this function is to build a list of the names of documents satisfying some user-specified search criteria.

Function Name: build document name list
Function Description:
  Inputs: document name
  Outputs: document name list
  Transformation: add document name to document name list
         return document name list

A.4 IDENTIFYING CONSTRAINTS AND SPECIFYING OPTIMIZATION CRITERIA

Any constraints, or functional dependencies, between objects should be noted. Additionally, any pre- or postconditions on functions must be specified in our analysis model. Pre- and postconditions on functions are constraints that the input and output values of functions must hold, respectively.

The only constraint between objects that we have identified so far is that only nonempty documents may be filed in the system. Pre- and postconditions on functions have already been noted in the description of each function.

Optimization criteria are values or operations to be maximized or minimized. Optimization criteria frequently turn out to be performance requirements for your program or system, e.g., minimize the time it takes to conduct a file and/or search operation. No optimization criteria have been specified.

Windowing Concepts and
GUI Tools

Sɪɴᴄᴇ ᴏᴜʀ ᴘʀᴏɢʀᴀᴍ is being designed to run in a windowing environment, a discussion of basic windowing concepts is in order before presenting detailed formats of the user interface. Although we are presenting the basic elements of a graphical user interface under Microsoft Windows, the structure also has a lot in common with other GUI systems such as the Apple Macintosh, Motif/X Windows, and the OS/2 Presentation Manager.

The various types of menus that can be used in both a windows and nonwindows environment is shown in Figure B.1. The window caption is the top-most element in the window. The window caption usually contains the name of the program being run in the window. The menu bar shows the main categories of interaction that are available between a user and the program. The menu bar connects to the windows caption. Both the windows caption and the menu bar are the elements of the window that are displayed on the screen when the program is executed by a user.

When a menu-bar item is selected from the menu bar, a pop-up menu is displayed on the screen and the menu-bar item is highlighted on the screen. When a pop-up menu item with an adjoining arrow is selected, a nested menu is also displayed on the screen. The user can now select one of the elements in the nested menu and some function will be performed and/or more information will be displayed on the screen.

The systems-menu box is in the upper left-hand corner of the window—see Figure B.2. By selecting the systems-menu box with a click of the mouse, the systems menu will appear on the screen. The systems menu provides a standard set of operations that can be performed on a window in the Microsoft Windows environment.

Figure B.3 shows additional standard parts of a window. The minimize box and the maximize box allow a user to make the current window smaller or larger, respectively. The vertical and horizontal scroll bars permit a user to scroll through the information in the window either

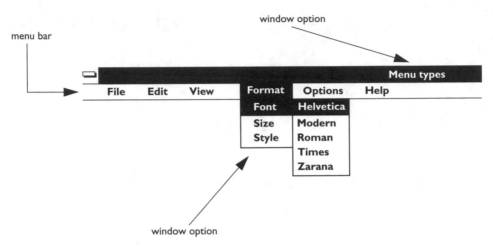

Figure B.1. Window Menu Types.

vertically or horizontally, respectively. Window frames are sizable. By placing the cursor at the edge of a window, a double-headed arrow will appear, The user may then hold down the mouse button and drag the window in some direction. This will either enlarge the window or make it smaller, depending on the direction in which the mouse is moved.

Another window component that will be used in the construction of the electronic filing program is a dialog box. A dialog box is used for gathering input from a user and then performing some input-related task. A dialog box contains entry fields and controls. Controls are items such as push-button, text boxes, and scroll bars. Our dialog boxes can be modal or modeless. A modal dialog box requires a user to finish with the dialog box before accessing other parts of the applica-

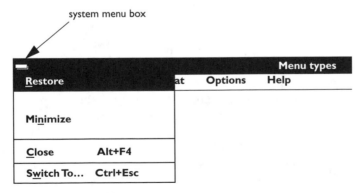

Figure B.2. The System Menu.

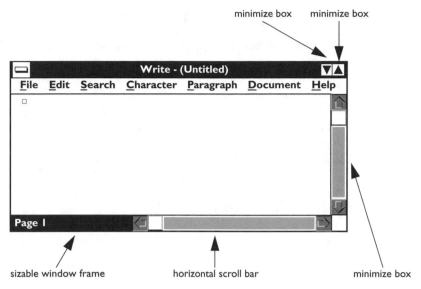

Figure B.3. Additional Standard Window Parts.

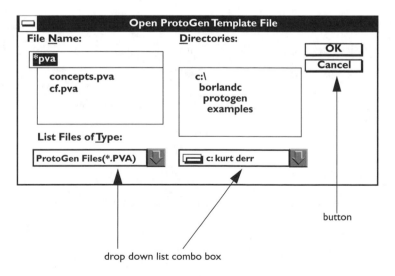

Figure B.4. Dialog Box.

tion. With a modeless dialog box, the user can switch to other parts of the application or to other applications before finishing with the dialog box.

Figure B.4 shows a dialog box from ProtoGen, a graphical user interface design tool that generates C++ code and runs in a PC Windows environment. This dialog box is used for choosing the menu resource file that will be edited by the user. The user may select both a directory and a file name and then complete the transaction by selecting the *OK* push-button, or canceling the transaction by selecting the *Cancel* push-button. The user may also select a different file type or drive by using the drop-down-list combo boxes shown at the bottom of the dialog box. By selecting the down arrow in the drop-down-list combo box, a list of items is displayed on the screen. The user may then select one of these items.

B.1 DESIGNING THE GUI USING PROTOGEN

ProtoGen will be used to design the electronic filing user interface menu bar and pull-down menus shown in Chapter 6 and to generate C++ code using Borland's Application Frameworks. A dialog box may be created separately with the Windows SDK or with another tool such as Borland's Resource Workshop. We will use Borland's Resource Workshop to create, edit, and test our dialog boxes. This tool generates a resource compiler file (.RC) containing definitions of one or more resources (such as a dialog box, bitmap, icon, cursor, etc.). ProtoGen then generates a resource file (.RES) from the .RC file. The compiler then binds the .RES file to the executable file.

The process that we will use to develop the user interface using ProtoGen consists of the following steps:

1. Develop all dialog boxes for electronic filing using Borland's Resource Workshop

2. Link the dialog boxes to the GUI using ProtoGen

3. Generate and compile the code, and test the GUI using ProtoGen

We'll use ProtoGen to design, generate, and test the user interface windows and their menus. The following steps will be taken to create the electronic filing window and its associated menus:

1. Invoke ProtoGen

2. Select File | New from the main menu

3. Click Design Menu and the Menu Designer screen is displayed

4. Design the menu bar

5. Design the pop-up menus for each item in the menu bar

6. Save the menus

7. Exit from ProtoGen

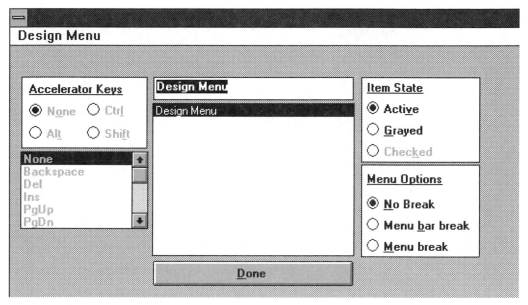

Figure B.5. ProtoGen Design Menu.

The main application window, the pop-up menus, and nested menus will be designed and developed using ProtoGen. After invoking ProtoGen, select the *New* item from the *File* pop-up menu. Next, click *Design Menu* (Fig. B.5) and the Menu Designer screen is displayed. You may now specify all of the elements for the application's menu bar and all associated pop-up menus and nested menus. ProtoGen is very easy to use, so we won't specify all of the details of its usage here. When you are done designing the menu, click *Done* at the bottom of the Menu Designer screen. Now select *File | SaveAs* to save the menu you just designed using ProtoGen. The main window and all pop-up and nested menus have now been designed for the electronic filing application.

B.1.1   Developing All Dialog Boxes Using Borland's Resource Workshop

The next step is to develop all of the needed dialog boxes using Borland's Resource Workshop dialog editor. The dialog editor will be used to create, edit, and test the dialog boxes. The following dialog boxes, as identified in Chapter 3, need to be created using the Resource Workshop (RW):

- ❑ File A Document
- ❑ Document Reference Information
- ❑ Search For A Document(s)
- ❑ Search Results
- ❑ Delete A Document

❑ Print A Document

❑ Electronic Filing Character Set

❑ Changing Junk Words

Dialog boxes generally contain a number of controls. Controls are used to display static text and graphics in the dialog box and also allow a user to specify information. The designer may specify, on paper, the controls that will be used to represent the elements of the dialog box prior to invoking RW. The basic types of controls implemented in the RW Dialog editor are:

❑ Push-button

❑ Radio button

❑ Horizontal and vertical scroll bars

❑ List box

❑ Check box

❑ Group box

❑ Combo box

❑ Edit text control

❑ Text static control

❑ Iconic static control

❑ Custom control

The *Document Reference Information*, *File A Document*, and *Print A Document* dialog boxes along with their controls are shown in Figure B.6 through Figure B.8, respectively. All of the other electronic filing dialog boxes use the same types of controls as are used in these dialog boxes, and therefore are not shown in the text. These dialog boxes are recalled from Chapter 3 and annotated to indicate the controls that will be used for the various elements. The dialog boxes have had some slight modifications to accommodate the types of controls available in the class library. Also, draft quality was expunged from the Print dialog box as a feature because it was determined to be unnecessary.

The following steps will be taken to create the File A Document dialog box:

1. Invoke the Resource Workshop

2. Select the *File | New* project

3. In the New Project dialog box, set the program file type equal to RC

4. Select *Resource | New*

5. Select *Dialog* as the resource type and click the *OK* push-button. The dialog editing box is now displayed along with alignment and tool palettes.

6. Select the dialog box, and then press the enter key or double click with a mouse inside of the dialog box. The Window Style dialog box now appears.

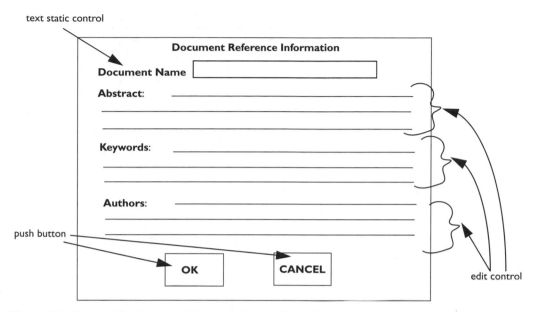

Figure B.6. Controls For *Document Reference Information* Dialog Box

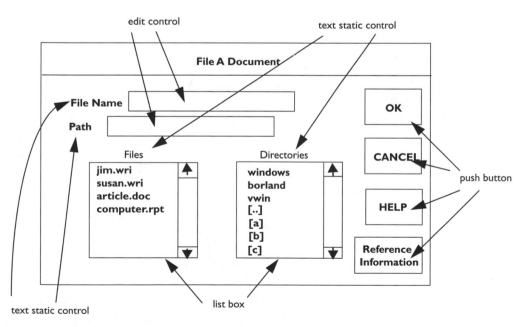

Figure B.7. Controls For *File A Document* Dialog Box.

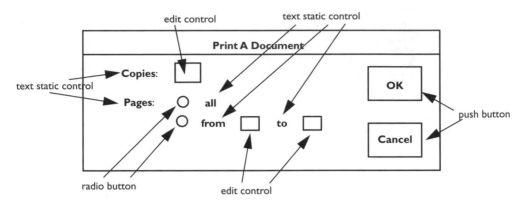

Figure B.8. Controls For *Print A Document* Dialog Box.

7. Change the caption field of the Window Style dialog box to *File A Document*. Click the *OK* push-button. The dialog box and the RW screens are shown in Figure B.7.

8. Select a push-button and move the cursor to the location in the dialog box for the *OK* push-button. Click the mouse and the push-button appears. Now double click the push-button and a Button Style window is displayed. Change the caption to OK and click the *OK* push-button inside of the Button Style window. Repeat this step for the *Cancel, Help,* and *Reference Information* push-buttons.

9. Select the text static control from the tool palette and move the cursor to the location in the dialog box for the "File Name." Click the mouse and the text box appears. Now double click the text box and a Static Style window is displayed. Change the caption to File Name and click the *OK* push-button inside of the Static Style window. Repeat this step for both the "Files" and "Directories" text elements to place in the dialog box.

10. Select the list box from the tool palette and move the cursor to the location in the dialog box under the "Files" text box. Click the mouse and the list box appears. Now double click the list box and a List Box Style window is displayed. Just go with the default options. Click the *OK* push-button inside of the List box style window. Repeat this step for placing a list box under the "Directories" text element.

11. Select the edit control tool from the tool palette and move the cursor to the location in the dialog box next to the "File Name" text element. Click the mouse and the edit control box appears. Now double click the edit control box and an Edit Text Style window is displayed. Just go with the default options. Click the *OK* push-button inside of the Edit Text Style window.

12. Now save this file as a DLG resource script (i.e.,.dlg file). The dialog box for "File A Document" is shown inside of the Resource Workshop window in Figure B.4. Exit from RW.

13. Repeat this basic process for generating all of the identified dialog boxes.

The electronic filing dialog boxes are shown in the subsequent sections during the discussions of each user interface function.

B.1.2 Linking Dialog Boxes to the GUI Using ProtoGen

The next step is to link the dialog box with the File item in the Document Storage pop-up menu. Do the following steps:

1. Invoke ProtoGen and open the menu that you previously designed. Select the Document *Storage | File* item in the menu.

2. The Add Application Dialog screen is now displayed. Retain the *modal* default option for the dialog mode. Select the appropriate dialog file and directory. Now select the *open file* push-button and the dialogs contained in the dialog file will be displayed in the Dialogs Contained list box.

3. Now select the *view dialog* push-button to view the dialog box and to ensure that you are selecting the correct dialog box. After verifying that you have selected the correct dialog box double click on the system menu box in the left corner of the dialog box. This closes the dialog box.

4. Now select the *OK* push-button in the Add Application Dialog screen. The dialog box is now linked to the pop-up menu. Save your menu.

5. Repeat this basic process for linking all of the identified dialog boxes to the electronic filing menu.

B.1.3 Generate and Compile the Code, and Test the GUI Using ProtoGen

Now that the user interface menu and all of the dialog boxes have been developed, it is time to generate, compile, and test the code for the user interface. Take the following steps:

1. Select *Application | Generate* from the ProtoGen main menu. The Set Compiler Options dialog box is displayed on the screen.

2. Select Borland C++ Generation and enter the Include and Library Directory files necessary for Borland C++. Select the Generate push-button. The C++ code is now generated by ProtoGen.

3. Select *Application | Compile*. The Application Compile dialog box is displayed on the screen. Select the *OK* push-button.

4. A Make window appears on the screen with messages being displayed in this window as the code is compiled. Enter *ctrl c* when the code has finished compiling and this will take you back to the main ProtoGen menu.

5. Select *Application | Run* from the ProtoGen menu. The Execute Application dialog box is displayed on the screen.

6. Enter the application filename if you choose to change the default name. Now select the *OK* push-button and execute the application.

7. The application window should now be up and running. Close the application when you are done by double clicking on the system menu box. Next, exit from ProtoGen.

We have now implemented the basic elements of our user interface design and generated the C++ code using ProtoGen, a graphically oriented user-interface design tool for quickly designing menus for Windows applications.

B.1.3.1 Designing the GUI Using Window Builder

The Window Builder tool will be used to design the electronic filing user interface menu bar and pull-down menus shown in Chapter 6 and to generate Smalltalk code using Digitalk's Smalltalk/ V for Windows. All dialog boxes and the main application menu are created using Window Builder.

The process that we will use to develop the user interface using Window Builder consists of the following steps:

1. Install and invoke Window Builder.

2. Develop and test the main application menu.

3. Develop and test all dialog boxes.

4. Link the dialog boxes to the main application window.

The first step, of course, is to install the Window Builder tool developed by Objectshare Systems, Inc. The installation of Window Builder consists of compiling it into your Smalltalk image. As

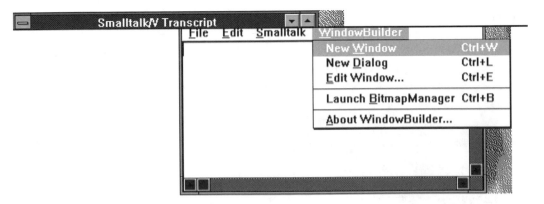

Figure B.9. Window Builder Pulldown Menu in Smalltalk V.

shown in Figure B.9, a Window Builder pulldown menu has been added to the standard Smalltalk menu bar after compiling Window Builder into the Smalltalk image.

Next, we'll use Window Builder to design, generate, and test the main application menu. The main application menu is created by taking the following steps:

1. Select the Window Builder item from the Smalltalk menu bar.

2. Select the New Window item from the Window Builder pull-down menu.

3. Design the main menu bar and the associated pull-down menus.

Figure B.10 shows the main Window Builder screen after selecting the New Window item. The main application window's attributes, such as the title of our application, Electronic Filing, can be entered in the Text: field at the bottom of the screen. To create the menu bar for our window, select the *Menubar* push-button in the lefthand side of the Window Builder screen. A menu bar editor dialog box now appears on the screen. All of the elements for the application's menu bar menu and associated pull-down/pop-up menus are specified here. Window Builder is very easy to use, so we won't specify all of the details of its usage here. When you are done designing the

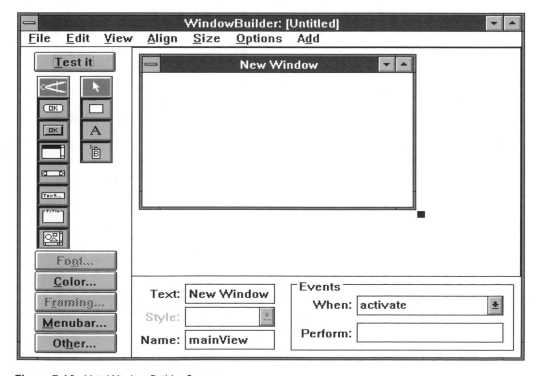

Figure B.10. Main Window Builder Screen.

window and its menus, click the *OK* push-button in the menu bar editor and save the application by selecting the *SaveAs* item under the File pull-down menu of the main Window Builder screen.

The next step is to develop and test all of the dialog boxes. A dialog box may be created by first selecting the File item from the Window Builder menu bar and then the New Dialog item from the File pull-down menu. A new dialog box then appears on the Window Builder screen. The subpane palettes or the Add menu item on the Window Builder's menu bar may then be used to add push-buttons, edit boxes, static text, etc. to the dialog box.

The following steps will be taken to create a File A Document dialog box using Window Builder:

1. Invoke the Window Builder

2. Select the *File | New Dialog* items from the main menu

3. Go to the Add menu on the Window Builder's menu bar

4. Select the *Button | Button* items. Now move the cursor to the location within the dialog box for the *OK* push-button. Now click the mouse and a push-button is displayed. Go to the Name field and specify a push-button name of your choosing. Notice that a combo box at the bottom of the Window Builder screen is labeled When: and contains the word clicked. Specify the name of the method in the Perform: entry field that is to be associated with the When: #clicked event. Repeat this process for the *Cancel, Help*, and *Reference Information* push-buttons.

5. Select the *Static | StaticText* items from the Add menu item. Now move the cursor to the location within the dialog box for the File Name static text. Now click the mouse and a static text element is displayed. Go to the Name field and specify the static text of your choosing. Repeat this process for the Path, Files, and Directories static text elements.

6. Select the *Text | EntryField* items from the Add menu item. Now move the cursor to the location within the dialog box for the File Name entry field. Now click the mouse and an entry field element is displayed. Go to the Name field and specify the name of your choosing for the entry field. Specify the name of the method in the Perform: entry field that is to be associated with the When: display event. Repeat this process for the Path entry field.

7. Select the *List | ListBox* items from the Add menu item. Now move the cursor to the location within the dialog box for the Files list box. Now click the mouse and a list box element is displayed. Go to the Name field and specify the name of your choosing for the list box. Specify the name of the method in the Perform: entry field that is to be associated with the When: select event. Repeat this process for the Directories list box.

8. Select the *Test It* push-button on the Window Builder screen to verify the operation of the dialog box.

9. Repeat this process for generating all of the electronic filing dialog boxes.

The last step in the design of the user interface is to link the dialog boxes to the main application window. We will need to write some code to tie these dialog boxes both to the main application window and to the behavior of our application.

In the Smalltalk code the menu items have selectors associated with them. The selectors are messages sent to the Efiling application window when the menu item is selected by the user. The dialog boxes are tied to the main application window by simply adding code to these messages. The selector items and their message names are specified in the open method of the Efiling class. These messages are fileItem, deleteItem, exitItem, searchItem, etc. For example, to tie the main application menu File selector to the File dialog box we would add the following code to the fileItem message: FileADocument new open. In this example, FileADocument is the class name of the dialog box for filing a document. This code opens and displays the FileADocument dialog box on the screen when the user selects the File item from the Document Storage pull-down menu.

In C++, dialog boxes are linked to the main application window, and dialog boxes are linked to other dialog boxes as well, using the ProtoGen tool as previously described. However, code must be added to the dialog box so that it will close. For example, TDIALOG_1Dlg is the class for the dialog box for filing a document. The code CloseWindow () must be added to the member function for the *OK* push-button (RTDIALOG_1101) for this class so that the dialog box will close after a document is filed in the system.

We have now implemented the basic elements of our user interface design and generated the Smalltalk code using Window Builder. The user interface we have developed in Smalltalk using Window Builder has the same look and feel as the user interface developed in C++ using the ProtoGen tool.

Events and Methods

C.1 FILE A DOCUMENT USE CASE

File A Document Dialog Box

The *document reference information button selected, ok button selected, cancel button selected* events will need explicit methods as event handlers. These methods will be called *dri button selected, ok button selected,* and *cancel button selected.*

Scrolling list boxes will be used to display the file and directory names to the user. Event handlers are needed to respond to the selection of an item in a scrolling list. The *record file name* and *record directory name* activities are named as event handlers. Attributes will be necessary to record both the file and directory names. These attributes will be named *selected file* and *selected directory.*

Document Reference Information Dialog Box

A separate entry field or edit box is used for keyword, author, and abstract entry. The *record keywords, record authors,* and *record abstract* activities are named as event handlers. Attributes will be necessary to record the keyword, author, and abstract names. These attributes will be named keyword, author, and abstract.

The *ok button selected* and *cancel button selected* events will need explicit methods as event handlers. These methods will be called *ok button selected* and *cancel button selected.*

C.2 DELETE A DOCUMENT USE CASE

Delete A Document Dialog Box

The *record file name* and *record directory name* activities are named as event handlers. Attributes selected directory and selected file are created to retain this information. The *ok button selected* and *cancel button selected* events will be named as event handlers with the same names.

C.3 SEARCH FOR A DOCUMENT USE CASE

Search For A Document Dialog Box

A separate entry field or edit box is used for keyword, author, content, and abstract queries. The *record keyword query, record author query,* and *record abstract query* are named as event handlers for the record query actions associated with each query. Content query, abstract query, author query, and keyword query will be named as attributes to record this information. The *ok button selected, done button selected,* and *cancel button selected* events will be named as event handlers with the same names.

Search Results Dialog Box

The *record file name* and *record directory name* activities are named as event handlers. Attributes selected directory and selected file are created to retain this information. The *print button selected, done button selected,* and *view button selected* events will be named as event handlers with the same names.

C.4 FILING CHARACTER CHANGE USE CASE

Filing Character Set Dialog Box

The *include button selected, discard button selected, cancel button selected,* and *ok button selected* events will be named as event handlers with the same names. The *filing character selected* event will be renamed as the event handler for getting the filing character selected in the scrolling list by the user.

C.5 JUNK WORD CHANGE USE CASE

Junk Word Dialog Box

The *add button selected, delete button selected, cancel button selected,* and *ok button selected* events will be named as event handlers with the same names. The *junk word selected* event will be renamed as the event handler for getting the junk word entered in the entry field by the user.

Analysis Document

THE ANALYSIS DOCUMENT consists of the:

1. problem statement

2. object model (data dictionary, class diagrams, and possible object diagrams)

3. dynamic model (user interface formats, use cases, scenarios, event flow diagram for electronic filing, state diagrams)

4. functional model (context diagram, data flow diagrams, any constraints, process descriptions)

Other requirements that are not necessarily related to a specific analysis or design methodology should also be addressed here. Some examples of these requirements are:

❑ performance requirements

❑ availability requirements

❑ communication protocols for interaction

❑ software engineering standards

D.1 PROBLEM STATEMENT

An electronic filing program can be used to store and retrieve documents. Documents are first created by a word processor, editor, or other means. A document may then be filed along with document reference information. Document reference information contains keyword(s), author(s), and an abstract that describes the text document. Document indexes, maintained in a filing directory, are created for documents that are filed in the system. The indexes then reference the text documents that are filed in the system.

A text document may contain multiple pages, and each page contains multiple lines, and each line contains multiple words. The words may be junk words (i.e., common vernacular not used by the program for filing or finding documents) or nonjunk words that are used by the electronic filing program. The words used by electronic filing may contain one or more ASCII characters. Each ASCII character may or may not be a character that is used in electronic filing.

Documents filed in the system may later be retrieved by using a query and conducting a search. A query is an author query, keyword query, abstract query, and/or content query. A query contains phrases separated by query operators. A search results in a document name list, or search hit list. The user may select one of the documents in the document name list to view or print. Alternatively, the user may continue to specify additional queries or search criteria, successively narrowing down the search until the required documents are found.

The user is provided with the capability of specifying any extraneous or "junk" words, which if found in the content of the document will not be searched or indexed; e.g., and, or, not, the, if. The user can also specify which alphanumeric characters will be indexed and searchable, thereby limiting the search and index to only portions of a document(s).

D.2 OBJECT MODEL

The object model consists of a data dictionary, class diagrams, and possible object diagrams.

Data Dictionary

All of the definitions in the data dictionary reflect top-down partitioning of data. Entries exist in the data dictionary for data flows, files, processes, and data elements.

The following set of relational operators are used in the data dictionary to explain data flows

=	is equivalent to
+	and
|	either-or, i.e., select one of the options
{}	**iteration of** the component enclosed; bounds are typically indicated next to the brackets
()	that the enclosed component is **optional**

A data flow will be described in the data dictionary using the following entry:

Dataflow Name:
Aliases:
Composition:
Notes:

An alias is a synonymous name for the data flow name or element. The composition section is left blank if the entry is for an alias data flow. The composition section describes the definition of the data flow name or element using data flows and elements combined with the previously defined set of relational operators. The notes section can be used to record information that you would like to keep track of about the entry, other than the physical character of it.

A data element will be described in the data dictionary using the following entry:

Data Element Name:
Aliases:
Values and Meanings:
Notes:

The values and meanings portion of the data element entry is used to record what values the data element may take on and what those values mean.

A file or database name will be described in the data dictionary using the following entry:

File or Database Name
Aliases
Composition
Organization
Notes

The organization portion of the file or database name entry is used to record information on how the file or database is organized and therefor accessed.

The entries in the data dictionary are presented in alphabetical order to facilitate easy lookup.

Dataflow Name:	abstract
Composition:	$_1\{phrase\}^n$
Notes:	A brief statement of the essential thoughts of a document. This is carried over from the initial data dictionary described in Chapter 2.

Data Element Name:	abstract match indicator
Values and Meanings:	match, nomatch
Notes:	

Dataflow Name:	abstract query
Composition:	(word | phrase) + $_0\{query\ operator + (word \| phrase)\}^n$
Notes:	An abstract query must have at least one word or phrase. Additional words or phrases require a query operator between them. An abstract query is used to search for similar words or phrases in the abstract of a document(s).

Dataflow Name:	author
Aliases:	author name
Composition:	word | phrase
Notes:	This entry is carried over from the initial data dictionary described in Chapter 2.

Data Element Name:	author match indicator
Values and Meanings:	match, nomatch
Notes:	

Dataflow Name:	author query
Composition:	author name + $_0\{$query operator + author name$\}^n$
Notes:	An author query must have at least one author name. Additional author names require a query operator between them. An author query is used to search for author names in the authors portion of document reference information for a document(s).

Dataflow Name:	authors
Composition:	$_0\{$author$\}^n$
Notes:	The authors specified as part of document reference information.

Dataflow Name:	content query
Composition:	(word | phrase) + $_0\{$query operator + (word | phrase)$\}^n$
Notes:	A content query must have at least one word or phrase. Additional words or phrases require a query operator between them.

Dataflow Name:	document directory name
Aliases:	directory name
Composition:	$_1\{$alphanumeric characters$\}^n$
Notes:	A string of ASCII characters representing the name of a directory for the location of a document. The maximum number of characters in the name, n, is dependent upon the operating software platform.

Dataflow Name:	document file name
Aliases:	document name
Composition:	$_1\{$alphanumeric characters$\}^n$
Notes:	A string of ASCII characters representing the name of a file which is a document. The maximum number of characters in the name, n, is dependent upon the operating software platform.

Dataflow Name:	document index
Aliases:	index
Composition:	An index of all of the words in a document text file.
Notes:	The document index facilitates rapid retrieval of any nonjunk word in the content of the document. The document index is a file.

Dataflow Name:	document index file name
Composition:	$_1\{$alphanumeric characters$\}^n$
Notes:	An ASCII string of characters representing the name of the document index file. The maximum number of characters in the name, n, is dependent upon the operating software platform.

Dataflow Name:	document name
Composition:	$_1\{$alphanumeric characters$\}^n$
Notes:	An ASCII string of characters. used to identify the name of a document. The maximum number of characters in the name, n, is dependent upon the operating software platform.

Dataflow Name:	document name list
Composition:	$_0\{$document name$\}^n$
Notes:	This represents a list of document names that have satisfied some search criteria.

Dataflow Name:	document path
Composition:	document directory name + document file name
Notes:	A document path is a document file name concatenated to a document directory name.

Dataflow Name:	document record
Composition:	$_1\{$word$\}^n$
Notes:	A document consists of one or more records. Each record must contain one or more words.

Dataflow Name:	document reference information
Composition:	(abstract) + (keywords) + (authors)
Notes:	Each text document may have document reference information associated with it.

Dataflow Name:	file
Aliases:	text document
Composition:	program or data
Notes:	Files organize information used by a computer. A program or data is stored as a file on disk.

Dataflow Name:	file directory name
Composition:	$_1\{$alphanumeric characters$\}^n$
Notes:	A directory name specifying the location of a file. The maximum number of characters in the name, n, is dependent upon the operating software platform.

Dataflow Name:	file name
Composition:	$_1\{$alphanumeric characters$\}^n$
Notes:	A name of a file. The maximum number of characters in the name, n, is dependent upon the operating software platform.

File or Database Name:	Filing Character Set file
Composition:	string of filing characters
Organization:	sequential based on ASCII ordering
Notes:	

File or Database Name:	Filing Directory
Composition:	$_0\{$document index$\}^n$
Organization:	Based on the operating system.
Notes:	

Dataflow Name:	hashed block
Composition:	$_1\{$hashed record$\}^n$
Notes:	A collection of some number of hashed records representing a portion of a document. A document index typically will have a number of hashed blocks, n, depending on the size of the text document.

Dataflow Name:	hashed query element
Composition:	A string of bits based on a hashing of a word or phrase.
Notes:	

Dataflow Name:	hashed record
Composition:	A string of bits based on a hashing of all of the records in a document.
Notes:	

Dataflow Name:	hashed word
Composition:	A string of bits based on a hashing of all of the filing characters in a word.
Notes:	

File or Database Name:	Junk word file
Composition:	$_0\{$word$\}^n$
Organization:	listing of words in alphabetic order
Notes:	

Dataflow Name:	keyword
Composition:	word	phrase
Notes:	A keyword is a word that helps the user to uniquely identify a document. This entry is carried over from the initial data dictionary described in Chapter 2.

Data Element Name:	keyword match indicator
Values and Meanings:	match, nomatch
Notes:	

Dataflow Name:	keyword query
Composition:	keyword + $_0\{$query operator + keyword$\}^n$
Notes:	A keyword query must have at least one keyword. Additional keywords require a query operator between them. A keyword query is used to search for keywords in the keywords portion of document reference information for a document(s).

Dataflow Name:	keywords
Composition:	$_0\{$keyword$\}^n$
Notes:	The keywords specified as part of document reference information.

Data Element Name:	logical query operator

Aliases:	query operator, logical operator
Values and Meanings:	and | or
Notes:	

Dataflow Name:	phrase
Composition:	word $+_1\{$space + word$\}^n$
Notes:	A phrase is a sequence of two or more words that convey a single thought.

Dataflow Name:	query element
Composition:	a nonjunk word of a phrase
Notes:	

Data Element Name:	record number
Values and Meanings:	From 0 to n-1, where n = the maximum number of fixed data records in the file.
Notes:	

Dataflow Name:	search criteria
Composition:	(content query) + (logical query operator + abstract query) + (logical query operator + keyword query) + (logical query operator + author query)
Notes:	All the elements of a search criteria are optional. However, one element must be present in order for a search criteria to exist. Logical query operators must separate the elements of the search criteria.

Dataflow Name:	search vector
Composition:	A string of bits based on a hashing of all of the elements in a content query.
Notes:	A search vector is used to determine the records of the document index that should be read. The document index is then read to determine the data records of the document file to read. Specific records of the document file are then read to determine if there is a match between the content query and the content of a document.

Dataflow Name:	text document record
Composition:	$_1\{$alphanumeric character$\}^{80}$
Notes:	The data record of a text file, or document, represented by a string of ASCII characters.

Dataflow Name:	text document type
Composition:	$_1\{$alphanumeric character$\}^n$
Notes:	An alphanumeric string of characters representing a type of text document.

Data Element Name:	word
Values and Meanings:	$_1\{$alphanumeric character$\}^n$
Notes:	An alphanumeric character or some meaningful combination of alphanumeric characters that represent a unit of language. This is carried over from the initial data dictionary described in Chapter 2

Class Diagrams

The class diagrams developed for electronic filing are shown in Figures D.1 and D.2.

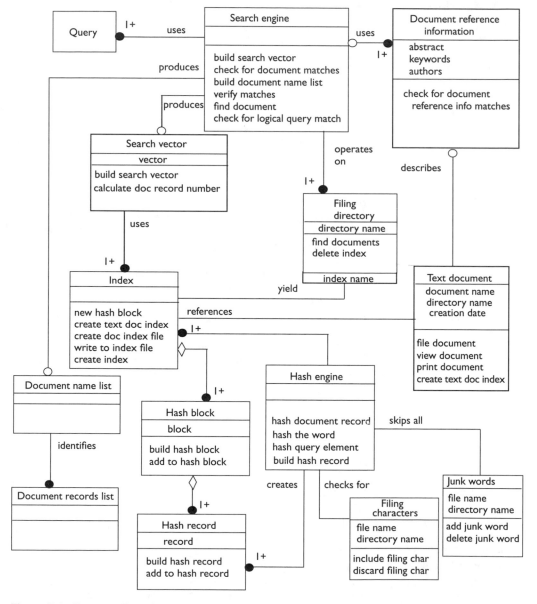

Figure D.1. Electronic Filing Class Diagram.

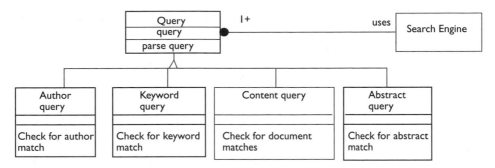

Figure D.2. Query Module Class Diagram.

D.3 DYNAMIC MODEL

The dynamic model consists of user interface formats, scenarios, an event flow diagram for electronic filing, and state diagrams. The user interface for electronic filing is shown in Figure D.3.

D.3.1 Main Application User Interface

The use cases, which represent the invocation of the application functions, are

1. filing a document

2. searching for, or finding, a document(s)

3. deleting a document

4. changing the filing character set

5. changing the junk words

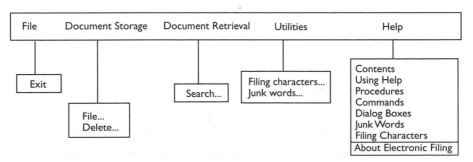

Figure D.3. Electronic Filing Menu Bar and Pull-Down Menus.

Each use case involves multiple scenarios. Each use case represents the dialog for an application function. A scenario is like a thread through a use case. Presentation formats, scenarios, event traces, and statecharts exist for each use case.

Some sequence of steps are common in several scenarios. These common steps are grouped and noted for each scenario to promote reuse and to minimize redundancy.

> **Important:** The normal and exception scenarios represent some variations of user input and system response. Many other variations are possible! Modern user interfaces allow flexible input. The intent here is only to illustrate some possible variations of user input that bring out all of the graphical elements of the user interface for a particular scenario. The rigid interaction sequences subsequently depicted in scenarios and event traces represent only one or two possibilities.

D.3.2 File a Document Operation

Detailed Presentation Formats

The *file a document* operation utilizes the following dialog boxes from the user interface:

- ❏ File a Document
- ❏ Document Reference Information
- ❏ Filing in Progress
- ❏ Invalid Filing Characters Error Message

The dialog box for *Filing a Document* is shown in Figure D.4. Figure D.5 shows the dialog box for specifying *Document Reference Information* when filing a document. A detailed scenario for filing a document is shown in Scenario 2. This scenario requires a "filing in progress" message

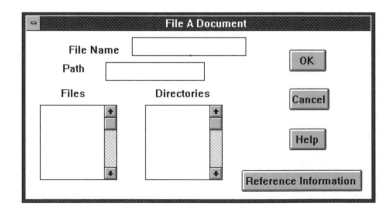

Figure D.4. File A Document Dialog Box.

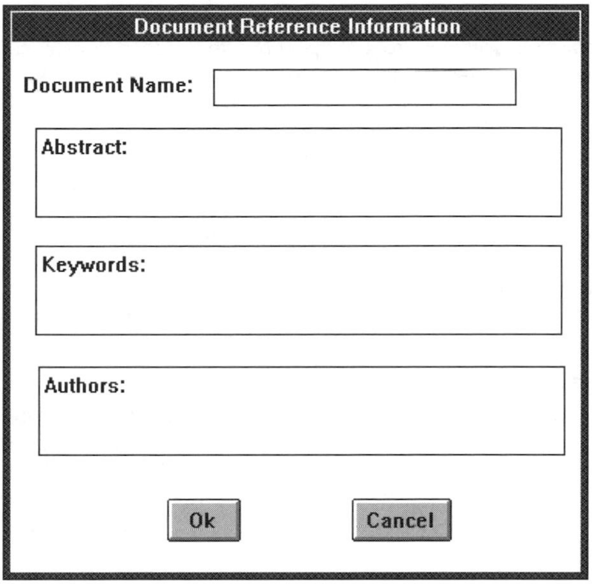

Figure D.5. Document Reference Information Dialog Box.

to be displayed after the user has requested the filing of the document. This message will demonstrate a visible sign of filing progress by showing a percent filing complete as part of the message. The message box that will be displayed to the user while the document is being filed is shown in Figure D.6.

Scenarios

The sequence of events, or steps, that are common to both normal and exceptions scenarios are shown in Scenario 1. This setup sequence of events precedes both the detailed filing scenario and detailed filing scenario with exceptions. A detailed filing scenario is depicted in Scenario 2.

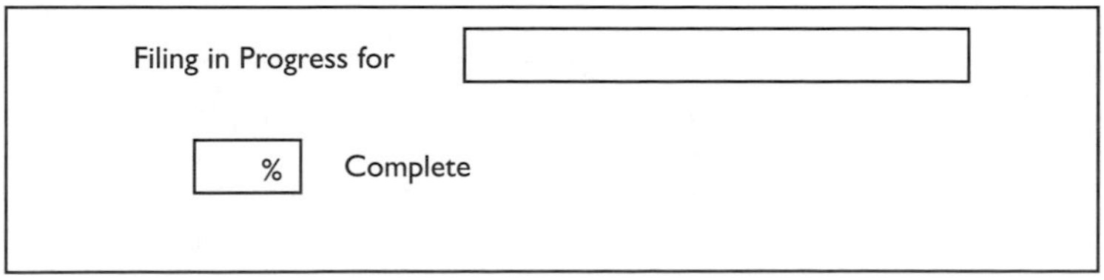

Figure D.6. Filing In Progress Message Box.

Scenario 1. Setup Sequence of Events Preceding All Filing Scenarios.

The user selects the Document Storage menu-bar item from the menu bar.
A pop-up menu for Document Storage appears.
The user selects the File item from the pop-up menu.
The File a Document dialog box is displayed.
The user selects a directory from the scrolling list of directories.
The directory name is displayed in the Path edit control box.
The user selects a document file from the scrolling list of files.
The document file name is displayed in the path and file name edit control boxes.
The user selects the Reference Information push-button in the dialog box.
A Document Reference Information dialog box is displayed.
The document name is displayed inside of the document name edit box.

Scenario 2. Detailed Filing Scenario.

The user enters a description of the document in the edit field for the abstract.
The user enters keywords for the document in the edit field for the keywords.
The user enters authors for the document in the edit field for the authors.
The user selects the OK push-button in the Document Reference Information dialog box.
A filing in progress message box is displayed while the document is being indexed.
The filing in progress message box is cleared from the screen when the indexing of the document is completed.
The Document Reference Information and File a Document dialog boxes are cleared from the screen.
The main application window is redisplayed.

Scenario 3. Detailed Filing Scenario with Exceptions.

The user enters keywords, consisting of all invalid filing characters, for the document in the edit field for the keywords.
The user selects the OK push-button in the Document Reference Information dialog box.
The EFP displays an error message and asks the user to reenter the keywords, or change the filing character set.
The user selects the OK push-button in the error message box.
The error message box is cleared from the screen.
The keywords are cleared from the Document Reference Information dialog box.
The user selects the Cancel push-button in the Document Reference Information dialog box.
The Document Reference Information and File a Document dialog boxes are cleared from the screen.
The main application window is redisplayed.

```
Invalid Filing Characters were specified in your data entry.

Please reenter the data or cancel your operation.

                    OK
```

Figure D.7. Invalid Filing Characters Error Message Box.

A detailed scenario for filing a document, with exceptions, is shown in Scenario 3. This scenario requires an error message to be displayed if the user enters invalid filing characters for the abstract, authors, or keywords. The error message dialog box requires the user to acknowledge the error by selecting the OK push-button before continuing with the program. The error message box that may be displayed to the user is shown in Figure D.7.

Event Trace

A detailed event trace for filing a document is shown in Figure D.8. The main window, file dialog box, and the document reference information dialog box objects represent the user interface sub-

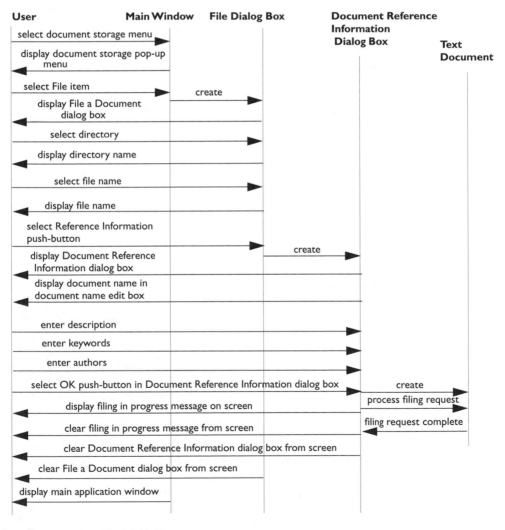

Figure D.8. Detailed Filing Event Trace.

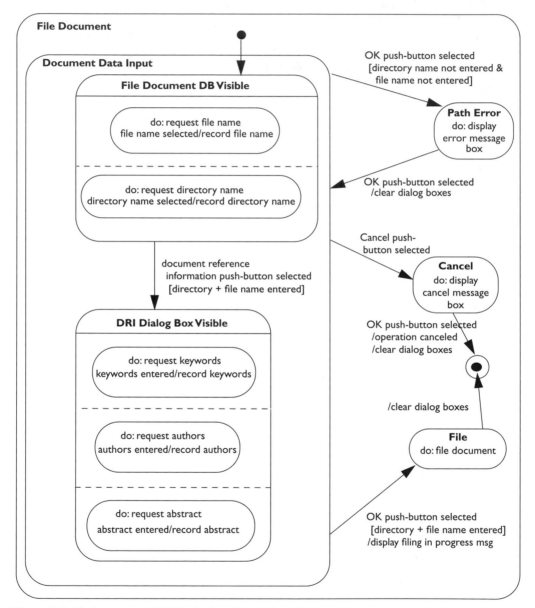

Figure D.9. *File Document* and *DRI* Dialog Box Classes Statechart.

system. The "create" event in this diagram denotes the creation of an object. The file dialog box object is created and opened by the main window object. The document reference information object is created and opened by the file dialog box object. And finally, the text document object is created and opened by the document reference information object.

Statechart

The *File Document* statechart is shown in Figure D.9.

D.3.3 Delete Operation

Detailed Presentation Formats

The *delete a document* operation utilizes the following dialog boxes from the user interface:

- ❑ Delete a Document
- ❑ Delete Error Message Box

The *Delete a Document* dialog box is shown in Figure D.10. Only the directories that contain index files and the index file names themselves will be shown in the scrolling list boxes within the dialog box. This also allows the user to see all of the documents that were filed in the electronic filing system; i.e., each of the documents filed in the system must have an index file. The user may select and delete a document or just survey the document indexes and then cancel the operation. The

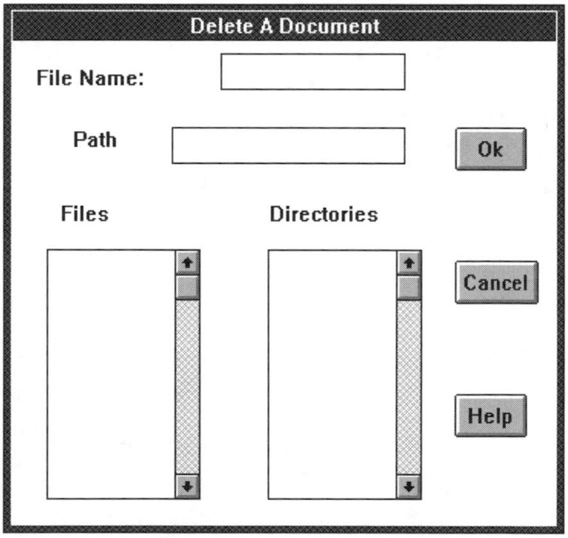

Figure D.10. Delete a Document Dialog Box.

document name is displayed in the file name edit control box. The path edit control box displays the location of a file within the directory tree.

Scenario 4. Setup Sequence of Events Preceding All Delete Scenarios.

    The user selects the Document Storage menu-bar item from the menu bar.
    The pop-up menu for Document Storage appears.
    The user selects the Delete item from the pop-up menu.
    The Delete a Document dialog box is displayed.

Scenario 5. Delete Scenario.

    The user selects a directory from the scrolling list of directories.
    The directory name is displayed in the Path edit control box.
    The user selects a document file from the scrolling list of files.
    The document file name is displayed in the file name edit control boxes.
    The user selects the OK push-button in the dialog box.
    The document index is deleted.
    The Delete a Document dialog box is cleared from the screen.
    The main application window is redisplayed.

Scenarios

The sequence of events, or steps, that is common to both normal and exceptions delete scenarios is shown in Scenario 4. This setup sequence of events precedes both the detailed delete scenario and the detailed delete scenario with exceptions.

A detailed scenario for deleting a document is shown in Scenario 5. A detailed scenario for deleting a document, with exceptions, is shown in Scenario 6. This scenario requires an error message to be displayed if the user selects the OK push-button before specifying any directory and file. The delete error message dialog box (see Figure D.11) requires the user to acknowledge the error by selecting the OK push-button before continuing with the program.

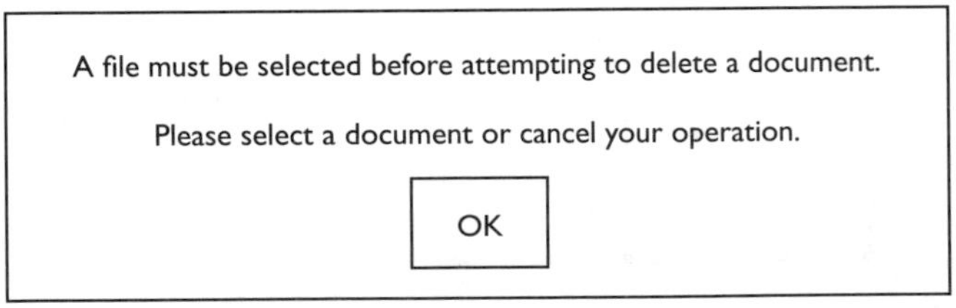

A file must be selected before attempting to delete a document.

Please select a document or cancel your operation.

OK

Figure D.11. Delete Error Message Box.

Scenario 6. Delete Scenario with Exceptions.

> The user selects the OK push-button in the dialog box.
> Delete error message box is displayed showing error message and asking user to specify directory and file name.
> The user selects the OK push-button in the delete error message box.
> The delete error message box is cleared from the screen.
> The user selects the Cancel push-button in the dialog box.
> The Delete a Document dialog box is cleared from the screen.
> The main application window is redisplayed.

Event Trace

A detailed event trace for deleting a document is shown in Figure D.12. The main window and the delete dialog box objects represent the user interface subsystem. The delete dialog box object is created and opened by the main window object. The filing directory object is created when the application is first started and is destroyed at the completion of the application.

Statechart

A *Delete Document* statechart is shown in Figure D.13.

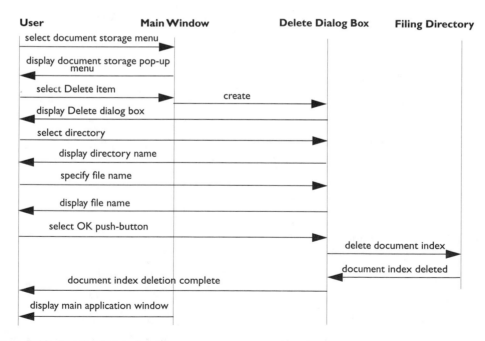

Figure D.12. Detailed Delete Event Trace.

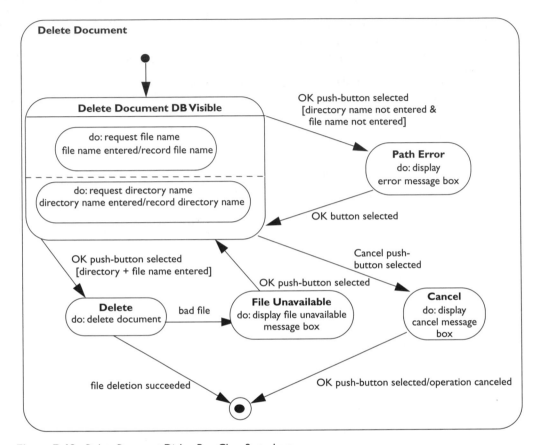

Figure D.13. *Delete Document* Dialog Box Class Statechart.

D.3.4 Search Operation

Detailed Presentation Formats

The *search* operation uses the following dialog boxes from the user interface:

- ❑ Search for a Document
- ❑ Search Results
- ❑ Search error message box

The dialog box for searching for a document is shown in Figure D.15. Here the user enters specific search criteria for locating one or more documents. Logical operators (i.e., AND and OR) may be used between words or phrases within a search query category (i.e, content, ab-

This file is no longer available.

Please select another file or cancel your operation.

OK

Figure D.14. Invalid File Message Box.

stract, keyword, or author searches). The search query categories are also connected via logical operators. The logical connecting operators default to AND. A tab or enter key moves the cursor across fields in the search dialog box.

A search error message box (see Figure D.19) is displayed if the user selects the OK push-button before entering any search criteria. The search results are presented to the user via a

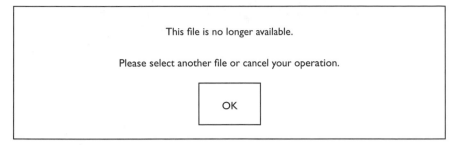

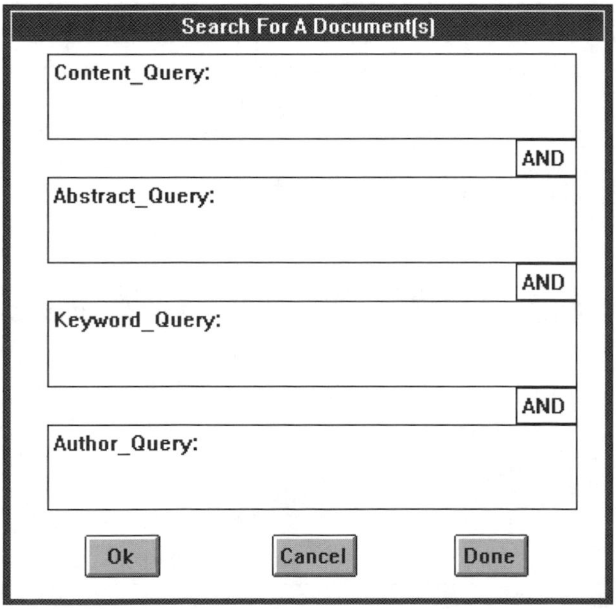

Search For A Document(s)

Content_Query:

AND

Abstract_Query:

AND

Keyword_Query:

AND

Author_Query:

Ok   Cancel   Done

Figure D.15. Search Dialog Box.

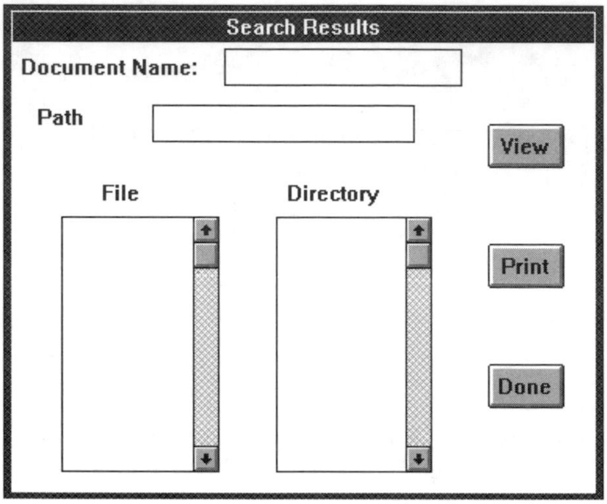

Figure D.16. Search Results Dialog Box.

search results dialog box shown in Figure D.16. The search results are displayed as a scrolling list of document and directory names that were found to meet the search criteria. The user may then select one of those documents to view or print and then select the View or Print push-button. If the user selects a document to view, the document will appear in a new window, enabling the user to scroll through the document and examine its contents. The locations of the hits (i.e., places in the document where the search criteria were found) in the document may be highlighted. Highlighting the hits is left as an exercise to the reader. The view operation uses the *Viewing A Document* window shown in Figure D.17. The print operation uses the *Print a Document* dialog box shown in Figure D.18.

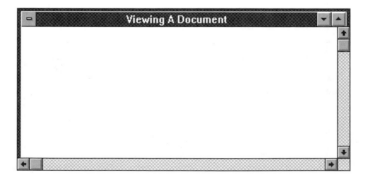

Figure D.17. Viewing a Document Window.

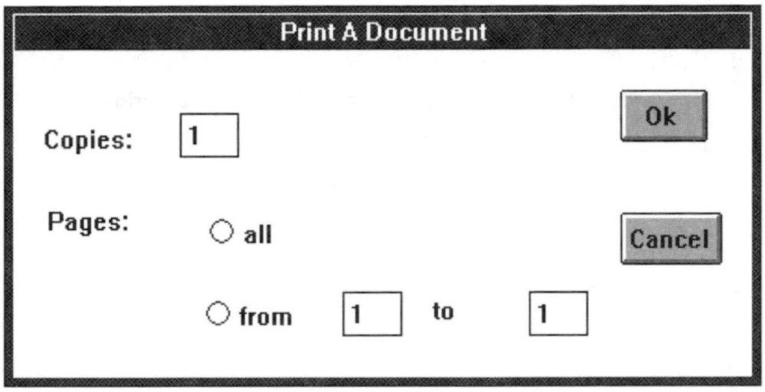

Figure D.18. Print a Document Dialog Box.

Scenarios

The sequence of events, or steps, that is common to both normal and exceptions search scenarios is shown in Scenario 7. This setup sequence of events precedes both the detailed search scenario and the detailed search scenario with exceptions.

A detailed scenario for searching for a document is shown in Scenario 9. This also includes the scenario for viewing a document, since the only documents that may be viewed or printed are those that have been retrieved as the result of a search. This scenario assumes that the user is not changing the logical operators that connect the query categories. A scenario that requires multiple searches to find a document is simply a repetition of a single search and will not be shown.

Scenario 7. Setup Sequence of Events Preceding All Search Scenarios.

> The user selects the Document Retrieval menu-bar item from the menu bar.
> A pop-up menu for Document Retrieval appears.
> The user selects the Search item from the pop-up menu.
> The Search for a Document(s) dialog box is displayed.

Scenario 8. Search Scenario with Exceptions.

> The user selects the OK push-button in the Search for Document(s) dialog box.
> A search error message box is displayed showing an error message and asking the user to enter content, abstract, keyword, or author information as a query.
> The user selects the OK push-button in the search error message box.
> The search error message box is cleared from the screen.
> The Search for Documents dialog box is redisplayed.
> The user selects the Cancel push-button in the Search for Document(s) dialog box.
> The Search for Document(s) dialog box is cleared from the screen.
> The main application window is redisplayed.

A detailed scenario for searching for a document, with exceptions, is shown in Scenario 8. This scenario requires an error message to be displayed if the user selects the OK push-button before entering any search criteria. The search error message dialog box (see Figure D.19) requires the

Figure D.19. Search Error Message Box.

user to acknowledge the error by selecting the OK push-button before continuing with the program.

A detailed scenario for searching for a document, including print, is shown in Scenario 9. No meaningful exception conditions exist for print.

Event Trace

The event trace for a normal search scenario, including print and view operations, is shown in Figures D.20 and D.21, respectively. Several details have been left out of the event trace because of its size (e.g., display pop-up system menu, and clear system menu, search, and search results dialog boxes from screen). Notice that the search dialog box, search results dialog box, and view a document window are objects that are created and destroyed during the course of the application. Also, a document is printed when the user selects OK in the print dialog box.

Scenario 9. Search Scenario Including Print.

> The user enters a query in the content query edit field.
> The user tabs over to the content query logical operator and changes it from AND to OR.
> The user tabs over to the abstract query edit field.
> The user enters a query in the abstract query edit field.
> The user tabs over to the keyword query edit field.
> The user enters one or more keywords and logical operators in the keyword edit field.
> The user tabs over to the author query edit field.
> The user enters one or more authors in the author query edit field.
> The user selects the OK push-button in the Search for Document(s) dialog box.
> The Search Results dialog box is displayed, showing the names of several documents found meeting the search criteria.
> The user selects a directory from the scrolling list of directories.
> The directory name is displayed in the Path edit control box.
> The user selects a document file from the scrolling list of files.
> The document file name is displayed in the document name edit control box.
> The user selects the Print push-button in the dialog box.
> The print dialog box is displayed.

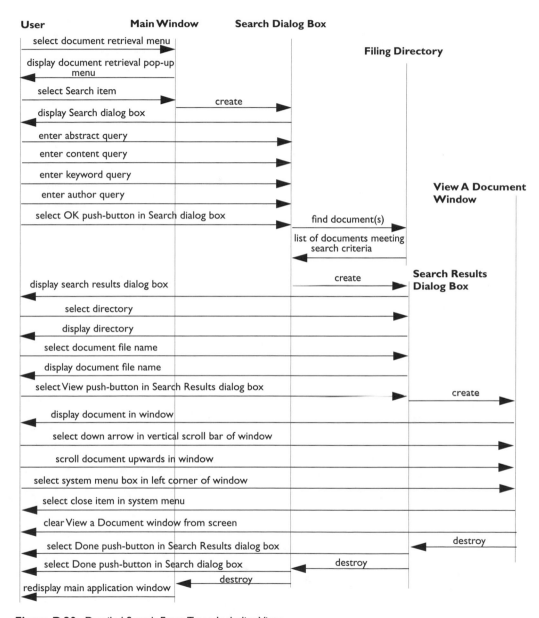

Figure D.20. Detailed Search Event Trace Including View.

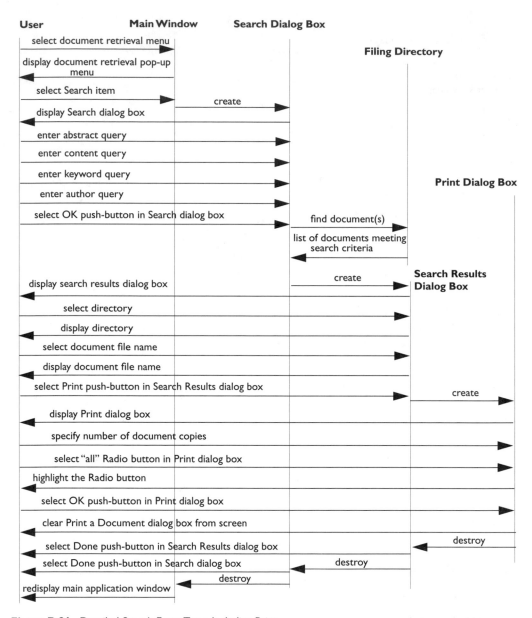

Figure D.21. Detailed Search Event Trace Including Print.

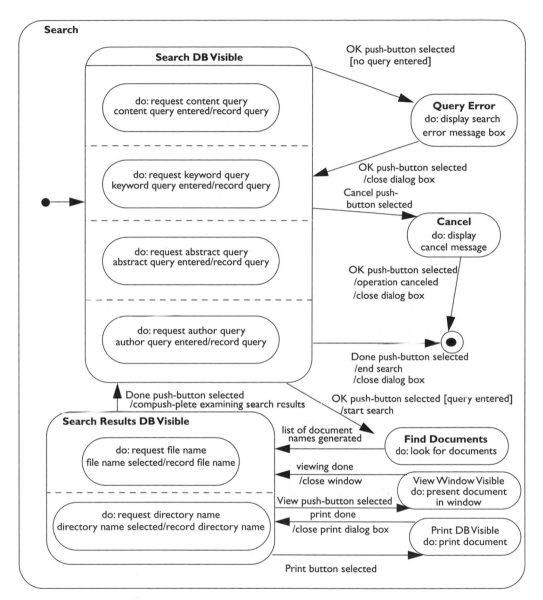

Figure D.22. *Search* and *Search Results* Dialog Box Classes Statecharts.

The user specifies the number of document copies.
The user selects the "all" radio button.
The radio button is highlighted.
The user selects the OK push-button in the print dialog box.
The document is printed.
The print dialog box is cleared from the screen.
The user selects the Done push-button from the search results dialog box.
The search results dialog box is cleared from the screen.
The user selects the Done push-button from the search for a document dialog box.
The search for a document dialog box is cleared from the screen.
The main application window is redisplayed.

Statechart

The statechart for the search dialog box, including both view and print activities, is shown in Figure D.22. The search results may either be viewed or printed by the user. The *look for documents* activity of the *Find Documents* substate in Figure D.22 is the basic search for documents.

D.3.5 Filing Character Set Change Operation

Detailed Presentation Formats

The *filing character set change* operation uses the following dialog boxes from the user interface:

❑ Filing Character Set

❑ Are You Sure?

The *Filing Character Set* dialog box is shown in Figure D.23. The scrolling list box displays all of the possible ASCII character that may be part of the filing character set. Characters that were once discarded from the filing set may again be selected and included in the filing set. An *Are You Sure?* message box is used to verify that a user wants to cancel an include or discard operation.

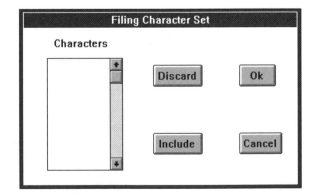

Figure D.23. Filing Character Set Dialog Box.

Scenario 10. Setup Sequence of Events Preceding All Filing Character Scenarios.

> The user selects the Utilities menu-bar item from the menu bar.
> A pop-up menu for Utilities appears.
> The user selects the Filing Characters item from the pop-up menu.
> The Filing Character Set dialog box is displayed.
> The user selects a character in the scrolling list.
> The character is highlighted.
> The user selects the Discard push-button in the dialog box.
> The selected character is redisplayed in gray.

Scenario 11. Filing Character Set Scenario.

> The user selects the OK push-button in the Character Set dialog box.
> The Character Set dialog box is cleared from the screen.
> The main application window is redisplayed.

Scenarios

The sequence of events, or steps, that is common to both normal and exceptions filing character set scenarios is shown in Scenario 10. This setup sequence of events precedes both the detailed filing character set scenario and detailed filing character set scenario with exceptions.

A detailed scenario for discarding or including a character in the filing character set is shown in Scenario 11. This allows the user to scroll through the list box and see all of the characters that are included in or have been excluded from the current filing character set.

Characters that are included in the current filing character set are shown in black, while characters that have been discarded from the filing character set will be shown in gray.

Scenario 12. Filing Character Set Scenario with Exceptions.

> The user selects the Cancel push-button in the Character Set dialog box.
> A message box asking Are You Sure? is displayed.
> The user selects the Yes push-button.
> The Are You Sure? message box is cleared from the screen.
> The Filing Character Set dialog box is cleared from the screen.
> The main application window is redisplayed.

A detailed scenario for discarding or including a character in the filing character set, with exceptions, is shown in Scenario 12. If a user decides to cancel this operation after discarding or including a character in the filing character set, an *Are You Sure?* message box (see Figure D.24) is displayed on the screen. The user may then cancel the cancel operation or select the Yes push–button and complete the cancel operation.

Event Trace

A detailed event trace for changing the filing character set is shown in Figure D.25. The program retains a global set of filing characters, and each filed document retains its own local set of filing characters. The global set is used when filing a document, and the local set is used when searching for a document. The filing character set object is created and destroyed during the course of the

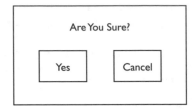

Figure D.24. Are You Sure? Message Box.

application. The filing character set object is created when the program is started and exists until the application is terminated by the user.

Statechart

The statechart for changing the filing character set is shown in Figure D.26. Note the use of several conditions associated with events. These conditions are used as guards on transitions. For example, the *select discard push-button* event is only allowed if *a character is selected*. *Character selected* is the guard on the transition. The *Are You Sure?* message box is referred to as the *cancel message box*.

D.3.6 Junk Word Set Change Operation

Detailed Presentation Formats

The *junk word set change* operation uses the following dialog boxes from the user interface:

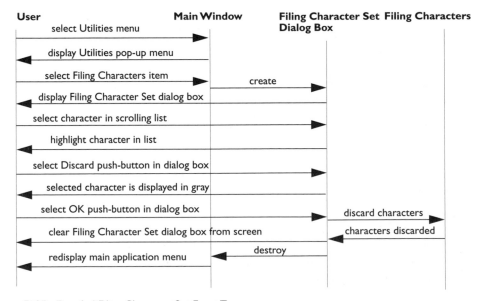

Figure D.25. Detailed Filing Character Set Event Trace.

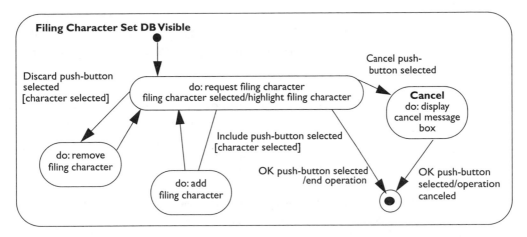

Figure D.26. *Filing Character Set* Dialog Box Class Statechart.

❏ Junk Words

❏ Are You Sure?

The *Junk Words* dialog box is shown in Figure D.27. The scrolling list box displays all of the junk words that are part of the junk word set. Junk words may be added to or deleted from the current set. An *Are You Sure?* message box is used to verify that a user wants to cancel an add or delete operation. The *Are You Sure?* message box is referred to as the *cancel message box*. The electronic filing program comes with a basic set of junk words that it always retains, whether or not a user deletes one or more of the basic junk words.

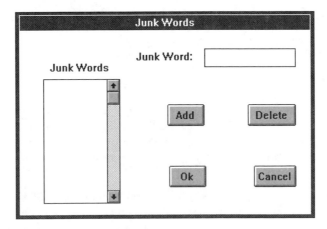

Figure D.27. Junk Words Dialog Box.

Junk words that are included in the current set are shown in black, while junk words that have been deleted from the program's basic junk words set will be shown in gray (left as an exercise for the reader). Junk words that a user adds to the program are not shown in the scrolling list after they have been deleted.

Scenarios

The sequence of events, or steps, that is common to both normal and exceptions junk word scenarios is shown in Scenario 13. This setup sequence of events precedes both the detailed junk word scenario and detailed junk word scenario with exceptions.

A detailed scenario for adding or deleting a junk word from the set of junk words specified for the electronic filing program is shown in Scenario 14.

Scenario 13. Setup Sequence of Events Preceding All Junk Word Scenarios.

> The user selects the Utilities menu-bar item from the menu bar.
> A pop-up menu for Utilities appears.
> The user selects the junk words item from the pop-up menu.
> The Junk Words dialog box is displayed.
> The user selects the down arrow in the scroll bar for junk words.
> The junk word display is scrolled upward.
> The user enters a junk word into the junk word edit box.
> The user selects the Add push-button.
> The word is added to the list of junk words in the scrolling list.

Scenario 14. Junk Words Scenario.

> The user selects the OK push-button in the Junk Words dialog box.
> The Junk Words dialog box is cleared from the screen.
> The main application window is redisplayed.

Scenario 15. Junk Words Scenario with Exceptions.

> The user selects the Cancel push-button in the junk words dialog box.
> A message box asking Are You Sure? is displayed.
> The user selects the Yes push-button in the message box.
> The Are You Sure? message box is cleared from the screen.
> The junk words dialog box is cleared from the screen.
> The main application window is redisplayed.

A detailed scenario, with exceptions, for adding or deleting a junk word from the set of junk words is shown in Scenario 15. If a user decides to cancel this operation after adding or deleting a junk word, an *Are You Sure?* message box (see Figure D.24) is displayed on the screen. The user may then either cancel the cancel operation or select the Yes push-button and complete the cancel operation.

Event Trace

A detailed event trace for changing the junk word set is shown in Figure D.28. The program retains a global set of junk words, and each filed document retains its own local set of junk words. The global set is used when filing a document, and the local set is used when searching for a document.

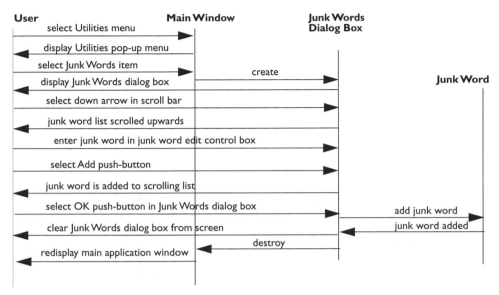

Figure D.28. Detailed Junk Words Event Trace.

The junk words object (dialog box) is created and destroyed during the course of the application. The junk word object is created when the program is first executed and exists until the application is terminated by the user.

Statechart

The statechart for changing the junk word set is shown in Figure D.29.

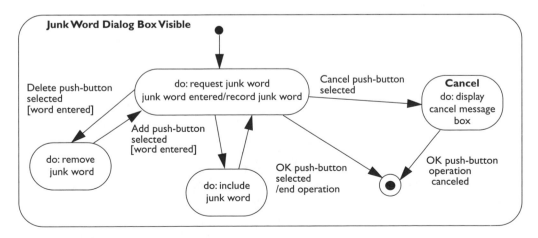

Figure D.29. *Junk Word* Dialog Box Class Statechart.

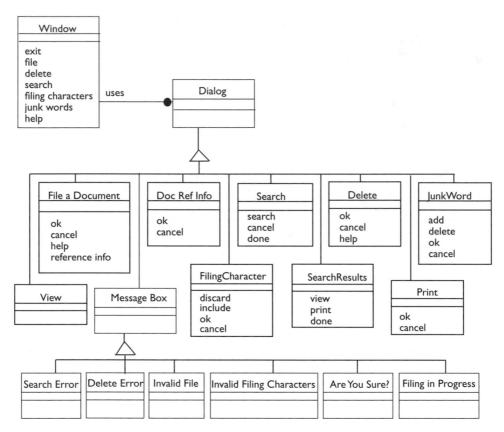

Figure D.30. User Interface Class Diagram.

D.3.7 Application Objects and Domain Objects

Application object classes are object classes that are visible to the outside users (Rumbaugh, 1993), i.e., user interface object classes. Domain objects represent the problem domain. Utility objects are the generic class library object classes that you buy from a vendor, e.g., set, bag, dictionary, string, etc. Utility objects are used to implement programs. The user interface subsystem module that will be part of the OMT object model is shown in Figure D.30. This figure depicts only the application object classes. The relationships between some of the application object classes and the domain object classes is shown in Figure D.31.

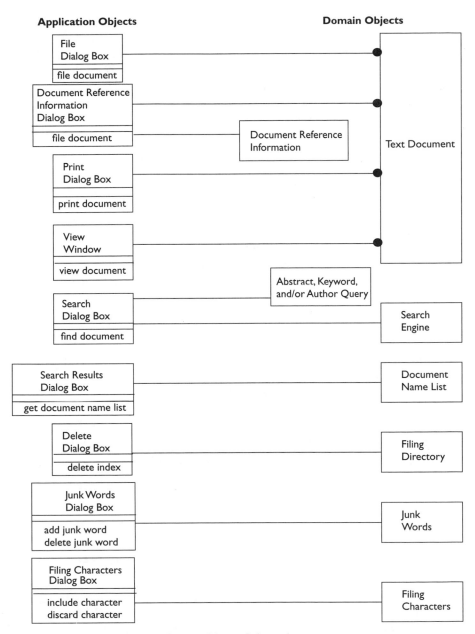

Figure D.31. Application Objects and Domain Objects Relationships.

D.4 FUNCTIONAL MODEL

The input and output values between the electronic filing application and the outside world are shown in Figure D.32. All interactions between the electronic filing program and the outside world pass through the user interface. Therefore all input and output values are parameters of user interface events. The most important events in our application are a file request and a search request. The input values for the EFP are parameters to these events:

- ❑ file name
- ❑ file directory name
- ❑ document reference information (author, keyword, abstract)
- ❑ search criteria (author, keyword, word or phrase)
- ❑ a file (the document itself)

The file name and file directory are necessary to locate and read a file (i.e., text document) that is to be filed in the system. The document reference information captures information about the document itself, which can be used to locate the document later on. Search criteria must be specified by a user when trying to search for one or more documents. The last major input is the file, or text document, which the user has put away in the electronic filing system so that it can be retrieved quickly and easily.

The output values are parameters of the event which signals that the search request has been completed. The output values for the EPF are the document name list (list of document names representing the documents found meeting the search criteria). Users put information, in the form of documents, into the system and expect to be able to retrieve them quickly and easily later on.

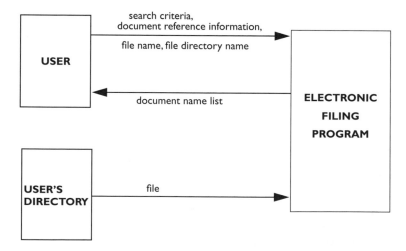

Figure D.32. Input and Output Values for the EFP.

The major output value of the EFP is a document name list that contains the names of documents that satisfy some search criteria. The user can then either view or print these documents.

D.4.1 Top-Level Data Flow Diagram for Electronic Filing Program

The top-level data flow diagram for the Electronic Filing Program is shown in Figure D.33; input and output values are supplied and consumed by external objects, such as *User* and *User's Directory*.

One data store is shown in the top-level data flow diagram: a filing directory. A filing directory, used exclusively by the EFP, maintains document indexes and document reference information. A document index and document reference information are stored in the filing directory when a document is filed in the system. This information is later retrieved from the filing directory and used when searching for documents.

The user represents an actor outside the context of the system. The user provides document reference information, a document file name, and a document directory name when filing a document, and search criteria when the EFP is trying to find a document(s) for the user. A text document in the form of a file comes from a source outside of the filing system—the user's directory.

As the result of the filing process, a document index is created and stored in the filing directory along with document reference information. The document index and document reference information are used to find a document(s) for the user. A list of the names of documents that have satisfied the search request are returned to the user.

The next step is to decompose and expand each nontrivial process in Figure D.33. If this results in more nontrivial processes, then continue to decompose and expand each nontrivial process again, resulting in another layer of data flow diagrams.

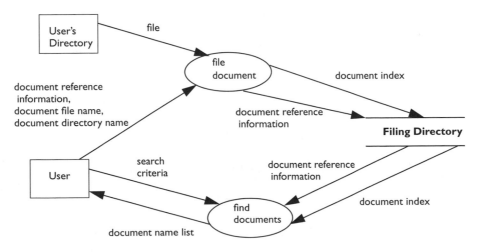

Figure D.33. Top-Level Data Flow Diagram.

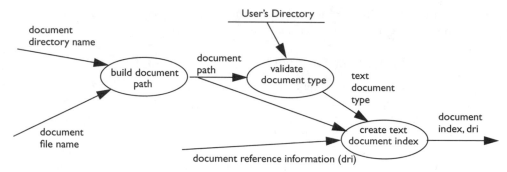

Figure D.34. DFD for File Document Process.

D.4.2 File Document Process

Figure D.34 represents the process of filing a document. Note that the net inputs and outputs of this diagram are equivalent to the data flows into and out of the *file document* process in Figure D.33.

D.4.3 Create Text Document Index Process

Text document type, document file name, and document reference information are the net inputs for the *create text document index* process of Figure D.35. The net output is a document index. Note that a hashing mechanism will be used to create an index of the document file.

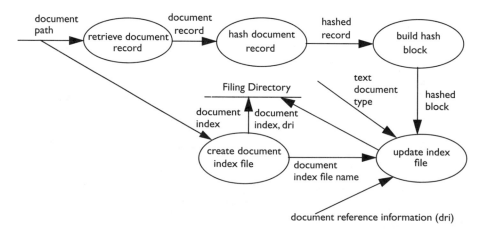

Figure D.35. DFD for Create Text Document Index Process.

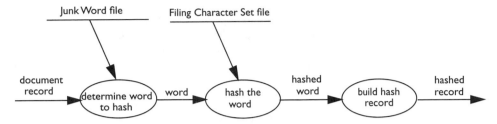

Figure D.36. DFD for Hash Document Record Process.

D.4.4 Hash Document Record Process

The net inputs and outputs to the *hash document record* process, shown in Figure D.36, are *document record* and *hashed record*, respectively. The *hash document record* process of Figure D.36 is balanced with respect to Diagram 1.3, since the inputs and outputs are the same.

D.4.5 Find Documents Process

Figure D.37 represents the process of finding one or more documents based on some search criteria. The net inputs to this process are *content query, abstract query, keyword query, author query, logical query operators, document reference information,* and *document index.* A *document name list* is the output data flow from the *build document name list* process.

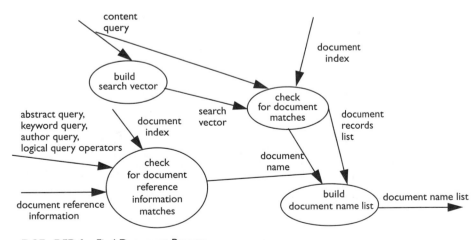

Figure D.37. DFD for Find Document Process.

D.4.6 Build Search Vector Process

The net inputs to the build search vector process are phrase and logical operator (see Figure D.38). However, the parent process for build search vector (see Figure D.37) shows content query as the input data flow. Content query is made up of some combination of phrases and logical operators. A *search vector* represents the output data flow.

D.4.7 Check for Document Matches Process

The net inputs to the check for document matches DFD of Figure D.39 are *search vector, content query,* and *document index.* The net outputs are a *document name* and a *document records list.*

D.4.8 Check for Document Reference Information Matches Process

The net inputs to the *check for document reference information matches* process are *abstract query, keyword query, author query, abstract, keywords, authors,* and *logical query operators* (see Figure D.40). *Document reference information* is made up of some combination of *abstract, keywords,* and *authors.* A *document name* is the output data flow for the check for logical query match process. This is the name of the document found as the result of a search.

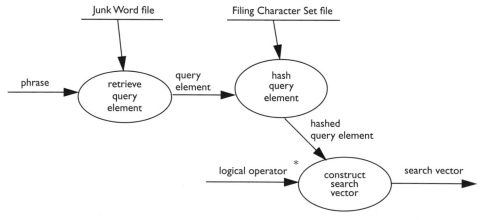

Figure D.38. DFD for Build Search Vector Process.

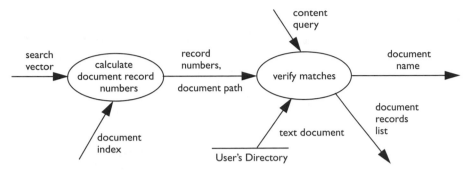

Figure D.39. DFD for Check For Document Matches Process.

D.4.9 Event Flow Diagram

Figure D.41 shows an event flow diagram for the EFP. The event flow diagram for the EFP clearly shows that there is a significant amount of interaction between the user and the user interface.

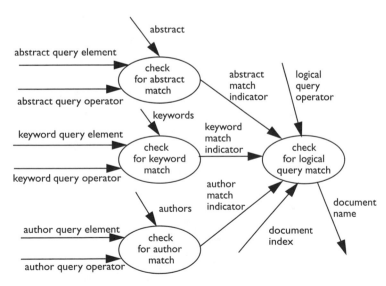

Figure D.40. DFD for Check for Document Reference Information Matches Process.

D.4.10 Process Descriptions

The process descriptions for the data flow diagrams should also be a part of this document. They are shown in Appendix A.

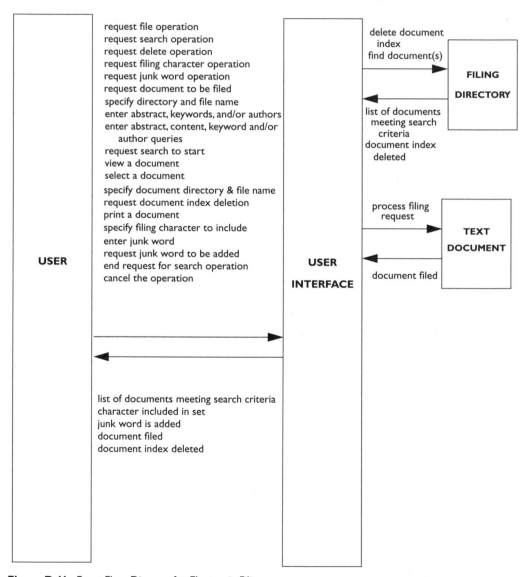

Figure D.41. Event Flow Diagram for Electronic Filing.

System Design Document

THE SYSTEM DESIGN document represents the basic approach to solving the problem. The steps identified by the OMT that make sense for the scale of our application are

- ❏ specifying high-level strategy decisions
- ❏ organizing the system into subsystems
- ❏ identifying concurrency inherent in the problem
- ❏ allocating subsystems to processors and tasks
- ❏ choosing an approach for the safe, efficient management of data stores

The deliverables for the system design consist of

- ❏ a data flow diagram showing the information flow among subsystems
- ❏ a list of the high-level strategy decisions
- ❏ a list and description of the subsystems that are part of the system
- ❏ a subsystem block diagram showing the layers and partitions of the system
- ❏ a class diagram of subsystems
- ❏ a list of potential concurrent tasks and their object representations
- ❏ one or more process diagrams showing possible allocations of subsystems to processors and tasks, and the recommended approach
- ❏ a diagram of the data stores represented as objects

E.1 SUBSYSTEMS

System design for the electronic filing application is extremely trivial. The scale of the problem is small; therefore, so is the number and size of the subsystems. However, the application is logically divided into a number of small subsystems, providing a coherent way of looking at various aspects of the problem.

Electronic filing has an interactive interface which is dominated by the dynamic model. The interactive interface consists of many application interface objects. These object classes share a common property and provide the same type of service: they are all application interface object classes. The *user interface,* or *application interface,* is a part of the system that should be represented as a subsystem.

A query module was identified in the analysis document as a subsystem of our application. The query module represents a group of classes and their associations and operations, which also share a common property. They all are functionally related to representing and processing queries—this is their purpose. Also, there is minimal coupling between this subsystem and the rest of the system—through the *search engine* object class.

Another group of classes that share common properties and serve the same purpose are the *document name list* and *document records list* classes. The purpose of these classes is to represent the search results from a search operation, where a user has specified some query and is trying to find one or more documents. These objects will be grouped to form a subsystem known as a *search results module* in the object model. They represent a self-contained piece of functionality. The *search engine* and the *search results dialog box* are the only classes that access this subsystem.

The object model shows another group of classes that share common properties. The *text document, index,* and *document reference information* object classes all operate on the same conceptual entity—a document and the information representing a text document that has been provided by a user. There purpose is to represent a document and the processing of that document. These objects will be grouped to form a subsystem known as a *document module* in the object model.

The *hash engine, filing character, junk word, hash block,* and *hash record* classes also share common properties. They are all associated with the hashing operation. Each class fulfills the goals of the subsystem—creating an indexed representation of a text document. We'll call this subsystem the hashing subsystem. The superimposed coding techniques specified in Knuth (1973) will be used for indexing and retrieval of text.

The *search engine* and *search vect*or classes along with the query and search result subsystems also form a subsystem. These subsystems and classes all share a common property: they all work together in performing a search requested by the user. The interactions of the query subsystem are strongly coupled to the *search engine* class. The query subsystem has interactions only with the *search engine* class. We'll call this new subsystem the search subsystem.

To summarize, the subsystems of the electronic filing program are

❑ user interface

❑ document

❏ query

❏ search results

❏ hashing

❏ search

E.2 LAYERS AND PARTITIONS

Figure E.1 shows a subsystem block diagram of the electronic filing program representing various types of subsystems in layers and partitions. Several of the electronic filing classes that are not part of a subsystem are omitted from this diagram. The computer hardware and the electronic filing application represent the bottom and top layers of our system, respectively. The operating system is part of our computer platform. Our application has a user interface subsystem that uses the services of several application modules/subsystems: document subsystem, query subsystem, and search results subsystem. The user interface subsystem also interfaces with a component library to provide its functionality. And the component library interfaces with a windowing subsystem, such as Microsoft Windows or Motif or Presentation Manager, and the computer operating system. The component library will be a commercial off-the-shelf class library that will provide windowing functionality and will include a basic, generic object library.

Figure E.2 shows the relationships among the system's subsystems and classes, along with their public operations. This diagram is not part of the OMT notation. Public operations/methods that are used by other operations are shown in the figure, with no regard to sequence. Also, the

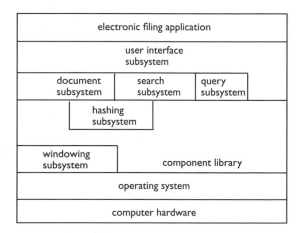

Figure E.1. Subsystem Block Diagram of Electronic Filing.

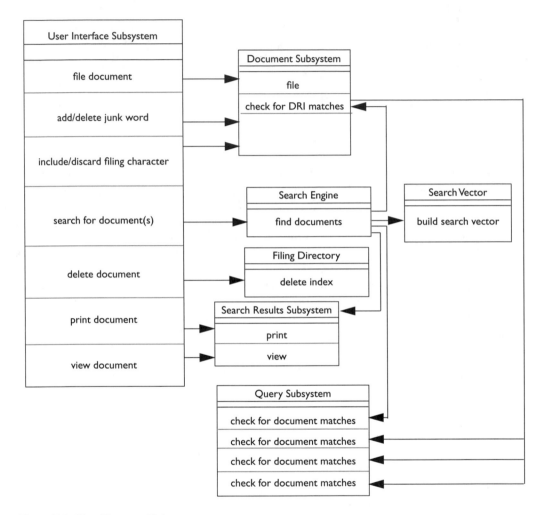

Figure E.2. Class Diagram of Subsystems.

supplier of a method/operation that a client operation of some subsystem/class uses is also listed in the Figure E.2.

E.3 CONCURRENCY

The dynamic model for our program mainly involves the user interface. We choose to use an event-driven system for the user interface. Event-driven systems are more modular than procedural-driven systems and are also well suited to graphical user interfaces. Several parts of the user interface are concurrent, i.e., selecting directory and file names, entering query information. However, we will specify that the programming environment for our event-driven user interface will provide a dispatcher or monitor that will handle events.

The following could be concurrent activities:

- ❏ the event-driven user interface—root of main program

- ❏ printing of a document—create a print operation object

- ❏ viewing of a document—create a view document window object

- ❏ document subsystem associated with the filing of a document

- ❏ hashing subsystem associated with both the filing and retrieval of a document

- ❏ filing directory object and search subsystem associated with the finding and deleting of a document(s)

E.4 ALLOCATING SUBSYSTEMS TO PROCESSORS AND TASKS

Process diagrams as shown in Booch (1994) are used to show the allocation of processes/concurrent activities/tasks to processors in the physical design of a system. The three-dimensional box in Figure E.3 denotes a processor. The root of a main program and active objects are listed under each processor box with which they are associated.

The electronic filing application could be designed to operate on multiple processors or on a single processor. The single processor could simulate logical concurrency with separate threads of control being known as *tasks* or *daemons*. Many different possible allocations of subsystems to processors and tasks are possible. Some of these possibilities are subsequently discussed.

In Figure E.3 a LAN ties all computers together for shared Email, office automation, directory, computational, and printing services. The LAN requires basic communication hardware and software, such as Ethernet, in order for these computers to communicate with each other. The electronic filing client and server also require an application-level protocol in order to share information and perform the functions of an electronic filing system. The event–driven user interface, the objects necessary for the viewing of a document, and the application protocol exist on the client machine running as independent tasks. The print server provides the ability to print a document. The electronic filing server has the document, query, and search results subsystems and filing directory object running as independent tasks. The advantage of this approach is that higher performance is achievable using multiple processors and multiple tasks.

Figure E.4 combines the client and server subsystems and objects on one processor. The respective subsystems and objects are each running as independent tasks. In this configuration, an application level protocol is still necessary in order to share information and perform the functions of an electronic filing system. The disadvantage of this approach is that the overall throughput for filing and retrieving documents under heavy load will be less than for the multiple processor approach.

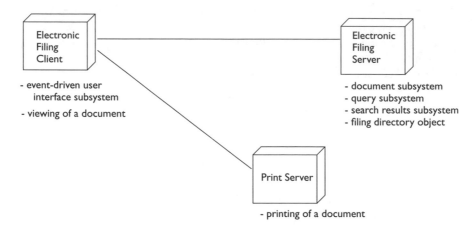

Figure E.3. Electronic Filing Client-Server Process Diagram.

In Figure E.5 all subsystems and objects for the electronic filing application are packaged together into a single task running on a single processor. This configuration provides the simplest implementation but under heavy or moderate loads will not perform as well as the previously discussed configurations.

The configurations depicted in Figures E.3 and E.4 require the use of a multitasking operating system for each processor. Figure E.5 does not require the use of a multitasking operating system. We will assume that this application is being developed for Microsoft Windows and that it will run as a single task. Therefore we will opt for the configuration shown in Figure E.5. However, various

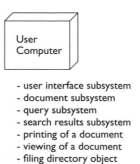

Figure E.4. Electronic Filing with Multiple Tasks Process Diagram.

- all electronic filing subsystems and objects

Figure E.5. Electronic Filing with Single Task Process Diagram.

multitasking operating systems (OS2, Windows NT, a number of different Unix systems) could be used on a PC to support the configuration shown in Figure E.4.

E.5 IMPLEMENTING DATA STORES

Several possible data stores are shown in the data flow diagrams for the functional model: junk word file, filing character file, user's directory, and filing directory. Junk word, filing character, and filing directory are already represented as objects in the electronic filing object model. *Junk word* and *filing character* interface to the junk word file and filing characters file, respectively. The *filing directory* object maintains a list of the index files in memory that are part of the filing directory.

The user directory has little behavior and state associated with it. We choose to access files in the user directory through file and directory names. The user directory is generated prior to invoking the electronic filing program; i.e, the electronic filing program does not store data in the user's directory—text documents are accessed only if they already exist in the user's directory.

The data stores for electronic filing are shown pictorially in Figure E.6. Objects have already been identified to represent the filing characters, junk words, and the filing directory. Access to these data stores is managed through the identified objects.

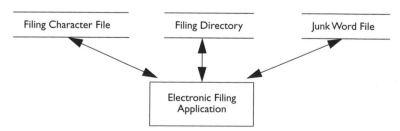

Figure E.6. Data Stores for Electronic Filing.

E.6 SUMMARY OF HIGH-LEVEL STRATEGY DECISIONS

The following summarizes the high-level strategy decisions for the development of our electronic filing program:

❑ The user interface will be an event-driven graphical user interface.

❑ Standard files and directories along with the indexing techniques specified in Knuth (1973) will be used for index and retrieval of text.

❑ Component libraries in C++ and Smalltalk will insulate us from the details of the application programming interface of the windowing environment for our platform(s).

❑ This application is being developed for a PC Microsoft Windows environment and will run on a single processor and as a single task, negating the requirement to allocate subsystems among processors and tasks.

Electronic Filing Methods: Methods for the Domain Objects

fileDoc Method

The *fileDoc* method creates an Index object and then sends a message to the Index object to create the document index, which invokes the *createDocIndex* method.

Implementing Classes: TextDocument

Inputs: TextDocumentName   DirectoryName

Outputs:

Data Structures:

Algorithm:
```
create an Index object
Index.createDocIndex (TextDocumentName, DirectoryName)
```

buildHashBlock Method

Implementing Classes: HashEngine

Inputs: IndexFileStreamDocumentFileStream

Outputs:

Data Structures: DocumentRecord:String of 80 characters;   HashedRecord:String of 640 bits;   HashedBlock: Integer (16384)

Algorithm:
```
FOR each DocumentRecord
   DocumentRecord := DocumentFileStream.get the next document record
```

```
    HashedRecord := self.hashDocumentRecord (DocumentRecord)
    IF hash block full THEN
       IndexFileStream.output the HashedBlock
       clear HashedBlock
    ENDIF
ENDFOR
```

hashDocumentRecord Method

Implementing Classes: HashEngine

Inputs: DocumentRecord

Outputs:

Data Structures: Word:String

Algorithm:

```
read a record
DO
   Word := self.GetWordToHash ()
   self.hashTheWord (Word)
UNTIL all words in the record have been processed
```

getWordToHash Method

This method gets the next word in the data record about to be hashed.

Implementing Classes: Hash Engine

Inputs: DataRecord:String   RecordPosition:Integer

Outputs: WordSize:Integer

Data Structures: Word:String

Algorithm:

```
find first real character of word using RecordPosition
find last real character of word
WordSize := last real char position - first real char position + 1
RecordPosition := last real char position + 1
```

hashTheWord Method

The hashTheWord method hashes an individual word consisting of two or more characters. The pseudocode for the hashTheWord method is as follows:

Implementing Classes: Hash Engine

Inputs: Word:String   WordSize:Integer

Outputs: HashedWord

Data Structures:

Algorithm:

```
IF WordSize > 2 characters
   get the first character
   hashFirstChar(Character, HashedWord)      //hash the first character 6 times
   get the second character
   hashSecondChar(Character, HashedWord)     //hash the second character 4 times
   WHILE not at end of word
      get the next character
      hashOtherChar(Character, HashedWord) //hash the third character 2 times
   END WHILE
ENDIF
```

hashFirstChar Method

The first character is hashed a unique number of times using a table lookup technique. The hashFirstChar method is as follows:

Implementing Classes: Hash Engine

Inputs: Character   HashedWord:String of bits

Outputs: HashedWord:String of bits

Data Structures: TranslateTable:Integer (128)   HashedBlock: Integer (16384)

Algorithm:

```
translate character = TranslateTable[ASCII character value]
offset = (translate character) Modulo 1024
index = random number table[offset] + number of data records indexed in this
   block
WHILE counter <= 6
   hashCharacter (index, number of data records)
   offset = offset + translate character
   index = random number table[offset] + number of data records indexed in
      this block
ENDWHILE
```

hashCharacter Method

Implementing Classes: Hash Engine

Inputs: Index   number of data records indexed in this block

Outputs:

Data Structures: HashedBlock: Integer (16384)

Algorithm:

```
mask number = number of data records indexed in this block Modulo 8
char mask = mask table[mask number]
hashed_block[index] = hashed_block[index] | char mask
```

hashSecondChar Method

Implementing Classes: Hash Engine

Inputs: Character   HashedWord:String of bits

Outputs: HashedWord:String of bits

Data Structures: TranslateTable:Integer (128)

Algorithm:
```
translate character = TranslateTable[ASCII character value]
offset = (translate character) Modulo 1024
index = random number table[offset] + number of data records indexed in this
  block
WHILE counter <= 4
  hashCharacter (Index, number of data records)
  offset = offset + translate character
  index = random number table[offset] + number of data records indexed in
    this block
ENDWHILE
```

hashOtherChar Method

Implementing Classes: Hash Engine

Inputs: Character   HashedWord:String of bits

Outputs: HashedWord:String of bits

Data Structures: TranslateTable:Integer (128)

Algorithm:
```
translate character = TranslateTable[ASCII character value]
offset = (translate character) Modulo 1024
index = random number table[offset] + number of data records indexed in this
  block
WHILE counter <= 2
  hashCharacter (index, number of data records indexed in this block)
  offset = offset + translate character
  index = random number table[offset] + number of data records indexed in
    this block
ENDWHILE
```

addToHashRecord Method

Implementing Classes: Hash Engine

Inputs: HashedWord:String of bits   HashedRecord:String of 640 bits

Outputs: HashedRecord:String of 640 bits

Data Structures:

Algorithm:

```
HashedRecord := HashedRecord | HashedWord
```

addToHashBlock Method

Implementing Classes: Index

Inputs: HashedRecord:String of 640 bits

Outputs: HashedBlock   HashedRecord

Data Structures:

Algorithm:

```
HashedBlock = HashedBlock | HashedRecord
```

Searching and retrieving one or more documents based on an index method that uses hashing is a nontrivial operation. In this section we will write the pseudocode for implementing this algorithm, specify the data structures necessary for the algorithm, and define any new internal classes and operations needed to hold intermediate results. The rest of the code that is needed to implement the search operation is fairly straightforward and will not be specified here in pseudocode.

findDocument Method

The *findDocument* method searches for one or more documents satisfying the user-specified search criteria. A document name list is built by the methods that check for document and document reference information matches. The pseudocode for the *findDocument* method is as follows:

Implementing Classes: SearchEngine

Inputs: AuthorQuery:String, KeywordQuery:String, ContentQuery:String, AbstractQuery:String

Outputs:

Data Structures: SearchVector:String   DocumentNameList:List

Algorithm:

```
IF ContentQuery specified by the user THEN
   SearchVector := build the search vector (ContentQuery)
   DocumentNameList := check for document matches (SearchVector)
ENDIF
IF document reference information specified by the user THEN
   DocumentNameList := check for document reference information matches
      (AuthorQuery, KeywordQuery,
         AbstractQuery, DocumentReferenceInformation)
ENDIF
build the document name list based on current matches
```

```
IF document name list is NOT empty THEN
   display Search Results Dialog box
ELSE
   display message indicating no matches were found meeting the search criteria
ENDIF
```

buildSearchVector Method

The buildSearchVector method uses the content query to construct a search vector.

Implementing Classes: SearchVector

Inputs: ContentQuery:String

Outputs: SearchVector:String

Data Structures: SearchVector:String   WordString:String   HashedWordString

Algorithm:

```
DO
   WordString := get next query element (ContentQuery)
   HashedWordString := hashTheWord (WordString)
   LogicalOperator := get next logical operator (WordString)
   SearchVector := construct search vector (HashedWordString, LogicalOperator)
UNTIL end of content query
```

checkForDocumentMatches Method

This method uses the search vector and the document index files to determine which documents satisfy the user-specified search criteria. The result of this process is a list of document names that meet the user's search criteria.

Implementing Classes: SearchEngine

Inputs: SearchVector:String

Outputs: DocumentNameList:List

Data Structures: RecordNumberList:List   matches:Boolean

Algorithm:

```
create an empty document name list
FOR each document index file
   RecordNumberList := calculate document record numbers (SearchVector)
   matches := verify matches (DocumentIndex, RecordNumberList, ContentQuery)
   IF matches THEN
      add document name and RecordNumberList to DocumentNameList
   ENDIF
ENDFOR
```

getQueryElement Method

Implementing Classes: Query

Inputs: Query:String

Outputs: QueryElement:String   QueryOperator:String

Data Structures:

Algorithm:

```
QueryOperator := find logical query operator (Query)
QueryElement := get query element prior to operator (Query)
```

hashQueryElement Method

Implementing Classes: HashEngine

Inputs: QueryElement:String

Outputs: HashedQueryElement

Data Structures: Word:String

Algorithm:

```
DO
   Word := get next word (QueryElement)
   HashedQueryElement := hash the word (Word, number of characters in word)
   HashedQueryElement := HashedQueryElement | HashedQueryElement
UNTIL end of QueryElement
```

constructVector Method

Implementing Classes: SearchVector

Inputs: HashedQueryElement   Logical Operator:String   SearchVector:String

Outputs: SearchVector

Data Structures:

Algorithm:

```
IF Logical Operator == OR THEN
   SearchVector := SearchVector OR HashedQueryElement
ELSE
   SearchVector := SearchVector AND HashedQueryElement
ENDIF
```

calculateDocRecNumbers Method

Implementing Classes: SearchVector

Inputs: SearchVector:String   DocumentIndex

Outputs: DocumentRecordNumberList:List

Data Structures: DocumentRecordNumberList:List   DocumentIndexRecord:String of bits

Algorithm:

```
FOR each bit in the SearchVector
   IF bit is set THEN
      read document index record (bit number)
      FOR each bit in the DocumentIndexRecord
         IF bit is set THEN
            add bit number to DocumentRecordNumberList
         ENDIF
      ENDFOR
   ENDIF
ENDFOR
```

verifyMatches Method

Implementing Classes: SearchEngine

Inputs: DocumentRecordNumberList:List   ContentQuery:String

Outputs: DocumentRecordNumberList:List   MatchIndicator:Boolean

Data Structures: DocumentRecordNumber:Integer   documentRecord:String

Algorithm:

```
FOR all document record numbers
   DocumentRecordNumber := get document record number (DocumentRecordNumberList)
   DocumentRecord := read document record(DocumentRecordNumber)
   search document record for content query
   IF ContentQuery NOT found THEN
      MatchIndicator := FALSE
      delete document record number (DocumentRecordNumberList)
   ENDIF
ENDFOR
```

checkForDRIMatches Method

Implementing Classes: SearchEngine

Inputs: DocumentReferenceInformation, AbstractQuery:String, KeywordQuery:String, AuthorQuery:String, LogicalQueryOperatorList:List

Outputs: DocumentNameList:List

Data Structures: Abstract, Keyword, Author, LogicalQueryMatchIndicator:Boolean

Algorithm:

```
parse query (AbstractQuery, AbstractQueryPhraseList, AbstractQueryOperatorList)
parse query (AuthorQuery, AuthorQueryPhraseList, AuthorQueryOperatorList)
parse query (KeywordQuery, KeywordQueryPhraseList, KeywordQueryOperatorList)
FOR each DocumentReferenceInformation
   AbstractMatchIndicator := check for abstract match (Abstract, Abstract-
                             QueryPhraseList, AbstractQueryOperatorList)
   AuthorMatchIndicator := check for author match (Author, AuthorQuery-
                             PhraseList, AuthorQueryOperatorList)
   KeywordMatchIndicator := check for keyword match (Keyword, KeywordQuery-
                             PhraseList, KeywordQueryOperatorList)
   LogicalQueryMatchIndicator := check for logical query match (LogicalQuery-
                             OperatorList, AbstractMatchIndicator, Author-
                             MatchIndicator, KeywordMatchIndicator)
   IF LogicalQueryMatchIndicator THEN
      get document name from document name list
      add document name to the document name list
   ENDIF
ENDFOR
```

parseQuery

Implementing Classes: Query

Inputs: AbstractQuery:String or AuthorQuery:String or KeywordQuery:String

Outputs: QueryPhraseList :List   QueryOperatorList:List

Data Structures:

Algorithm:

```
get first query elements (QueryPhraseList, QueryOperatorList)
DO WHILE not at end of query
   get next query element (QueryPhraseList, QueryOperatorList)
ENDDO
```

checkForAbstractMatch Method

Implementing Classes: AbstractQuery

Inputs: Abstract:String   AbstractQueryPhraseList:List
                     AbstractQueryOperatorList:List

Outputs: AbstractMatchIndicator:Boolean

Data Structures: NextIndicator:Boolean   AbstractMatchIndicator:Boolean

Algorithm:

```
first phrase := remove abstract phrase from AbstractQueryPhraseList
abstract indicator := check if phrase in abstract
DO WHILE AbstractQueryPhraseList is NOT empty
   next phrase := remove next abstract phrase from AbstractQueryPhraseList
```

```
   next indicator := check if next phrase in abstract
   remove operator from AbstractQueryOperatorList
   IF operator == AND THEN
      abstract match indicator := first indicator AND next indicator
   ELSE
      abstract match indicator := first indicator OR next indicator
   ENDIF
UNTIL
```

checkForAuthorMatch Method

Implementing Classes: AuthorQuery

Inputs: Author:String   AuthorQueryPhraseList:List
                          AuthorQueryOperatorList:List

Outputs: AuthorMatchIndicator:Boolean

Data Structures: NextIndicator:Boolean   AuthorMatchIndicator:Boolean

Algorithm:

```
first phrase := remove author phrase from AuthorQueryPhraseList
author indicator := check if phrase in author
DO WHILE AuthorQueryPhraseList is NOT empty
   next phrase := remove next author phrase from AuthorQueryPhraseList
   next indicator := check if next phrase in author
   remove operator from AuthorQueryOperatorList
   IF operator == AND THEN
      author match indicator := first indicator AND next indicator
   ELSE
      author match indicator := first indicator OR next indicator
   ENDIF
UNTIL
```

checkForKeywordMatch Method

Implementing Classes: KeywordQuery

Inputs: Keyword:String   KeywordQueryPhraseList:List
                          KeywordQueryOperatorList:List

Outputs: KeywordMatchIndicator:Boolean

Data Structures: NextIndicator:Boolean   KeywordMatchIndicator:Boolean

Algorithm:

```
first phrase := remove keyword phrase from KeywordQueryPhraseList
keyword indicator := check if phrase in keyword
DO WHILE KeywordQueryPhraseList is NOT empty
   next phrase := remove next keyword phrase from KeywordQueryPhraseList
   next indicator := check if next phrase in keyword
   remove operator from KeywordQueryOperatorList
```

```
    IF operator == AND THEN
       keyword match indicator := first indicator AND next indicator
    ELSE
       keyword match indicator := first indicator OR next indicator
    ENDIF
UNTIL
```

checkForLogicalQueryMatch Method

Implementing Classes: DocumentReferenceInformation

Inputs: LogicalQueryOperatorList   AbstractMatchIndicator,
                     AuthorMatchIndicator, KeywordMatchIndicator

Outputs: LogicalMatchIndicator:Boolean

Data Structures:

Algorithm:

```
retrieve abstract query operator from list
IF operator == OR THEN
   LogicalMatchIndicator := AbstractMatchIndicator OR KeywordMatchIndicator
ELSE
   LogicalMatchIndicator := AbstractMatchIndicator AND KeywordMatchIndicator
ENDIF
retrieve keyword query operator from list
IF operator == OR THEN
   LogicalMatchIndicator := LogicalMatchIndicator OR AuthorMatchIndicator
ELSE
   LogicalMatchIndicator := LogicalMatchIndicator AND AuthorMatchIndicator
ENDIF
```

Subsystems and Coherence of Entities

User Interface Subsystem

Purpose: To enable the user to perform the functionality specified for this application. This means that the user interface subsystem should obtain the necessary information from the user that is required to run this application and then pass this information off to the application objects. The user interface should interface to as few domain objects as possible; i.e., the user interface should be loosely coupled to the other objects in the application.

Review of Coherence: The interface between the user interface item and the application objects was depicted at the end of Chapter 7. The user interface classes are view, observer, or actor types of classes. They present information to the user on an output device and operate upon other objects but are never operated upon.

Section 8.2.6 specifies the pseudocode for each of the main methods of the user interface classes. Reviewing the actual code and the pseudocode against the user interface to application object diagram in Chapter 7 is left as an exercise for the reader. After examining the code and pseudocode, we can see that the user interface objects intermediate between the user and the application, allowing the user to specify the information needed to run the application. The user interface objects have no other purpose. The methods of the user interface classes are all tied to the functioning of the user interface elements.

Document Subsystem

Purpose: The document subsystem consists of the text document and document reference information classes. These entities are all related to a document. Their purpose is to represent a document and the processing of that document.

Review of Coherence: Document reference information is associated with a document. Document reference information is information about a document that is entered by a user. These classes are logically related even though they don't collaborate much with each other. They mostly collaborate with the user interface classes.

Classes:

1. **DocRefInfo:** The *DocRefInfo* (document reference information) class is also a data manager type of class which maintains data (i.e., author, keyword, and abstract information) about a text document. The public methods of this class—getAbstract, getAuthors, getDocumentName, getKeywords, and setDRI—are all related to the purpose of maintaining and providing access to document reference information.

2. **TextDocument:** A *TextDocument* class represents a text document as it is being filed in the system. This is also a data manager type of class. The public methods of this class, fileDoc, serve a single purpose—to file the document in the system.

Search Results Subsystem

Purpose: The purpose of the search results subsystem is to provide the results of a search to the application for the users perusal. The search results subsystem classes are *DocumentNameList* and *DocumentRecordsList*.

Review of Coherence: A *DocumentNameList* and one or more *DocumentRecordsList* objects are produced as a result of a successful search. A *DocumentNameList* creates a *DocumentRecordsList* object for each document found meeting the search criteria. These classes are very tightly related.

Classes:

1. **DocumentNameList:** A *DocumentNameList* class is a list of document names that represent documents that have satisfied the search criteria. This is another data manager type of class, which retains document names. However, this class also operates on another class—the *DocumentRecordsList* class. A object that can both operate on other objects and be operated upon is known as an *agent* type of object. The public methods of this class—addToDNL, do, getRecordsList, putRecordsList, and removeFromDNL. The public methods of this class, fileDoc, serve a single purpose—to create and provide access to search results information.

2. **DocumentRecordsList:** A *DocumentRecordsList* class is a list of document record numbers that point to data records in a specific document that have satisfied the search criteria. This is another data manager type of class, which retains document record numbers. The public methods of this class—addToDRL, atPut, removeFromDRL, and removeIndex—all exist to create and provide access to document record numbers associated with a document.

Query Subsystem

Purpose: The purpose of the Query subsystem is to represent the queries posed by a user and to provide access to the component parts of the query. The query subsystem classes are *Query, AbstractQuery, AuthorQuery, ContentQuery,* and *KeywordQuery.*

Review of Coherence: *Query* is the abstract superclass for all the other classes in this subsystem, so these classes are tightly bound by function.

Classes:

1. **Query:** The abstract superclass for this subsystem. This class defines the attributes and common methods for the subsystem. The methods for this class—checkForElement-Match, getLogicalOperators, getQueryElements, parseQuery, and query—are all related to the processing of a query.

2. **AbstractQuery, AuthorQuery, ContentQuery, KeywordQuery:** These query type of classes all have methods for getting and setting operators related to their specific queries. All methods are closely related by function.

Search Subsystem

Purpose: The purpose of the search subsystem is to find documents that satisfy user-specified search criteria. The Search subsystem classes are *SearchEngine* and *SearchVector.*

Review of Coherence: *SearchEngine* and *SearchVector* are associated with a search for a document. The *SearchEngine* object produces a SearchVector object.

Classes:

1. **SearchEngine:** The *SearchEngine* is an example of an *agent* type of object. The only function it performs is to conduct a search. The findDocument and calculateDocRec-Numbers methods are both related to finding documents that satisfy the search criteria and calculating the document record numbers for the search results.

2. **SearchVector:** The *SearchVector* object is produced by the *SearchEngine*. It simply builds the vector used to determine which documents satisfy the search criteria. The public method for this class is buildSearchVector, which is closely related to the construction of the search vector.

Data Storage Subsystem

Purpose: The purpose of the data storage subsystem is to represent, construct, and provide access to the indexes associated with the text documents filed in the system. The Data Storage subsystem classes are *Index* and *FilingDirectory.*

Review of Coherence: The *FilingDirectory* object represents the collection of index files that have been created by filing documents in the system. The *Index* object is used during the creation of the index file representing the text document.

Classes:

1. **Index:** The *Index* object is a data-sink object—it generates data on demand for a data source. It does not hold the data for a period of time, but simply generates it and outputs it to disk. The createDocIndex is the only public method; all other methods support this method.

2. **FilingDirectory:** The *FilingDirectory* is a data manager type of class. Its responsibility is to maintain the list of index file names for text documents that have been filed in the system. All of its methods support the addition and removal of names to this list.

Hashing Subsystem

Purpose: The purpose of this subsystem is to provide the hashing functions that are used to index text document for later retrieval. This subsystem consists of the *HashEngine*, *JunkWords*, and *FilingCharacters* classes. Junk words and filing characters may be entered by a user, or default to the system set of junk words and filing characters.

Classes:

1. **HashEngine:** All of the methods of this class are functionally related—they are all concerned with hashing various data types such as documents, words, and characters.

2. **JunkWords:** This is a data manager type of class, which maintains data, i.e., junk words, related to the processing of a document. The public methods of this class—addWord, deleteWord, getCurrentWords, getDeletedWords, initialize, and saveJunkWords—are all related to the purpose of maintaining and providing access to junk word data.

3. **FilingCharacters:** This is also a data manager type of class, which maintains data, i.e., filing characters, related to the processing of a document. The public methods of this class—addToDiscardChars, addToIncludeChars, getIncludedChars, and saveFilingCharacters—are all related to the purpose of maintaining and providing access to filing character data.

All of the classes in each of the subsystems are closely related functionally.

Design Document

THE OBJECT DESIGN phase of the electronic filing system application has taken the analysis document and added implementation details and refinements. The object design phase has defined the classes, their methods and attributes, and the association between classes, and implemented them. This has helped to validate and refine the current design, and to test the implementation to date.

The design document consists of the detailed object, functional, and dynamic models. Our functional and dynamic models remain the same as those shown in the analysis document. However, the object model has undergone considerable revision. Operations have been added to the object model, and associations among objects have changed based on what we have learned during our design and implementation so far.

The object design document consists of

- ❑ data dictionary (updated)

- ❑ object model

- ❑ message hierarchy diagrams

- ❑ event traces

- ❑ object representations

- ❑ association designs

- ❑ description of the physical packaging of the programs

H.1 DATA DICTIONARY

The data dictionary remains the same as in the analysis document with the exception of one additional entry:

File or Database Name: Index file

Composition:	hash block word vector size + total block count + total record count + filing characters + junk words + random number table + $_1${hashed block}^{n}
Organization:	Blocks are sequential.
Notes:	Each block contains up to 512 data records that have been hashed.

H.2 OBJECT MODEL

The class diagram for the electronic filing design model is shown in Figures H.1 and H.2.

The search engine uses a query to determine what criteria to use in finding documents for the user. A query may be an author query, keyword query, abstract query, or content query. An author query consists of author names separated by logical query operators. A keyword query consists of one or more keywords separated by logical operators. An abstract query is one or more words or phrases separated by logical operators that might be found in some document abstract. A content query is also one or more words or phrases separated by logical operators that might be found in the content of a text document.

The search engine produces a search vector based on a content query. The search engine uses a document index to determine which document records might have words or phrases that match a word or phrase in a document record.

The search engine also operates on one filing directory that has document indexes. The search engine uses document reference information that describes a text document filed in the system. A text document creates only one index.

A document index contains one or more hash blocks. Each hash block contains one or more hash records.

A hash engine checks for filing characters when hashing a text document. A hash engine also checks for junk words when hashing a text document.

The user interface subsystem classes interface to several electronic filing domain classes. The file, document reference information, and print dialog boxes use a text document. The search dialog box uses the search engine. The search engine uses a search results dialog box. The delete dialog box uses a filing directory. The filing characters dialog box uses the filing characters object class. The junk words dialog box uses the junk words object class. The filing characters and junk words objects represent the filing characters file and the junk words file, respectively.

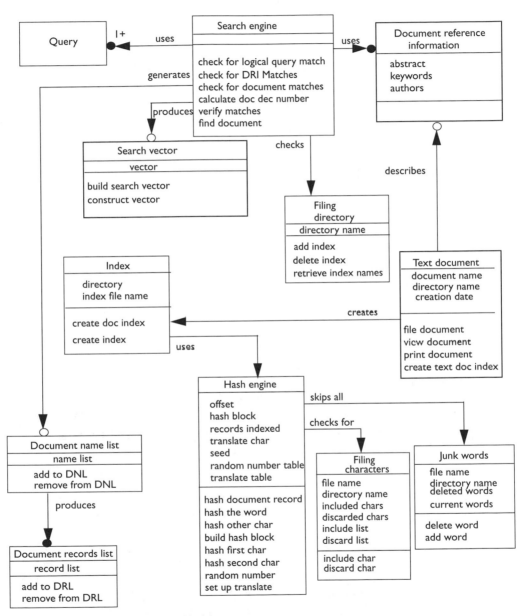

Figure H.1. Class Diagram—Design Model.

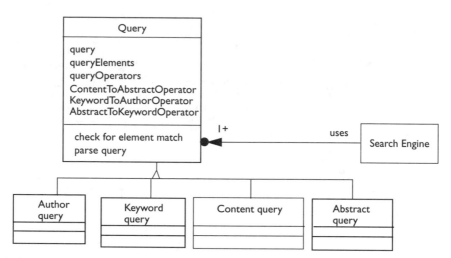

Figure H.2. Query Module.

H.3 USE CASES

Message hierarchy diagrams and event traces are shown for each use case: file, search, delete, change junk word, change filing character. Object interaction diagrams are developed for the most interesting search and file scenarios.

An object-oriented pseudocode, as discussed in Blaha (1994), is used to describe the algorithms for each method. The syntax for sending a message is receiver object.method.argument. A data structure will be identified as follows: data structure: type of data structure. Method names will begin with a lowercase letter. A data structure will begin with an uppercase letter.

File Operation

The message hierarchy diagram for the *file* operation is shown in Figure H.3. This diagram describes the single execution scenario of filing a document with document reference information. An execution scenario for filing a document with no document reference information is the same as in Figure H.3, except with all pseudocode referencing the DRIDB and document reference information must be removed from the message hierarchy diagram. The following abbreviations are used in the message hierarchy diagram: File_Dialog_Box = FDB, Text_Document = TD, Document_Reference_Information_Dialog_Box = DRIDB.

A new File dialog box object is created by the *TMainWindow* object (C++ Application Frameworks implementation) and the *Efiling* object (Smalltalk implementation) when the user selects the File item from the Document Storage pop-up menu. The user then selects the directory and file name of the document to be filed in the system. When the user selects the Reference Information

```
user selects File item
   new FDB()
   user selects directory and file
   FDB.referenceInformation()
        new DRIDB ()
      user enters document reference information
      DRIDB.ok()
           new TD()
           TD.fileDoc ()
              new Index()
           Index.createDocIndex ()
              Filing.addIndexFile ()
              Index.createIndex ()
              Index.buildIndexFileHeader()
              new HashEngine()
           HE.buildHashBlock()
               HE.hashDocRec ()
                  HE.hashTheWord ()
                     HE.hash1stChar ()
                     HE.hash2ndChar ()
                     HE.hash3rdChar ()
                     HE.hashOtherChar ()
      clear DRI dialog box from screen
    clear File dialog box from screen
display main application window
```

Figure H.3. File Operation Message Hierarchy Diagram with Document Reference Information.

push-button in the File dialog box, a document reference information (DRI) dialog box object is created by the File dialog box object. The DRI dialog box then displays itself and awaits user input. When the user has completed entering DRI information and has selected the OK push-button, a text document object is created by the DRI dialog box object. The DRI dialog box then sends a message, *fileDoc*, to the TextDocument object, which is responsible for filing the document in the system.

The TextDocument object then invokes the *fileDoc* method, which calls methods in the Text-Document object to fulfill its responsibilities. The TextDocument *fileDoc* method creates an Index object and then sends a message to the Index object, invoking the *createDocIndex* method. The *createDocIndex* method calls the *createIndex* method in the Index object. The *createIndex* method then invokes the *buildIndexFileHeader* method. Next, the *createIndex* method creates a new *HashEngine* object and sends a message to the *HashEngine* object, invoking the *buildHashBlock* method.

The *buildHashBlock* method of the *HashEngine* object first clears the hash block and then retrieves document records from the text document file using a *DocumentFileStream* object. A *hashDocumentRecord* message is next sent to the hash engine object, which creates a hashed record by calling the *hashTheWord* internal method. The *buildHashBlock* method continues this process until the hash block is full or all of the document records have been processed.

After the hash block is full or all document records in the text document have been processed, the *buildHashBlock* method of the *HashEngine* object sends a message to the *IndexFileStream* object to write the hash block to disk. The *IndexFileStream* object is used for all output to the text document index file.

A data dictionary entry that will be added for the index file is as follows:

File or Database Name: Index file

Composition: hash block word vector size + total block count + total record count + filing characters + junk words + random number table + $_1${hashed block}^{n}

Organization: Blocks are sequential.

Notes: Each block contains a represents up to 512 data records that have been hashed.

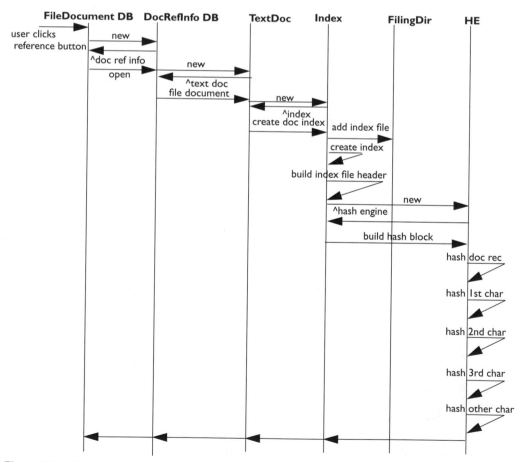

Figure H.4. File Document Event Trace.

An event trace diagram for a file operation is shown in Figure H.4. Like the message hierarchy diagram, the event trace describes a single execution scenario. This scenario includes the filing of document reference information, i.e., author, abstract, and/ keyword information.

The object interaction diagram shown in Figure H.8 shows the flow of control and data at a high level for a filing scenario. When a user selects the OK push-button in the document reference information dialog box object, a *file document* message with path information and document reference information is sent to the *TextDocument* object. File document is the main operation for this scenario. A number of suboperations (1.1 through 1.5) are executed to carry out the *file document* operation. The *TextDocument* object sends a *create text document index* message with path information as a parameter to the *Index* object. The *Index* object sends an *add to index file* message with an index file name as a parameter to the *FilingDirectory* object, followed by a *build hash block* message and

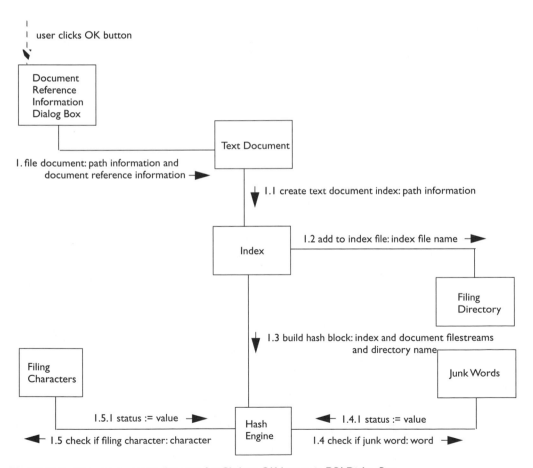

Figure H.5. Object Interaction Diagram for Clicking OK button in DRI Dialog Box.

some parameters to the *HashEngine* object. The OID also shows that the *HashEngine* object sends a *check if junk word* message with a word as a parameter to the *JunkWords* object. Note that the *check if junk word* method returns a value. The result of calling the *check if junk word* method on the *JunkWords* object is the value that we call *status*. The *HashEngine* object also sends a *check if filing character* message to the *FilingCharacters* object, and a value is returned, which we also call *status*.

Search Operation

The *search* operation is also referred to as the *find* operation. The message hierarchy diagram for the *search* operation is shown in Figure H.6. Some of the details have been abstracted out to focus on the essentials and to fit within a single diagram. The following abbreviations are used in this figure:

```
Search_Dialog_Box = SDB
Text_Document = TD
Search_Results_Dialog_Box = SRDB
Document_Reference_Information_Dialog_Box = DRIDB
Search_Engine = SE
```

```
user selects Search item
   new SDB ()
   SDB.ok ()
      new Search Engine
      SE.findDocument()
         new SearchVector
         SV.buildSearchVector ()
            CQ.parseQuery ()
            HE.hashQueryElement ()
         SV.constructVector ()
         SE.checkForDocumentMatches ()
            DO
            SE.calculateDocRecNumbers ()
            SE.verifyMatches ()
            DocumentNameList. put records list ()
            UNTIL all document index files processed
         SE.checkForDRIMatches ()
            parse all queries
               FOR each document reference information object
            ABSQ.checkForAbstractMatch ()
            AUTQ.checkForAuthorMatch ()
            KEYQ.checkForKeywordMatch ()
            SE.checkForLogicalQueryMatch ()
               DocumentNameList.add document name
            ENDFOR
         new SRDB()
         SRDB.view ()
         new ViewDB ()
         clear SRDB from screen
      clear SDB from screen
   display main application window
```

Figure H.6. Search Operation Hierarchy.

A new Search dialog box is created when the user selects the Search item from the Document Retrieval pop-up menu. The user then enters the content, abstract, keyword, and/or author queries with the connecting logical operators. When the user selects the Ok push-button in the Search dialog box, a *SearchEngine* object is created. A *findDocument* message is then sent to the *SearchEngine* object to locate the documents meeting the specified search criteria entered by the user.

The *findDocument* method of the *SearchEngine* object creates a new *SearchVector* object. It then sends a message to the *SearchVector* object to build the actual search vector, invoking the *buildSearchVector* method. The *buildSearchVector* method sends a *parseQuery* message to the *ContentQuery* object to parse the query. Next, a *hashQueryElement* message is sent to the *HashEngine* object to hash the query element. The *buildSearchVector* method now calls the *constructVector* method to create the actual search vector with this hashing information.

Now that the search vector has been built to do a content search, the next thing to do is to read specific records of each document using the search vector, and then to verify the matches. The *findDocument* method of the *SearchEngine* object now invokes the *checkForDocumentMatches* method. The *checkForDocumentMatches* method processes each document index file to see if any matches actually exist within the document(s).

The *checkForDocumentMatches* method sends a *calculateDocRecNumbers* message to the *SearchVector* object to retrieve document record numbers to read. The *checkForDocumentMatches* method next sends a *verifyMatches* message to the *SearchEngine* object to verify that a match exists within these records of the document. This process is repeated for each and every document index file in the system. The *verifyMatches* method removes any record numbers from the document record list for which there is no match. The *checkForDocumentMatches* method checks to see if this list is not empty. If the document record list is not empty, the document record list is associated with the document name in the document name list and the document name remains in the document name list.

Next, the *findDocument* method of the *SearchEngine* object invokes the *checkForDRIMatches* method. This method first parses all queries. Then for each and every *DocumentReferenceInformation* object it sends a *checkForAbstractMatch* message to the *AbstractQuery* object. A *checkForAuthorMatch* message is sent to the *AuthorQuery* element in the same fashion. And finally, a *checkForKeywordMatch* message is also sent to the *KeywordQuery* element in a similar fashion. Lastly, a *checkForLogicalQueryMatch* message is sent to the *SearchEngine* object. A result indicating whether or not a DRI match occurred is returned to the *checkForDRIMatches* method. The *checkForDRIMatches* method now creates a document name list (DNL) if none exists, a document records list if necessary, and then adds the document name to the DNL.

The search operation has now been completed, and it remains to present the results to the user. A Search Results dialog box is created by the *SearchEngine* object and displayed on the screen. The user may now select the Print or the View push-button within the dialog box. The Search Results dialog box is cleared from the screen when the user selects the Done push-button. The Search dialog box still remains on the screen. The user may conduct another search at this point or select the Done push-button and terminate the search process, clearing the Search dialog box from the screen.

An event trace diagram for the search operation is shown in Figure H.7. This search is of the content of the document only, i.e., no search of abstract, author, or keyword information. This

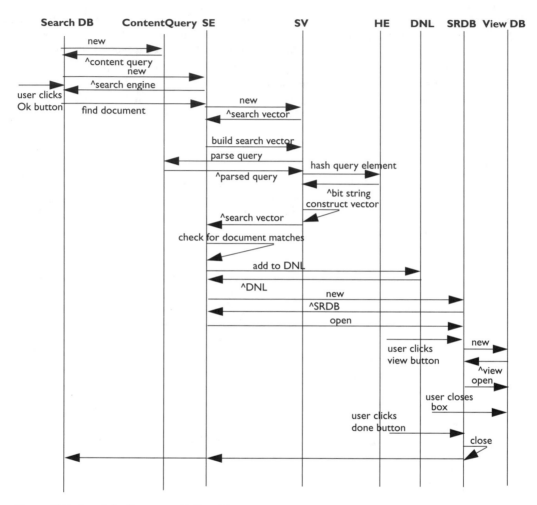

Figure H.7. Search for Document(s) Event Trace.

represents only one possible scenario for the search use case. Some details have been abstracted out due to lack of space in the diagram.

An object interaction diagram for the search operation is shown in Figure H.8. When a user selects the Ok push–button in the search dialog box object, a *find document* message with the user-entered queries is sent to the *SearchEngine* object. Find document is the main operation for this scenario. A number of suboperations (1.1 through 1.11) are executed to carry out the *find document* operation. The reader may trace through the execution of message sending in this diagram using the same technique used for the object interaction diagram for the *file operation*.

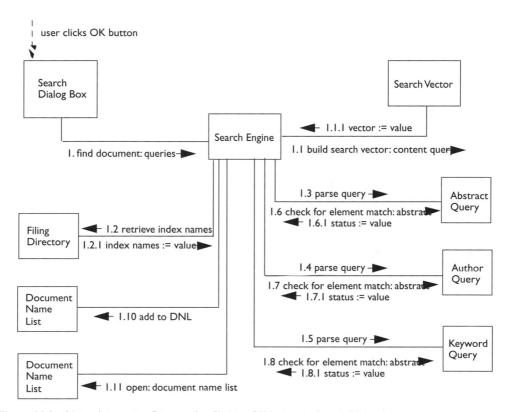

Figure H.8. Object Interaction Diagram for Clicking OK button in Search Dialog Box.

Delete Operation

The message hierarchy diagram for the delete operation is shown in Figure H.9. The following abbreviations are used in this figure:

Delete Dialog Box = DDB
Filing Directory = FD

A new Delete dialog box is created when the user selects the Delete item from the Document Storage pop-up menu. The Delete dialog box event handlers for the file list box and the directories list box retrieve the list of files for the current filing directory and the list of filing directories, respectively. This information is then displayed in the scrolling list boxes of the delete dialog box. When the user selects the OK push-button in the Delete dialog box, the selected index file is deleted from the specified directory. The deletion is accomplished by sending a *deleteIndex* message

```
user selects Delete item
   new DDB ()
      display filing directories
      display filing directory files
      DDB.ok ()
         FD.delete index
   clear DDB from screen
display main application window
```

Figure H.9. Delete Operation Hierarchy.

to the *FilingDirectory* object. The Delete dialog box is then cleared from the screen and the main application window is redisplayed.

Filing Characters Operation

The message hierarchy diagram for the filing character operation is shown in Figure H.10. The following abbreviations are used in this description:

    Filing_Characters = FC
    Filing_Characters_Dialog_Box = FCDB

Note that curly brackets, {}, are used to mark off several alternative blocks of code. Each block of code is separated by an *OR* statement. A specific block of code is executed depending upon the event that is received by the program.

A new Filing Characters dialog box is created when the user selects the Filing Characters item from the Utilities pop-up menu. The Filing Characters dialog box sends the *getIncludedCharacters* and *getDiscardedCharacters* messages to the *FilingCharacter* object. These messages return the included

```
user selects Filing Character item
   new FCDB ()
      FC.getIncludedCharacters ()
      FC.getDiscardedCharacters()
      FCDB.displayCharacters ()
      {FCDB.discard ()
         FC.addToDiscardList ()
   OR
      FCDB.include ()
         FC.addToIncludeList ()}
      DDB.Ok ()
         {FC.setDiscardChars()
   OR
         FC.setIncludeChars()}
   clear FCDB from screen
display main application window
```

Figure H.10. Filing Character Operation Hierarchy.

and discarded filing characters, which are then displayed in black and gray, respectively, in the scrolling list box of the Filing Characters dialog box. The *displayCharacters* method from the Filing Characters dialog box object is invoked to display these characters.

The user may now select a character and then either discard it *or* include it in the filing character set by selecting the Discard *or* Include push-button. The *addToIncludeList* or *addToDiscardList* methods are invoked to carry out these operations. These methods add characters to temporary include/discard lists.

When the user selects the OK push-button in the Filing Characters dialog box, the characters in the temporary include/discard lists are moved to the permanent set of include/discard characters by invoking the *setDiscardChar* and *setIncludeChar* methods. These changes are also written to the filing characters file. The Filing Characters dialog box is then cleared from the screen.

Junk Words Operation

The message hierarchy diagram for the junk words operation is shown in Figure H.11. The following abbreviations are used in this description:

```
Junk_Words = JW
Junk_Words_Dialog_Box = JWDB
```

Note that curly brackets, {}, are used to mark off several alternative blocks of code, in the same manner as in the Filing Characters operation.

A new Junk Words dialog box is created when the user selects the Junk Words item from the Utilities pop-up menu. The Junk Words dialog box sends the *getCurrentJunkWords* and *getDeletedJunkWords* messages to the Junk Words object. These messages return the current and deleted junk words, which are then displayed in black and gray, respectively, in the scrolling list box of the Junk Words dialog box. The *displayWords* method from the Junk Words dialog box object is invoked to display these words.

```
user selects Junk Word item
   new JWDB ()
      JW.getCurrentJunkWords ()
      JW.getDeletedJunkWords()
      JWDB.displayWords ()
      {JWDB.delete ()
         JW.deleteWord ()
   OR
      JWDB.add ()
         JW.addWord ()}
      JWDB.ok ()
         {JW.setDeletedWords()
   OR
         JW.setAddedWords()}
   clear JWDB from screen
display main application window
```

Figure H.11. Junk Words Operation Hierarchy.

The user may now select a word and then either add it *or* delete it in the junk words set by selecting the Add *or* Delete push-button. The *addToCurrentList* or *addToDeleteList* methods are invoked to carry out these operations. These methods add words to temporary add/delete lists. The user may alternatively enter a junk word in the edit box and the word will either be added to or deleted from the junk word set depending upon the option selected by the user.

When the user selects the OK push-button in the Junk Words dialog box, the words in the temporary add/delete lists are moved to the permanent set of added/deleted words by invoking the *setAddedWord* and *setDeleteWord* methods. These changes are also written to the junk words file. The Junk Words dialog box is then cleared from the screen.

Object Representations

Object representations are dependent upon the language and class library that is used during the implementation. The Smalltalk object representations for each electronic filing domain object are as follows:

SearchEngine: The *SearchEngine* class collects the high-level search functions together in one place. An instance of the *SearchEngine* class acts as an agent responsible for carrying out the search algorithm. No existing class in the class library is similar to the *SearchEngine* class. The *SearchEngine* class will be a subclass of *Object* (i.e., self-standing).

HashEngine: The *HashEngine* class collects the indexing functions together in one place. An instance of the *HashEngine* class acts as an agent responsible for carrying out the indexing algorithm. No existing class in the class library is similar to the *HashEngine* class. The *HashEngine* class will be a subclass of *Object*.

DocRefInfo: Document reference information may be entered by a user when filing a document. Document reference information consists of an abstract/description, author(s), and/or keyword(s) associated with the document. There are no classes similar to the *DocRefInfo* class in the class library. The *DocRefInfo* class will be a subclass of *Object*.

SearchVector: A search vector is used during the search of the content of a document(s). A search vector is used to determine the records of the document index that should be read. The document index is then read to determine the data records of the document file to read. Specific records of the document file are then read to determine if there is a match between the content query and the content of a document. The behavior and state information of the SearchVector class is unique to the application. Search Vector will also be a subclass of class *Object*.

TextDocument: The *TextDocument* class represents a document that is filed by the electronic filing program. The *File* class contains the behavior necessary for opening, closing, reading, and writing data from/to a file. However, the operations of the *TextDocument* class are at a higher level of abstraction than the *File* class. The *TextDocument* class will be a subclass of *Object*.

FilingDirectory: A FilingDirectory object represents all of the document index files, keeping track of all of the names of the documents that have been indexed by the program. The *Directory* class contains the behavior necessary to get the directory name. The *File* class provides sequential or random access to a file. Since a *FilingDirectory* represents a collection of files, a *Collection* type of class is more in order. An *OrderedCollection* can be used like a dynamic array, stack, or queue, and allows elements to be dynamically added or removed from the collection. However, an *OrderedCollection* has about 25 instance methods, and most of this behavior is inappropriate for our needs. A more appropriate way of representing a filing directory would be to make *FilingDirectory* a subclass of *Object* and an *OrderedCollection* of file names an attribute of the *FilingDirectory* class. Only meaningful operations should be delegated to the *OrderedCollection* object. Additional behavior beyond that provided by the *OrderedCollection* class will be included in the *FilingDirectory* class.

JunkWords: Junk words are extraneous words, which if found in the content of a document are not indexed and are not retrievable via a search operation using a content query; e.g., junk words are words such as and, the, we, him then, that, from. The junk words in the electronic filing system represent a group or collection of objects (words). These objects or junk words need to be presented to the user in some sort of order. The class library has a *SortedCollection* class that seems appropriate to represent this structure. However, most of the behavior of the *SortedCollection* class is unnecessary for junk words. A more appropriate way of representing junk words would be to make *JunkWords* a subclass of *Object* and a *SortedCollection* of junk words an attribute of the *Junk-Words* class. Only meaningful operations should be delegated to the *SortedCollection* object. Junk words can be added or removed from the collection of junk words, and the collection will still remain in sorted order. Application specific behavior in addition to the *add* and *remove* operations of the *SortedCollection* class will need to be included in the *JunkWords* class.

FilingCharacters: Filing characters are ASCII characters that allow the user to restrict the indexing and retrieval operations to only certain characters. The filing characters in the electronic filing system represent a group or collection of objects (characters). These objects or filing characters need to be presented to the user in some sort of order (i.e., alphabetical). The *SortedCollection* class in the Smalltalk/V class library seems appropriate to represent this structure. However, most of the behavior of the *SortedCollection* class is unnecessary for filing characters. A more appropriate way of representing filing characters would be to make *FilingCharacters* a subclass of *Object* and a *SortedCollection* of filing characters an attribute of the *FilingCharacters* class. Only meaningful operations should be delegated to the *SortedCollection* object. Objects can be added or removed from the collection, and the collection will still remain in sorted order. Application specific behavior in addition to the *add* and *remove* operations of the *SortedCollection* class will need to be included in the *FilingCharacters* class.

DocumentNameList: The electronic filing program presents the user with a list of file names (documents) that satisfy the search request—commonly known as a *search hit list* or *document name list*. So a document name list in the electronic filing system represents a group or collection of objects (document names). The *OrderedCollection* class in the Smalltalk/V class library seems appropriate for this purpose. However, most of the behavior of the *OrderedCollection* class is unnecessary for the *DocumentNameList*. A more appropriate way of representing a document name list would be to make *DocumentNameList* a subclass of *Object* and an *OrderedCollection* of document names an attribute of the *DocumentNameList* class. Only meaningful operations should be delegated to the *OrderedCollection* object. Application specific behavior beyond that provided by the *OrderedCollection* class will need to be included in the *DocumentNameList* class.

DocumentRecordsList: A document records list is a list of record numbers where a word or phrase specified in a search query has been found in the content of a document. A document records list in the electronic filing system represents a group or collection of document record numbers. The *OrderedCollection* class in the Smalltalk/V class library again seems appropriate for this purpose. However, most of the behavior of the *OrderedCollection* class is unnecessary for the *DocumentRecordsList*. A more appropriate way of representing a document records list would be to make *DocumentRecordsList* a subclass of *Object* and an *OrderedCollection* of document records an attribute of the *DocumentRecordsList* class. Only meaningful operations should be delegated to the *OrderedCollection* object. Application specific behavior beyond that provided by the *OrderedCollection* class will need to be included in the *DocumentRecordsList* class.

Index: An index represents an indexed document file, so that an index is a type of file. The *File* class conceptually represents a file and contains the behavior necessary for opening, closing, reading, and writing data from/to a file. However, the operations of the *Index* class are at a higher level of abstraction than the *File* class; i.e., an *Index* object does not do low-level I/O operations. The *Index* class will be a subclass of *Object*.

Query: A query represents words and/or phrases that may be separated by logical operators (AND or OR). A query class is an abstract class for all of the query type classes. It provides some of the behavior common to all query classes, such as parsing the query, getting the query elements, and getting the logical operators. This class will be a subclass of *Object*—no other classes in the Smalltalk/V class library seem appropriate for this purpose.

AuthorQuery: An author query is one or more author names separated by logical operators. *AuthorQuery* is one type of query and is made a subclass of *Query*. *AuthorQuery* also has some unique behavior.

KeywordQuery: A keyword query is one or more keywords separated by logical operators. *KeywordQuery* is one type of query and is made a subclass of *Query*. *KeywordQuery* also has some unique behavior.

ContentQuery: A content query is one or more words or phrases separated by logical operators. *ContentQuery* is one type of query and is made a subclass of *Query*. *ContentQuery* also has some unique behavior.

AbstractQuery: An abstract query is one or more words or phrases separated by logical operators. *AbstractQuery* is one type of query and is made a subclass of *Query*. *AbstractQuery* also has some unique behavior.

The C++ object representations are as follows: Borland C++ with Application Frameworks provides the following class libraries: streamable classes, standard ObjectWindows classes, ObjectWindows miscellaneous components, and container class libraries (one is based on templates and the other is not). These classes do not provide the functionality needed by any of the electronic filing application classes. Therefore, all of the application classes for electronic filing are stand-alone classes in C++. However, many of the application classes will use the streamable classes and the container classes to provide their behavior and representation.

Here is how some electronic filing classes will choose to internally represent their data structures.

JunkWords, FilingCharacters: HashTable, Bag, List, DoubleList, Deque, Queue, and BTree classes are all inappropriate to represent these collections. A *Set* is a collection that allows only one instance of any one object and seems the most suited of the Collection classes to represent these groupings of words and characters.

DocumentNameList: A collection of unique document names is best represented by the *Set* class. The *Set* class provides behavior to add, remove, or retrieve objects in the container.

DocumentRecordsList: Record numbers in the DocumentRecordsList should be unique. The Set class allows only one instance of any particular object in its collection.

Query: A *Query* class is an abstract class for all of the query type classes. It provides some of the behavior common to all query classes.

AuthorQuery, KeywordQuery, ContentQuery, AbstractQuery: All the specialized query classes can inherit behavior from the *Query* class. The words or phrases and the logical operators that form the queries should always be processed on a first-in–first-out basis because the author query is parsed from left to right starting with the first word or phrase and the first logical operator that enter the queue.

Association Designs

The following is a list of all the associations (indicated in *italics*) and the multiplicity (indicated in parentheses) between object classes. All of the listed associations are traversed in the forward direction only (i.e., the direction implied by the name), unless otherwise indicated. We'll select a particular technique for implementing each association depending on how it is used in the application.

SearchEngine *uses* (one or more) Query: Although a *SearchEngine* may use one or more *Query* objects, it can use only one *ContentQuery*, one *AuthorQuery*, one *AbstractQuery*, and one *KeywordQuery* at a time. Attributes are used in the *SearchEngine* object to refer to each one of these types of *Query* objects.

SearchEngine *uses* (zero or more) DocRefInfo: A global name, *DRIs*, will represent a *Set* of *DocRefInfo* objects. *DocRefInfo* objects can then be referenced anywhere in the application. Document reference information objects are used during both filing and searching operations.

TextDocument is *described by* (zero or one) DocRefInfo: An attribute in the *TextDocument* object referring to the *DocRefInfo* object.

SearchEngine *generates* (zero or one) DocumentNameList: An attribute in the *SearchEngine* object referring to the *DocumentNameList* object.

DocumentNameList *identifies* (zero or more) DocumentRecordsList: An attribute in the *DocumentNameList* object is a *Dictionary* type of object. The *Dictionary* object uses index file names as the keys and *DocumentRecordsList* objects as the values.

SearchEngine *produces* (zero or one) SearchVector: An attribute in the *SearchEngine* object referring to the *SearchVector* object.

SearchVector *utilizes* (one or more) Index: An attribute in the *SearchVector* object referring to a *Set* of *Index* objects.

SearchEngine *checks* (one or more) FilingDirectory: A FilingDirectory object will be common to several operations: delete, file, and search. We'll use a global name, *Filing*, to represent a *FilingDirectory* so that universal access can be provided. Also, for now we will restrict the program to have one *FilingDirectory.*

FilingDirectory plus index name yield an Index: The *FilingDirectory* will be used only to maintain the names of index files. Therefore the association between *FilingDirectory* and *Index* classes can be removed. Index objects are created and used only during the filing of a document. *FilingDirectory* has an attribute, which is a *Collection* of index names.

Index *references* (one) TextDocument: An attribute in the *Index* object referring to the *TextDocument* object.

HashEngine *services* (one or more) Index: An attribute in the *HashEngine* object referring to a *Set* of *Index* objects.

HashEngine *skips all* (one) JunkWords: An attribute in the *HashEngine* object referring to the *JunkWords* object.

HashEngine *checks for* (one) FilingCharacters: An attribute in the *HashEngine* object referring to the *FilingCharacters* object.

H.4 PHYSICAL PACKAGING OF THE PROGRAMS

The basic elements in Smalltalk are objects. The Smalltalk/V "image" is all of the objects, including both data and code. No other physical modules are developed in the Smalltalk implementation. The development environment must be stripped from the Smalltalk environment, leaving the basic application and the Smalltalk classes necessary to support that application. Care must be taken in removing object classes that could or will be referenced in the runtime environment.

The C++ program is organized as a set of header files and source files. The header files contain class declarations, types and names of external variables, structure definitions, constants, macros, etc. The class declaration lists the members (i.e., data and methods/operations) of the class. The class implementations are contained in the source files. The class implementation defines the methods for the class. One header file and one source file will be defined for each subsystem in the electronic filing implementation as well as for each class that is not part of a subsystem.

Smalltalk Electronic Filing Application Code

I.1 USER INTERFACE SUBSYSTEM

```
ViewManager subclass: #Efiling
    instanceVariableNames: ''
    classVariableNames: ''
    poolDictionaries:
    'ColorConstants WBConstants '!

!Efiling class methods !

wbCreated
    ^true! !

!Efiling methods !

aboutItem
    "Callback for the menu item titled 'About Electronic Filing'.
    (Generated by WindowBuilder)"
    AboutFiling new open.!

charItem
    "Callback for the menu item titled 'Filing Characters'.
    (Generated by WindowBuilder)"
    FilingCharacterDialog new open.!

contentItem
    "Callback for the menu item titled 'Contents'.
    (Generated by WindowBuilder)"
    MessageBox message: 'Help Not Implemented For This Version of Electronic Filing'!

deleteItem
```

```
   "Callback for the menu item titled 'Delete'.
   (Generated by WindowBuilder)"
   DeleteADocument new open.!

exitItem
   "Callback for the menu item titled 'Exit'.
   (Generated by WindowBuilder)"
   self close.!

fileItem
   "Callback for the menu item titled 'File'.
   (Generated by WindowBuilder)"
   FileADocument new open.!

junkItem
   "Callback for the menu item titled 'Junk Words'.
   (Generated by WindowBuilder)"
   JunkWordsDialog new open.!

open
   "WARNING!! This method was automatically generated by WindowBuilder. Code you
   add here which does not conform to the WindowBuilder API will probably be lost
   the next time you save your layout definition."

   | v |

   self addView: (
   v := self topPaneClass new
      owner: self;
      labelWithoutPrefix:'Electronic Filing';
      noSmalltalkMenuBar;
      viewName: 'mainFiling';
      framingBlock: ( FramingParameters new iDUE: 1088 @ 568; xC; yC;   cRDU: (9 @
         560 rightBottom: 1079 @ 84));
      pStyle: #(sysmenu maximize titlebar sizable minimize);
   yourself
   ).

   v menuWindow
   yourself;
   addMenu: (
      Menu new
         title: 'File';
         owner: self;
         appendItem: 'Exit' selector: #exitItem acceleratorString: ''
   );
   addMenu: (
      Menu new
      title: 'Document Storage';
      owner: self;
      appendItem: 'File...' selector: #fileItem acceleratorString: '';
      appendItem: 'Delete...' selector: #deleteItem acceleratorString: ''
   );
   addMenu: (
      Menu new
      title: 'Document Retrieval';
```

```
      owner: self;
      appendItem: 'Search...' selector: #searchItem acceleratorString: ''
   );
   addMenu: (
      Menu new
      title: 'Utilities';
      owner: self;
      appendItem: 'Filing Characters...' selector: #charItem acceleratorString: '';
      appendItem: 'Junk Words...' selector: #junkItem
   );
   addMenu: (
      Menu new
      title: 'Help';
      owner: self;
      appendItem: 'Contents' selector: #contentItem;
      appendSeparator;
      appendItem: 'About Electronic Filing' selector: #aboutItem
   ).

   self openWindow!

searchItem
   "Callback for the menu item titled 'Search'.
   (Generated by WindowBuilder)"
   SearchForDocument new.! !


WindowDialog subclass: #DeleteADocument
   instanceVariableNames:
   'selectedDirectory selectedFile directoryList pathNameArray '
   classVariableNames: ''
   poolDictionaries:
   'ColorConstants WBConstants '!

!DeleteADocument class methods !

wbCreated
   ^true! !

!DeleteADocument methods !

buildDirectoryList
   "Private - Build an OrderedCollection of
   directory name Strings for all filing directories on the disk. Precede names with
      spaces to indicate directory hierarchy."

   selectedDirectory := Directory new drive: $C; pathName: '\filing'.
   directoryList := OrderedCollection new.
   pathNameArray := OrderedCollection new.
   directoryList add: '\filing'.
   pathNameArray add: '\filing'.!

deleteCancel: aPane
   "Callback for the #clicked event in an unnamed Button (contents is 'Cancel').
   (Generated by WindowBuilder)"
   ((MessageBox confirm: 'Are You Sure?') = true)
```

```
    ifTrue: [self close]!

deleteHelp: aPane
    "Callback for the #clicked event in an unnamed Button (contents is 'Help').
    (Generated by WindowBuilder)"
    MessageBox message: 'Help Not Implemented For This Version of Electronic Filing'!

deleteOk: aPane
    "Callback for the #clicked event in an unnamed Button (contents is 'Ok').
    (Generated by WindowBuilder)"
    | currentPath driFileName newFileName|

DRIs do: [ :aDri | driFileName := aDri getDocumentName.
                   newFileName := driFileName fileName , '.sam'.
                   newFileName = selectedFile
    " if TRUE then delete the DRI."
          ifTrue: [DRIs remove: aDri ifAbsent: [MessageBox message:
             'Tried to remove a nonexistent element from the DRIs']]].

    selectedDirectory isNil
    ifFalse: [selectedFile isNil
      ifFalse: [Filing deleteIndexFile: selectedFile]].
    self close.!

directories: directoryListBox
       "Private - Fill the directoryListBox with the list
       of filing directories."

    directoryList isNil
       ifTrue: [self buildDirectoryList].
    directoryListBox contents: directoryList.!

dirSelect: aPane
    "Callback for the #select event in an unnamed ListBox.
    (Generated by WindowBuilder)"

    | directoryIndex |
    directoryIndex := aPane selection.
    selectedDirectory pathName: (pathNameArray at: directoryIndex).
    self changed: #files:.
    self changed: #displayPath:.
    selectedFile := ' '.
    self changed: #displayFileName:.!

displayFileName: aPane
    "Callback for the #display event in an unnamed EntryField (contents is '').
    (Generated by WindowBuilder)"
    aPane contents: selectedFile.!

displayPath: aPane
    "Callback for the #display event in an unnamed EntryField (contents is '').
    (Generated by WindowBuilder)"
    aPane contents: (selectedDirectory drivePathName).!

files: aPane
    "Callback for the #getContents event in the files ListBox'.
```

```
(Generated by WindowBuilder)"

   "Private - Fill the ListBox with a sorted list of files for the selected
      directory."
| answer sortedFileList |
sortedFileList := SortedCollection
   sortBlock: [ :a :b | (a at: 1) < (b at: 1)].
sortedFileList := SortedCollection sortBlock:
   sortedFileList sortBlock.
answer := SortedCollection new.
selectedDirectory == nil
   ifTrue: [^aPane contents: answer].
sortedFileList addAll: selectedDirectory formatted.
sortedFileList do: [ :each | answer add: (each at: 1)].
aPane contents: answer.!

fileSelect: aPane
   "Callback for the #select event in an unnamed ListBox.
   (Generated by WindowBuilder)"
   selectedFile := aPane selectedItem.
   self changed: #displayFileName:.!

open
   "WARNING!! This method was automatically generated by WindowBuilder. Code you
      add here which does not conform to the WindowBuilder API will probably be
      lost the next time you save your layout definition."

   | v |

   self addView: (
      v := self topPaneClass new
         owner: self;
         labelWithoutPrefix:'Delete A Document';
         noSmalltalkMenuBar;
         viewName: 'mainView';
         framingBlock: ( FramingParameters new iDUE: 805 @ 544; xC; yC; cRDU: (11
            @ 534 rightBottom: 793 @ 48));
         pStyle: #(sysmenu modal titlebar);
         addSubpane: (
            Button new
               owner: self;
               framingBlock: ( FramingParameters new iDUE: 142 @ 60; lDU: 601 r:
                  #left; rDU: 743 r: #left; tDU: 70 r: #top; bDU: 130 r: #top);
               idOK;
               startGroup;
               when: #clicked perform: #deleteOk:;
               contents: 'Ok';
               yourself
         );
         addSubpane: (
            Button new
               owner: self;
               framingBlock: ( FramingParameters new iDUE: 142 @ 60; lDU: 603 r:
                  #left; rDU: 745 r: #left; tDU: 214 r: #top; bDU: 274 r: #top);
               idCancel;
               startGroup;
```

```
        when: #clicked perform: #deleteCancel:;
        contents: 'Cancel';
        yourself
);
addSubpane: (
    Button new
        owner: self;
        framingBlock: ( FramingParameters new iDUE: 142 @ 60; lDU: 603 r:
            #left; rDU: 745 r: #left; tDU: 358 r: #top; bDU: 418 r: #top);
        startGroup;
        when: #clicked perform: #deleteHelp:;
        contents: 'Help';
        yourself
);
addSubpane: (
    StaticText new
        owner: self;
        framingBlock: ( FramingParameters new iDUE: 217 @ 34; lDU: 30 r: #left;
            rDU: 247 r: #left; tDU: 28 r: #top; bDU: 62 r: #top);
        startGroup;
        contents: 'File Name:';
        yourself
);
addSubpane: (
    StaticText new
        owner: self;
        framingBlock: ( FramingParameters new iDUE: 158 @ 32; lDU: 27 r: #left;
            rDU: 185 r: #left; tDU: 108 r: #top; bDU: 140 r: #top);
        startGroup;
        contents: 'Path';
        yourself
);
addSubpane: (
    StaticText new
        owner: self;
        framingBlock: ( FramingParameters new iDUE: 158 @ 32; lDU: 39 r: #left;
            rDU: 197 r: #left; tDU: 218 r: #top; bDU: 250 r: #top);
        startGroup;
        contents: 'Files';
        yourself
);
addSubpane: (
    StaticText new
        owner: self;
        framingBlock: ( FramingParameters new iDUE: 158 @ 32; lDU: 313 r:
            #left; rDU: 471 r: #left; tDU: 218 r: #top; bDU: 250 r: #top);
        startGroup;
        contents: 'Directories';
        yourself
);
addSubpane: (
    ListBox new
        owner: self;
        framingBlock: ( FramingParameters new iDUE: 229 @ 200; lDU: 32 r:
            #left; rDU: 261 r: #left; tDU: 264 r: #top; bDU: 464 r: #top);
        startGroup;
```

```
                 when: #select perform: #fileSelect:;
                 when: #getContents perform: #files:;
                 yourself
            );
         addSubpane: (
            ListBox new
               owner: self;
               framingBlock: ( FramingParameters new iDUE: 229 @ 200; lDU: 309 r:
                  #left; rDU: 537 r: #left; tDU: 262 r: #top; bDU: 462 r: #top);
               startGroup;
               when: #select perform: #dirSelect:;
               when: #getContents perform: #directories:;
               yourself
            );
         addSubpane: (
            EntryField new
               owner: self;
               framingBlock: ( FramingParameters new iDUE: 229 @ 48; lDU: 247 r:
                  #left; rDU: 475 r: #left; tDU: 16 r: #top; bDU: 64 r: #top; indent:
                  3 @ 4);
               startGroup;
               when: #getContents perform: #displayFileName:;
               yourself
            );
         addSubpane: (
            EntryField new
               owner: self;
               framingBlock: ( FramingParameters new iDUE: 398 @ 48; lDU: 149 r:
                  #left; rDU: 546 r: #left; tDU: 100 r: #top; bDU: 148 r: #top; indent:
                  3 @ 4);
               startGroup;
               when: #getContents perform: #displayPath:;
               yourself
            );
      yourself
   ).

   self openWindow! !


WindowDialog subclass: #FileADocument
   instanceVariableNames:
   'selectedDirectory selectedFile directoryList pathNameArray '
   classVariableNames: ''
   poolDictionaries:
   'ColorConstants WBConstants '!

!FileADocument class methods !

wbCreated
   ^true! !

!FileADocument methods !

buildDirectoryList
      "Private - Build an OrderedCollection of directory name Strings for all
```

```
        directories on the disk. Precede names with spaces to indicate directory
        hierarchy."
    | dir subDirectoryList listSize aStream index totalPath backSlash |
    backSlash := '\'.
    selectedDirectory isNil
        ifTrue: [dir := Directory new
        drive: $C;
        pathName: backSlash.
    selectedDirectory := dir].

    selectedFile := ' '.
    subDirectoryList := SortedCollection
        sortBlock: [ :a :b | (a at: 1) < (b at: 1)].
    dir := selectedDirectory.
    subDirectoryList add: (Array with: backSlash with: backSlash).
    dir subdirectories do: [ :subdir |
        subDirectoryList add: subdir].
    listSize := subDirectoryList size.
    directoryList := OrderedCollection new: listSize.
    pathNameArray := OrderedCollection new: listSize.
    aStream := WriteStream on: (String new: 30).
    index := 1.
    subDirectoryList do: [ :subdir |
        totalPath := subdir at: 1.
        aStream reset.
        totalPath= backSlash
            ifFalse: [
                (totalPath occurrencesOf: $\)
                    timesRepeat: [aStream space]].
        aStream nextPutAll: (subdir at: 2).
        index > 1 ifTrue: [
            aStream nextPutAll: '...'].
        directoryList add: aStream contents.
        pathNameArray add: totalPath.
        index := index + 1].!

dirDoubleClicked: aPane
    "Private. Event handler for #doubleClickSelect: event. A directory name was
        double clicked. Get the directories subdirectories, if any."
    | directoryIndex |
    directoryIndex := aPane selection.
    selectedDirectory := Directory new
        drive: $C;
        pathName: (pathNameArray at: directoryIndex).
    self buildDirectoryList.
    self changed: #directories:.
    self changed: #files:.
    self changed: #displayPath:.
    selectedFile := ' '.
    self changed: #displayFileName:.!

directories: directoryListBox
    "Private - Fill the directoryListBox with the list of directories for the
        selected device."
    directoryList isNil
        ifTrue: [self buildDirectoryList].
```

```
    directoryListBox contents: directoryList.!

dirSelect: aPane
    | directoryIndex |
    "Callback for the #select event in an unnamed ListBox.
    (Generated by WindowBuilder)"
    directoryIndex := aPane selection.
    selectedDirectory := Directory new
       drive: $C;
       pathName: (pathNameArray at: directoryIndex).
    self changed: #files:.
    self changed: #displayPath:.
    selectedFile := ' '.
    self changed: #displayFileName:.!

displayFileName: aPane
    "Callback for the #getContents event in the EntryField named 'fileNameEntryField'.
    (Generated by WindowBuilder)"
    aPane contents: selectedFile.!

displayPath: aPane
    "Callback for the #getContents event in the EntryField named 'pathEntryField'.
    (Generated by WindowBuilder)"
    aPane contents: (selectedDirectory drivePathName).!

fileCancel: aPane
    "Callback for the #clicked event in an unnamed Button (contents is 'Cancel').
    (Generated by WindowBuilder)"
    ((MessageBox confirm: 'Are You Sure?')= true)
       ifTrue: [self close]!

fileHelp: aPane
    "Callback for the #clicked event in an unnamed Button (contents is 'Help').
    (Generated by WindowBuilder)"
    MessageBox message: 'Help Not Implemented For This Version of Electronic Filing'!

fileOk: aPane
    | document |
    "Callback for the #clicked event in an unnamed Button (contents is 'Ok').
    (Generated by WindowBuilder)"

    "Create the TextDocument object and file the document. "
    document := TextDocument new.
    document fileDoc: selectedFile with: selectedDirectory.
    self close.!

fileRefInfo: aPane
    | reference |
    "Callback for the #clicked event in an unnamed Button (contents is 'Reference
       Information').
    (Generated by WindowBuilder)"

    "Pass the document name that is being filed to the DocRefInfo dialog box object.
       Then open the dialog box."
    reference := DocRefInfoDialog new.
    reference setDocName: selectedFile withDir: selectedDirectory; open.
```

```
    self close.!

files: aPane
    "Callback for the #getContents event in the ListBox named 'fileListBox'.
    (Generated by WindowBuilder)"
        "Private - Fill the ListBox with a sorted list of files for the selected
            directory."
    | answer sortedFileList |
    sortedFileList := SortedCollection
        sortBlock: [ :a :b | (a at: 1) < (b at: 1)].
    sortedFileList := SortedCollection sortBlock:
        sortedFileList sortBlock.
    answer := SortedCollection new.
    selectedDirectory == nil
        ifTrue: [^aPane contents: answer].
    sortedFileList addAll: selectedDirectory formatted.
    sortedFileList do: [ :each | answer add: (each at: 1)].
    aPane contents: answer.!

fileSelect: aPane
    "Callback for the #select event in an unnamed ListBox.
    (Generated by WindowBuilder)"
    selectedFile := aPane selectedItem.
    self changed: #displayFileName:.!

open
    "WARNING!! This method was automatically generated by WindowBuilder. Code you
        add here which does not conform to the WindowBuilder API will probably be
        lost the next time you save your layout definition."

    | v |

    self addView: (
        v := self topPaneClass new
            owner: self;
            labelWithoutPrefix:'File A Document';
            noSmalltalkMenuBar;
            viewName: 'fileDocumentDialog';
            framingBlock: ( FramingParameters new iDUE: 919 @ 536; xC; yC; cRDU: (11
                @ 526 rightBottom: 907 @ 48));
            pStyle: #(sysmenu modal titlebar);
            addSubpane: (
                Button new
                    owner: self;
                    framingBlock: ( FramingParameters new iDUE: 142 @ 60; lDU: 722 r:
                        #left; rDU: 864 r: #left; tDU: 72 r: #top; bDU: 132 r: #top);
                    paneName: 'fileOkButton';
                    idOK;
                    startGroup;
                    when: #clicked perform: #fileOk:;
                    contents: 'Ok';
                    yourself
            );
            addSubpane: (
                Button new
                    owner: self;
```

```
        framingBlock: ( FramingParameters new iDUE: 142 @ 60; lDU: 718 r:
           #left; rDU: 859 r: #left; tDU: 172 r: #top; bDU: 232 r: #top);
        paneName: 'fileCancelButton';
        idCancel;
        startGroup;
        when: #clicked perform: #fileCancel:;
        contents: 'Cancel';
        yourself
);
addSubpane: (
   Button new
      owner: self;
      framingBlock: ( FramingParameters new iDUE: 142 @ 60; lDU: 725 r:
         #left; rDU: 866 r: #left; tDU: 274 r: #top; bDU: 334 r: #top);
      paneName: 'fileHelpButton';
      startGroup;
      when: #clicked perform: #fileHelp:;
      contents: 'Help';
      yourself
);
addSubpane: (
   Button new
      owner: self;
      framingBlock: ( FramingParameters new iDUE: 398 @ 62; lDU: 473 r:
         #left; rDU: 871 r: #left; tDU: 390 r: #top; bDU: 452 r: #top);
      paneName: 'fileRefInfoButton';
      startGroup;
      when: #clicked perform: #fileRefInfo:;
      contents: 'Reference Information';
      yourself
);
addSubpane: (
   ListBox new
      owner: self;
      framingBlock: ( FramingParameters new iDUE: 263 @ 202; lDU: 23 r:
         #left; rDU: 286 r: #left; tDU: 170 r: #top; bDU: 372 r: #top);
      paneName: 'fileListBox';
      startGroup;
      when: #getContents perform: #files:;
      when: #select perform: #fileSelect:;
      yourself
);
addSubpane: (
   ListBox new
      owner: self;
      framingBlock: ( FramingParameters new iDUE: 263 @ 200; lDU: 354 r:
         #left; rDU: 617 r: #left; tDU: 170 r: #top; bDU: 370 r: #top);
      paneName: 'directoryListBox';
      startGroup;
      when: #getContents perform: #directories:;
      when: #select perform: #dirSelect:;
      when: #doubleClickSelect perform: #dirDoubleClicked:;
      yourself
);
addSubpane: (
   StaticText new
```

```
            owner: self;
            framingBlock: ( FramingParameters new iDUE: 158 @ 32; lDU: 57 r: #left;
               rDU: 215 r: #left; tDU: 130 r: #top; bDU: 162 r: #top);
            startGroup;
            contents: 'Files';
            yourself
     );
     addSubpane: (
        StaticText new
            owner: self;
            framingBlock: ( FramingParameters new iDUE: 158 @ 32; lDU: 377 r:
               #left; rDU: 535 r: #left; tDU: 130 r: #top; bDU: 162 r: #top);
            startGroup;
            contents: 'Directories';
            yourself
     );
     addSubpane: (
        EntryField new
            owner: self;
            framingBlock: ( FramingParameters new iDUE: 416 @ 48; lDU: 210 r:
               #left; rDU: 626 r: #left; tDU: 70 r: #top; bDU: 118 r: #top; indent:
               3 @ 4);
            paneName: 'pathEntryField';
            startGroup;
            when: #getContents perform: #displayPath:;
            yourself
     );
     addSubpane: (
        EntryField new
            owner: self;
            framingBlock: ( FramingParameters new iDUE: 414 @ 48; lDU: 210 r:
               #left; rDU: 624 r: #left; tDU: 10 r: #top; bDU: 58 r: #top; indent:
               3 @ 4);
            paneName: 'fileNameEntryField';
            startGroup;
            when: #getContents perform: #displayFileName:;
            yourself
     );
     addSubpane: (
        StaticText new
            owner: self;
            framingBlock: ( FramingParameters new iDUE: 158 @ 32; lDU: 27 r: #left;
               rDU: 185 r: #left; tDU: 16 r: #top; bDU: 48 r: #top);
            startGroup;
            contents: 'File Name';
            yourself
     );
     addSubpane: (
        StaticText new
            owner: self;
            framingBlock: ( FramingParameters new iDUE: 158 @ 32; lDU: 34 r: #left;
               rDU: 192 r: #left; tDU: 78 r: #top; bDU: 110 r: #top);
            startGroup;
            contents: 'Path';
            yourself
     );
```

```
    yourself
  ).

  self openWindow! !


WindowDialog subclass: #FilingCharacterDialog
  instanceVariableNames:
    'filingCharactersObject selectedFilingChar '
  classVariableNames: ''
  poolDictionaries:
    'ColorConstants WBConstants ' !

!FilingCharacterDialog class methods !

wbCreated

  ^true! !

!FilingCharacterDialog methods !

filingCharCancel: aPane
  "Callback for the #clicked event in an unnamed Button (contents is 'Cancel').
  (Generated by WindowBuilder)"
  ((MessageBox confirm: 'Are You Sure?') = true)
    ifTrue: [self close]!

filingCharDiscard: aPane
  "Callback for the #clicked event in an unnamed Button (contents is 'Discard').
  (Generated by WindowBuilder)"
  selectedFilingChar isNil
    ifFalse: [filingCharactersObject deleteFilingChar: selectedFilingChar.
            selectedFilingChar := nil].
  self changed: #getFilingCharacters:.
  self changed: #getEnteredFilingCharacter:.!

filingCharInclude: aPane
  "Callback for the #clicked event in an unnamed Button (contents is 'Include').
  (Generated by WindowBuilder)"
  self changed: #getEnteredFilingCharacter:.
  filingCharactersObject addFilingChar: selectedFilingChar.
  self changed: #getFilingCharacters:.!

filingCharOk: aPane
  "Callback for the #clicked event in an unnamed Button (contents is 'Ok').
  (Generated by WindowBuilder)"
  filingCharactersObject saveFilingCharacters.
  self close.!

getEnteredFilingCharacter: aPane
    "Private. Get the filing character entered by the user."
  selectedFilingChar := aPane contents.!

getFilingCharacters: aPane
  "Private. Callback for the #getContents event in an unnamed ListBox. Display
    the FilingCharacters in the FilingCharacters ListBox in a sorted fashion."
```

```
    aPane contents: (filingCharactersObject getFilingChars).!

open
    "WARNING!! This method was automatically generated by WindowBuilder. Code you
       add here which does not conform to the WindowBuilder API will probably be
       lost the next time you save your layout definition."

    | v |

    self addView: (
       v := self topPaneClass new
          owner: self;
          labelWithoutPrefix:'Filing Character Set';
          noSmalltalkMenuBar;
          viewName: 'mainView';
          framingBlock: ( FramingParameters new iDUE: 677 @ 434; xC; yC; cRDU: (11
             @ 424 rightBottom: 665 @ 48));
          pStyle: #(sysmenu modal titlebar);
          addSubpane: (
             Button new
                owner: self;
                framingBlock: ( FramingParameters new iDUE: 142 @ 60; lDU: 299 r:
                   #left; rDU: 441 r: #left; tDU: 140 r: #top; bDU: 200 r: #top);
                startGroup;
                when: #clicked perform: #filingCharDiscard:;
                contents: 'Discard';
                yourself
          );
          addSubpane: (
             Button new
                owner: self;
                framingBlock: ( FramingParameters new iDUE: 142 @ 60; lDU: 485 r:
                   #left; rDU: 626 r: #left; tDU: 140 r: #top; bDU: 200 r: #top);
                idOK;
                startGroup;
                when: #clicked perform: #filingCharOk:;
                contents: 'Ok';
                yourself
          );
          addSubpane: (
             Button new
                owner: self;
                framingBlock: ( FramingParameters new iDUE: 142 @ 60; lDU: 299 r:
                   #left; rDU: 441 r: #left; tDU: 262 r: #top; bDU: 322 r: #top);
                startGroup;
                when: #clicked perform: #filingCharInclude:;
                contents: 'Include';
                yourself
          );
          addSubpane: (
             Button new
                owner: self;
                framingBlock: ( FramingParameters new iDUE: 142 @ 60; lDU: 485 r:
                   #left; rDU: 626 r: #left; tDU: 262 r: #top; bDU: 322 r: #top);
                idCancel;
                startGroup;
```

```
                when: #clicked perform: #filingCharCancel:;
                contents: 'Cancel';
                yourself
        );
        addSubpane: (
            StaticText new
                owner: self;
                framingBlock: ( FramingParameters new iDUE: 158 @ 66; lDU: 23 r: #left;
                    rDU: 181 r: #left; tDU: 28 r: #top; bDU: 94 r: #top);
                startGroup;
                contents: 'Filing Characters';
                yourself
        );
        addSubpane: (
            ListBox new
                owner: self;
                framingBlock: ( FramingParameters new iDUE: 229 @ 246; lDU: 21 r:
                    #left; rDU: 249 r: #left; tDU: 112 r: #top; bDU: 358 r: #top);
                startGroup;
                when: #getContents perform: #getFilingCharacters:;
                when: #select perform: #selectFilingChar:;
                yourself
        );
        addSubpane: (
            StaticText new
                owner: self;
                framingBlock: ( FramingParameters new iDUE: 158 @ 32; lDU: 281 r:
                    #left; rDU: 439 r: #left; tDU: 32 r: #top; bDU: 64 r: #top);
                startGroup;
                contents: 'Character';
                yourself
        );
        addSubpane: (
            EntryField new
                owner: self;
                framingBlock: ( FramingParameters new iDUE: 133 @ 48; lDU: 473 r:
                    #left; rDU: 606 r: #left; tDU: 26 r: #top; bDU: 74 r: #top; indent:
                    3 @ 4);
                paneName: 'filingCharacterEntryField';
                startGroup;
                when: #getContents perform: #getEnteredFilingCharacter:;
                yourself
        );
    yourself
).
filingCharactersObject := FilingCharacters new.
self openWindow!

selectFilingChar: aPane
    "Callback for the #select event in an unnamed ListBox.
    (Generated by WindowBuilder)"
    selectedFilingChar := aPane selectedItem.! !


WindowDialog subclass: #JunkWordsDialog
    instanceVariableNames:
```

```
      'selectedJunkWord junkWords junkWordsObject '
   classVariableNames: ''
   poolDictionaries:
      'ColorConstants WBConstants '!

!JunkWordsDialog class methods !

wbCreated
   ^true! !

!JunkWordsDialog methods !

getEnteredJunkWord: aPane
   "Private. Callback for the #getContents event in an unnamed EntryField.
     Display the selectedJunkWord in the EntryField.
   (Generated by WindowBuilder)"
      "Perform this method when a word has been entered in the EntryField. Get the
         junk word entered in the EntryField. The user may then add this word to
         the junk word set."
   aPane contents: selectedJunkWord.!

getJunkWords: junkWordsListBox
   "Private. Callback for the #getContents event in an unnamed ListBox. Display
     the JunkWords in the JunkWords ListBox in a sorted fashion."
   junkWordsListBox contents: (junkWordsObject getJunkWords).!

junkWordAdd: aPane
   "Callback for the #clicked event in an unnamed Button (contents is 'Add').
   (Generated by WindowBuilder) Add the word to the current JunkWords set."
   self changed: #getEnteredJunkWord:.
   junkWordsObject addJunkWord: selectedJunkWord.
   selectedJunkWord := ''.
   self changed: #getJunkWords:.
   self changed: #getEnteredJunkWord:.!

junkWordCancel: aPane
   "Callback for the #clicked event in an unnamed Button (contents is 'Cancel').
   (Generated by WindowBuilder)"
   ((MessageBox confirm: 'Are You Sure?')= true)
      ifTrue: [self close]!

junkWordDelete: aPane
   "Callback for the #clicked event in an unnamed Button (contents is 'Delete').
   (Generated by WindowBuilder) Change the ListBox entries and the entry in the
      EntryField."
   selectedJunkWord isNil
      ifFalse: [junkWordsObject deleteJunkWord: selectedJunkWord.
               selectedJunkWord := nil].
   self changed: #getJunkWords:.
   self changed: #getEnteredJunkWord:.!

junkWordEntered: aPane
   "Callback for the #textChanged event in an unnamed EntryField .
   (Generated by WindowBuilder) This callback is executed if a user enters a carriage
     return in the EntryField. The Ok button is then automatically executed."
   selectedJunkWord := aPane contents.!
```

```
junkWordOk: aPane
   "Callback for the #clicked event in an unnamed Button (contents is 'Ok').
   (Generated by WindowBuilder) All of the JunkWords changes should now be committed
      to the JunkWord file."
   junkWordsObject saveJunkWords.
   self close.!

open
   "WARNING!! This method was automatically generated by WindowBuilder. Code you
      add here which does not conform to the WindowBuilder API will probably be
      lost the next time you save your layout definition."

   | v |

   self addView: (
      v := self topPaneClass new
         owner: self;
         labelWithoutPrefix:'Junk Words';
         noSmalltalkMenuBar;
         viewName: 'mainView';
         framingBlock: ( FramingParameters new iDUE: 718 @ 376; xC; yC; cRDU: (11
            @ 366 rightBottom: 706 @ 48));
         pStyle: #(sysmenu modal titlebar);
         addSubpane: (
            Button new
               owner: self;
               framingBlock: ( FramingParameters new iDUE: 142 @ 60; lDU: 322 r:
                  #left; rDU: 464 r: #left; tDU: 128 r: #top; bDU: 188 r: #top);
               startGroup;
               when: #clicked perform: #junkWordAdd:;
               contents: 'Add';
               yourself
         );
         addSubpane: (
            Button new
               owner: self;
               framingBlock: ( FramingParameters new iDUE: 142 @ 60; lDU: 512 r:
                  #left; rDU: 654 r: #left; tDU: 128 r: #top; bDU: 188 r: #top);
               startGroup;
               when: #clicked perform: #junkWordDelete:;
               contents: 'Delete';
               yourself
         );
         addSubpane: (
            Button new
               owner: self;
               framingBlock: ( FramingParameters new iDUE: 142 @ 60; lDU: 322 r:
                  #left; rDU: 464 r: #left; tDU: 242 r: #top; bDU: 302 r: #top);
               idOK;
               startGroup;
               when: #clicked perform: #junkWordOk:;
               contents: 'Ok';
               yourself
         );
         addSubpane: (
            Button new
```

```
            owner: self;
            framingBlock: ( FramingParameters new iDUE: 142 @ 60; lDU: 512 r:
               #left; rDU: 654 r: #left; tDU: 242 r: #top; bDU: 302 r: #top);
            idCancel;
            startGroup;
            when: #clicked perform: #junkWordCancel:;
            contents: 'Cancel';
            yourself
        );
        addSubpane: (
          ListBox new
            owner: self;
            framingBlock: ( FramingParameters new iDUE: 229 @ 200; lDU: 23 r:
               #left; rDU: 251 r: #left; tDU: 106 r: #top; bDU: 306 r: #top);
            startGroup;
            when: #getContents perform: #getJunkWords:;
            when: #select perform: #selectJunkWord:;
            yourself
        );
        addSubpane: (
          StaticText new
            owner: self;
            framingBlock: ( FramingParameters new iDUE: 181 @ 32; lDU: 23 r: #left;
               rDU: 203 r: #left; tDU: 60 r: #top; bDU: 92 r: #top);
            startGroup;
            contents: 'Junk Words';
            yourself
        );
        addSubpane: (
          StaticText new
            owner: self;
            framingBlock: ( FramingParameters new iDUE: 181 @ 32; lDU: 233 r:
               #left; rDU: 414 r: #left; tDU: 24 r: #top; bDU: 56 r: #top);
            startGroup;
            contents: 'Junk Word:';
            yourself
        );
        addSubpane: (
          EntryField new
            owner: self;
            framingBlock: ( FramingParameters new iDUE: 215 @ 48; lDU: 430 r:
               #left; rDU: 645 r: #left; tDU: 20 r: #top; bDU: 68 r: #top; indent:
               3 @ 4);
            startGroup;
            when: #getContents perform: #getEnteredJunkWord:;
            when: #textChanged perform: #junkWordEntered:;
            yourself
        );
      yourself
    ).
    junkWordsObject := JunkWords new.
    self openWindow!

selectJunkWord: aPane
    "Callback for the #select event in an unnamed ListBox.
    (Generated by WindowBuilder) When a user selects a JunkWord from the list of
```

```
    JunkWords, the selected JunkWord should be displayed in the EntryField."
    selectedJunkWord := aPane selectedItem.
    self changed: #getEnteredJunkWord:.! !


WindowDialog subclass: #SearchForDocument
    instanceVariableNames:
        'contentQuery abstractQuery keywordQuery authorQuery contentToAbstract-
        Operator keywordToAuthorOperator abstractToKeywordOperator '
    classVariableNames: ''
    poolDictionaries:
        'ColorConstants WBConstants '!

!SearchForDocument class methods !

new
     "Answer a new instance of the receiver."
    ^super new initialize open!

wbCreated
    ^true! !

!SearchForDocument methods !

abstractToKeywordAnd: aPane
    "Callback for the #clicked event in an unnamed RadioButton (contents is 'AND').
    (Generated by WindowBuilder)"

    "Get the current button state and then set the query operator."
    aPane selection
        ifTrue: [abstractToKeywordOperator := 'AND']
        ifFalse: [abstractToKeywordOperator := 'OR'].!

abstractToKeywordOr: aPane
    "Callback for the #clicked event in an unnamed RadioButton (contents is 'OR').
    (Generated by WindowBuilder)"

    "Get the current button state and then set the query operator."
    aPane selection
        ifTrue: [abstractToKeywordOperator := 'OR']
        ifFalse: [abstractToKeywordOperator := 'AND'].!

contentToAbstractAnd: aPane
    "Callback for the #clicked event in an unnamed RadioButton (contents is 'AND').
    (Generated by WindowBuilder)"
    "Get the current button state and then set the query operator."
    aPane selection
        ifTrue: [contentToAbstractOperator := 'AND']
        ifFalse: [contentToAbstractOperator := 'OR'].!

contentToAbstractOr: aPane
    "Callback for the #clicked event in an unnamed RadioButton (contents is 'OR').
    (Generated by WindowBuilder)"

    "Get the current button state and then set the query operator."
    aPane selection
```

```
        ifTrue: [contentToAbstractOperator := 'OR']
        ifFalse: [contentToAbstractOperator := 'AND'].!

getAbstractQuery: aPane
    "Callback for the #textChanged event in an unnamed EntryField.
    (Generated by WindowBuilder)"
    abstractQuery := aPane contents.!

getAuthorQuery: aPane
    "Callback for the #textChanged event in an unnamed EntryField.
    (Generated by WindowBuilder)"
    authorQuery := aPane contents.!

getContentQuery: aPane
    "Callback for the #textChanged event in an unnamed EntryField.
    (Generated by WindowBuilder)"
    contentQuery := aPane contents.!

getKeywordQuery: aPane
    "Callback for the #textChanged event in an unnamed EntryField.
    (Generated by WindowBuilder)"
    keywordQuery := aPane contents.!

initialize
        "Set the logical operators linking each query to be equal to AND."
    super initialize.
    keywordToAuthorOperator := 'AND'.
    contentToAbstractOperator := 'AND'.
    abstractToKeywordOperator := 'AND'.!

keywordToAuthorAnd: aPane
    "Callback for the #clicked event in an unnamed RadioButton (contents is 'AND').
    (Generated by WindowBuilder)"
    "Get the current button state and then set the query operator."
    aPane selection
        ifTrue: [keywordToAuthorOperator := 'AND']
        ifFalse: [keywordToAuthorOperator := 'OR'].!

keywordToAuthorOr: aPane
    "Callback for the #clicked event in an unnamed RadioButton (contents is 'OR').
    (Generated by WindowBuilder)"
    "Get the current button state and then set the query operator."
    aPane selection
        ifTrue: [keywordToAuthorOperator := 'OR']
        ifFalse: [keywordToAuthorOperator := 'AND'].!

open
    "WARNING!! This method was automatically generated by WindowBuilder. Code you
        add here which does not conform to the WindowBuilder API will probably be
        lost the next time you save your layout definition."

    | v |

    self addView: (
      v := self topPaneClass new
        owner: self;
```

```
labelWithoutPrefix:'Search For A Document(s)';
noSmalltalkMenuBar;
viewName: 'searchForDocumentMenu';
framingBlock: ( FramingParameters new iDUE: 709 @ 560; xC; yC; cRDU: (11
    @ 550 rightBottom: 697 @ 48));
pStyle: #(sysmenu modal titlebar);
addSubpane: (
  Button new
     owner: self;
     framingBlock: ( FramingParameters new iDUE: 142 @ 60; lDU: 279 r:
        #left; rDU: 421 r: #left; tDU: 424 r: #top; bDU: 484 r: #top);
     paneName: 'cancelPushButton';
     idCancel;
     startGroup;
     when: #clicked perform: #searchCancel:;
     contents: 'Cancel';
     yourself
);
addSubpane: (
  Button new
     owner: self;
     framingBlock: ( FramingParameters new iDUE: 142 @ 60; lDU: 494 r:
        #left; rDU: 635 r: #left; tDU: 424 r: #top; bDU: 484 r: #top);
     paneName: 'donePushButton';
     startGroup;
     when: #clicked perform: #searchDone:;
     contents: 'Done';
     yourself
);
addSubpane: (
  StaticText new
     owner: self;
     framingBlock: ( FramingParameters new iDUE: 233 @ 36; lDU: 69 r: #left;
        rDU: 302 r: #left; tDU: 0 r: #top; bDU: 36 r: #top);
     startGroup;
     contents: 'Content Query:';
     yourself
);
addSubpane: (
  StaticText new
     owner: self;
     framingBlock: ( FramingParameters new iDUE: 258 @ 32; lDU: 69 r: #left;
        rDU: 327 r: #left; tDU: 100 r: #top; bDU: 132 r: #top);
     startGroup;
     contents: 'Abstract Query:';
     yourself
);
addSubpane: (
  StaticText new
     owner: self;
     framingBlock: ( FramingParameters new iDUE: 263 @ 34; lDU: 73 r: #left;
        rDU: 336 r: #left; tDU: 196 r: #top; bDU: 230 r: #top);
     startGroup;
     contents: 'Keyword Query:';
     yourself
);
```

```
addSubpane: (
   StaticText new
      owner: self;
      framingBlock: ( FramingParameters new iDUE: 249 @ 34; lDU: 71 r: #left;
         rDU: 320 r: #left; tDU: 294 r: #top; bDU: 328 r: #top);
      startGroup;
      contents: 'Author Query:';
      yourself
);
addSubpane: (
   EntryField new
      owner: self;
      framingBlock: ( FramingParameters new iDUE: 555 @ 48; lDU: 69 r: #left;
         rDU: 624 r: #left; tDU: 40 r: #top; bDU: 88 r: #top; indent: 3 @ 4);
      paneName: 'contentEntryField';
      startGroup;
      tabStop;
      when: #textChanged perform: #getContentQuery:;
      yourself
);
addSubpane: (
   RadioButton new
      owner: self;
      framingBlock: ( FramingParameters new iDUE: 114 @ 44; lDU: 391 r:
         #left; rDU: 505 r: #left; tDU: 98 r: #top; bDU: 142 r: #top);
      paneName: 'contentToAbstractAnd';
      startGroup;
      tabStop;
      when: #clicked perform: #contentToAbstractAnd:;
      when: #getContents perform: #setContentToAbstractAnd:;
      contents: 'AND';
      yourself
);
addSubpane: (
   RadioButton new
      owner: self;
      framingBlock: ( FramingParameters new iDUE: 101 @ 42; lDU: 514 r:
         #left; rDU: 615 r: #left; tDU: 100 r: #top; bDU: 142 r: #top);
      paneName: 'contentToAbstractOr';
      when: #clicked perform: #contentToAbstractOr:;
      when: #getContents perform: #setContentToAbstractOr:;
      contents: 'OR';
      yourself
);
addSubpane: (
   EntryField new
      owner: self;
      framingBlock: ( FramingParameters new iDUE: 555 @ 48; lDU: 69 r: #left;
         rDU: 624 r: #left; tDU: 140 r: #top; bDU: 188 r: #top; indent: 3 @ 4);
      paneName: 'abstractEntryField';
      startGroup;
      tabStop;
      when: #textChanged perform: #getAbstractQuery:;
      yourself
);
addSubpane: (
```

```
        RadioButton new
          owner: self;
          framingBlock: ( FramingParameters new iDUE: 126 @ 42; lDU: 391 r:
            #left; rDU: 517 r: #left; tDU: 196 r: #top; bDU: 238 r: #top);
          paneName: 'abstractToKeywordAnd';
          startGroup;
          tabStop;
          when: #clicked perform: #abstractToKeywordAnd:;
          when: #getContents perform: #setAbstractToKeywordAnd:;
          contents: 'AND';
          yourself
    );
    addSubpane: (
        RadioButton new
          owner: self;
          framingBlock: ( FramingParameters new iDUE: 105 @ 40; lDU: 514 r:
            #left; rDU: 619 r: #left; tDU: 196 r: #top; bDU: 236 r: #top);
          paneName: 'abstractToKeywordOr';
          when: #clicked perform: #abstractToKeywordOr:;
          when: #getContents perform: #setAbstractToKeywordOr:;
          contents: 'OR';
          yourself
    );
    addSubpane: (
        EntryField new
          owner: self;
          framingBlock: ( FramingParameters new iDUE: 560 @ 48; lDU: 69 r: #left;
            rDU: 629 r: #left; tDU: 240 r: #top; bDU: 288 r: #top; indent: 3 @ 4);
          paneName: 'keywordEntryField';
          startGroup;
          tabStop;
          when: #textChanged perform: #getKeywordQuery:;
          yourself
    );
    addSubpane: (
        RadioButton new
          owner: self;
          framingBlock: ( FramingParameters new iDUE: 112 @ 42; lDU: 391 r:
            #left; rDU: 503 r: #left; tDU: 290 r: #top; bDU: 332 r: #top);
          paneName: 'keywordToAuthorAnd';
          startGroup;
          tabStop;
          when: #clicked perform: #keywordToAuthorAnd:;
          when: #getContents perform: #setKeywordToAuthorAnd:;
          contents: 'AND';
          yourself
    );
    addSubpane: (
        RadioButton new
          owner: self;
          framingBlock: ( FramingParameters new iDUE: 98 @ 38; lDU: 514 r: #left;
            rDU: 613 r: #left; tDU: 292 r: #top; bDU: 330 r: #top);
          paneName: 'keywordToAuthorOr';
          when: #clicked perform: #keywordToAuthorOr:;
          when: #getContents perform: #setKeywordToAuthorOr:;
          contents: 'OR';
```

```
                    yourself
            );
            addSubpane: (
                EntryField new
                    owner: self;
                    framingBlock: ( FramingParameters new iDUE: 571 @ 48; lDU: 66 r: #left;
                        rDU: 638 r: #left; tDU: 336 r: #top; bDU: 384 r: #top; indent: 3 @ 4);
                    paneName: 'authorEntryField';
                    startGroup;
                    tabStop;
                    when: #textChanged perform: #getAuthorQuery:;
                    yourself
            );
            addSubpane: (
                Button new
                    owner: self;
                    framingBlock: ( FramingParameters new iDUE: 142 @ 60; lDU: 64 r: #left;
                        rDU: 206 r: #left; tDU: 424 r: #top; bDU: 484 r: #top);
                    paneName: 'okPushButton';
                    idOK;
                    startGroup;
                    tabStop;
                    when: #clicked perform: #searchOk:;
                    contents: 'Ok';
                    yourself
            );
        yourself
    ).

    self openWindow!

searchCancel: aPane
    "Callback for the #clicked event in an unnamed Button (contents is 'Cancel').
    (Generated by WindowBuilder)"
    ((MessageBox confirm: 'Are You Sure?')= true)
        ifTrue: [self close]!

searchDone: aPane
    "Callback for the #clicked event in an unnamed Button (contents is 'Done').
    (Generated by WindowBuilder)"
    self close.!

searchOk: aPane
    "Callback for the #clicked event in an unnamed Button (contents is 'Ok').
    (Generated by WindowBuilder)"
| keywordQueryObject abstractQueryObject authorQueryObject contentQuerySize
    contentQueryObject searchEngine keywordQuerySize abstractQuerySize
        authorQuerySize |

    "Create query objects for each query type."
    abstractQueryObject := AbstractQuery new.
    abstractQueryObject setAbstractQuery: abstractQuery.
    abstractQueryObject setContentToAbstractOperator: contentToAbstractOperator.

    keywordQueryObject := KeywordQuery new.
    keywordQueryObject setKeywordQuery: keywordQuery.
```

```
    keywordQueryObject setAbstractToKeywordOperator: abstractToKeywordOperator.

    authorQueryObject := AuthorQuery new.
    authorQueryObject setAuthorQuery: authorQuery.
    authorQueryObject setKeywordToAuthorOperator: keywordToAuthorOperator.

    contentQueryObject := ContentQuery new.
    contentQueryObject setContentQuery: contentQuery.
    FalseHits := 0.

    keywordQuerySize := keywordQuery size.
    abstractQuerySize := abstractQuery size.
    authorQuerySize := authorQuery size.
    contentQuerySize := contentQuery size.

    searchEngine := SearchEngine new.

    ((contentQuerySize = 0) & ((keywordQuerySize = 0) & (authorQuerySize = 0) &
      (abstractQuerySize = 0)))
      ifTrue: [MessageBox message: 'A Query Must Be Specified In Order To Perform
        A Search']
      ifFalse: [

    ((contentQuerySize > 0) & ((keywordQuerySize > 0) | (authorQuerySize > 0) |
      (abstractQuerySize > 0)))
      "Search both document content and document reference information."
      ifTrue: [searchEngine findDocument: authorQueryObject with: keywordQuery-
        Object with: contentQueryObject with: abstractQueryObject].

    ((contentQuerySize = 0) & ((keywordQuerySize > 0) | (authorQuerySize > 0) |
      (abstractQuerySize > 0)))
      "Search document reference information ONLY."
      ifTrue: [searchEngine findDocument: authorQueryObject with: keywordQuery-
        Object with: abstractQueryObject].

    ((contentQuerySize > 0) & ((keywordQuerySize = 0) & (authorQuerySize = 0) &
      (abstractQuerySize = 0)))
      "Search document content ONLY."
      ifTrue: [searchEngine findDocument: contentQueryObject]].!

setAbstractToKeywordAnd: aPane
    "Callback for the #getContents event in the RadioButton named 'abstractTo-
      KeywordAnd'.
    (Generated by WindowBuilder)"
    "This method is only invoked during the initial setup of the Search For Document(s)
      dialog box."

    aPane selection: true.
    abstractToKeywordOperator := 'AND'!

setAbstractToKeywordOr: aPane
    "Callback for the #getContents event in the RadioButton named 'abstractTo-
      KeywordOr'.
    (Generated by WindowBuilder)"
    "This method is only invoked during the initial setup of the Search For Document(s)
      dialog box."
```

```
    aPane selection: false.!

setContentToAbstractAnd: aPane
    "Callback for the #getContents event in the RadioButton named 'contentTo-
      AbstractAnd'.
    (Generated by WindowBuilder)"
    "This method is only invoked during the initial setup of the Search For Document(s)
      dialog box."

    aPane selection: true.
    contentToAbstractOperator := 'AND'!

setContentToAbstractOr: aPane
    "Callback for the #getContents event in the RadioButton named 'contentToAbstractOr'.
    (Generated by WindowBuilder)"
    "This method is only invoked during the initial setup of the Search For Document(s)
      dialog box."

    aPane selection: false.!

setKeywordToAuthorAnd: aPane
    "Callback for the #getContents event in the RadioButton named 'keywordTo-
      AuthorAnd'.
    (Generated by WindowBuilder)"
    "This method is only invoked during the initial setup of the Search For Document(s)
    dialog box."

    aPane selection: true.
    keywordToAuthorOperator := 'AND'!

setKeywordToAuthorOr: aPane
    "Callback for the #getContents event in the RadioButton named 'keywordToAuthorOr'.
    (Generated by WindowBuilder)"
    "This method is only invoked during the initial setup of the Search For Document(s)
      dialog box."

    aPane selection: false.! !


WindowDialog subclass: #SearchResultsDialog
    instanceVariableNames:
      'documentNames selectedFile '
    classVariableNames: ''
    poolDictionaries:
      'ColorConstants WBConstants '!

!SearchResultsDialog class methods !

wbCreated
    ^true! !

!SearchResultsDialog methods !

displayDocumentPathName: aPane
    "Callback for the #display event in an unnamed EntryField (contents is '').
    (Generated by WindowBuilder)"
```

```
      aPane contents: selectedFile.!

getFile: aPane
      "Callback for the #getContents event in an unnamed ListBox.
      (Generated by WindowBuilder)"
      | answer anOrderedCollection |
      aPane contents: documentNames.!

open
      "WARNING!! This method was automatically generated by WindowBuilder. Code you
       add here which does not conform to the WindowBuilder API will probably be
       lost the next time you save your layout definition."

      | v |

      self addView: (
         v := self topPaneClass new
            owner: self;
            labelWithoutPrefix:'Search Results';
            noSmalltalkMenuBar;
            viewName: 'searchResultsDialog';
            framingBlock: ( FramingParameters new iDUE: 795 @ 492; xC; yC; cRDU: (11
               @ 482 rightBottom: 784 @ 48));
            pStyle: #(sysmenu modal titlebar);
            addSubpane: (
               ListBox new
                  owner: self;
                  framingBlock: ( FramingParameters new iDUE: 286 @ 200; lDU: 23 r:
                     #left; rDU: 309 r: #left; tDU: 210 r: #top; bDU: 410 r: #top);
                  startGroup;
                  when: #getContents perform: #getFile:;
                  when: #select perform: #selectFile:;
                  yourself
            );
            addSubpane: (
               Button new
                  owner: self;
                  framingBlock: ( FramingParameters new iDUE: 142 @ 60; lDU: 354 r:
                     #left; rDU: 496 r: #left; tDU: 180 r: #top; bDU: 240 r: #top);
                  startGroup;
                  when: #clicked perform: #searchResultsView:;
                  contents: 'View';
                  yourself
            );
            addSubpane: (
               Button new
                  owner: self;
                  framingBlock: ( FramingParameters new iDUE: 142 @ 60; lDU: 583 r:
                     #left; rDU: 725 r: #left; tDU: 180 r: #top; bDU: 240 r: #top);
                  startGroup;
                  when: #clicked perform: #searchResultsPrint:;
                  contents: 'Print';
                  yourself
            );
            addSubpane: (
               Button new
```

```
                owner: self;
                framingBlock: ( FramingParameters new iDUE: 142 @ 60; lDU: 469 r:
                    #left; rDU: 610 r: #left; tDU: 320 r: #top; bDU: 380 r: #top);
                startGroup;
                when: #clicked perform: #searchResultsDone:;
                contents: 'Done';
                yourself
            );
        addSubpane: (
            StaticText new
                owner: self;
                framingBlock: ( FramingParameters new iDUE: 91 @ 30; lDU: 126 r: #left;
                    rDU: 217 r: #left; tDU: 170 r: #top; bDU: 200 r: #top);
                startGroup;
                contents: 'File';
                yourself
            );
        addSubpane: (
            StaticText new
                owner: self;
                framingBlock: ( FramingParameters new iDUE: 427 @ 40; lDU: 185 r:
                    #left; rDU: 613 r: #left; tDU: 16 r: #top; bDU: 56 r: #top);
                startGroup;
                contents: 'Path and Document Name:';
                yourself
            );
        addSubpane: (
            EntryField new
                owner: self;
                framingBlock: ( FramingParameters new iDUE: 608 @ 48; lDU: 75 r: #left;
                    rDU: 683 r: #left; tDU: 64 r: #top; bDU: 112 r: #top; indent: 3 @ 4);
                startGroup;
                when: #getContents perform: #displayDocumentPathName:;
                yourself
            );
        yourself
    ).

    self openWindow!

openWith: listOfDocumentNames
    "Set the documentNameList reference and then open the dialog box."
    documentNames := listOfDocumentNames.
    self open!

searchResultsDone: aPane
    "Callback for the #clicked event in an unnamed Button (contents is 'Done').
    (Generated by WindowBuilder)"
    self close!

searchResultsPrint: aPane
    "Callback for the #clicked event in an unnamed Button (contents is 'Print').
    (Generated by WindowBuilder)"
    | printer |
    printer := Printer new.
" printer startPrintJob."
```

```
"  printer endPrintJob."
    self close!

searchResultsView: aPane
    "Callback for the #clicked event in an unnamed Button (contents is 'View').
    (Generated by WindowBuilder)"
    selectedFile isNil
       ifFalse: [DocumentView new openWith: selectedFile].
    selectedFile := nil.
    self changed: #getFile:.
    self changed: #displayDocumentPathName:!

selectFile: aPane
    "Callback for the #select event in an unnamed ListBox.
    (Generated by WindowBuilder)"
    selectedFile := aPane selectedItem.
    self changed: #displayDocumentPathName:.! !


WindowDialog subclass: #DocumentView
    instanceVariableNames:
       'documentName'
    classVariableNames: ''
    poolDictionaries:
       'ColorConstants WBConstants '!

!DocumentView class methods !

wbCreated

    ^true! !

!DocumentView methods !

open
    "WARNING!! This method was automatically generated by WindowBuilder. Code you
       add here which does not conform to the WindowBuilder API will probably be
       lost the next time you save your layout definition."

    | v |

    self addView: (
       v := self topPaneClass new
          owner: self;
          labelWithoutPrefix:'Viewing A Document';
          noSmalltalkMenuBar;
          viewName: 'mainView';
          framingBlock: ( FramingParameters new iDUE: 1058 @ 592; xC; yC; cRDU: (11
             @ 582 rightBottom: 1047 @ 48));
          pStyle: #(sysmenu modal titlebar);
          addSubpane: (
             StaticText new
                owner: self;
                framingBlock: ( FramingParameters new iDUE: 256 @ 36; lDU: 117 r:
                   #left; rDU: 373 r: #left; tDU: 24 r: #top; bDU: 60 r: #top);
                startGroup;
```

```
                contents: 'Document Name:';
                yourself
        );
        addSubpane: (
           EntryField new
              owner: self;
              framingBlock: ( FramingParameters new iDUE: 427 @ 48; lDU: 400 r:
                 #left; rDU: 827 r: #left; tDU: 14 r: #top; bDU: 62 r: #top; indent:
                 3 @ 4);
              startGroup;
              when: #getContents perform: #updateDocumentEntryField:;
              yourself
        );
        addSubpane: (
           TextPane new
              owner: self;
              framingBlock: ( FramingParameters new iDUE: 1013 @ 450; lDU: 11 r:
                 #left; rDU: 1024 r: #left; tDU: 78 r: #top; bDU: 528 r: #top);
              startGroup;
              when: #getContents perform: #updateTextPane:;
              yourself
        );
     yourself
  ).

  self openWindow!

openWith: aDocumentName
     "Set the documentName reference and then open the dialog box."
  documentName := aDocumentName.
  self open!

updateDocumentEntryField: aPane
  "Callback for the #getContents event in an unnamed EntryField.
  (Generated by WindowBuilder)"
  aPane contents: documentName.!

updateTextPane: aPane
  | fileStream |
  "Callback for the #getContents event in an unnamed TextPane.
  (Generated by WindowBuilder)"
  "fill up the textPane with the contents of the file documentName refers to"
  fileStream := File pathName: documentName.
  aPane nextPutAll: fileStream contents.! !


WindowDialog subclass: #DocRefInfoDialog
  instanceVariableNames:
     'documentName directoryName authors keywords abstract documentPathName '
  classVariableNames: ''
  poolDictionaries:
     'ColorConstants WBConstants '!

!DocRefInfoDialog class methods !

wbCreated
```

```
    ^true! !

!DocRefInfoDialog methods !

displayDocName: aPane
    "Callback for the #display event in an unnamed EntryField.
    (Generated by WindowBuilder)"
    aPane contents: documentPathName.!

docRefInfoCancel: aPane
    "Callback for the #clicked event in an unnamed Button (contents is 'Cancel').
    (Generated by WindowBuilder)"
    ((MessageBox confirm: 'Are You Sure?') = true)
        ifTrue: [self close]!

docRefInfoOk: aPane
    | document reference |
    "Callback for the #clicked event in an unnamed Button (contents is 'Ok').
    (Generated by WindowBuilder)"

    " Create a new TextDocument object and file the document. "
    document := TextDocument new.

    " Create a new Document Reference Information object and pass it the DRI info. "
    reference := DocRefInfo new: document.

    reference setDRI: authors with: abstract with: keywords with: documentName with:
        documentPathName.
    DRIs isNil
        ifTrue: [
            DRIs := Set new: DRISize].
    DRIs add: reference.

    "File the document."
    document fileDoc: documentName with: directoryName with: reference.

    self close!

getAbstract: aPane
    "Callback for the #textChanged event in an unnamed EntryField.
    (Generated by WindowBuilder)"
    abstract := aPane contents.!

getAuthors: aPane
    "Callback for the #textChanged event in an unnamed EntryField.
    (Generated by WindowBuilder)"
    authors := aPane contents.!

getKeywords: aPane
    "Callback for the #textChanged event in an unnamed EntryField.
    (Generated by WindowBuilder)"
    keywords := aPane contents.!

open
    "WARNING!! This method was automatically generated by WindowBuilder. Code you
        add here which does not conform to the WindowBuilder API will probably be
```

```
        lost the next time you save your layout definition."
    | v |

    self addView: (
        v := self topPaneClass new
            owner: self;
            labelWithoutPrefix:'Document Reference Information';
            noSmalltalkMenuBar;
            viewName: 'mainView';
            framingBlock: ( FramingParameters new iDUE: 887 @ 600; xC; yC; cRDU: (11
                @ 590 rightBottom: 875 @ 48));
            pStyle: #(sysmenu modal titlebar);
            addSubpane: (
                StaticText new
                    owner: self;
                    framingBlock: ( FramingParameters new iDUE: 279 @ 34; lDU: 34 r: #left;
                        rDU: 313 r: #left; tDU: 40 r: #top; bDU: 74 r: #top);
                    startGroup;
                    contents: 'Document Name:';
                    yourself
            );
            addSubpane: (
                EntryField new
                    owner: self;
                    framingBlock: ( FramingParameters new iDUE: 503 @ 48; lDU: 309 r:
                        #left; rDU: 811 r: #left; tDU: 30 r: #top; bDU: 78 r: #top; indent:
                        3 @ 4);
                    startGroup;
                    when: #getContents perform: #displayDocName:;
                    yourself
            );
            addSubpane: (
                Button new
                    owner: self;
                    framingBlock: ( FramingParameters new iDUE: 142 @ 60; lDU: 229 r:
                        #left; rDU: 370 r: #left; tDU: 440 r: #top; bDU: 500 r: #top);
                    idOK;
                    startGroup;
                    when: #clicked perform: #docRefInfoOk:;
                    contents: 'Ok';
                    yourself
            );
            addSubpane: (
                Button new
                    owner: self;
                    framingBlock: ( FramingParameters new iDUE: 142 @ 60; lDU: 514 r:
                        #left; rDU: 656 r: #left; tDU: 440 r: #top; bDU: 500 r: #top);
                    idCancel;
                    startGroup;
                    when: #clicked perform: #docRefInfoCancel:;
                    contents: 'Cancel';
                    yourself
            );
            addSubpane: (
                EntryField new
```

```
            owner: self;
            framingBlock: ( FramingParameters new iDUE: 754 @ 48; lDU: 57 r: #left;
               rDU: 811 r: #left; tDU: 140 r: #top; bDU: 188 r: #top; indent: 3 @ 4);
            startGroup;
            when: #textChanged perform: #getAbstract:;
            yourself
         );
      addSubpane: (
         EntryField new
            owner: self;
            framingBlock: ( FramingParameters new iDUE: 754 @ 48; lDU: 57 r: #left;
               rDU: 811 r: #left; tDU: 240 r: #top; bDU: 288 r: #top; indent: 3 @ 4);
            startGroup;
            when: #textChanged perform: #getKeywords:;
            yourself
         );
      addSubpane: (
         EntryField new
            owner: self;
            framingBlock: ( FramingParameters new iDUE: 754 @ 48; lDU: 57 r: #left;
               rDU: 811 r: #left; tDU: 340 r: #top; bDU: 388 r: #top; indent: 3 @ 4);
            startGroup;
            when: #textChanged perform: #getAuthors:;
            yourself
         );
      addSubpane: (
         StaticText new
            owner: self;
            framingBlock: ( FramingParameters new iDUE: 158 @ 32; lDU: 80 r: #left;
               rDU: 238 r: #left; tDU: 100 r: #top; bDU: 132 r: #top);
            startGroup;
            contents: 'Abstract:';
            yourself
         );
      addSubpane: (
         StaticText new
            owner: self;
            framingBlock: ( FramingParameters new iDUE: 158 @ 32; lDU: 80 r: #left;
               rDU: 238 r: #left; tDU: 200 r: #top; bDU: 232 r: #top);
            startGroup;
            contents: 'Keywords:';
            yourself
         );
      addSubpane: (
         StaticText new
            owner: self;
            framingBlock: ( FramingParameters new iDUE: 158 @ 32; lDU: 80 r: #left;
               rDU: 238 r: #left; tDU: 300 r: #top; bDU: 332 r: #top);
            startGroup;
            contents: 'Authors:';
            yourself
         );
   yourself
).

self openWindow!
```

```
setDocName: aDocName withDir: aDirectory
    " Save the document name. "
  | aChar |

  documentPathName := aDirectory drivePathName.
  aChar := documentPathName at: documentPathName size.
  aChar = $\
     ifFalse: [documentPathName := documentPathName , '\'].
  documentPathName := documentPathName , aDocName.
  documentName := aDocName.
  directoryName := aDirectory.! !
```

I.2 SEARCH SUBSYSTEM

```
Object subclass: #SearchEngine
   instanceVariableNames:
      'aKeywordQueryObject aAbstractQueryObject aAuthorQueryObject '
   classVariableNames: ''
   poolDictionaries: ''!

!SearchEngine class methods ! !

!SearchEngine methods !

calculateDocRecNumbers: indexFileStream with: searchVectorStream
     "Private. Calculate the document record numbers where hits are possible for
        this search query and this document. Answer with a documentRecordList."

  " This algorithm can be made more efficient by only processing the number of
    records that actually exist in the last block. To do this, the HashEngine
    must save the number of records processed in the last block in the file header
    and the number of blocks."
  | filingDirectory index recordList anIndexRecordvectorStreamPosition
      startPosition endPosition indexPosition totalDataRecordsProcessed
      indexFileStreamEndtotalIndexRecordsProcessed indexFileStreamStart
      indexFileStreamRecords resultVector documentPath maxRecordNumber|

  "Get the maximum number of data records."
  indexFileStream position: 0.
  documentPath := indexFileStream nextLine.
  maxRecordNumber := indexFileStream nextLine asInteger.

     "create an empty document record list."
  recordList := DocumentRecordsList new.
  endPosition := 1.
  indexFileStream position: XHashBlock.
  indexFileStreamRecords := ((indexFileStream size) - XHashBlock) //
        XHashBlock.
  indexFileStreamEnd := (indexFileStream size) - 1.
  indexFileStreamStart := XHashBlock.
  totalDataRecordsProcessed := 0.
  totalIndexRecordsProcessed := XHashBlock.
"debug code"
```

```
searchVectorStream position: 0.
SearchRecs isNil
   ifTrue: [SearchRecs := OrderedCollection new].
index := 1.
searchVectorStream do: [:each | each = $1
                            ifTrue: [SearchRecs add: index.
                                       index := index + 1]
                            ifFalse: [index := index + 1]].

   "Initialize the result vector returned to the client. Set all positions to 1,
         since we are ANDing."
   resultVector := String new: XHashBlock.
   resultVector replaceFrom: 1 to: XHashBlock withObject: $1.

   "[indexFileStream atEnd]"
   [totalIndexRecordsProcessed < indexFileStreamRecords]
      whileTrue: [
         "Process a hash block."
         totalIndexRecordsProcessed := totalIndexRecordsProcessed + XHashBlock.
         searchVectorStream position: 1.
         "Examine the searchVectorStream for each Index File Hash Block."
         [searchVectorStream atEnd]
            whileFalse: [vectorStreamPosition := searchVectorStream position.
               " For each char that equals 1 in the searchVector, read the corresponding
                  record in the index file. "
               (searchVectorStream next = $1) & (endPosition < indexFileStreamEnd)
                  ifTrue: [vectorStreamPosition := searchVectorStream position.
                     startPosition := (vectorStreamPosition - 1) * XHashBlock +
                        indexFileStreamStart + 1.
                     endPosition := vectorStreamPosition * XHashBlock +
                        (XHashBlock - 1) + 1.
                     endPosition >= indexFileStreamEnd
                        ifTrue: [endPosition := indexFileStreamEnd].
                     anIndexRecord := indexFileStream copyFrom: startPosition to:
                        endPosition.

                     "For each char that equals 1 in anIndexFileRecord, AND it with
                        the result vector."
                     indexPosition := 1.
                     [indexPosition <= XHashBlock]
                        whileTrue: [(anIndexRecord at: indexPosition) = $1
                           ifTrue: [(resultVector at: indexPosition) = $1
                              ifFalse: [resultVector at: indexPosition put: $0.
                                 indexPosition := indexPosition + 1]
                              ifTrue: [indexPosition := indexPosition + 1]]
                           ifFalse: [resultVector at: indexPosition put: $0.
                              indexPosition := indexPosition + 1].
                              ]. " END whileTrue"
                  ]. "END ifTrue"
            ]. "END whileFalse"
         "For each char that equals 1 in the resultVector, add the record number to
            the documentRecordList. Add to the document records list by evaluating
            each bit in the resultVector."
         indexPosition := 1.
         [indexPosition <= XHashBlock]
            whileTrue: [(resultVector at: indexPosition) = $1
```

```
            ifTrue: [((indexPosition + totalDataRecordsProcessed) <= maxRecord-
                Number)
                    ifTrue: [recordList addToDRL: indexPosition
                                              + totalDataRecordsProcessed].
                    indexPosition := indexPosition + 1]
                ifFalse: [indexPosition := indexPosition + 1].
                ]. " END whileTrue"
        totalDataRecordsProcessed := totalDataRecordsProcessed + XHashBlock.
        "Set up the vector for processing the next block."
        resultVector replaceFrom: 1 to: XHashBlock withObject: $1.
]. "END whileTrue"

^recordList!

checkForDocumentMatches: theSearchVector using: contentQuery
    "Private. Uses the search vector and the document index files to determine
        which documents satisfy the user specified search criteria. Returns a list
        of document names that were found to meet the user's specified search
        criteria. "

  | documentRecordList indexFileName indexFileStream filingDirectory
    nameList searchVectorStream indexNames filePathName |

  "create an empty document record list."
  nameList := DocumentNameList new.

  " Create a directory object to represent the existing filing directory. "
  filingDirectory := Directory new drive: $C; pathName: '\filing'.
  searchVectorStream := theSearchVector asStream.

  indexNames := Filing retrieveIndexNames.

  "For each document index file name DO"
  indexNames do: [:eachDocumentIndex | indexFileName := eachDocumentIndex.
      indexFileStream := filingDirectory file: indexFileName.
      documentRecordList := self calculateDocRecNumbers: indexFileStream with:
          searchVectorStream.

      "Now verify the record matches. If no match exists for a record number,
          then remove the record number form the documentRecordList."
      filePathName := self verifyMatches: documentRecordList with:
          indexFileStream using: contentQuery.
      indexFileStream close.

      "Associate the documentRecordList with a document in the
          documentNameList."
          documentRecordList size > 0
            ifTrue: [nameList putRecordsList: documentRecordList with: filePath-
                Name].
          ]. "END DO"
  searchVectorStream close.
  ^nameList!

checkForDRIMatches
    "Private. Using the abstract, author, and keyword queries, examine each
        document reference information item to see if there is a match. Answer with
```

```
        a document name list."
    | authorMatchIndicator keywordMatchIndicator
   abstractMatchIndicator matchIndicator driDocumentNameList |

   "First parse the queries into query elements and logical operators. Then get
      the query elements and logical operators for each query."
   ((aAbstractQueryObject query size) = 0)
      ifFalse: [aAbstractQueryObject parseQuery].
   ((aAuthorQueryObject query size) = 0)
      ifFalse: [aAuthorQueryObject parseQuery].
   ((aKeywordQueryObject query size) = 0)
      ifFalse: [aKeywordQueryObject parseQuery].

   "For each document reference information object, check the query elements for
      a match against the document reference information for each text document.
      If a match occurs, then add the document name to the document name list. The
      queries are already parsed at this point into query elements and logical
      operators."

   authorMatchIndicator := false.
   keywordMatchIndicator := false.
   abstractMatchIndicator := false.
   matchIndicator := false.

   "create an empty document name list."
   driDocumentNameList := DocumentNameList new.

   DRIs do: [ :aDri |
        authorMatchIndicator := aAuthorQueryObject checkForElementMatch: (aDri ge-
           tAuthors).
        keywordMatchIndicator := aKeywordQueryObject checkForElementMatch: (aDri
           getKeywords).
        abstractMatchIndicator := aAbstractQueryObject checkForElementMatch: (aDri
           getAbstract).
        matchIndicator := self checkForLogicalQueryMatch: abstractMatchIndicator
                         with: keywordMatchIndicator with: authorMatchIndicator.
      " if the matchIndicator is TRUE then add the document name to the document-
        NameList."
        matchIndicator
           ifTrue: [driDocumentNameList addToDNL: (aDri getDocumentAndPathName)]].
   ^driDocumentNameList!

checkForLogicalQueryMatch: abstractMatchIndicator with: keywordMatchIndicator
   with: authorMatchIndicator
      "Private. Answer with a False or True matchIndicator. matchIndicator indicates
         wheither or not a document satisfied the document reference information
         query."
   | matchIndicator |

   matchIndicator := false.
   aAbstractQueryObject getAbstractToKeywordOperator = 'AND'
      ifTrue: [matchIndicator := abstractMatchIndicator & keywordMatchIndicator]
      ifFalse: [matchIndicator := abstractMatchIndicator | keywordMatchIndicator].

   aKeywordQueryObject getKeywordToAuthorOperator = 'AND'
      ifTrue: [matchIndicator := matchIndicator & authorMatchIndicator]
```

```
        ifFalse: [matchIndicator := matchIndicator | authorMatchIndicator].
    ^matchIndicator!

findDocument: contentQueryObject
        " A method for searching for one or more documents based on a content search
            only. "
    | searchVectorObject aSearchVector documentNamesList |

    "First build the search vector."
    searchVectorObject := SearchVector new.
    aSearchVector := searchVectorObject buildSearchVector: contentQueryObject.

    "Next, check for document matches. Use the search vector, verify the matches,
        and if a match occurs, then add the document name to the documentNamesList. "
    documentNamesList := self checkForDocumentMatches: aSearchVector using:
        contentQueryObject.

    " Now open the Search Results Dialog Box and allow the user to examine one of
        the documents found meeting the search criteria."
    documentNamesList size > 0
        ifFalse: [MessageBox message: 'No documents found meeting search criteria']
        ifTrue: [SearchResultsDialog new openWith: documentNamesList retrieveDocu-
            mentNames].!

findDocument: authorQueryObject with: keywordQueryObject with: abstractQueryObject
        " The method for searching for one or more documents based ONLY on document
            reference information search criteria. "
    | searchVectorObject vector documentNamesList |

    aAuthorQueryObject := authorQueryObject.
    aKeywordQueryObject := keywordQueryObject.
    aAbstractQueryObject := abstractQueryObject.

    "Check the author, keyword, and abstract queries for matches against document
        reference information. A list of document names satisfying the search criteria
        is returned."

    documentNamesList := self checkForDRIMatches.

    " Now open the Search Results Dialog Box and allow the user to examine one of
        the documents found meeting the search criteria."
    documentNamesList size > 0
        ifFalse: [MessageBox message: 'No documents found meeting search criteria']
        ifTrue: [SearchResultsDialog new openWith: documentNamesList retrieveDocu-
            mentNames].!

findDocument: authorQueryObject with: keywordQueryObject with: contentQueryObject
    with: abstractQueryObject
        " The method for searching for one or more documents based on a content and
            document reference information search criteria."
    | searchVectorObject vector contentDocumentNameList combinedDocumentNameList
        driDocumentNameList |

    aAuthorQueryObject := authorQueryObject.
    aKeywordQueryObject := keywordQueryObject.
    aAbstractQueryObject := abstractQueryObject.
```

```
"First build the search vector."
searchVectorObject := SearchVector new.
vector := searchVectorObject buildSearchVector: contentQueryObject.

"Next, check for document matches. Use the search vector, verify the matches,
    and build the contentDocumentNameList. "
contentDocumentNameList := self checkForDocumentMatches: vector using:
    contentQueryObject.

"Now check the author, keyword, and abstract queries for matches against document
    reference information. For each DRI with a match, add the document name to
    the driDocumentNameList."

driDocumentNameList := self checkForDRIMatches.

"Produce a new document name list based on the logical operation performed
    between the content query and the DRI query. If the 'content to abstract
    operator' is an OR, then the document name lists from both the content search
    and the DRI search are added together. If the 'content to abstract operator'
    is an AND, then a new document name list is created based on the union of
    these two lists."

"create an empty document record list."
combinedDocumentNameList := DocumentNameList new.

contentQueryObject getContentToAbstractOperator = 'OR'
    ifTrue: [contentDocumentNameList do: [:contentElement |
            combinedDocumentNameList addToDNL: contentElement].
          driDocumentNameList do: [:driElement |
              (combinedDocumentNameList includes: driElement)
                 ifFalse: [combinedDocumentNameList addToDNL: driElement]]]
    ifFalse: [contentDocumentNameList do: [:contentElement |
              (driDocumentNameList includes: contentElement)
                 ifTrue: [combinedDocumentNameList addToDNL: contentElement]]].

" Now open the Search Results Dialog Box and allow the user to examine one of
    the documents found meeting the search criteria."
combinedDocumentNameList size > 0
    ifFalse: [MessageBox message: 'No documents found meeting search criteria']
    ifTrue: [SearchResultsDialog new openWith: combinedDocumentNameList
        retrieveDocumentNames].!

verifyMatches: docRecordNumberList with: indexFileStream using: contentQuery
        "Private. Use the document record list to verify that the specified content
            query actually exists in the document record. The docRecordNumberList is
            changed accordingly. This method operates on a specific document."
    "Answer with a String representing a document name, if the matches are verified."

    | path textFileStream startPosition endPosition documentRecordSubstrings
        contentQueryElements duplicateRecordList textFileStreamEnd queryFound |

    duplicateRecordList := docRecordNumberList deepCopy.
    "First get the complete path of the text document. Read the directory and document
        name of the text document file from the index file header - up to the line
        terminating character."
```

```
    indexFileStream position: 0.
    path := indexFileStream nextLine.

    "Now set up a textFileStream so that the text document records can be read."
    textFileStream := File pathName: path.

    "For all record numbers in the docRecordNumberList, read the document record
       and verify that some element of the content query exists within that record.
       If not, then remove the document record number from the docRecordNumberList.
       All record numbers start with 1, not 0."
    textFileStreamEnd := textFileStream size.
    duplicateRecordList do: [:recordNumber | startPosition := (recordNumber - 1) *
       FilingRecordSize + 1.
          endPosition := recordNumber * FilingRecordSize.
          endPosition >= textFileStreamEnd
             ifTrue: [endPosition := textFileStreamEnd].
          documentRecordSubstrings := (textFileStream copyFrom: startPosition to:
       endPosition) asArrayOfSubstrings.
          contentQueryElements := contentQuery getQueryElements.
          queryFound := false.
          contentQueryElements do: [:eachQueryElement |
          (documentRecordSubstrings select: [:eachSubstring | eachSubstring =
       eachQueryElement]) size > 0
             ifTrue: [queryFound := true]].
          queryFound
             ifFalse: [FalseHits := FalseHits + 1.
                      docRecordNumberList removeRecordNumber: recordNumber].
                         ].
    textFileStream close.
    docRecordNumberList size > 0
       ifTrue: [^path]
       ifFalse: [^nil].! !

Object subclass: #SearchVector
    instanceVariableNames: ''
    classVariableNames: ''
    poolDictionaries: '' !

!SearchVector class methods ! !

!SearchVector methods !

buildSearchVector: contentQueryObject
       "Uses the content query to build a search vector. Produces a search vector. "
    | contentQuery contentQueryElements contentQueryOperators theHashEngine
      numberOfElements numberOfOperators index aHashString initChar
      logicalOperator duplicateQueryElements duplicateQueryOperators
      queryVector elementVector junkWords aWord |

    queryVector := String new: YHashBlock.
    queryVector replaceFrom: 1 to: YHashBlock withObject: $0.
    elementVector := queryVector deepCopy.

    contentQuery := contentQueryObject query.
    "First parse the queries into query elements and logical operators. Then get
       the query elements and logical operators for each query. Assumes that multiword
```

```
                query elements are a single substring."
        ((contentQuery size) = 0)
            ifFalse: [contentQueryObject parseQuery.
                    contentQueryElements := contentQueryObject getQueryElements.
                    contentQueryOperators := contentQueryObject getLogicalOperators].

    duplicateQueryElements := contentQueryElements deepCopy.
    duplicateQueryOperators := contentQueryOperators deepCopy.
        "Now hash each query element and AND or OR the results from each element
            together depending upon the query operator. "
    theHashEngine := HashEngine new.   " create a new hash engine object "
    logicalOperator := 'OR'.
    junkWords := JunkWords new.
    [duplicateQueryElements size > 0]
        whileTrue: [aWord := duplicateQueryElements removeFromQueue.
                    (junkWords checkIfJunkWord: aWord)
                        ifFalse: [theHashEngine hashTheWord: aWord using: elementVector.
                            self constructVector: queryVector with: elementVector using:
                                logicalOperator.
                            (duplicateQueryOperators size) > 0
                            ifTrue: [logicalOperator := duplicateQueryOperators remove-
                                FromQueue]]].
    ^queryVector!

constructVector: queryVectorString with: elementVectorString using: operator
        "Private. Perform the AND or OR operation between the queryVector and the
            elementVector. The result is placed in the queryVector."
    | queryStreamChar elementStreamChar queryVectorStream elementVectorStream |
    queryVectorStream := queryVectorString asStream.
    elementVectorStream := elementVectorString asStream.
    queryVectorStream position: 0.
    elementVectorStream position: 0.
    [queryVectorStream atEnd]
        whileFalse: [elementStreamChar := elementVectorStream next.
                    queryStreamChar := queryVectorStream peek.
                    operator = 'AND'
                        ifTrue: [(elementStreamChar asInteger) = (queryStreamChar
                            asInteger)
                            ifFalse: [queryVectorStream nextPut: $0]
                            ifTrue: [queryVectorStream next]]
                        ifFalse: [(elementStreamChar asInteger) = (queryStreamChar as-
                            Integer)
                            ifFalse: [queryVectorStream nextPut: $1]
                            ifTrue: [queryVectorStream next]].
                    ].! !
```

I.3 SEARCH RESULTS SUBSYSTEM

```
Object subclass: #DocumentNameList
    instanceVariableNames:
        'documentNameList recordDictionary '
    classVariableNames: ''
    poolDictionaries: '' !
```

```smalltalk
!DocumentNameList class methods !

new
    "Answer a new instance of the receiver."
  ^super new initialize! !

!DocumentNameList methods !

addToDNL: anObject
    "Add an object to the tail of the documentNameList."
  documentNameList add: anObject!

do: aBlock
    "Answer the receiver. For each element in the receiver,
    evaluate aBlock with that element as the argument. this is from an Ordered-
        Collection"

  | index listSize |
  listSize := documentNameList size.
  index := 0.
  [(index := index + 1) <= listSize]
    whileTrue: [aBlock value: (documentNameList at: index)].!

getRecordsList: indexFileName
    "Answer with the DocumentRecordsList object."
  ^recordDictionary at: indexFileName!

includes: anObject
    "Answer True if anObject is included in the DNL, else answer False."
  ^documentNameList includes: anObject!

initialize
    "This method is private. Set up a DocumentNameList as an OrderedCollection
        able to hold 12 elements initially."
  documentNameList := OrderedCollection new.
  recordDictionary := Dictionary new.!

putRecordsList: theRecordsListObject with: indexFileName
    "Associate a DocumentRecordsList object with the indexFileName."
  recordDictionary at: indexFileName put: theRecordsListObject.
  documentNameList add: indexFileName.!

removeFromDNL
    "Answer a removed object from the head of the documentNameList."
  ^documentNameList removeFirst!

retrieveDocumentNames
    "Answer with the documentNameList."
  ^documentNameList!

size
    "Answer an Integer which is the size of the documentNameList."
  ^documentNameList size! !
```

```
Object subclass: #DocumentRecordsList
   instanceVariableNames:
      'documentRecordsList '
   classVariableNames: ''
   poolDictionaries: ''!

!DocumentRecordsList class methods !

new
     "Answer a new instance of the receiver."
   ^super new initialize! !

!DocumentRecordsList methods !

addToDRL: anObject
     "Add an object to the tail of the documentRecordsList."
   documentRecordsList add: anObject!

at: anInteger put: aRecordNumber
     "Replace the element of the receiver at index position anInteger with
        aRecordNumber. "
   documentRecordsList at: anInteger put: aRecordNumber!

do: aBlock
     "Answer the receiver. For each element in the receiver, evaluate aBlock with
        that element as the argument. this is from an OrderedCollection"

   | index listSize |
   listSize := documentRecordsList size.
   index := 0.
   [(index := index + 1) <= listSize]
      whileTrue: [aBlock value: (documentRecordsList at: index)].!

initialize
     "This method is private. Set up a DocumentRecordsList as an OrderedCollection
        able to hold 12 elements initially."
   documentRecordsList := OrderedCollection new.!

removeFromDRL
     "Answer a removed object from the head of the documentRecordsList."
   ^documentRecordsList removeFirst!

removeIndex: anInteger
     "Remove the document record number at index position anInteger."
   documentRecordsList removeIndex: anInteger!

removeRecordNumber: recordNumber
     "Remove the document record number at index position anInteger."
   documentRecordsList remove: recordNumber ifAbsent: [].!

size
     "Answer an Integer which is the size of the documentRecordsList."
   ^documentRecordsList size! !
```

I.4 DOCUMENT SUBSYSTEM

```
Object subclass: #DocRefInfo
   instanceVariableNames:
      'abstract authors keywords textDocument documentName pathAndDocumentName '
   classVariableNames: ''
   poolDictionaries: '' !

!DocRefInfo class methods !

new: theTextDocument
      "Answer a new instance of the receiver."
   ^super new initialize: theTextDocument! !

!DocRefInfo methods !

getAbstract
      "Answer with the abstract String of this text document."
   ^abstract!

getAuthors
      "Answer with the authors String of this text document."
   ^authors!

getDocumentAndPathName
      "Answer with the pathAndDocumentName String for this text document."
   ^pathAndDocumentName!

getDocumentName
      "Answer with the documentName String for this text document."
   ^documentName!

getKeywords
      "Answer with the keywords String of this text document."
   ^keywords!

initialize: theTextDocument
      "Have the document reference information object be associated with a specific
         text document."
   textDocument := theTextDocument!

setDRI: allAuthors with: theAbstract with: allKeywords with: textDocumentName with:
   docAndPathName
      "Set up the document reference information as part of the DRI object. The
         abstract, authors, and keywords are all strings."
   abstract := theAbstract.
   authors := allAuthors.
   keywords := allKeywords.
   documentName := textDocumentName.
   pathAndDocumentName := docAndPathName! !


Object subclass: #TextDocument
   instanceVariableNames:
      'name directory '
```

```
    classVariableNames: ''
    poolDictionaries: ''!

!TextDocument class methods ! !

!TextDocument methods !

fileDoc: documentName with: directoryName
        " A document has been filed with no document reference information."
    | newIndex |

    name := documentName.
    directory := directoryName.

    " Create an Index object. "
    newIndex := Index new.

       " File the document. "
    newIndex createDocIndex: documentName withDir: directoryName.!

fileDoc: documentName with: directoryName with: theDriObject
    | newIndex |

    name := documentName.
    directory := directoryName.

    " Create an Index object. "
    newIndex := Index new.

       " File the document. "
    newIndex createDocIndex: documentName withDir: directoryName.! !


Object subclass: #Index
    instanceVariableNames:
        'indexFileName name directory '
    classVariableNames: ''
    poolDictionaries: '' !

!Index class methods ! !

!Index methods !

buildIndexFileHeader: indexFileWriteStream with: documentName with: directoryName
        "Private. This method builds the IndexFile header and outputs it to the index
          file. The file header is equal to the number of columns in the hash block."
    | dirName aChar textDocumentStream docSizeInAscii quotient remainder |
    "Initialize the file header to all zeros."
    [(indexFileWriteStream position) = XHashBlock]
        whileFalse: [indexFileWriteStream nextPut: $0].

    " Write the directory and document names of the text document file to the index
        file header."
    indexFileWriteStream position: 0.
    dirName := directoryName drivePathName.
    aChar := dirName at: dirName size.
```

```
    aChar = $\
      ifFalse: [dirName := dirName , '\'].
    indexFileWriteStream nextPutAll: dirName.

    "Terminate the document path name with a line terminating character to make it
      easy to read back in during the search process."
    indexFileWriteStream nextPutAll: documentName; cr.

    "Determine the number of records in the text document and save in the index file
      to expedite the search process later on."
    textDocumentStream := File pathName: dirName , documentName.
    quotient := textDocumentStream size // FilingRecordSize.
    remainder := textDocumentStream size rem:FilingRecordSize.
    remainder > 0
      ifTrue: [quotient := quotient + 1].
    docSizeInAscii := (quotient radix: 10).
    textDocumentStream close.
    indexFileWriteStream nextPutAll: docSizeInAscii; cr.!

createDocIndex: documentName withDir: directoryName
      " Public. Create the actual text document index. "
    | indexFileStream filingDirectory docFileStream |
      directory := directoryName.

    " Create a copy of the documentName object including its instance variables. "
      name := documentName deepCopy.

    " Create an input FileStream for our document. "
    docFileStream := directoryName fileReadOnly: documentName.
    indexFileName := (name upTo: $.) , '.sam'.   "Index file name"

    " Create a directory object to represent the existing filing directory. "
    filingDirectory := Directory new drive: $C; pathName: '\filing'.

    " Create the actual index file. The result is our output FileStream. "
    indexFileStream := filingDirectory newFile: indexFileName.

    "Make sure that the FilingDirectory is alive and well."
    Filing isNil
      ifTrue: [
          Filing := FilingDirectory new].
    Filing addIndexFile: indexFileName.

    " Create an index of the text document file contents. "
    self createIndex: indexFileStream with: docFileStream with: documentName with:
      directoryName.
    docFileStream close.
    indexFileStream close.!

createIndex: indexFileStream with: docFileStream with: documentName with:
    directoryName
    " Private. Create an index of the contents of the text document.
      indexFileStream = file stream for text document
      docFileStream = file stream for index file. "
    | hashEngine |
```

```
" First create the index file header."
self buildIndexFileHeader: indexFileStream with: documentName with: directoryName.
" Next, build the hash blocks in the index file."
hashEngine := HashEngine new.            " create a new hash engine object "
hashEngine buildHashBlock: indexFileStream with: docFileStream.    "build hash
  blocks"! !
```

I.5 QUERY SUBSYSTEM

```
Object subclass: #Query
   instanceVariableNames:
      'queryElements logicalOperators query '
   classVariableNames:
      'ContentToAbstractOperator KeywordToAuthorOperator AbstractToKeywordOperator '
   poolDictionaries: ''!

!Query class methods ! !

!Query methods !

checkForElementMatch: typeOfQueryElements
      "Check each element of the typeOfQueryElements query for a match against each
         of the documents typeOfQueryElements that are part of a document reference
         information object."
   | flags aFlag nextFlag operator arrayOfSubstrings newOrderedCollection |

   typeOfQueryElements isNil
     ifTrue: [^false].
   (queryElements size) = 0
     ifTrue: [^false].
   "Compare each typeOfQueryElements query element with each element in the
      typeOfQueryElements list from the document reference information."
   "Create a queue to save the True or False booleans for each query element that
      is found in the list of typeOfQueryElements."
   flags := Queue new: MaxQueryOperators.

   "Check to see if each and every typeOfQueryElements query element is included
      in the list of typeOfQueryElements. Save a False or True boolean in the flags
      to indicate yes or no."
   "make the typeOfQueryElements into an array of substrings"
   "make the array of substrings into an ordered collection"
   arrayOfSubstrings := typeOfQueryElements asArrayOfSubstrings.
   newOrderedCollection := OrderedCollection new: MaxQueryElements.
   arrayOfSubstrings do: [:aSubString | newOrderedCollection add: aSubString].
   queryElements do: [ :element | flags addToQueue: (newOrderedCollection includes:
      element)].

   "If there were no logical operators, then return the match indicator. If there
      were one or more logical operators, then AND and OR the match indicators
      together and return the Boolean result."
   ((logicalOperators size) = 0)
     ifTrue: [^flags removeFromQueue]
     ifFalse: [aFlag := flags removeFromQueue.
```

```
            [(flags size) > 0]
               whileTrue:   [nextFlag := flags removeFromQueue.
                             operator := logicalOperators removeFromQueue.
                             (operator = 'AND')
                                ifTrue: [aFlag := aFlag & nextFlag]
                                ifFalse: [aFlag := aFlag | nextFlag]]].
      ^aFlag!

getLogicalOperators
      "Answer an array of substrings of logical operators."
   ^logicalOperators!

getQueryElements
      "Answer an array of substrings of query elements."
   ^queryElements!

parseQuery
      " This is an abstract class. No instances of this class exist. Parse the query
         into query elements, which are words or phrases, and logical operators. "
   | substringArray |
   (queryElements = nil)
      ifTrue: [queryElements := Queue new: MaxQueryOperators].
   (logicalOperators = nil)
      ifTrue: [logicalOperators := Queue new: MaxQueryOperators].
   substringArray := query asArrayOfSubstrings.
   substringArray do: [:element |
      (element = 'OR' or: [element = 'AND'])
         ifTrue: [logicalOperators addToQueue: element]
         ifFalse: [queryElements addToQueue: element]].!

query
      "Answer the query."
   ^query! !


Query subclass: #AbstractQuery
   instanceVariableNames: ''
   classVariableNames: ''
   poolDictionaries: '' !

!AbstractQuery class methods ! !

!AbstractQuery methods !

getAbstractToKeywordOperator
      "Answer with the AbstractToKeywordOperator."
   ^AbstractToKeywordOperator!

setAbstractQuery: abstractQuery
      "Set the abstract query up. "
   query := abstractQuery.!

setContentToAbstractOperator: operator
      "Set up the ContentToAbstractOperator. "
   ContentToAbstractOperator := operator! !
```

```
Query subclass: #AuthorQuery
    instanceVariableNames: ''
    classVariableNames: ''
    poolDictionaries: ''!

!AuthorQuery class methods ! !

!AuthorQuery methods !

setAuthorQuery: authorQuery
      "Set the author query up. "
    query := authorQuery.!

setKeywordToAuthorOperator: operator
      "Set up the KeywordToAuthorOperator. "
    KeywordToAuthorOperator := operator! !


Query subclass: #ContentQuery
    instanceVariableNames: ''
    classVariableNames: ''
    poolDictionaries: ''!

!ContentQuery class methods ! !

!ContentQuery methods !

getContentToAbstractOperator
      "Get the ContentToAbstractOperator. "
    ^ContentToAbstractOperator!

setContentQuery: contentQuery
      "Set the content query up. "
    query := contentQuery.! !


Query subclass: #KeywordQuery
    instanceVariableNames: ''
    classVariableNames: ''
    poolDictionaries: ''!

!KeywordQuery class methods ! !

!KeywordQuery methods !

getKeywordToAuthorOperator
      "Answer with the KeywordToAuthorOperator."
    ^KeywordToAuthorOperator!

setAbstractToKeywordOperator: operator
      "Set up the AbstractToKeywordOperator. "
    AbstractToKeywordOperator := operator!

setKeywordQuery: keywordQuery
      "Set the keyword query up. "
    query := keywordQuery.! !
```

I.6 HASHING SUBSYSTEM

```
Object subclass: #HashEngine
   instanceVariableNames:
      'hashBlock translateChar offset hashBlockIndex seed recordsIndexed junkWords
         filingCharacters '
   classVariableNames:
      'RandomNumberTable TranslateTable '
   poolDictionaries: '' !

!HashEngine class methods !

new
      "Answer a new instance of the receiver."
   ^super new initialize!

setupTranslateTable
      "Initialize the translate table."
   TranslateTable := OrderedCollection new: 128.
   TranslateTable addAllFirst: #(0 0 0 0 0 0 0 0 0 0 0 0 0 0 0 0
                                 0 0 0 0 0 0 0 0 0 0 0 0 0 0 0 0
                                 0 0 0 0 0 0 0 0 0 0 0 0 0 0 0 0
                                 97 15 118 228 91 179 200 29 125 69 0 0 0 0 0 0
                                 0 35 67 170 24 86 121 176 74 36 119 83 37 139 212 42
                                 9 41 109 201 26 78 101 183 49 122 149 0 0 0 0 0
                                 0 35 67 170 24 86 121 176 74 36 119 83 37 139 212 42
                                 941 109 201 26 78 101 183 49 122 149 0 0 0 0 0).!  !

!HashEngine methods !

buildHashBlock: indexFileStream with: docFileStream
      "Build the hash blocks for the index file. indexFileStream is a read/write
         FileStream, and docFileStream is a read-only FileStream. A text document
         may require multiple blocks be hashed and output to the index file, depending
         upon the size of the text document. Hash blocks are contiguous; i.e., a
         new hash block starts immediately after a previous hash block ends."
   | first last initChar hashStream documentRecord
      streamEnd totalRecordsIndexed index |

   " Create an empty hash block and initialize it to all zeros. "
   hashBlock := String new: (YHashBlock * XHashBlock).
   initChar := $0.
   hashStream := ReadWriteStream on: hashBlock.
   [hashStream atEnd]
      whileFalse: [hashStream nextPut: initChar].

   " Hash each record in a block. Read fixed sized records of FilingRecordSize
      characters each. Each hashed record in put in the hashBlock. Do this UNTIL
      the last document record is processed."
   streamEnd := docFileStream size.
   first := 1.
   last := FilingRecordSize.
   last > streamEnd
      ifTrue: [last := streamEnd].
   recordsIndexed := 0.
```

```
totalRecordsIndexed := 0.
docFileStream position: 0.

"Set the initial indexFileStream position to go directly after the file header."
indexFileStream position: XHashBlock.
[ docFileStream atEnd]
    whileFalse: [
        last > streamEnd
            ifTrue: [last := streamEnd].
        documentRecord := docFileStream copyFrom: first to: last.  "read a record"
        docFileStream position: last.
        self hashDocumentRecord: documentRecord.                  "hash a record"
        first := first + FilingRecordSize.
        last := last + FilingRecordSize.
        recordsIndexed := recordsIndexed +1.
        totalRecordsIndexed := totalRecordsIndexed + 1.
        " Check if the hashBlock is full. If so, write the hashBlock to the
           indexFileStream. "
        recordsIndexed = XHashBlock
            ifTrue: [recordsIndexed := 0.
                    indexFileStream nextPutAll: hashBlock.
                    "hashStream position: 1."
                    hashStream position: 0.
                    [hashStream atEnd]
                        whileFalse: [hashStream nextPut: initChar]]].

"Make sure that 1) the text document file wasn't empty, and 2) that the last
   hashed block was not already output to the index file."
(recordsIndexed) ~= 0 & (totalRecordsIndexed ~= 0)
    ifTrue: [indexFileStream nextPutAll: hashBlock].

"debug code"
"hashStream position: XHashBlock.
index := XHashBlock.
FilingRecs isNil
    ifTrue: [FilingRecs := OrderedCollection new].
hashStream do: [:each | each = $1
                ifTrue: [FilingRecs add: ((index - XHashBlock) // XHashBlock +
                    1 + recordsIndexed).
                        index := index + 1]
                ifFalse: [index := index + 1]]."
"debug code
hashStream position: 0.
index := 1.
FilingRecs isNil
    ifTrue: [FilingRecs := OrderedCollection new].
hashStream do: [:each | each = $1
                ifTrue: [FilingRecs add: ((index // XHashBlock) + 1).
                    index := index + 1]
                ifFalse: [index := index + 1]]. "
hashStream close.!

hashDocumentRecord: documentRecord
    " Hash an 80 character documentRecord and puts the hashed record in the
        hashBlock. The hash values for each word in the record are ORed together. "
  | words |
```

```
words := documentRecord asArrayOfSubstrings.
words do: [:aWord | (junkWords checkIfJunkWord: aWord)
                    ifFalse: [self hashTheWord: aWord]].!

hashFirstChar: aChar
    "Hash the first character."
 | maxIndexNumber randomNumber |
  maxIndexNumber := YHashBlock.
  translateChar := 0.
  6 timesRepeat: [
      translateChar := translateChar + (TranslateTable at: (aChar asInteger))
          asInteger.
      offset := translateChar rem: 1024.
      offset > 0
          ifTrue: [randomNumber := (RandomNumberTable at: offset) rem: maxIndex-
Number.
                  hashBlockIndex := ((randomNumber - 1) abs) * XHashBlock + 1 +
                      recordsIndexed.
                  hashBlock at: hashBlockIndex put: $1]].!

hashFirstChar: aChar using: theHashBlock
    "Hash the first character."
 | maxIndexNumber |
  maxIndexNumber := YHashBlock.
  translateChar := 0.
  6 timesRepeat: [
      translateChar := translateChar + (TranslateTable at: (aChar asInteger))
          asInteger.
      offset := translateChar rem: 1024.
      offset > 0
          ifTrue: [hashBlockIndex := (RandomNumberTable at: offset) rem:
              maxIndexNumber.
                  theHashBlock at: hashBlockIndex put: $1]].!

hashOtherChar: aChar
    "Hash the first character."
 | maxIndexNumber randomNumber |
  maxIndexNumber := YHashBlock.
  translateChar := 0.
  2 timesRepeat: [
      translateChar := translateChar + (TranslateTable at: (aChar asInteger))
          asInteger.
      offset := translateChar rem: 1024.
      offset > 0
          ifTrue: [randomNumber := (RandomNumberTable at: offset) rem: maxIndex-
              Number.
                  hashBlockIndex := ((randomNumber - 1) abs) * XHashBlock + 1 +
                      recordsIndexed.
                  hashBlock at: hashBlockIndex put: $1]].!

hashOtherChar: aChar using: theHashBlock
    "Hash the first character."
 | maxIndexNumber |
  maxIndexNumber := YHashBlock.
  translateChar := 0.
  2 timesRepeat: [
```

```
            translateChar := translateChar + (TranslateTable at: (aChar asInteger))
               asInteger.
            offset := translateChar rem: 1024.
            offset > 0
               ifTrue: [hashBlockIndex := (RandomNumberTable at: offset) rem:
                  maxIndexNumber.
                     theHashBlock at: hashBlockIndex put: $1]].!

hashSecondChar: aChar
      "Hash the first character."
    | maxIndexNumber randomNumber |
    maxIndexNumber := YHashBlock.
    translateChar := 0.
    4 timesRepeat: [
         translateChar := translateChar + (TranslateTable at: (aChar asInteger))
            asInteger.
         offset := translateChar rem: 1024.
         offset > 0
            ifTrue: [randomNumber := (RandomNumberTable at: offset) rem: maxIndex-
               Number.
                  hashBlockIndex := ((randomNumber - 1) abs) * XHashBlock + 1 +
                     recordsIndexed.
                  hashBlock at: hashBlockIndex put: $1]].!

hashSecondChar: aChar using: theHashBlock
      "Hash the first character."
    | maxIndexNumber |
    maxIndexNumber := YHashBlock.
    translateChar := 0.
    4 timesRepeat: [
         translateChar := translateChar + (TranslateTable at: (aChar asInteger))
            asInteger.
         offset := translateChar rem: 1024.
         offset > 0
            ifTrue: [hashBlockIndex := (RandomNumberTable at: offset) rem: maxIn-
               dexNumber.
                  theHashBlock at: hashBlockIndex put: $1]].!

hashTheWord: word
      " Hash the ASCII word. Words must be greater than 2 characters in length to
        be hashed. Non-filing characters may preceed a word and must be contiguous.
        Non-filing characters may not follow valid filing characters in a word."
    | wordSize index filingCharacterCount firstFilingCharacterPosition |
    wordSize := word size.
    index := 1.

    filingCharacterCount := 0.
    word do: [:aCharacter | (filingCharacters checkIfFilingCharacter: aCharacter)
                     ifTrue: [filingCharacterCount := filingCharacterCount + 1]].
    (filingCharacterCount > 2)
       ifTrue: [firstFilingCharacterPosition := filingCharacters getFirstFiling-
          Character: word.
               self hashFirstChar: (word at: firstFilingCharacterPosition).
               self hashSecondChar: (word at: firstFilingCharacterPosition + 1).
               filingCharacterCount := filingCharacterCount - 2.
               self hashOtherChar: (word at: firstFilingCharacterPosition + 2).
```

```
        index := firstFilingCharacterPosition + 3.
        [(filingCharacterCount := filingCharacterCount - 1) > 0]
          whileTrue: [self hashOtherChar: (word at: index).
                        index := index + 1]].!

hashTheWord: word using: theHashBlock
    " Hash the ASCII word. Words must be greater than 2 characters in length to
      be hashed. Non-filing characters may preceed a word and must be contiguous.
      Non-filing characters may not follow valid filing characters in a word."
    | wordSize index filingCharacters filingCharacterCount firstFilingCharacter-
    Position |

    wordSize := word size.
    index := 1.
    filingCharacters := FilingCharacters new.
    filingCharacterCount := 0.
    word do: [:aCharacter | (filingCharacters checkIfFilingCharacter: aCharacter)
                    ifTrue: [filingCharacterCount := filingCharacterCount + 1]].
    (filingCharacterCount > 2)
      ifTrue: [firstFilingCharacterPosition := filingCharacters getFirstFilingChar-
        acter: word.
          self hashFirstChar: (word at: firstFilingCharacterPosition) using: the-
            HashBlock.
          self hashSecondChar: (word at: firstFilingCharacterPosition + 1) using:
            theHashBlock.
          filingCharacterCount := filingCharacterCount - 2.
          self hashOtherChar: (word at: firstFilingCharacterPosition + 2) using:
            theHashBlock.
          index := firstFilingCharacterPosition + 3.
          [(filingCharacterCount := filingCharacterCount - 1) > 0]
            whileTrue: [self hashOtherChar: (word at: index) using: theHashBlock.
                          index := index + 1]].!

initialize
    "Private. Set up the random number table."
    | tempCollection randomNumber index numberOfRandomNumbers maxIndexNumber |
    self class setupTranslateTable.
    seed := 17451.
    numberOfRandomNumbers := 1024.
    RandomNumberTable := OrderedCollection new: numberOfRandomNumbers.
    index := 1.
    maxIndexNumber := (YHashBlock * XHashBlock) - XHashBlock.
    "[index <= numberOfRandomNumbers]
      whileTrue: [RandomNumberTable add:
                    (((((self randomNumber) * YHashBlock) * XHashBlock) rem: (YHash-
                      Block * XHashBlock)).
                    index := index + 1]."
    [index <= numberOfRandomNumbers]
      whileTrue: [RandomNumberTable add:
                      ((self randomNumber) rem: maxIndexNumber).
                      index := index + 1].
    junkWords := JunkWords new.
    filingCharacters := FilingCharacters new!

randomNumber
    "Generate a random number based on a seed."
```

```
"| x newSeed modulo randomNumber |"
| product divisor quotient remainder multiplier |
" code must be added to limit seed and randomNumber to 32 bits max. this can be
   done by doing a rem: seed and a rem: randomNumber."
" x := 3125.
modulo := 67108864.
seed := (seed * x) rem: 4294967295.
newSeed := seed."
"randomNumber := newSeed - ((newSeed // modulo) * modulo).
randomNumber := (randomNumber // modulo) rem: 4294967295."
"randomNumber := (seed // modulo) rem: 4294967295."
multiplier:= 19683.
divisor := 65536.
(seed = 0)
   ifTrue: [seed := 1 - multiplier + 65536.
            "seed := seed negated .
            seed := 65536 - seed"]
   ifFalse: [product := seed * multiplier.
             quotient := product // divisor.
             remainder := product rem: divisor.
             (remainder > quotient)
                ifTrue: [seed := remainder -quotient]
                ifFalse: [seed := 1 + remainder -quotient]].
" i might want to change the algorithm to only generate numbers from 1 to 1024??"
   seed < 0
      ifTrue: [seed := (seed negated) + 1].
   ^ seed! !


Object subclass: #FilingCharacters
   instanceVariableNames:
      'filingCharactersFileStream '
   classVariableNames:
      'IncludedCharacters '
   poolDictionaries: ''!

!FilingCharacters class methods !

new
     "Answer a new instance of the receiver."
   ^super new initialize! !

!FilingCharacters methods !

addFilingChar: aChar
     "Add the specified character to the set of Filing characters."
   IncludedCharacters add: aChar.!

checkIfFilingCharacter: aChar
     "Answer True if aChar is a filing character, else answer False."
   ^IncludedCharacters includes: aChar!

deleteFilingChar: aChar
     "Delete the specified character from the set of Filing characters."
   IncludedCharacters remove: aChar ifAbsent: [].!
```

```
getFilingChars
    " Answer a SortedCollection of containing all of the included characters. "
    ^IncludedCharacters!

getFirstFilingCharacter: aWord
    "Answer the position of the first filing character in the word. Answer 0 if not
        found."
    | position firstChar |
    position := 0.
    firstChar := true.
    aWord do: [:char | position := position + 1.
                    (IncludedCharacters includes: char) & [firstChar]
                        ifTrue: [^position]].
    ^0.!

initialize
        "This Class method reads the filing characters file from disk and establishes
            a SortedCollection of filing characters."
    | fileContents |

    filingCharactersFileStream := File pathName: FCFile.
    fileContents := filingCharactersFileStream contents.
    filingCharactersFileStream close.
    IncludedCharacters := SortedCollection new: fileContents size.
    IncludedCharacters addAll: fileContents.!

replaceFilingCharactersFile
        "Private. Replace the FilingCharacters File."
    File remove: FCFile.
    filingCharactersFileStream := File newFile: FCFile.!

saveFilingCharacters
        "Save the FilingCharacters to the filing characters file. Do this by first
            combining the DiscardedCharacters and the IncludedCharacters into the In-
            cludedCharacters SortedCollection. Then, create a string out of a sorted
            collection of substrings. Then write the string to the filing characters
            file."
    | aFilingCharactersString |
    aFilingCharactersString := ''.
    IncludedCharacters do: [:each | aFilingCharactersString := aFilingCharacters-
        String, (' ', each)].
    aFilingCharactersString := aFilingCharactersString trimBlanks.
    self replaceFilingCharactersFile.
    filingCharactersFileStream position: 0.
    filingCharactersFileStream putBytesFrom: aFilingCharactersString.
    filingCharactersFileStream close.! !


Object subclass: #JunkWords
    instanceVariableNames:
        'junkWordFileStream '
    classVariableNames:
        'CurrentWords '
    poolDictionaries: ''!
```

```
!JunkWords class methods !

new
     "Answer a new instance of the receiver."
    ^super new initialize! !

!JunkWords methods !

addJunkWord: word
     " Add the specified word to the JunkWord set of words. "
    (CurrentWords includes: word)
    ifFalse: [CurrentWords add: word].!

checkIfJunkWord: aWord
     "Answer True if aWord is a junk word, else answer False."
    ^CurrentWords includes: aWord!

deleteJunkWord: word
     " Remove the specified word from the junk word set. "
    CurrentWords remove: word ifAbsent: [].!

getJunkWords
     " Answer a SortedCollection of substrings containing all of the current junk
        words. "
    ^CurrentWords!

initialize
     "This Class method reads the junk words file from disk and establishes a
        SortedCollection of junk words."
    | fileSubStrings |

    junkWordFileStream := File pathName: JWFile.
    fileSubStrings := junkWordFileStream contents asArrayOfSubstrings.
    junkWordFileStream close.
    CurrentWords := SortedCollection new: fileSubStrings size.
    CurrentWords addAll: fileSubStrings.!

replaceJunkWordFile
     "Private. Replace the Junk Word File."
    File remove: JWFile.
    junkWordFileStream := File newFile: JWFile.!

saveJunkWords
     "Save the JunkWords to the junk word file. Do this by first combining the
        DeletedWords and the CurrentWords into the CurrentWords SortedCollection.
        Then, create a string out of a sorted collection of substrings. Then write
        the string to the junk words file."
    | aJunkWordsString |
    aJunkWordsString := ''.
    CurrentWords do: [:each | aJunkWordsString := aJunkWordsString, (' ', each)].
    aJunkWordsString := aJunkWordsString trimBlanks.
    self replaceJunkWordFile.
    junkWordFileStream position: 0.
    junkWordFileStream putBytesFrom: aJunkWordsString.
    junkWordFileStream close.! !
```

I.7 MISCELLANEOUS CLASSES

```
Object subclass: #FilingDirectory
   instanceVariableNames:
      'directoryName files '
   classVariableNames: ''
   poolDictionaries: ''!

!FilingDirectory class methods !

new
     "Answer a FilingDirectory."
   ^super new initialize! !

!FilingDirectory methods !

addIndexFile: fileName
     "Add a fileName to the FilingDirectory object. "
   files add: fileName!

deleteIndexFile: indexName
     "Delete the specified index file from disk."
   | indexNumber |
   "Remove the index file name from the files OrderedCollection."
   ((indexNumber := files indexOf: indexName) = 0)
   ifFalse: [files removeIndex: indexNumber].

   " Delete the file from the Filing directory on disk."
   File remove: (directoryName , '\' , indexName).!

initialize
     "Set up the FilingDirectory."
   files := OrderedCollection new.
   directoryName := 'C:\FILING'.!

retrieveIndexNames
     "Answer a SortedCollection containing the elements (index file names) of the
       receiver."
   "answer should point to an OrderedCollection of index file names."
   ^files! !


Object subclass: #Queue
   instanceVariableNames:
      'queue '
   classVariableNames: ''
   poolDictionaries: ''!

!Queue class methods !

new
     "Answer a new instance of the receiver."
   ^super new initialize!

new: sizeOfQueue
```

```
        "Answer a new instance of the receiver."
    ^super new initialize: sizeOfQueue! !

!Queue methods !

addToQueue: anObject
        "Add an object to the tail of the queue."
    queue add: anObject!

at: anInteger
        "Answer the element of the receiver at index position anInteger."
    queue at: anInteger!

do: aBlock
        "Answer the receiver. For each element in the receiver, evaluate aBlock with
            that element as the argument. this is from an OrderedCollection"

    | index qSize |
    qSize := queue size.
    index := 0.
    [(index := index + 1) <= qSize]
        whileTrue: [aBlock value: (queue at: index)].!

initialize
        "This method is private. Set up a queue as an OrderedCollection able to hold
            12 elements initially."
    queue := OrderedCollection new.!

initialize: sizeOfQueue
        "This method is private. Set up a queue as an OrderedCollection able to holding
            sizeOfQueue number of elements."
    queue := OrderedCollection new: sizeOfQueue.!

removeFromQueue
        "Answer a removed object from the head of the queue."
    ^queue removeFirst!

size
        "Answer an Integer which is the size of the queue."
    ^queue size! !
```

C++ Electronic Filing Application Code

J.1 USER INTERFACE SUBSYSTEM

```
//REGEN_FILEHEADING
//REGEN_FILEHEADING

    /****************************************************************
    *                                                              *
    *     Source File: EF.h                                        *
    *     Description: Header file for EF application              *
    *     Date:          Sun Jan 01 05:51:17 1995                  *
    *                                                              *
    ****************************************************************/

#ifndef __EF__H
#define __EF__H

//REGEN_HEADER
//REGEN_HEADER


//REGEN_VARS
//REGEN_VARS



#endif // __EF__H


//REGEN_FILEHEADING
//REGEN_FILEHEADING
```

```
/****************************************************************
 *                                                              *
 *    Source File: EF.cpp                                       *
 *    Description: C++ Source file for EF application           *
 *    Date:        Sun Jan 01 05:51:17 1995                     *
 *                                                              *
 ****************************************************************/

#include <owl.h>
#include <edit.h>
#include <listbox.h>
#include <combobox.h>
#include <bchkbox.h>
#include <checkbox.h>
#include <bradio.h>
#include <radiobut.h>
#include <scrollba.h>
#include <dialog.h>
#include <bwcc.h>
#include <dtctl.h>
#include "EF.H"
#include "EFID.h"
#include "EF.h"

//REGEN_VARIABLES
// GLOBALS
#include <dir.h>
#include <dos.h>
#include "misc.h"
#include "defines.h"
#include "datassub.h"
#include "querysub.h"
#include <strng.h>
#include "docsub.h"
#include "serchsub.h"
#include <dirent.h>
#include <stdio.h>
#include <stdlib.h>

String contentToAbstractOperator = "AND";    // Logical operator between content
                                             // query and abstract query
String keywordToAuthorOperator = "AND";      // Logical operator between keyword
                                             // query and author query
String abstractToKeywordOperator = "AND";    // Logical operator between
                                             // keyword query
String& conToAbsOp = contentToAbstractOperator;
String& keyToAutOp = keywordToAuthorOperator;
String& absToKeyOp = abstractToKeywordOperator;

FilingDirectory    *Filing;              //create the FilingDirectory object
List               *DRIs;                // document reference information objects
DocumentNameList*  docNameListObjPtr;    // DocNameList returned from search

const WORD ID_LISTBOX7 = 107;
const WORD ID_LISTBOX6 = 106;
const WORD ID_LISTBOX4 = 104;
```

```
char currentFile[MAXPATH];              // document name selected by user
char currentDirectory[MAXPATH];         // current directory selected by user
char selectedDirectory[MAXPATH];        // selected directory selected by user
char fullDocumentPath[MAXPATH];         // full path including document name
char searchResultsFile[MAXPATH];        // file selected as result of search

//REGEN_VARIABLES

// Define application class derived from TApplication
class TEF : public TApplication
{
public:
  TEF(LPSTR AName, HINSTANCE hInstance, HINSTANCE hPrevInstance,
                LPSTR lpCmdLine, int nCmdShow)
    : TApplication(AName, hInstance, hPrevInstance, lpCmdLine, nCmdShow) {};
    virtual void InitMainWindow();
    virtual void InitInstance();
    //REGEN_APPCLASS
    void initApplication ();        // I added this for app-specific init
    // Electronic Filing Application Class
    //REGEN_APPCLASS
};

void TEF::InitInstance()
{
  TApplication::InitInstance();
  HAccTable = LoadAccelerators(hInstance, "EF");

}
// Declare TMainWindow, a TWindow descendant
class TMainWindow : public TWindow
{
public:
  TMainWindow(PTWindowsObject AParent, LPSTR ATitle);
  ~TMainWindow();
  virtual void EXIT(RTMessage Msg) = [CM_FIRST + IDM_EXIT];
  virtual void FILE(RTMessage Msg) = [CM_FIRST + IDM_FILE];
  virtual void DELETE(RTMessage Msg) = [CM_FIRST + IDM_DELETE];
  virtual void SEARCH(RTMessage Msg) = [CM_FIRST + IDM_SEARCH];
  virtual void FILINGCHARACTERS(RTMessage Msg) = [CM_FIRST +
                                          IDM_FILINGCHARACTERS];
  virtual void JUNKWORDS(RTMessage Msg) = [CM_FIRST + IDM_JUNKWORDS];
  //REGEN_MAINCLASS
  // Electronic Filing Main Application Window Class
  //REGEN_MAINCLASS

};


/****************************************************
 * TMainWindow implementations:
 ****************************************************/

// Define TMainWindow, a TWindow constructor
TMainWindow::TMainWindow(PTWindowsObject AParent, LPSTR ATitle)
                        : TWindow(AParent, ATitle)
```

```
{
   AssignMenu("EF");
   //REGEN_MAINCONSTRUCT
      //
   // Initialize the Filing and DRIs objects
   //    - add all the names of the index files to Filing
   //    - create DRI objects for all index files that have DRI
   //

   DIR          *dir;
   struct       dirent *ent;
   char         dirname[] = "c:\\filing";
   char         *indexString = ".SAM";
   char         *driString = ".DRI";
   char         *ptr;
   char         driAbstract[MaxAbstractSize];
   char         driKeywords[MaxKeywordsSize];
   char         driAuthors[MaxAuthorsSize];
   DocRefInfo   *docRefInfoObj;
   char         documentPath[MAXPATH];// full path including document name
   char         driFileName[MAXPATH]; // file name of .DRI file
   int          status;
   char         *backSlash = "\\";


   if ((status = chdir (dirname)) == -1)
   {
      MessageBox(HWindow, dirname, "Error in changing directoty:", MB_OK);
      perror ("chdir()");
      exit (1);
   }
   if ((dir = opendir (dirname)) == NULL)
   {
      MessageBox(HWindow, "Unable to open filing directory", "Error",
     MB_OK);
      exit (1);
   }

   Filing = new FilingDirectory;
   DRIs = new List;

   while ((ent = readdir (dir)) != NULL)
   {
      if ((ptr = strstr (ent->d_name, indexString)) != NULL)
      {

String *aPtr = new String (ent->d_name);
String& anIndexReference = *aPtr;

// Add an index file to the existing Filing Directory Object
Filing->addIndexFile (anIndexReference);
      }
      else if ((ptr = strstr (ent->d_name, driString)) != NULL)
      {
// For each DRI file, read the DRI file and place the DRI info
//  in a DRI object
```

```
  strcpy (driFileName, ent->d_name);
  ifstream fin (driFileName);
       if (!fin)
  {
    delete Filing;
        delete DRIs;
    MessageBox(HWindow, "ifstream fin (file)", "Errno in creating input file
 stream :", MB_OK);
    fin.close ();
        }
        else
        {
     // abstract
     fin.getline (driAbstract, MaxAbstractSize, '\n');
     // keywords
     fin.getline (driKeywords, MaxKeywordsSize, '\n');
     // authors
     fin.getline (driAuthors, MaxAuthorsSize, '\n');
     fin.close();

     strcpy (documentPath, dirname);
     strcat (documentPath, backSlash);
     strncat (documentPath, ent->d_name, strlen(ent->d_name));

     //Assume that all document files are of the .txt extension
     //  so replace the .dri extension with .txt

     char txtExtension[] = ".TXT\0";
     char driExtension[] = ".DRI\0";
     char*  driPtr;

     driPtr = strstr (documentPath, driExtension);
     strcpy (driPtr, txtExtension);

     docRefInfoObj = new DocRefInfo (driAbstract, driAuthors, driKeywords,
          ent->d_name, documentPath);

     DocRefInfo& theDRIObject = *docRefInfoObj;

     // Add the Document Reference Info object to the DRIs holder
     DRIs->add ((Object&)theDRIObject);
   }
      }
  }

  if (closedir (dir) != 0)
     MessageBox(HWindow, "Unable to close filing directory", "Error",
    MB_OK);

  //REGEN_MAINCONSTRUCT

}

// Define TMainWindow destructor
TMainWindow::~TMainWindow()
{
```

```
   //REGEN_MAINDESTRUCT
   delete Filing;
   delete DRIs;
   //REGEN_MAINDESTRUCT


}


_CLASSDEF(TDIALOG_1Dlg)


// Declare TDIALOG_1Dlg, a TDialog descendant
class TDIALOG_1Dlg : public TDialog
{
public:
   PTEdit Edit105;
   PTListBox LBox106;
   PTListBox LBox107;
   PTEdit Edit108;

   TDIALOG_1Dlg(PTWindowsObject AParent, LPSTR AName);
   ~TDIALOG_1Dlg();
   virtual void SetupWindow();
   virtual void RTDIALOG_1104(RTMessage Msg) = [ID_FIRST + 104];
   virtual void RTDIALOG_1101(RTMessage Msg) = [ID_FIRST + 101];
   virtual void RTDIALOG_1102(RTMessage Msg) = [ID_FIRST + 102];
   virtual void RTDIALOG_1103(RTMessage Msg) = [ID_FIRST + 103];
   //REGEN_DIALOG_1_CLASS
   // RT constant represents the available type of Windows resources.
   // File A Document Dialog Box Declaration
   // RTDIALOG_1104Reference Information Push Button
   // RTDIALOG_1101Ok Push Button
   // RTDIALOG_1102Cancel Push Button
   // RTDIALOG_1103Help Push Button
   virtual void handleDirListBoxMsg(RTMessage Msg)   = [ID_FIRST + ID_LISTBOX7];
   virtual void handleFileListBoxMsg(RTMessage Msg)   = [ID_FIRST + ID_LISTBOX6];
   charselectedFile[13];// document name to file
   //REGEN_DIALOG_1_CLASS

};


_CLASSDEF(TDIALOG_2Dlg)


// Declare TDIALOG_2Dlg, a TDialog descendant
class TDIALOG_2Dlg : public TDialog
{
public:
   PTEdit Edit103;
   PTEdit Edit104;
   PTEdit Edit111;
   PTEdit Edit112;

   TDIALOG_2Dlg(PTWindowsObject AParent, LPSTR AName);
   ~TDIALOG_2Dlg();
   virtual void SetupWindow();
   virtual void RTDIALOG_2101(RTMessage Msg) = [ID_FIRST + 101];
   virtual void RTDIALOG_2102(RTMessage Msg) = [ID_FIRST + 102];
   //REGEN_DIALOG_2_CLASS
```

```
   // Document Reference Information Dialog Box
   //REGEN_DIALOG_2_CLASS

};

_CLASSDEF(TDIALOG_5Dlg)

// Declare TDIALOG_5Dlg, a TDialog descendant
class TDIALOG_5Dlg : public TDialog
{
public:
   PTListBox LBox104;
   PTListBox LBox105;
   PTEdit Edit106;
   PTEdit Edit107;

   TDIALOG_5Dlg(PTWindowsObject AParent, LPSTR AName);
   ~TDIALOG_5Dlg();
   virtual void SetupWindow();
   virtual void RTDIALOG_5101(RTMessage Msg) = [ID_FIRST + 101];
   virtual void RTDIALOG_5102(RTMessage Msg) = [ID_FIRST + 102];
   virtual void RTDIALOG_5103(RTMessage Msg) = [ID_FIRST + 103];
   //REGEN_DIALOG_5_CLASS
   // Delete A Document Dialog Box
   //REGEN_DIALOG_5_CLASS

};

_CLASSDEF(TDIALOG_3Dlg)

// Declare TDIALOG_3Dlg, a TDialog descendant
class TDIALOG_3Dlg : public TDialog
{
public:
   PTEdit Edit104;
   PTEdit Edit105;
   PTEdit Edit106;
   PTEdit Edit107;

   TDIALOG_3Dlg(PTWindowsObject AParent, LPSTR AName);
   ~TDIALOG_3Dlg();
   virtual void SetupWindow();
   virtual void RTDIALOG_3101(RTMessage Msg) = [ID_FIRST + 101];
   virtual void RTDIALOG_3102(RTMessage Msg) = [ID_FIRST + 102];
   virtual void RTDIALOG_3103(RTMessage Msg) = [ID_FIRST + 103];
   virtual void RTDIALOG_3110(RTMessage Msg) = [ID_FIRST + 110];
   virtual void RTDIALOG_3111(RTMessage Msg) = [ID_FIRST + 111];
   virtual void RTDIALOG_3108(RTMessage Msg) = [ID_FIRST + 108];
   virtual void RTDIALOG_3109(RTMessage Msg) = [ID_FIRST + 109];
   virtual void RTDIALOG_3112(RTMessage Msg) = [ID_FIRST + 112];
   virtual void RTDIALOG_3113(RTMessage Msg) = [ID_FIRST + 113];
   //REGEN_DIALOG_3_CLASS
   // Search Dialog Box
private:
   SearchEngine   *searchEngineObj;
   ContentQuery *contentQueryObj;
```

```cpp
    AuthorQuery *authorQueryObj;
    AbstractQuery *abstractQueryObj;
    KeywordQuery *keywordQueryObj;

    //REGEN_DIALOG_3_CLASS

};

_CLASSDEF(TDIALOG_4Dlg)

// Declare TDIALOG_4Dlg, a TDialog descendant
class TDIALOG_4Dlg : public TDialog
{
public:
    PTListBox LBox104;
    PTEdit Edit107;

    TDIALOG_4Dlg(PTWindowsObject AParent, LPSTR AName);
    ~TDIALOG_4Dlg();
    virtual void SetupWindow();
    virtual void RTDIALOG_4101(RTMessage Msg) = [ID_FIRST + 101];
    virtual void RTDIALOG_4102(RTMessage Msg) = [ID_FIRST + 102];
    virtual void RTDIALOG_4103(RTMessage Msg) = [ID_FIRST + 103];
    //REGEN_DIALOG_4_CLASS
    // Search Results Dialog Box
    virtual void handleSRListBoxMsg(RTMessage Msg)   = [ID_FIRST + ID_LISTBOX4];
    //REGEN_DIALOG_4_CLASS

};

_CLASSDEF(TDIALOG_9Dlg)

// Declare TDIALOG_9Dlg, a TDialog descendant
class TDIALOG_9Dlg : public TDialog
{
public:
    PTEdit Edit101;

    TDIALOG_9Dlg(PTWindowsObject AParent, LPSTR AName);
    ~TDIALOG_9Dlg();
    virtual void donePushButton(RTMessage Msg) = [ID_FIRST + 102];
    virtual void SetupWindow();
    //REGEN_DIALOG_9_CLASS
    // View A Document Dialog Box
    //REGEN_DIALOG_9_CLASS

};

_CLASSDEF(TDIALOG_6Dlg)

// Declare TDIALOG_6Dlg, a TDialog descendant
class TDIALOG_6Dlg : public TDialog
{
public:
    PTEdit Edit101;
    PTEdit Edit104;
```

```
   PTEdit Edit105;

   TDIALOG_6Dlg(PTWindowsObject AParent, LPSTR AName);
   ~TDIALOG_6Dlg();
   virtual void SetupWindow();
   virtual void RTDIALOG_6102(RTMessage Msg) = [ID_FIRST + 102];
   virtual void RTDIALOG_6103(RTMessage Msg) = [ID_FIRST + 103];
   virtual void RTDIALOG_6106(RTMessage Msg) = [ID_FIRST + 106];
   virtual void RTDIALOG_6107(RTMessage Msg) = [ID_FIRST + 107];
   //REGEN_DIALOG_6_CLASS
   // Print A Document Dialog Box
   //REGEN_DIALOG_6_CLASS

};

_CLASSDEF(TDIALOG_7Dlg)

// Declare TDIALOG_7Dlg, a TDialog descendant
class TDIALOG_7Dlg : public TDialog
{
public:
   PTListBox LBox101;
   PTEdit Edit106;

   TDIALOG_7Dlg(PTWindowsObject AParent, LPSTR AName);
   ~TDIALOG_7Dlg();
   virtual void SetupWindow();
   virtual void RTDIALOG_7102(RTMessage Msg) = [ID_FIRST + 102];
   virtual void RTDIALOG_7103(RTMessage Msg) = [ID_FIRST + 103];
   virtual void RTDIALOG_7104(RTMessage Msg) = [ID_FIRST + 104];
   virtual void RTDIALOG_7105(RTMessage Msg) = [ID_FIRST + 105];
   //REGEN_DIALOG_7_CLASS
   // Filing Character Dialog Box
   //REGEN_DIALOG_7_CLASS

};

_CLASSDEF(TDIALOG_8Dlg)

// Declare TDIALOG_8Dlg, a TDialog descendant
class TDIALOG_8Dlg : public TDialog
{
public:
   PTListBox LBox101;
   PTEdit Edit102;

   TDIALOG_8Dlg(PTWindowsObject AParent, LPSTR AName);
   ~TDIALOG_8Dlg();
   virtual void SetupWindow();
   virtual void RTDIALOG_8103(RTMessage Msg) = [ID_FIRST + 103];
   virtual void RTDIALOG_8104(RTMessage Msg) = [ID_FIRST + 104];
   virtual void RTDIALOG_8105(RTMessage Msg) = [ID_FIRST + 105];
   virtual void RTDIALOG_8106(RTMessage Msg) = [ID_FIRST + 106];
   //REGEN_DIALOG_8_CLASS
   // Junk Words Dialog Box
   //REGEN_DIALOG_8_CLASS
```

```
};

void TDIALOG_1Dlg::handleDirListBoxMsg(RTMessage Msg)
{
  int Idx;
  char*ptr;
  charnewDirectory[MAXPATH];
  charfilesDirectory[MAXPATH];
  unsigneddrive;
  intsearchPathFlag;

  //
  // Handle the Directories List Box when the selection in the list box
  //   has changed
  //

  if ( Msg.LP.Hi == LBN_SELCHANGE )
  {
    _dos_getdrive(&drive);
    filesDirectory[0] = '\\';
    filesDirectory[1] = 0;
    newDirectory[0] = drive + 'A' - 1;
    newDirectory[1] = ':';
    newDirectory[2] = '\\';
    newDirectory[3] = 0;
    DlgDirSelect (HWindow, currentDirectory, 107);

    // set the selectedDirectory
    strcpy (selectedDirectory, currentDirectory);

    strncat (filesDirectory, currentDirectory, strlen (currentDirectory));
    strncat (newDirectory, currentDirectory, strlen (currentDirectory));
    strcpy (selectedDirectory, newDirectory); // new directory in proper format
    if ((ptr = strrchr (selectedDirectory, '\\')) != 0)
        *ptr = 0;
    strncat (filesDirectory, "*.*", 3);

    // fill Directories list box
    searchPathFlag = DlgDirList(HWindow, newDirectory, 106, 108, 0);

  // fill Files list box
    searchPathFlag = DlgDirList(HWindow, filesDirectory, 106, 0, 0);
  }
  else if ( Msg.LP.Hi == LBN_DBLCLK)
  {
  //
  // A directory item in the Directories list box has been double clicked
  //
    _dos_getdrive(&drive);
    filesDirectory[0] = '\\';
    filesDirectory[1] = 0;
    newDirectory[0] = drive + 'A' - 1;
    newDirectory[1] = ':';
    newDirectory[2] = '\\';
    newDirectory[3] = 0;
```

```
      DlgDirSelect (HWindow, currentDirectory, 107);
      strncat (filesDirectory, currentDirectory, strlen (currentDirectory));
      strcpy (selectedDirectory, newDirectory); // new directory in proper format
      if ((ptr = strrchr (selectedDirectory, '\\')) != 0)
          *ptr = 0;
      strncat (filesDirectory, "*.*", 3);

      // fill Directories list box
      searchPathFlag = DlgDirList(HWindow, filesDirectory, 107, 108, 0xC010);

   // fill Files list box
      searchPathFlag = DlgDirList(HWindow, filesDirectory, 106, 0, 0);

   }
}

void TDIALOG_1Dlg::handleFileListBoxMsg(RTMessage Msg)
{
  int Idx;
  int stringSize;

  //
  // Handle the File List Box when the selection in the File list box
  //    has changed
  //

  if ( Msg.LP.Hi == LBN_SELCHANGE )
  {
    DlgDirSelect (HWindow, selectedFile, 106);
    strcpy (currentFile, selectedFile);
  }
}


void TDIALOG_9Dlg::donePushButton(RTMessage Msg)
{

   //REGEN_VAR
   //REGEN_VAR

   switch(Msg.LP.Hi)
   {
     case BN_CLICKED :
     // Execute modal dialog
     CloseWindow ();

     //REGEN_END
     //REGEN_END

    break;
   }
}


// Place all Window or field interaction here, not in the constructor.
```

```
void TDIALOG_1Dlg::SetupWindow()
{
   TDialog::SetupWindow();

   //REGEN_DIALOG_1_SETUP
   //  File Dialog Box - setup the dialog box
   DIR*dir;
   struct dirent *ent;
   char *mydir = "\\";

   selectedDirectory[0] = '\\';
   selectedDirectory[1] = '\0';
   currentDirectory[0] = '\\';
   currentDirectory[1] = '\0';
   // fill the Directories list box
   DlgDirList(HWindow, mydir, 107, 108, 0xC010);

   // fill Files list box
   DlgDirList(HWindow, mydir, 106, 0, 0);

   //REGEN_DIALOG_1_SETUP

}

// Define TDIALOG_1Dlg, a TDialog constructor
TDIALOG_1Dlg::TDIALOG_1Dlg(PTWindowsObject AParent, LPSTR AName)
              :TDialog(AParent, AName)
{

   Edit105 = new TEdit(this, 105, 81);
   LBox106 = new TListBox(this, 106);
   LBox107 = new TListBox(this, 107);
   Edit108 = new TEdit(this, 108, 81);
   //REGEN_DIALOG_1_CONSTRUCTOR

   // File A Document Dialog Box Constructor

   //REGEN_DIALOG_1_CONSTRUCTOR

}

// Define TDIALOG_1Dlg destructor
TDIALOG_1Dlg::~TDIALOG_1Dlg()
{

   //REGEN_DIALOG_1_DESTRUCTOR
   // File A Document Destructor
   //REGEN_DIALOG_1_DESTRUCTOR

}

void TDIALOG_1Dlg::RTDIALOG_1101(RTMessage Msg)
{
   //REGEN_VAR
   //REGEN_VAR
   switch(Msg.LP.Hi)
```

```
   {
      case BN_CLICKED :
      //REGEN_DIALOG_1101_ROUTING
      //  File Dialog Box Ok Push Button
      // Index the document
   TextDocument   *textDocumentObj;

   textDocumentObj = new TextDocument;
   //send text document a file message
   textDocumentObj->fileDoc(HWindow, selectedFile, selectedDirectory);
   delete textDocumentObj;
   CloseWindow();
      //REGEN_DIALOG_1101_ROUTING
      break;
   }
   //REGEN_END
   //REGEN_END
}

void TDIALOG_1Dlg::RTDIALOG_1102(RTMessage Msg)
{
   //REGEN_VAR
   //REGEN_VAR
   switch(Msg.LP.Hi)
   {
      case BN_CLICKED :
      //REGEN_DIALOG_1102_ROUTING
      //  File Dialog Box Cancel Push Button
   if (MessageBox(HWindow, "Are you sure?", "Cancel File Operation",
     MB_YESNO) == IDYES)
     CloseWindow();

      //REGEN_DIALOG_1102_ROUTING
      break;
   }
   //REGEN_END
   //REGEN_END
}

void TDIALOG_1Dlg::RTDIALOG_1103(RTMessage Msg)
{
   //REGEN_VAR
   //REGEN_VAR
   switch(Msg.LP.Hi)
   {
      case BN_CLICKED :
      //REGEN_DIALOG_1103_ROUTING
      // File Dialog Box Help Push Button
      MessageBox(HWindow, "Help Not Implemented", "Help",
     MB_OK);
   CloseWindow();
      //REGEN_DIALOG_1103_ROUTING
      break;
   }
   //REGEN_END
   //REGEN_END
```

```
}

// Place all Window or field interaction here, not in the constructor.
void TDIALOG_2Dlg::SetupWindow()
{
   TDialog::SetupWindow();

   //REGEN_DIALOG_2_SETUP
   // Document Reference Information Dialog Box
   //REGEN_DIALOG_2_SETUP

}

// Define TDIALOG_2Dlg, a TDialog constructor
TDIALOG_2Dlg::TDIALOG_2Dlg(PTWindowsObject AParent, LPSTR AName)
             :TDialog(AParent, AName)
{

   Edit103 = new TEdit(this, 103, 81);
   Edit104 = new TEdit(this, 104, 81);
   Edit111 = new TEdit(this, 111, 81);
   Edit112 = new TEdit(this, 112, 81);
   //REGEN_DIALOG_2_CONSTRUCTOR
   // Document Reference Information Dialog Box
   //REGEN_DIALOG_2_CONSTRUCTOR

}

// Define TDIALOG_2Dlg destructor
TDIALOG_2Dlg::~TDIALOG_2Dlg()
{

   //REGEN_DIALOG_2_DESTRUCTOR
   // Document Reference Information Dialog Box
   //REGEN_DIALOG_2_DESTRUCTOR

}

void TDIALOG_2Dlg::RTDIALOG_2101(RTMessage Msg)
{
   //REGEN_VAR
   //REGEN_VAR
   switch(Msg.LP.Hi)
   {
      case BN_CLICKED :
      //REGEN_DIALOG_2101_ROUTING
      // Document Reference Information Dialog Box Ok Push Button
   TextDocument  *textDocumentObj;
   DocRefInfo   *docRefInfoObj;
   intmaxAbstractChars, maxKeywordChars, maxAuthorChars;
   charabstractString[MaxAbstractSize],
      authorString[MaxAuthorsSize],
      keywordString[MaxKeywordsSize];
   char    *objectName;
   List    myClassId;
```

```
      maxAbstractChars = Edit103->GetText (abstractString, MaxAbstractSize);
   maxKeywordChars = Edit111->GetText (keywordString, MaxKeywordsSize);
   maxAuthorChars = Edit112->GetText (authorString, MaxAuthorsSize);

   // Append a newline character to each piece of document reference
   //   information to simplify the input and output using streams
   strncat (abstractString, "\n\0", 2);
   strncat (keywordString, "\n\0", 2);
   strncat (authorString, "\n\0", 2);

   textDocumentObj = new TextDocument;
   docRefInfoObj = new DocRefInfo;

   docRefInfoObj->setDri (authorString, abstractString, keywordString, current-
       File, fullDocumentPath);
   DocRefInfo& theDRIObject = *docRefInfoObj;

   // Add the Document Reference Info object to the DRIs holder
   DRIs->add ((Object&)theDRIObject);

   //send text document a file message
   textDocumentObj->fileDocAndDri (HWindow, currentFile, selectedDirectory, doc-
       RefInfoObj);
   delete textDocumentObj;
   CloseWindow();
      //REGEN_DIALOG_2101_ROUTING
      break;
   }
   //REGEN_END
   //REGEN_END
}

void TDIALOG_2Dlg::RTDIALOG_2102(RTMessage Msg)
{
   //REGEN_VAR
   //REGEN_VAR
   switch(Msg.LP.Hi)
   {
      case BN_CLICKED :
      //REGEN_DIALOG_2102_ROUTING
      // Document Reference Information Dialog Box Cancel Push Button
   CloseWindow();
      //REGEN_DIALOG_2102_ROUTING
      break;
   }
   //REGEN_END
   //REGEN_END
}

// Place all Window or field interaction here, not in the constructor.
void TDIALOG_5Dlg::SetupWindow()
{
   TDialog::SetupWindow();

   //REGEN_DIALOG_5_SETUP
   // Delete Document Dialog Box
```

```
   //REGEN_DIALOG_5_SETUP

}

// Define TDIALOG_5Dlg, a TDialog constructor
TDIALOG_5Dlg::TDIALOG_5Dlg(PTWindowsObject AParent, LPSTR AName)
             :TDialog(AParent, AName)
{

  LBox104 = new TListBox(this, 104);
  LBox105 = new TListBox(this, 105);
  Edit106 = new TEdit(this, 106, 81);
  Edit107 = new TEdit(this, 107, 81);
  //REGEN_DIALOG_5_CONSTRUCTOR
  // Delete Document Dialog Box
  //REGEN_DIALOG_5_CONSTRUCTOR

}

// Define TDIALOG_5Dlg destructor
TDIALOG_5Dlg::~TDIALOG_5Dlg()
{

  //REGEN_DIALOG_5_DESTRUCTOR
  // Delete Document Dialog Box
  //REGEN_DIALOG_5_DESTRUCTOR

}

void TDIALOG_5Dlg::RTDIALOG_5101(RTMessage Msg)
{
  //REGEN_VAR
  // Delete Document Dialog Box Ok Push Button
  //REGEN_VAR
  switch(Msg.LP.Hi)
  {
     case BN_CLICKED :
     //REGEN_DIALOG_5101_ROUTING
       CloseWindow();
     //REGEN_DIALOG_5101_ROUTING
     break;
  }
  //REGEN_END
  //REGEN_END
}

void TDIALOG_5Dlg::RTDIALOG_5102(RTMessage Msg)
{
  //REGEN_VAR
  // Delete Document Dialog Box Cancel Push Button
  //REGEN_VAR
  switch(Msg.LP.Hi)
  {
     case BN_CLICKED :
     //REGEN_DIALOG_5102_ROUTING
       CloseWindow();
```

```
         //REGEN_DIALOG_5102_ROUTING
         break;
      }
   //REGEN_END
   //REGEN_END
}

void TDIALOG_5Dlg::RTDIALOG_5103(RTMessage Msg)
{
   //REGEN_VAR
   // Delete Document Dialog Box Help Push Button
   //REGEN_VAR
   switch(Msg.LP.Hi)
   {
      case BN_CLICKED :
      //REGEN_DIALOG_5103_ROUTING
        CloseWindow();
      //REGEN_DIALOG_5103_ROUTING
      break;
   }
   //REGEN_END
   //REGEN_END
}

// Place all Window or field interaction here, not in the constructor.
void TDIALOG_3Dlg::SetupWindow()
{
   TDialog::SetupWindow();

   //REGEN_DIALOG_3_SETUP
   // Search for Document Dialog Box
   //REGEN_DIALOG_3_SETUP

}

// Define TDIALOG_3Dlg, a TDialog constructor
TDIALOG_3Dlg::TDIALOG_3Dlg(PTWindowsObject AParent, LPSTR AName)
              :TDialog(AParent, AName)
{

   Edit104 = new TEdit(this, 104, 81);
   Edit105 = new TEdit(this, 105, 81);
   Edit106 = new TEdit(this, 106, 81);
   Edit107 = new TEdit(this, 107, 81);
   //REGEN_DIALOG_3_CONSTRUCTOR
   // Search for Document Dialog Box
   //REGEN_DIALOG_3_CONSTRUCTOR

}

// Define TDIALOG_3Dlg destructor
TDIALOG_3Dlg::~TDIALOG_3Dlg()
{

   //REGEN_DIALOG_3_DESTRUCTOR
   // Search for Document Dialog Box
```

```cpp
   //REGEN_DIALOG_3_DESTRUCTOR

}

void TDIALOG_3Dlg::RTDIALOG_3102(RTMessage Msg)
{
   //REGEN_VAR
   //REGEN_VAR
   switch(Msg.LP.Hi)
   {
      case BN_CLICKED :
      //REGEN_DIALOG_3102_ROUTING
      // Search for Document Dialog Box Cancel Push Button
   if (MessageBox(HWindow, "Are you sure?", "Cancel Search Operation",
     MB_YESNO) == IDYES)
      CloseWindow();
      //REGEN_DIALOG_3102_ROUTING
      break;
   }
   //REGEN_END
   //REGEN_END
}

void TDIALOG_3Dlg::RTDIALOG_3103(RTMessage Msg)
{
   //REGEN_VAR
   //REGEN_VAR
   switch(Msg.LP.Hi)
   {
      case BN_CLICKED :
      //REGEN_DIALOG_3103_ROUTING
      // Search for Document Dialog Box Done Push Button
      CloseWindow();
      //REGEN_DIALOG_3103_ROUTING
      break;
   }
   //REGEN_END
   //REGEN_END
}

void TDIALOG_3Dlg::RTDIALOG_3110(RTMessage Msg)
{
   //REGEN_VAR
   //REGEN_VAR
   switch(Msg.LP.Hi)
   {
      case BN_CLICKED :
      //REGEN_DIALOG_3110_ROUTING
      //REGEN_DIALOG_3110_ROUTING
      break;
   }
   //REGEN_END
   //REGEN_END
}

void TDIALOG_3Dlg::RTDIALOG_3111(RTMessage Msg)
```

```
{
   //REGEN_VAR
   //REGEN_VAR
   switch(Msg.LP.Hi)
   {
      case BN_CLICKED :
      //REGEN_DIALOG_3111_ROUTING
      //REGEN_DIALOG_3111_ROUTING
      break;
   }
   //REGEN_END
   //REGEN_END
}

void TDIALOG_3Dlg::RTDIALOG_3108(RTMessage Msg)
{
   //REGEN_VAR
   //REGEN_VAR
   switch(Msg.LP.Hi)
   {
      case BN_CLICKED :
      //REGEN_DIALOG_3108_ROUTING
      //REGEN_DIALOG_3108_ROUTING
      break;
   }
   //REGEN_END
   //REGEN_END
}

void TDIALOG_3Dlg::RTDIALOG_3109(RTMessage Msg)
{
   //REGEN_VAR
   //REGEN_VAR
   switch(Msg.LP.Hi)
   {
      case BN_CLICKED :
      //REGEN_DIALOG_3109_ROUTING
      //REGEN_DIALOG_3109_ROUTING
      break;
   }
   //REGEN_END
   //REGEN_END
}

void TDIALOG_3Dlg::RTDIALOG_3112(RTMessage Msg)
{
   //REGEN_VAR
   //REGEN_VAR
   switch(Msg.LP.Hi)
   {
      case BN_CLICKED :
      //REGEN_DIALOG_3112_ROUTING
      //REGEN_DIALOG_3112_ROUTING
      break;
   }
   //REGEN_END
```

```
   //REGEN_END
}

void TDIALOG_3Dlg::RTDIALOG_3113(RTMessage Msg)
{
   //REGEN_VAR
   //REGEN_VAR
   switch(Msg.LP.Hi)
   {
      case BN_CLICKED :
      //REGEN_DIALOG_3113_ROUTING
      //REGEN_DIALOG_3113_ROUTING
      break;
   }
   //REGEN_END
   //REGEN_END
}

// Place all Window or field interaction here, not in the constructor.
void TDIALOG_4Dlg::SetupWindow()
{
   TDialog::SetupWindow();

   //REGEN_DIALOG_4_SETUP
      // Search Results Dialog Box

   // fill the scrolling list box with document names found as the
   //    result of a search

   const char*  aFileName;  // null terminated file name string
   String*  fileNamePtr;
   int  numberOfDocumentsFound;
   DWORD   valueReturned;

   numberOfDocumentsFound = docNameListObjPtr->size ();
   while (numberOfDocumentsFound-- > 0)
   {
      String& fileName = docNameListObjPtr->documentName();
      fileNamePtr = &fileName;
      aFileName = *fileNamePtr;
      docNameListObjPtr->removeFromDNL (fileName);
      valueReturned = SendDlgItemMessage (HWindow, 104, LB_ADDSTRING, 0, (DWORD)
   aFileName);
   }

   //REGEN_DIALOG_4_SETUP

}

void TDIALOG_4Dlg::handleSRListBoxMsg(RTMessage Msg)
{
   // a file name in the Search Results List Box and been selected
   //    or double clicked

   if ( (Msg.LP.Hi == LBN_SELCHANGE) || (Msg.LP.Hi == LBN_DBLCLK))
```

```
    {
       DlgDirSelect (HWindow, searchResultsFile, 104);
    }
}



// Define TDIALOG_4Dlg, a TDialog constructor
TDIALOG_4Dlg::TDIALOG_4Dlg(PTWindowsObject AParent, LPSTR AName)
              :TDialog(AParent, AName)
{

   LBox104 = new TListBox(this, 104);
   Edit107 = new TEdit(this, 107, 81);
   //REGEN_DIALOG_4_CONSTRUCTOR
   //REGEN_DIALOG_4_CONSTRUCTOR

}

// Define TDIALOG_4Dlg destructor
TDIALOG_4Dlg::~TDIALOG_4Dlg()
{

   //REGEN_DIALOG_4_DESTRUCTOR
   //REGEN_DIALOG_4_DESTRUCTOR

}

void TDIALOG_4Dlg::RTDIALOG_4103(RTMessage Msg)
{
   //REGEN_VAR
   //REGEN_VAR
   switch(Msg.LP.Hi)
   {
      case BN_CLICKED :
      //REGEN_DIALOG_4103_ROUTING
      CloseWindow ();
      //REGEN_DIALOG_4103_ROUTING
      break;
   }
   //REGEN_END
   //REGEN_END
}

// Place all Window or field interaction here, not in the constructor.
void TDIALOG_9Dlg::SetupWindow()
{
   TDialog::SetupWindow();

   //REGEN_DIALOG_9_SETUP

   // read in the text file and insert text into the edit control box
   chartextBuffer[81];

   ifstream docFStream (searchResultsFile);
```

```
   docFStream.clear ();// reset eof

   // Position document file stream to the beginning of file
   docFStream.seekg (0, ios::beg);

   while (!docFStream.eof())
   {
      fillBuffer (textBuffer, 0, sizeof (textBuffer));
      docFStream.getline (textBuffer, sizeof (textBuffer), '\n');
      Edit101->Insert (textBuffer); // insert text into edit control box
   }

   //REGEN_DIALOG_9_SETUP

}

// Define TDIALOG_9Dlg, a TDialog constructor
TDIALOG_9Dlg::TDIALOG_9Dlg(PTWindowsObject AParent, LPSTR AName)
            :TDialog(AParent, AName)
{

   Edit101 = new TEdit(this, 101, 81);
   //REGEN_DIALOG_9_CONSTRUCTOR
   //REGEN_DIALOG_9_CONSTRUCTOR

}

// Define TDIALOG_9Dlg destructor
TDIALOG_9Dlg::~TDIALOG_9Dlg()
{

   //REGEN_DIALOG_9_DESTRUCTOR
   //REGEN_DIALOG_9_DESTRUCTOR

}

// Place all Window or field interaction here, not in the constructor.
void TDIALOG_6Dlg::SetupWindow()
{
   TDialog::SetupWindow();

   //REGEN_DIALOG_6_SETUP
   //REGEN_DIALOG_6_SETUP

}

// Define TDIALOG_6Dlg, a TDialog constructor
TDIALOG_6Dlg::TDIALOG_6Dlg(PTWindowsObject AParent, LPSTR AName)
            :TDialog(AParent, AName)
{

   Edit101 = new TEdit(this, 101, 81);
   Edit104 = new TEdit(this, 104, 81);
   Edit105 = new TEdit(this, 105, 81);
   //REGEN_DIALOG_6_CONSTRUCTOR
   //REGEN_DIALOG_6_CONSTRUCTOR
```

```
}

// Define TDIALOG_6Dlg destructor
TDIALOG_6Dlg::~TDIALOG_6Dlg()
{

   //REGEN_DIALOG_6_DESTRUCTOR
   //REGEN_DIALOG_6_DESTRUCTOR

}

void TDIALOG_6Dlg::RTDIALOG_6102(RTMessage Msg)
{
   //REGEN_VAR
   //REGEN_VAR
   switch(Msg.LP.Hi)
   {
      case BN_CLICKED :
      //REGEN_DIALOG_6102_ROUTING
      //REGEN_DIALOG_6102_ROUTING
      break;
   }
   //REGEN_END
   //REGEN_END
}

void TDIALOG_6Dlg::RTDIALOG_6103(RTMessage Msg)
{
   //REGEN_VAR
   //REGEN_VAR
   switch(Msg.LP.Hi)
   {
      case BN_CLICKED :
      //REGEN_DIALOG_6103_ROUTING
      //REGEN_DIALOG_6103_ROUTING
      break;
   }
   //REGEN_END
   //REGEN_END
}

void TDIALOG_6Dlg::RTDIALOG_6106(RTMessage Msg)
{
   //REGEN_VAR
   // Ok push button for Print dialog box
   //REGEN_VAR
   switch(Msg.LP.Hi)
   {
      case BN_CLICKED :
      //REGEN_DIALOG_6106_ROUTING
      CloseWindow ();
      //REGEN_DIALOG_6106_ROUTING
      break;
   }
   //REGEN_END
   //REGEN_END
```

```
}

void TDIALOG_6Dlg::RTDIALOG_6107(RTMessage Msg)
{
   //REGEN_VAR
   // Cancel push button for Print dialog box
   //REGEN_VAR
   switch(Msg.LP.Hi)
   {
      case BN_CLICKED :
      //REGEN_DIALOG_6107_ROUTING
      CloseWindow ();
      //REGEN_DIALOG_6107_ROUTING
      break;
   }
   //REGEN_END
   //REGEN_END
}

// Place all Window or field interaction here, not in the constructor.
void TDIALOG_7Dlg::SetupWindow()
{
   TDialog::SetupWindow();

   //REGEN_DIALOG_7_SETUP
   //REGEN_DIALOG_7_SETUP

}

// Define TDIALOG_7Dlg, a TDialog constructor
TDIALOG_7Dlg::TDIALOG_7Dlg(PTWindowsObject AParent, LPSTR AName)
              :TDialog(AParent, AName)
{

   LBox101 = new TListBox(this, 101);
   Edit106 = new TEdit(this, 106, 81);
   //REGEN_DIALOG_7_CONSTRUCTOR
   //REGEN_DIALOG_7_CONSTRUCTOR

}

// Define TDIALOG_7Dlg destructor
TDIALOG_7Dlg::~TDIALOG_7Dlg()
{

   //REGEN_DIALOG_7_DESTRUCTOR
   //REGEN_DIALOG_7_DESTRUCTOR

}

void TDIALOG_7Dlg::RTDIALOG_7102(RTMessage Msg)
{
   //REGEN_VAR
   //REGEN_VAR
   switch(Msg.LP.Hi)
   {
```

```
      case BN_CLICKED :
      //REGEN_DIALOG_7102_ROUTING
      //REGEN_DIALOG_7102_ROUTING
      break;
   }
   //REGEN_END
   //REGEN_END
}

void TDIALOG_7Dlg::RTDIALOG_7103(RTMessage Msg)
{
   //REGEN_VAR
   //REGEN_VAR
   switch(Msg.LP.Hi)
   {
      case BN_CLICKED :
      //REGEN_DIALOG_7103_ROUTING
      //REGEN_DIALOG_7103_ROUTING
      break;
   }
   //REGEN_END
   //REGEN_END
}

void TDIALOG_7Dlg::RTDIALOG_7104(RTMessage Msg)
{
   //REGEN_VAR
   //REGEN_VAR
   switch(Msg.LP.Hi)
   {
      case BN_CLICKED :
      //REGEN_DIALOG_7104_ROUTING
      //REGEN_DIALOG_7104_ROUTING
      break;
   }
   //REGEN_END
   //REGEN_END
}

void TDIALOG_7Dlg::RTDIALOG_7105(RTMessage Msg)
{
   //REGEN_VAR
   //REGEN_VAR
   switch(Msg.LP.Hi)
   {
      case BN_CLICKED :
      //REGEN_DIALOG_7105_ROUTING
      //REGEN_DIALOG_7105_ROUTING
      break;
   }
   //REGEN_END
   //REGEN_END
}

// Place all Window or field interaction here, not in the constructor.
void TDIALOG_8Dlg::SetupWindow()
```

```
{
   TDialog::SetupWindow();

   //REGEN_DIALOG_8_SETUP
   //REGEN_DIALOG_8_SETUP

}

// Define TDIALOG_8Dlg, a TDialog constructor
TDIALOG_8Dlg::TDIALOG_8Dlg(PTWindowsObject AParent, LPSTR AName)
               :TDialog(AParent, AName)
{

   LBox101 = new TListBox(this, 101);
   Edit102 = new TEdit(this, 102, 81);
   //REGEN_DIALOG_8_CONSTRUCTOR
   //REGEN_DIALOG_8_CONSTRUCTOR

}

// Define TDIALOG_8Dlg destructor
TDIALOG_8Dlg::~TDIALOG_8Dlg()
{

   //REGEN_DIALOG_8_DESTRUCTOR
   //REGEN_DIALOG_8_DESTRUCTOR

}

void TDIALOG_8Dlg::RTDIALOG_8103(RTMessage Msg)
{
   //REGEN_VAR
   //REGEN_VAR
   switch(Msg.LP.Hi)
   {
      case BN_CLICKED :
      //REGEN_DIALOG_8103_ROUTING
      //REGEN_DIALOG_8103_ROUTING
      break;
   }
   //REGEN_END
   //REGEN_END
}

void TDIALOG_8Dlg::RTDIALOG_8104(RTMessage Msg)
{
   //REGEN_VAR
   //REGEN_VAR
   switch(Msg.LP.Hi)
   {
      case BN_CLICKED :
      //REGEN_DIALOG_8104_ROUTING
      //REGEN_DIALOG_8104_ROUTING
      break;
   }
   //REGEN_END
```

```
   //REGEN_END
}

void TDIALOG_8Dlg::RTDIALOG_8105(RTMessage Msg)
{
   //REGEN_VAR
   //REGEN_VAR
   switch(Msg.LP.Hi)
   {
      case BN_CLICKED :
      //REGEN_DIALOG_8105_ROUTING
      //REGEN_DIALOG_8105_ROUTING
      break;
   }
   //REGEN_END
   //REGEN_END
}

void TDIALOG_8Dlg::RTDIALOG_8106(RTMessage Msg)
{
   //REGEN_VAR
   // Reference Information Push Button from File Dialog Box
   fillBuffer (fullDocumentPath, 0, strlen(fullDocumentPath));
   strncat (fullDocumentPath, "C:\\n", 4);

   strncat (fullDocumentPath, currentDirectory, strlen(currentDirectory));
   strncat (fullDocumentPath, "\\n", 2);
   strncat (fullDocumentPath, currentFile, strlen(currentFile));

   //REGEN_VAR
   switch(Msg.LP.Hi)
   {
      case BN_CLICKED :
      //REGEN_DIALOG_8106_ROUTING
      //REGEN_DIALOG_8106_ROUTING
      break;
   }
   //REGEN_END
   //REGEN_END
}

void TMainWindow::EXIT(RTMessage)
{
   //REGEN_EXEC
   DRIs->flush(2);
   CloseWindow();   // Close the application window
   //REGEN_EXEC
}

void TMainWindow::FILE(RTMessage)
{

   //REGEN_VAR
   //REGEN_VAR

   // Execute modal dialog
```

```
   if (GetModule()->ExecDialog(
              new TDIALOG_1Dlg(this, "DIALOG_1")) == IDOK )
   {
   //REGEN_EXEC
   //REGEN_EXEC

   }

   //REGEN_END
   //REGEN_END

}

void TMainWindow::DELETE(RTMessage)
{

   //REGEN_VAR
   //REGEN_VAR

   // Execute modal dialog
   if (GetModule()->ExecDialog(
              new TDIALOG_5Dlg(this, "DIALOG_5")) == IDOK )
   {
   //REGEN_EXEC
   //REGEN_EXEC

   }

   //REGEN_END
   //REGEN_END

}

void TMainWindow::SEARCH(RTMessage)
{

   //REGEN_VAR
   //REGEN_VAR

   // Execute modal dialog
   if (GetModule()->ExecDialog(
              new TDIALOG_3Dlg(this, "DIALOG_3")) == IDOK )
   {
   //REGEN_EXEC
   //REGEN_EXEC

   }

   //REGEN_END
   //REGEN_END

}

void TMainWindow::FILINGCHARACTERS(RTMessage)
{
```

```
   //REGEN_VAR
   //REGEN_VAR

   // Execute modal dialog
   if (GetModule()->ExecDialog(
            new TDIALOG_7Dlg(this, "DIALOG_7")) == IDOK )
   {
   //REGEN_EXEC
   //REGEN_EXEC

   }

   //REGEN_END
   //REGEN_END

}

void TMainWindow::JUNKWORDS(RTMessage)
{

   //REGEN_VAR
   //REGEN_VAR

   // Execute modal dialog
   if (GetModule()->ExecDialog(
            new TDIALOG_8Dlg(this, "DIALOG_8")) == IDOK )
   {
   //REGEN_EXEC
   //REGEN_EXEC

   }

   //REGEN_END
   //REGEN_END

}

void TDIALOG_1Dlg::RTDIALOG_1104(RTMessage Msg)
{

   //REGEN_VAR
   //REGEN_VAR

   switch(Msg.LP.Hi)
   {
      case BN_CLICKED :
      // Execute modal dialog
      if (GetModule()->ExecDialog(
            new TDIALOG_2Dlg(this, "DIALOG_2")) == IDOK )
      {
      //REGEN_DIALOG_2_EXEC
      // File A Document Dialog Box  -  Reference Information Push Button
      //REGEN_DIALOG_2_EXEC
      }

      //REGEN_END
```

```
       //REGEN_END

    break;
    }
}

void TDIALOG_3Dlg::RTDIALOG_3101(RTMessage Msg)
{

   //REGEN_VAR
   //
   // Search Dialog Box  - Ok Push Button
   //

   intcontentSize, abstractSize, keywordSize, authorSize;
   intnumberOfDocumentsFound;
   static charabstractString[MaxAbstractSize],
   authorString[MaxAuthorsSize],
   keywordString[MaxKeywordsSize],
   contentString[MaxContentSize];

   numberOfDocumentsFound = 0;
   contentSize = Edit104->GetText (contentString, MaxAbstractSize);
   abstractSize = Edit105->GetText (abstractString, MaxAbstractSize);
   keywordSize = Edit106->GetText (keywordString, MaxKeywordsSize);
   authorSize = Edit107->GetText (authorString, MaxAuthorsSize);

   // Append a newline character to each piece of document reference
   //   information to simplify the input and output using streams

      contentQueryObj = new ContentQuery;
      contentQueryObj->setContentQuery (contentString);

      authorQueryObj = new AuthorQuery;
      authorQueryObj->setAuthorQuery (authorString);

      abstractQueryObj = new AbstractQuery;
      abstractQueryObj->setAbstractQuery (abstractString);

      keywordQueryObj = new KeywordQuery;
      keywordQueryObj->setKeywordQuery (keywordString);

   if ((contentSize == 0) & ((authorSize == 0) & (abstractSize == 0) & (keywordSize
   == 0)))
   {
     MessageBox(HWindow, "A Query Must Be Specified In Order To Perform A Search",
        "Error", MB_OK);
   }
   else if ((contentSize > 0) & ((authorSize > 0) | (abstractSize > 0) | (keywordSize
      > 0)))
   {
      // Search both document content and document reference information
      searchEngineObj = new SearchEngine (HWindow);
      docNameListObjPtr = searchEngineObj->findDocConAndDri(authorQueryObj,
              keywordQueryObj,
```

```
                 contentQueryObj, abstractQueryObj);   //send find a document message to
                                               search engine
    }
    else if ((contentSize == 0) & ((authorSize > 0) | (abstractSize > 0) | (keywordSize
        > 0)))
    {
       // Search document reference information only
       searchEngineObj = new SearchEngine (HWindow);
       docNameListObjPtr = searchEngineObj->findDocDri(authorQueryObj, keyword-
         QueryObj, abstractQueryObj);
    }
    else if ((contentSize > 0) & ((authorSize == 0) | (abstractSize == 0) | (keywordSize
        == 0)))
    {
       // Search document content only!
       searchEngineObj = new SearchEngine (HWindow);
       //send find a document message to search engine
       docNameListObjPtr = searchEngineObj->findDocCon(contentQueryObj);
    }
    //REGEN_VAR


    //REGEN_END
    numberOfDocumentsFound = docNameListObjPtr->size();
    if (numberOfDocumentsFound > 0)
    {
       if (GetModule()->ExecDialog(
             new TDIALOG_4Dlg(this, "DIALOG_4")) == IDOK )
       {
       //REGEN_DIALOG_4_EXEC
        //CloseWindow();
       //REGEN_DIALOG_4_EXEC
       }
    }
    else
       MessageBox(HWindow, "No Documents Found Meeting Search Criteria", "",
            MB_OK);

    delete searchEngineObj;
    delete docNameListObjPtr;

       //REGEN_END
}
void TDIALOG_4Dlg::RTDIALOG_4101(RTMessage Msg)
{

    //REGEN_VAR
    //REGEN_VAR

    switch(Msg.LP.Hi)
    {
       case BN_CLICKED :
       // Execute modal dialog
       if (GetModule()->ExecDialog(
             new TDIALOG_9Dlg(this, "DIALOG_9")) == IDOK )
```

```
    {
    //REGEN_DIALOG_9_EXEC
    // Search Results Dialog Box  -  View Push Button
     //CloseWindow();
    //REGEN_DIALOG_9_EXEC
    }

    //REGEN_END
    //REGEN_END

  break;
  }
}

void TDIALOG_4Dlg::RTDIALOG_4102(RTMessage Msg)
{

  //REGEN_VAR
  //REGEN_VAR

  switch(Msg.LP.Hi)
  {
    case BN_CLICKED :
    // Execute modal dialog
    if (GetModule()->ExecDialog(
          new TDIALOG_6Dlg(this, "DIALOG_6")) == IDOK )
    {
    //REGEN_DIALOG_6_EXEC
    // Search Results Dialog Box  -  Print Push Button
    //CloseWindow();
    //REGEN_DIALOG_6_EXEC
    }

    //REGEN_END
    //REGEN_END

  break;
  }
}


/***************************************************
 * TEFApp method implementations:
 ***************************************************/

// Construct the TEF's MainWindow of type TMainWindow
void TEF::InitMainWindow()
{
  MainWindow = new TMainWindow(NULL, Name);
  //REGEN_MAINCREATE
  //REGEN_MAINCREATE
}

// Main program
int PASCAL WinMain(HINSTANCE hInstance,
                   HINSTANCE hPrevInstance,
```

```
                      LPSTR lpCmdLine,
                      int nCmdShow)
{
   HINSTANCE hBorLibrary;

   hBorLibrary = LoadLibrary("bwcc.dll");

   if((UINT)hBorLibrary <= 32)
      MessageBox(NULL, "Unable to load Borland Controls", "System Error", MB_OK |
         MB_ICONHAND);

   //REGEN_INIT
   //REGEN_INIT

   TEF EF ("Electronic Filing", hInstance, hPrevInstance,
      lpCmdLine, nCmdShow);

   EF.Run();

   if((UINT)hBorLibrary > 32)
      FreeLibrary(hBorLibrary);

   //REGEN_CLEANUP
   //REGEN_CLEANUP

   return EF.Status;
}

//REGEN_CUSTOMCODE
//REGEN_CUSTOMCODE

Search Subsystem
//********************************************************************
//*                                                                  *
//*                   Electronic Filing in C++                       *
//*                        Version 1.0                               *
//*                 Copyright (c) 1993 Kurt Derr                     *
//*                        srcheng.h                                 *
//********************************************************************

#ifndef __SRCHENG_H
#define __SRCHENG_H
#include "ef.h"
#include "conquery.h"
#include "keyquery.h"
#include "absquery.h"
#include "autquery.h"
#include "docname1.h"
#include "docrecd1.h"
#include "srchvect.h"
#include <fstream.h>
#include <strstrea.h>

_CLASSDEF(SearchEngine)
```

```
class SearchEngine {

public:
    SearchEngine(HWND theHandle);
    ~SearchEngine();
    DocumentNameList* findDocCon (ContentQuery *conQryObj);
    DocumentNameList* findDocDri (AuthorQuery *autQryObj, KeywordQuery *keyQryObj,
            AbstractQuery *absQryObj);
    DocumentNameList* findDocConAndDri (AuthorQuery *autQryObj, KeywordQuery
            *keyQryObj, ContentQuery *conQryObj, AbstractQuery *absQryObj);
    HWND    searchHandle;

private:
    DocumentRecordsList* calcDocRecNumbers (ifstream *indexStream,
            istrstream *vectorStream);
    DocumentNameList* checkForDocMatches (SearchVector *searchVectorObj,
            ContentQuery *contentQueryObj);
    DocumentNameList* checkForDRIMatches ();
    int checkForLogicalQueryMatch (int abstractMatchIndicator,
    int keywordsMatchIndicator, int authorMatchIndicator);
    char* verifyMatches (DocumentRecordsList *docRecListObj, ifstream *indexStream,
            ContentQuery *conQueryObj);

    void checkEachIndex (String& indexDocName);
    AuthorQuery*aAutQryObj;// An author query object
    KeywordQuery*aKeyQryObj;// A keyword query object
    AbstractQuery*aAbsQryObj;    // An abstract query object
    ContentQuery*aConQryObj;// A content query object
    DocumentNameList*nameListObj;// A document name list object
    charresultVector[XHashBlock];// search vector
};

#endif

//**********************************************************************
//*                                                                    *
//*                  Electronic Filing in C++                          *
//*                        Version 1.0                                 *
//*            Copyright (c) 1993 Kurt Derr                            *
//*                       srcheng.cpp                                  *
//**********************************************************************

//#include "nowdefs.h"

#include <owl.h>
#include <list.h>
#include "srcheng.h"
#include "srchvect.h"
#include <stdio.h>
#include <string.h>
#include <fstream.h>
#include <strstrea.h>
#include "docnamel.h"
#include "externs.h"
#include "defines.h"
#include "docrefin.h"
```

```
//------------------------------------------------------------------
// Creates the Search Engine
//------------------------------------------------------------------

SearchEngine::SearchEngine(HWND theHandle)
{
   searchHandle = theHandle;
}

//------------------------------------------------------------------
// Disposes of the Search Engine
//------------------------------------------------------------------

SearchEngine::~SearchEngine(void)
{

}

//------------------------------------------------------------------
// Finds a document based on the content query only.
//------------------------------------------------------------------

DocumentNameList*  SearchEngine::findDocCon(ContentQuery *conQryObj)
{
   SearchVector  *searchVectorObj;
   DocumentNameList  *documentNameListObj;
   int     nop;
   int     numberOfDocumentsFound;

   aConQryObj = conQryObj;
   numberOfDocumentsFound = 0;
   // Build the search vector
   searchVectorObj = new SearchVector;
   searchVectorObj->buildSearchVector (aConQryObj);

   // Check for document matches
   documentNameListObj = checkForDocMatches (searchVectorObj, aConQryObj);

   return documentNameListObj;
}

//------------------------------------------------------------------
// Finds a document based on the DRI query only.
//------------------------------------------------------------------

DocumentNameList*  SearchEngine::findDocDri(AuthorQuery *autQryObj, KeywordQuery
   *keyQryObj, AbstractQuery *absQryObj)
{
   int     nop;
   int     numberOfDocumentsFound;

    aAutQryObj = autQryObj;
    aKeyQryObj = keyQryObj;
    aAbsQryObj = absQryObj;

   numberOfDocumentsFound = 0;
```

```
   // Check the author, keyword, and abstract queries for matches against
   // document reference information
   //
   nameListObj = checkForDRIMatches ();

   return nameListObj;
}
//-----------------------------------------------------------------
// Finds a document based on the content and DRI query.
//-----------------------------------------------------------------

DocumentNameList*  SearchEngine::findDocConAndDri(AuthorQuery *autQryObj, Key-
   wordQuery *keyQryObj,
       ContentQuery *conQryObj, AbstractQuery *absQryObj)
{
   SearchVector       *searchVectorObj;
   DocumentNameList  *contentDocumentNameListObj;
   int                nop;
   int                numberOfDocumentsFound;
   DocumentNameList  *newDocumentNameListObj;
   DocumentNameList  *driDocumentNameListObj;
   String             contentOperator;
   List*              temporaryList;
   ListIterator       it(*temporaryList);
   String             aFileName;
   int                numberOfItems;
   String*            aFileNamePtr;

   aAutQryObj = autQryObj;
   aKeyQryObj = keyQryObj;
   aAbsQryObj = absQryObj;
   aConQryObj = conQryObj;

   numberOfDocumentsFound = 0;
   // Build the search vector
   searchVectorObj = new SearchVector;
   searchVectorObj->buildSearchVector (aConQryObj);

   // Check for document matches
   contentDocumentNameListObj = checkForDocMatches (searchVectorObj, aConQryObj);

   // Check the author, keyword, and abstract queries for matches against
   // document reference information
   //
   driDocumentNameListObj = checkForDRIMatches ();

   //Produce a new documentNameList based on the logical operation performed
   // between the content query and the DRI query.
   String orOperator = "OR";
   contentOperator = conQryObj->getContentToAbstractOperator();

   if (contentOperator = orOperator)
   {
      newDocumentNameListObj = contentDocumentNameListObj;
```

```
        temporaryList = driDocumentNameListObj->retrieveDocumentNames();
        numberOfItems = driDocumentNameListObj->size();
        while (numberOfItems > 0)
        {
            numberOfItems--;
                (String&) aFileName = (String&) it++;
                aFileNamePtr = &aFileName;
                if (!newDocumentNameListObj->includes (aFileName))
                    newDocumentNameListObj->addToDNL(aFileNamePtr);
        }
    }
    else
    {
        temporaryList = contentDocumentNameListObj->retrieveDocumentNames();
        numberOfItems = contentDocumentNameListObj->size();
        while (numberOfItems > 0)
        {
            numberOfItems--;
                (String&) aFileName = (String&) it++;
                aFileNamePtr = &aFileName;
                if (driDocumentNameListObj->includes (aFileName))
                    newDocumentNameListObj->addToDNL(aFileNamePtr);
        }
    }
    return newDocumentNameListObj;
}

//----------------------------------------------------------------
// Calculate document record numbers where hits are possible.
//----------------------------------------------------------------

DocumentRecordsList* SearchEngine::calcDocRecNumbers(ifstream *indexStream,
            istrstream *vectorStream)
{
    char ch, buffer[80];
    int  maxDataRecords, indexFSRecords, indexFSEnd;
    int  indexFSStart, totalDataRecsRead, totalIndexRecsRead;
    int  startPos, endPos, indexPosition;
    long vectorStreamPosition;
    char indexFileBuffer[XHashBlock];
    DocumentRecordsList documentRecordsListObj;

    indexStream->getline (buffer, strlen (buffer), '\n');

    if ((maxDataRecords = atoi(buffer)) == 0)
    {
        MessageBox (searchHandle, "Exceeded Number of Data Records",
         "Error in Search - data records = \n", MB_OK);
    }
    else
    {
        indexFSRecords = 0;
        // Create an empty document records list object

        endPos = 1;
        indexStream->seekg (XHashBlock);// move to end of stream
```

```
// Calculate # of indexed stream records
while (indexStream->get (ch))
     indexFSRecords++;
indexFSEnd = indexFSRecords - 1;
indexFSRecords = (indexFSRecords - XHashBlock)/XHashBlock;
indexFSStart = XHashBlock;
totalDataRecsRead = 0;
totalIndexRecsRead = XHashBlock;

// Initialize the result vector to all ones, since we are ANDing
strnset (resultVector, '1', XHashBlock);

while (totalIndexRecsRead < indexFSRecords)
{
     // Process a hash block
     totalIndexRecsRead = totalIndexRecsRead + XHashBlock;

     // Examine search vector stream for each index file hash block
     vectorStream->seekg (1);

     while (vectorStream->get (ch))
     {
        vectorStreamPosition = vectorStream->tellg();

        // For each character that equals 1 in the SearchVector
        //    read the corresponding record in the index file
        if ((ch == '1') && (endPos < indexFSEnd))
        {
           startPos = (vectorStreamPosition - 1) * XHashBlock
   + (indexFSStart + 1);
           endPos = vectorStreamPosition * XHashBlock
   + (XHashBlock - 1) + 1;
           if (endPos >= indexFSEnd)
           {
     endPos = indexFSEnd;
           }
           vectorStream->seekg (startPos);
           indexStream->read (indexFileBuffer, XHashBlock);
           indexPosition = 1;
           while (indexPosition <= XHashBlock)
           {
     if (indexFileBuffer[indexPosition] == '1')
     {
        if (resultVector[indexPosition] == '1')
        {
   indexPosition++;
        }
        else
        {
   resultVector[indexPosition] = '0';
   indexPosition++;
        } // END If
     }
     else
     {
```

```
                    resultVector[indexPosition] = '0';
                    indexPosition++;
                } // END If
            } // END While
        } // END If
    } // END WHile
    // For each character = '1' in the result vector,
    //  add the record # to the docRecList. Add to the document
    //  records list by evaluating each bit in the resultVector.
    indexPosition = 1;
    while (indexPosition <= XHashBlock)
    {
        if (resultVector[indexPosition] == '1')
        {
            if (((indexPosition + totalDataRecsRead) <= maxDataRecords))
            {
            documentRecordsListObj.addToDRL
                (indexPosition + totalDataRecsRead);
            indexPosition++;
            }
        }
        else
        {
            indexPosition++;
        }
    } // End While
    totalDataRecsRead = totalDataRecsRead + XHashBlock;
    strnset (resultVector, '1', XHashBlock);
    }
    } // End If
    return &documentRecordsListObj;
}

//-----------------------------------------------------------------
// Check each index.
//-----------------------------------------------------------------

void SearchEngine::checkEachIndex (String& indexDocName)
//void SearchEngine::checkEachIndex (Object& o, char *indexDocName)
{
    char    *docName;
    SearchVector searchVector;
    DocumentRecordsList *docRecList;
    char    *theIndexDocName;

    theIndexDocName = (char *) *indexDocName;

    // Create an index file stream
    ifstream fin (theIndexDocName);

    // Create a stream on the search vector
    istrstream searchVectorStream (searchVector.returnVector(),
            strlen (searchVector.returnVector()));

    // Calculate the document record number hits
    docRecList = calcDocRecNumbers (&fin, &searchVectorStream);
```

```
   // Verify the record matches
   docName = verifyMatches (docRecList, &fin, aConQryObj);

   // Associate the document record list with a document name in the
   //    document name list
   if (docRecList->size () > 0)
      nameListObj->putRecordsList (docRecList, theIndexDocName);
   fin.close ();
}




//------------------------------------------------------------------
// Determine the documents that satisfy the search criteria.
//------------------------------------------------------------------

DocumentNameList* SearchEngine::checkForDocMatches(SearchVector *searchVectorObj,
            ContentQuery *contentQueryObj)
{
   List *indexNames;
   DocumentNameList  *nameListObj;
   int    val, numberOfItems;
   String aFileName;

   // Create an empty document name list object
   nameListObj = new DocumentNameList;

   // Retrieve index file names
   indexNames = Filing->retrieveIndexNames ();
   numberOfItems = Filing->numberOfIndexFiles();

   ListIterator   it((const List&)indexNames);

   // For each document index file DO
   while (numberOfItems-- > 0)
   {
      numberOfItems--;
      (String&) aFileName = (String&) it++;
      checkEachIndex (aFileName);
   }
   return nameListObj;
}

//------------------------------------------------------------------
// Determine what DRI satisfies the search criteria.
//------------------------------------------------------------------

DocumentNameList* SearchEngine::checkForDRIMatches(void)
{
   int    authorMatchIndicator = 0;
   int    abstractMatchIndicator = 0;
   int    keywordsMatchIndicator = 0;
   int    matchIndicator = 0;
   DocumentNameList    *driDocumentNameList;
```

```
    DocumentNameList  *nameListObj;
    int    numberOfItems;
    ListIterator   it(*DRIs);
    DocRefInfo   aDri;

    //String    theAuthorsStringObj;
    //String    theAbstractStringObj;
    //String    theKeywordsStringObj;
    //String    documentPathName;
//
// Using the abstract, keyword, and author queries, examine each document
// reference item and see if there is a match.
//

// First parse the queries into query elements and query operators
    if ((aAutQryObj->checkIfQueryEntered ()) == TRUE)
        aAutQryObj->parseQuery ();
    if ((aKeyQryObj->checkIfQueryEntered ()) == TRUE)
        aKeyQryObj->parseQuery ();
    if ((aAbsQryObj->checkIfQueryEntered ()) == TRUE)
        aAbsQryObj->parseQuery ();

    // For each document reference information object, check the query elements
    // for a match against the dri for each text document.

    // Create an empty document name list object
    driDocumentNameList = new DocumentNameList;

    // Retrieve number of document ref info object in container
    numberOfItems = DRIs->getItemsInContainer();

    // For each document reference information object DO
    while (numberOfItems-- > 0)
    {
//      numberOfItems--;
        (DocRefInfo&) aDri = (DocRefInfo&) it++;

        String& theAuthorsStringObj = aDri.getAuthors ();
        String* authorsObj = &theAuthorsStringObj;
        authorMatchIndicator = aAutQryObj->checkForElementMatch (authorsObj);

        String& theAbstractStringObj = aDri.getAbstract ();
        String* abstractObj = &theAbstractStringObj;
        abstractMatchIndicator = aAbsQryObj->checkForElementMatch (abstractObj);

        String& theKeywordsStringObj = aDri.getKeywords ();
        String* keywordsObj = &theKeywordsStringObj;
        keywordsMatchIndicator = aKeyQryObj->checkForElementMatch (keywordsObj);

        matchIndicator = checkForLogicalQueryMatch (abstractMatchIndicator,
          keywordsMatchIndicator, authorMatchIndicator);
        // If matchIndicator TRUE, then add the document name to the document
        //   NameList.

        if (matchIndicator)
        {
```

```
            String*    documentPathName;
            documentPathName = new String (aDri.getDocumentAndPathName ());
            driDocumentNameList->addToDNL (documentPathName);
        }
    }
    return driDocumentNameList;
}

//-----------------------------------------------------------------
// Perform logical operations between queries using query operators.
//-----------------------------------------------------------------

int SearchEngine::checkForLogicalQueryMatch(int abstractMatchIndicator,
    int keywordsMatchIndicator, int authorMatchIndicator)
{
    // Answer with a True or False matchIndicator. True indicates a document
    // satisfied a dri query.

    int    matchIndicator = 0;
    String firstOperator;
    String secondOperator;

    firstOperator = aAbsQryObj->getAbsToKeyOp ();
    secondOperator = aKeyQryObj->getKeyToAutOp ();
    if (firstOperator == "AND")
        matchIndicator = abstractMatchIndicator & keywordsMatchIndicator;
    else
        matchIndicator = abstractMatchIndicator | keywordsMatchIndicator;

    if (secondOperator == "AND")
        matchIndicator = matchIndicator & authorMatchIndicator;
    else
        matchIndicator = matchIndicator | authorMatchIndicator;

    return matchIndicator;
}

//-----------------------------------------------------------------
// Verify that the content query actually exists in the document.
//-----------------------------------------------------------------

char* SearchEngine::verifyMatches(DocumentRecordsList *docRecListObj, ifstream
    *indexStream, ContentQuery *conQueryObj)
{
    int    (*functionPtr)();
    Set    *recordsObj;
    int    documentStreamEnd = 0;
    char documentPath[80], ch;

    // Make a copy of the docRecListObj
    DocumentRecordsList dupDRLObj;
    dupDRLObj = *docRecListObj;

    // Get complete path of text document from index file header
    indexStream->seekg (1);
    indexStream->getline (documentPath, 80, '\n');
```

```
    // Set up a stream to read the text document
    ifstream documentStream;

    documentStream.open (documentPath);

    // For all record numbers in the docRecordNumberList, read the document
    //   record and verify that some element of the content query exists
    //   within that record. If not, then remove the document record number
    //   from the docRecordNumberList. All record numbers start with 1, not 0

    while (documentStream.get(ch))
       documentStreamEnd++;

    recordsObj = &(docRecListObj->getRecordsList ());
    return documentPath;
}
//*********************************************************************
//*                                                                 *
//*                    Electronic Filing in C++                     *
//*                         Version 1.0                             *
//*              Copyright (c) 1993 Kurt Derr                       *
//*                         srchvect.h                              *
//*********************************************************************

#ifndef __SRCHVECT_H
#define __SRCHVECT_H
#include "ef.h"
#include "conquery.h"
#include "defines.h"

_CLASSDEF(SearchVector)


class SearchVector {

public:
    SearchVector();
    ~SearchVector();
    String* buildSearchVector (ContentQuery *conQryObj);
    char* returnVector();

private:
    charqueryBuffer[YHashBlock];// the query search vector
    charelementBuffer[YHashBlock];
    void constructVector(String *queryVector, String *elementVector,
            String& logicalOpObj);
    String  *queryVector;
    String   *elementVector;
};

#endif

//*********************************************************************
//*                                                                 *
```

```
//*                    Electronic Filing in C++                    *
//*                         Version 1.0                           *
//*                  Copyright (c) 1993 Kurt Derr                 *
//*                         srchvect.cpp                          *
//****************************************************************

//#include "nowdefs.h"

#include <owl.h>

#include "srchvect.h"
#include "conquery.h"
#include "hasheng.h"
#include "junkword.h"
#include <queue.h>
#include <stdio.h>
#include "externs.h"
#include "strstrea.h"

//-----------------------------------------------------------------
// Creates the Search Vector
//-----------------------------------------------------------------

SearchVector::SearchVector()
{

   fillBuffer (queryBuffer, '0', YHashBlock);
   queryVector = new String (queryBuffer);

   fillBuffer (elementBuffer, '0', YHashBlock);
   elementVector = new String (elementBuffer);

}

//-----------------------------------------------------------------
// Disposes of the Search Vector
//-----------------------------------------------------------------

SearchVector::~SearchVector(void)
{
   delete queryVector;
}

//-----------------------------------------------------------------
// Answer a search vector.
//-----------------------------------------------------------------

String* SearchVector::buildSearchVector(ContentQuery *contentQueryObj)
{
   String   queryString;
   String   anElement;
   char     *stringPtr;
   int      numberOfOperators;
   int      junkWordStatus;

   String logicalOpObj = "OR";
```

```
   // Get the query entered by the user
   queryString = contentQueryObj->theQuery ();

   //
   // Parse the queries into query elements and logical operators
   //
   contentQueryObj->parseQuery ();
   Queue* contentQueryElements =  (Queue*) contentQueryObj->getQueryElements ();
   Queue* contentQueryOperators = (Queue*) contentQueryObj->getLogicalOperators ();
   //
   // Hash each query element and AND or OR the results from each element
   // together depending upon the query operator
   //

   Queue* duplicateQueryElements = contentQueryElements;
   Queue* duplicateQueryOperators = contentQueryOperators;
   JunkWords    *junkWordsObj = new JunkWords;

   HashEngine   *hashEngineObj = new HashEngine (junkWordsObj);

   while (!duplicateQueryElements->isEmpty ())
   {
       String& aWord = (String&) (duplicateQueryElements->get());
       String* wordPtr = &aWord;

       if ((junkWordStatus = junkWordsObj->checkIfJunkWord(aWord)) == FALSE)
       {
           hashEngineObj->hashTheWordUsing(wordPtr, elementVector);
           constructVector (queryVector, elementVector, logicalOpObj);
           if ((numberOfOperators = duplicateQueryOperators->getItemsInContain-
              er()) > 0)
           {
               String& logicalOpObj = (String&) duplicateQueryOperators->get();
           }
       }
   }
   return queryVector;
}

//----------------------------------------------------------------
// Perform logical operation between query and element vectors.
//----------------------------------------------------------------

void SearchVector::constructVector(String *queryVector, String *elementVector,
           String& logicalOpObj)
{
   const char    *queryVectorPointer;
   const char    *elementVectorPointer;
   String  andString ("AND");
   int  queryLength, elementLength;
   char   elementChar, queryChar;
   long    streamIndex;
   long   curStrPos, curIstrPos;

   queryVectorPointer = *queryVector;
   elementVectorPointer = *elementVector;
```

```
    queryLength = strlen (queryVectorPointer);
    elementLength = strlen (elementVectorPointer);
    istrstream    queryStream ((char *) queryVectorPointer, queryLength);
    ostrstream    outQueryStream ((char *) queryVectorPointer, queryLength);
    istrstream    elementStream ((char *) elementVectorPointer, elementLength);

    while (!queryStream.eof())
    {
        elementStream.get(elementChar);
        queryStream.get(queryChar);

        curStrPos = queryStream.tellg();
        curIstrPos = elementStream.tellg();

        if (logicalOpObj.isEqual (andString))
        {
                if (elementChar == queryChar)
                   outQueryStream.seekp(1, ios::cur);
                else
                   outQueryStream.put('0');
                }
                else
                {
                        if (elementChar == queryChar)
                          outQueryStream.seekp(1, ios::cur);
                        else
                          outQueryStream.put('1');
        }
    }
}

//-----------------------------------------------------------------
// Return the query search vector.
//-----------------------------------------------------------------

char* SearchVector::returnVector(void)
{
    // Return the actual search vector string
    return queryVector;
}

Search Results Subsystem

//*****************************************************************
//*                                                               *
//*              Electronic Filing in C++                         *
//*                    Version 1.0                                *
//*            Copyright (c) 1993 Kurt Derr                       *
//*                    docnamel.h                                 *
//*****************************************************************

#ifndef __DOCNAMEL_H
#define __DOCNAMEL_H
```

```
#include <list.h>
#include <dict.h>
#include <strng.h>
#include "docrecdl.h"

_CLASSDEF(DocumentNameList)

class DocumentNameList {

public:
    DocumentNameList();
    ~DocumentNameList();
    void addToDNL(String* documentName);
    List* getRecordsList ();
    void removeFromDNL (String& documentName);
    int size ();
    int includes (String& documentName);
    void putRecordsList (DocumentRecordsList *docRecListObj, char *indexName);
    List* retrieveDocumentNames ();
    String& documentName(void);


private:
    List*documentNameList;// Document name list
    Dictionary* recordDictionary;// Document records
};

#endif

//*********************************************************************
//*                                                                   *
//*                  Electronic Filing in C++                         *
//*                         Version 1.0                               *
//*              Copyright (c) 1993 Kurt Derr                         *
//*                       docnamel.cpp                                *
//*********************************************************************


#include <owl.h>

#include "docnamel.h"

#include <stdio.h>
#include <shddel.h>

//----------------------------------------------------------------
// Creates the Text Document Object
//----------------------------------------------------------------

DocumentNameList::DocumentNameList()
{
   documentNameList = new List ();
   recordDictionary = new Dictionary ();
}
```

```
//-------------------------------------------------------------------
// Disposes of the Text Document Object
//-------------------------------------------------------------------

DocumentNameList::~DocumentNameList(void)
{
   delete documentNameList;
   delete recordDictionary;
}

//-------------------------------------------------------------------
// Add an object to the document name list.
//-------------------------------------------------------------------

void DocumentNameList::addToDNL(String* documentName)
{
   String& name = *documentName;
   documentNameList->add ((Object&) name);
}

//-------------------------------------------------------------------
// Get the list of records for this document.
//-------------------------------------------------------------------

List* DocumentNameList::getRecordsList()
{

}


//-------------------------------------------------------------------
// Retrieve the document name removed from the document name list.
//-------------------------------------------------------------------

void DocumentNameList::removeFromDNL(String& documentName)
{
   documentNameList->detach (documentName, 2);
}

//-------------------------------------------------------------------
// Get the number of entries in the document name list.
//-------------------------------------------------------------------

int DocumentNameList::size(void)
{
   return documentNameList->getItemsInContainer();
}

//-------------------------------------------------------------------
// Determine if object is included in the document name list.
//-------------------------------------------------------------------

int DocumentNameList::includes(String& documentName)
{
   return documentNameList->hasMember ((Object&) documentName);
}
```

```
//-----------------------------------------------------------------
// Associate a document records list with the indexFileName.
//-----------------------------------------------------------------

void DocumentNameList::putRecordsList(DocumentRecordsList *docRecListObj, char
    *indexName)
{

}

//-----------------------------------------------------------------
// Answer with the document name list.
//-----------------------------------------------------------------

List* DocumentNameList::retrieveDocumentNames(void)
{
    return documentNameList;
}

//-----------------------------------------------------------------
// Answer with a document name from the DocumentNameList.
//-----------------------------------------------------------------

String& DocumentNameList::documentName(void)
{
    const char*   fileName;  // null terminated file name string
    String& searchResultsFileName = (String&) (documentNameList->peekHead ());
    return searchResultsFileName;
}


//******************************************************************
//*                                                               *
//*                  Electronic Filing in C++                     *
//*                       Version 1.0                             *
//*              Copyright (c) 1993 Kurt Derr                     *
//*                       docrecdl.h                              *
//******************************************************************

#ifndef __DOCRECDL_H
#define __DOCRECDL_H

#include <list.h>
#include <set.h>

_CLASSDEF(DocumentRecordsList)

class DocumentRecordsList {

public:
    DocumentRecordsList();
    ~DocumentRecordsList();
    void addToDRL(int recordNumber);
    void atPut();
    Set getRecordsList (void);
    int size ();
```

```
    void removeRecordNumber ();

private:
    SetdocumentRecordsList;    // List of document record #s
    int getFirstRecord();
    int getNextRecord ();
};

#endif

//**********************************************************************
//*                                                                    *
//*                    Electronic Filing in C++                        *
//*                         Version 1.0                                *
//*              Copyright (c) 1993 Kurt Derr                          *
//*                         docrecdl.cpp                               *
//**********************************************************************


#include <owl.h>

#include "docrecdl.h"

#include <stdio.h>

//----------------------------------------------------------------
// Creates the Text Document Object
//----------------------------------------------------------------

DocumentRecordsList::DocumentRecordsList()
{

}

//----------------------------------------------------------------
// Disposes of the Text Document Object
//----------------------------------------------------------------

DocumentRecordsList::~DocumentRecordsList(void)
{

}

//----------------------------------------------------------------
// Add an object to the document records list.
//----------------------------------------------------------------

void DocumentRecordsList::addToDRL(int recordNumber)
{

}

//----------------------------------------------------------------
// Replace an element of the receiver at an index position with a record #.
//----------------------------------------------------------------
```

```
void DocumentRecordsList::atPut(void)
{

}


//------------------------------------------------------------------
// Answer the document record list.
//------------------------------------------------------------------

Set DocumentRecordsList::getRecordsList(void)
{

}

//------------------------------------------------------------------
// Get the number of entries in the document record list.
//------------------------------------------------------------------

int DocumentRecordsList::size(void)
{

}

//------------------------------------------------------------------
// Remove the document record number at an index position.
//------------------------------------------------------------------

void DocumentRecordsList::removeRecordNumber(void)
{

}


int DocumentRecordsList::getFirstRecord (void)
{

}

int DocumentRecordsList::getNextRecord (void)
{

}
```

Document Subsystem

```
//*****************************************************************
//*                                                               *
//*                  Electronic Filing in C++                     *
//*                         Version 1.0                           *
//*               Copyright (c) 1993 Kurt Derr                    *
//*                         docrefin.h                            *
//*****************************************************************

#ifndef __DOCREF_H
#define __DOCREF_H
```

```cpp
#include <strng.h>

_CLASSDEF(DocRefInfo)


class DocRefInfo {

public:
   DocRefInfo ();
   DocRefInfo(const String& a, const String& b, const String& c,
  const String& d, const String& e) : abstract(a), authors(b), keywords(c),
       documentName(d), pathAndDocumentName(e) {};
   ~DocRefInfo();
   String getAbstract();
   String getAuthors ();
   String getKeywords ();
   String getDocumentName ();
   void setDri (char *theAuthors, char *theAbstract, char *theKeywords,
        char *docName, char *theDocPath);
   String getDocumentAndPathName ();

private:
   String     abstract;                // users abstract
   String     authors;                 // users authors
   String     keywords;                // users keywords
   String     documentName;            // Name of text document
   String     pathAndDocumentName;     // Path and text document name
};

#endif

//**********************************************************************
//*                                                                    *
//*                  Electronic Filing in C++                          *
//*                        Version 1.0                                 *
//*              Copyright (c) 1993 Kurt Derr                          *
//*                       docrefin.cpp                                 *
//**********************************************************************


#include <owl.h>

#include "docrefin.h"
#include <strng.h>
#include <stdio.h>



//-----------------------------------------------------------------
// Creates the Document Reference Information Object
//-----------------------------------------------------------------

DocRefInfo::DocRefInfo()
{

}
```

```
//--------------------------------------------------------------------
// Disposes of the Document Reference Information Object
//--------------------------------------------------------------------

DocRefInfo::~DocRefInfo(void)
{

}

//--------------------------------------------------------------------
// Retrieve the abstract.
//--------------------------------------------------------------------

String DocRefInfo::getAbstract(void)
{
   return abstract;
}

//--------------------------------------------------------------------
// Retrieve the authors.
//--------------------------------------------------------------------

String DocRefInfo::getAuthors(void)
{
   return authors;
}


//--------------------------------------------------------------------
// Retrieve the keywords.
//--------------------------------------------------------------------

String DocRefInfo::getKeywords(void)
{
   return keywords;
}

//--------------------------------------------------------------------
// Retrieve the document name.
//--------------------------------------------------------------------

String DocRefInfo::getDocumentName(void)
{
   return documentName;
}

//--------------------------------------------------------------------
// Set all of the Document Reference Information.
//--------------------------------------------------------------------

void DocRefInfo::setDri(char *theAuthors, char *theAbstract, char *theKeywords,
        char *docName, char *theDocPath)
{
   authors = theAuthors;
   abstract = theAbstract;
   keywords = theKeywords;
```

```
   pathAndDocumentName = theDocPath;
   documentName = docName;
}

//-----------------------------------------------------------------
// Retrieve the document and path name.
//-----------------------------------------------------------------

String DocRefInfo::getDocumentAndPathName(void)
{
   return pathAndDocumentName;
}



//*****************************************************************
//*                                                               *
//*                  Electronic Filing in C++                     *
//*                        Version 1.0                            *
//*               Copyright (c) 1993 Kurt Derr                    *
//*                        textdoc.h                              *
//*****************************************************************

#ifndef __TEXTDOC_H
#define __TEXTDOC_H
#include "docrefin.h"


_CLASSDEF(TextDocument)


class TextDocument {

public:
   TextDocument();
   ~TextDocument();
   void fileDoc(HWND handle, char *file, char *directory);
   void fileDocAndDri (HWND handle, char *file, char *directory, DocRefInfo *dri-
        Obj);
};

#endif

//*****************************************************************
//*                                                               *
//*                  Electronic Filing in C++                     *
//*                        Version 1.0                            *
//*               Copyright (c) 1993 Kurt Derr                    *
//*                        textdoc.cpp                            *
//*****************************************************************


#include <owl.h>

#include <windobj.h>

#include "textdoc.h"
```

```
#include "index.h"

#include <stdio.h>
#include <dir.h>
#include <dos.h>
#include <stdio.h>

#include <stdlib.h>
#include <fstream.h>
#include <iomanip.h>
#include <string.h>
#include <errno.h>
#include <dir.h>
#include <io.h>
#include "externs.h"

//-----------------------------------------------------------------
// Creates the Text Document Object
//-----------------------------------------------------------------

TextDocument::TextDocument()
{

}

//-----------------------------------------------------------------
// Disposes of the Text Document Object
//-----------------------------------------------------------------

TextDocument::~TextDocument(void)
{

}

//-----------------------------------------------------------------
// Files a document with no document reference information specified.
//-----------------------------------------------------------------

void TextDocument::fileDoc(HWND handle, char *file, char *directory)
{
      Index*indexObj;

      // Create the Index object
      indexObj = new Index;

      // File the document
      indexObj->createDocIndex (handle, file, directory);

      //Delete the Index object and reclaim memory
      delete indexObj;
}

//-----------------------------------------------------------------
// Files a document with document reference information specified.
//-----------------------------------------------------------------
```

```
void TextDocument::fileDocAndDri(HWND handle, char *file, char *directory,
        DocRefInfo *driObj)
{
     Index   *indexObj;
     char    pathName[MAXPATH];
     char    driFileName[13];
     char    *source = "dri";
     int     returnHandle;
     char    *errorString;
     char    *ptr;
     char    *partPath = "c:/filing/";
     String  stringPtr;

     //Create a Document Reference Information file for this document
     strcpy (driFileName, file);
     ptr = strrchr (driFileName, '.');

     if (ptr)
         {
         // '.' is in the string
         *(ptr + 1) = '\0';
         strncat (driFileName, source, 3);
         }
     else
         // no '.' in the string
         strncat (driFileName, ".dri", 4);

     strcpy (pathName, partPath);
     strcat (pathName,driFileName);

     // Create the actual dri file
     returnHandle = creatnew (pathName, FA_NORMAL);
     if (returnHandle == -1)
     {
         itoa (errno, errorString, 17);
         MessageBox(handle, errorString, "Errno in creating Index file:", MB_OK);
     }
     else
     {
         // Create the output file stream; steam is linked to file
         ofstream fout (pathName);

         // Write the abstract to the dri file
         stringPtr = driObj->getAbstract();
         stringPtr.printOn (fout);


         // Write the keywords to the dri file
         stringPtr = driObj->getKeywords();
         stringPtr.printOn (fout);


         // Write the authors to the dri file
         stringPtr = driObj->getAuthors();
         stringPtr.printOn (fout);
```

```
        // Close the output file stream
        fout.close ();
   }

        // Create the Index object
        indexObj = new Index;

        // File the document
        indexObj->createDocIndex (handle, file, directory);

        //Delete the Index object and reclaim memory
        delete indexObj;
}
//*********************************************************************
//*                                                                   *
//*                  Electronic Filing in C++                         *
//*                        Version 1.0                                *
//*             Copyright (c) 1993 Kurt Derr                          *
//*                        index.h                                    *
//*********************************************************************

#ifndef __INDEX_H
#define __INDEX_H

#include <strng.h>

_CLASSDEF(Index)


class Index {

public:
    Index();
    ~Index();
    void createDocIndex (HWND handle, char *file, char *directory);

private:
    void buildIndexFileHeader (ofstream *indexFileStream, ifstream *docFileStream,
            char *pathName);
    void createIndex(ofstream *indexFStream, ifstream *docFStream,
          char *pathName);

    String   indexFileName; // Name of the index file
    String   name;          // Name of the text document file
    String   directory;     // Directory name of text document file
};
#endif


//*********************************************************************
//*                                                                   *
//*                  Electronic Filing in C++                         *
//*                        Version 1.0                                *
//*             Copyright (c) 1993 Kurt Derr                          *
//*                        index.cpp                                  *
//*********************************************************************
```

```
#include <owl.h>
#include "defines.h"
#include "index.h"
#include <dos.h>
#include <stdio.h>
#include <stdlib.h>
#include <fstream.h>
#include <iomanip.h>
#include <string.h>
#include <errno.h>
#include <dir.h>
#include <io.h>
#include "hasheng.h"
#include "externs.h"

HWND myHandle;

//------------------------------------------------------------------
// Creates the Index Object
//------------------------------------------------------------------

Index::Index()
{

}

//------------------------------------------------------------------
// Disposes of the Index Object
//------------------------------------------------------------------

Index::~Index(void)
{

}

//------------------------------------------------------------------
// Create the actual text document index and its file.
//------------------------------------------------------------------

void Index::createDocIndex(HWND handle, char *file, char *directory)
{
        char        indexFileName[13];
        char        *source = "sam";
        char        pathName[MAXPATH];
        char        originalFilePath[MAXPATH];
        int         returnHandle;
        char        *errorString;
        char        *ptr;
        char        *partPath = "c:/filing/";
        fstream     myInput;        //create unopened fstream object
        int         status;

        myHandle = handle;
        if ((status = chdir (directory)) == -1)
        {
                MessageBox(myHandle, directory, "Error in changing directoty:",
```

```
                         MB_OK);
                 exit (1);
       }
     // Create an input file stream to read the text document
     ifstream fin (file);
     if (!fin)
     {
                 MessageBox(myHandle, directory, "The value of directoty is:",
                       MB_OK);
                 MessageBox(myHandle, "ifstream fin (file)", "Errno in creating input
                       file stream :", MB_OK);
                 fin.close ();
     }
     else
     {
// Create the index file name
strcpy (indexFileName, file);
ptr = strrchr (indexFileName, '.');
if (ptr)
       {
   // '.' is in the string
   *(ptr + 1) = '\0';
   strncat (indexFileName, source, 3);
       }
else
   // no '.' in the string
   strncat (indexFileName, ".sam", 4);
String *aPtr = new String (indexFileName);
String& anIndexReference = *aPtr;

// Add an index to the existing Filing Directory Object
Filing->addIndexFile (anIndexReference);

// Create the actual index file
strcpy (pathName, partPath);
strcpy (originalFilePath, partPath);
strcat (originalFilePath, file);
strcat (pathName,indexFileName);

// if the index file already exists, leave the file untouched
returnHandle = creatnew (pathName, FA_NORMAL);
if (returnHandle == -1)
       {
   itoa (errno, errorString, 10);
   MessageBox(myHandle, errorString, "Errno in creating Index file:", MB_OK);
   fin.close ();
}
else
       {
   // Create the output file stream; steam is linked to file
   ofstream fout (pathName);

   // Add the index file name to the Filing Directory


   // Create an index of the text document file contents
```

```
        createIndex (&fout, &fin, originalFilePath);

        // Close the input and output file steams
        fin.close ();
        fout.close ();
    }
      }
}

//------------------------------------------------------------------
// Build the index file header and output it to the index file.
//------------------------------------------------------------------

void Index::buildIndexFileHeader(ofstream *indexFileStream,
          ifstream *docFileStream, char *pathName)
{
 // Build the index file header and output it to the index file
   char    ch;
   int     count, stringSize;
   char    outbuf[80];
   div_t   x;       // holds quotient and remainder integers for division

   fillBuffer (outbuf, 0, sizeof (outbuf));

   // Write the pathName to the index file
   strcpy (outbuf, pathName);
   strcat (outbuf, "\n");
   stringSize = strlen (outbuf);
   indexFileStream->write (outbuf, stringSize);

   fillBuffer (outbuf, 0, sizeof (outbuf));

   // Determine the number of records in the text document and write to
   //  the index file. This will aid the search process later on.
   count = 0;
   while (docFileStream->get(ch))
   count++;

   x = div (count, FilingRecordSize);
   if (x.rem > 0)
      count = x.quot + 1;
   else
      count = x.quot;
   itoa (count, outbuf, 10);   // convert number of records to ascii string
   strcat (outbuf, "\n");
   stringSize = strlen (outbuf);
   indexFileStream->write (outbuf, stringSize);

}

//------------------------------------------------------------------
// Create an index of the contents of the text document.
//------------------------------------------------------------------

void Index::createIndex(ofstream *indexFStream, ifstream *docFStream, char *path-
   Name)
```

```
{
  HashEngine   *hashEngineObj;

//Create the index file header
  buildIndexFileHeader (indexFStream, docFStream, pathName);

// Build the hash blocks in the index file
  hashEngineObj = new HashEngine;
  hashEngineObj->buildHashBlock (indexFStream, docFStream);

  delete hashEngineObj;
}

Query Subsystem
//*********************************************************************
//*                                                                  *
//*                    Electronic Filing in C++                      *
//*                           Version 1.0                            *
//*                 Copyright (c) 1993 Kurt Derr                     *
//*                            query.h                               *
//*********************************************************************

#ifndef __QUERY_H
#define __QUERY_H
#include <strng.h>
#include <queue.h>
#include <list.h>


_CLASSDEF(Query)

class Query {
// Class Query is an abstract class
public:
    int       checkForElementMatch (String* element);
    List*     getLogicalOperators ();
    List*     getQueryElements ();
    void      parseQuery ();
    String    theQuery ();
    int       checkIfQueryEntered();

    List      *queryElementsObj;// Query elements
    List      *logicOperatorsObj;// Logical connecting query operators
    String    *queryObj;// The query entered by the user
    int       queryEntered;
private:
    char* getSubstring (char* ptrToString, int& strLengthPtr);
};
#endif

//*********************************************************************
//*                                                                  *
//*                    Electronic Filing in C++                      *
//*                           Version 1.0                            *
//*                 Copyright (c) 1993 Kurt Derr                     *
//*                           query.cpp                              *
```

```
//*********************************************************************


#include <owl.h>

#include "query.h"

#include <stdio.h>
#include <alloc.h>
#include <string.h>
#include "defines.h"
#include "externs.h"
#include <strstrea.h>

//------------------------------------------------------------------
// Check for match between author/keyword/abstract element and the DRI.
//------------------------------------------------------------------

int Query::checkForElementMatch(String* element)
{
  //
  // element = a DRI element (authors, keywords, or abstract String)
  // check a single dri element against the query element
  // element may be a string consisting of multiple authors, keywords, or
  //   words in an abstract
  //
  int stringLength, numberOfDriStrings, numberOfOperators, numberOfQueryElements;
  int     aFlag, nextFlag;
  char    textBuffer[MaxAbstractSize];
  List    *substrings, *theQueryElementsList;
  int trueFlag, falseFlag, comparisonValue, temp;
  char      andOperator[] = "AND";
  const    char*    stringPtr;
  const    char*    operatorString;
  const    char*    queryString;
  const    char*    driString;
  String* driStringPtr;
  String* queryStringPtr;
  int       testInt;
  int       flags[MaxQueryOperators + 1];
  int       flagsIndex;

  trueFlag = 1;
  falseFlag = 0;
  for (flagsIndex = 0; flagsIndex <= sizeof (flags); flagsIndex++)
  flags[flagsIndex] = 0;
  flagsIndex = 0;

  // a DRI element may have no authors or keywords or any abstract;
  // however, the DRI must have one of these at a minimum
  stringPtr = *element;
  stringLength = strlen (stringPtr);
  numberOfQueryElements = queryElementsObj->getItemsInContainer();

  if ((stringLength > 0) & (numberOfQueryElements > 0))
  {
```

```
    // Check to see if this DRI is part of the query
    substrings = new List;
    theQueryElementsList = new List;

    // process each of the words in the DRI string
    istrstream queryElementStream ((char *) stringPtr, stringLength);
    queryElementStream.clear ();// reset eof

// Position memory  stream to the beginning of the string
    queryElementStream.seekg (0, ios::beg);
    numberOfDriStrings = 0;

    // add each DRI element to substrings
    // substrings represents the dri elements
    while (!queryElementStream.eof())
    {
        fillBuffer (textBuffer, 0, sizeof (textBuffer));
        queryElementStream.getline (textBuffer, sizeof (textBuffer), ' ');
            String* newSubstring = new String (textBuffer);
            substrings->add ((Object&) *newSubstring);
            numberOfDriStrings++;
    }
    numberOfQueryElements = queryElementsObj->getItemsInContainer();
    temp = numberOfQueryElements;
    ListIterator   driIsIt(*substrings);

    ListIterator   queryIsIt(*queryElementsObj);
    queryIsIt.restart ();

    // now check to see if any of the query strings are part of any
    // of the DRI strings
    numberOfQueryElements = temp;
    while (numberOfQueryElements > 0)
    {
            numberOfQueryElements--;
            String& queryElement = (String&) queryIsIt++;
            while (numberOfDriStrings > 0)
            {
                    numberOfDriStrings--;
            String& driElement = (String&) driIsIt++;

            driStringPtr = &driElement;
            driString = *driStringPtr;
            queryStringPtr = &queryElement;
            queryString = *queryStringPtr;

            if ((strcmp (driString, queryString)) == 0)
        flags[flagsIndex++] = trueFlag;
            else
        flags[flagsIndex++] = falseFlag;
      }
    }
    numberOfOperators = logicOperatorsObj->getItemsInContainer();
    if (numberOfOperators == 0)
    {
            substrings->flush(2);
```

```
                delete substrings;
                        delete theQueryElementsList;
                return flags[0];
        }
        else
        {
                flagsIndex--;
                aFlag = flags[flagsIndex--];
                while (flagsIndex > 0)
                {
                   nextFlag = flags[flagsIndex--];
                   String& logicalOperator = ((String&) (logicOperatorsObj->peek-
                        Head())));
                        String* theLogicalOperator = &logicalOperator;
                        operatorString = *theLogicalOperator;
                        comparisonValue = strcmp(operatorString, andOperator);
                        if (comparisonValue == 0)
                                aFlag = aFlag & nextFlag;
                        else
                                aFlag = aFlag | nextFlag;
                }
                                substrings->flush(2);
                                delete substrings;
                                delete theQueryElementsList;
                        return aFlag;
        }
  }
  else
     return falseFlag;
}


//------------------------------------------------------------------
// Answer the query operators.
//------------------------------------------------------------------

List* Query::getLogicalOperators(void)
{
   return logicOperatorsObj;
}



//------------------------------------------------------------------
// Answer if a query has been entered.
//------------------------------------------------------------------

int Query::checkIfQueryEntered ()
{
   const char*  queryStringPointer;
   int  stringLength;

     queryStringPointer = *queryObj;

     stringLength = strlen (queryStringPointer);
     if (stringLength > 0)
         return TRUE;
     else
```

```
      return FALSE;
}


//----------------------------------------------------------------
// Answer the query elements.
//----------------------------------------------------------------

List* Query::getQueryElements(void)
{
   // Return a queue of substrings
   return   queryElementsObj;
}


//----------------------------------------------------------------
// Parse the query into query elements and operators.
//----------------------------------------------------------------

void Query::parseQuery(void)
{
   const char   *queryStringPointer;
   int   stringLength;
   char   *newString, *stringToDelete;
   char   *ptr;
//
// Parse the query string into substrings of logical operators and
//   query elements
//
   queryStringPointer = *queryObj;

   stringLength = strlen (queryStringPointer);

   // Make sure a query was really entered by the user
   if (stringLength > 0)
   {

      newString = (char *) malloc (stringLength + 1);
      stringToDelete = newString;

      strcpy (newString, queryStringPointer);
      while (*(ptr = getSubstring (newString, stringLength)) != NULL)
      {
            String *stringObj = new String (ptr);
            if ((strcmp (ptr, "AND")) == 0)
               logicOperatorsObj->add (*stringObj);
            else if ((strcmp (ptr, "OR")) == 0)
               logicOperatorsObj->add (*stringObj);
            else
               queryElementsObj->add (*stringObj);
            newString = newString + stringLength;
      }
      free (stringToDelete);
   }
}
```

```cpp
char* Query::getSubstring (char* ptrToString, int& strLengthPtr)
{
   static char   substring[50];
   char    *searchPtr;
   int     index;

   strLengthPtr = 0;
   index = 0;
   fillBuffer (substring, 0, sizeof substring);
   searchPtr = ptrToString;
   while (*searchPtr != ' ' & *searchPtr != NULL)
   {
      strLengthPtr++;
      substring[index++] = *searchPtr;
      searchPtr++;
   }
   return substring;
}


//-------------------------------------------------------------
// Answer the query.
//-------------------------------------------------------------

String Query::theQuery(void)
{
   return *queryObj;
}
//*********************************************************************
//*                                                                  *
//*                  Electronic Filing in C++                        *
//*                        Version 1.0                               *
//*            Copyright (c) 1993 Kurt Derr                          *
//*                       absquery.h                                 *
//*********************************************************************

#ifndef __ABSQRY_H
#define __ABSQRY_H
#include <strng.h>
#include "query.h"

_CLASSDEF(AbstractQuery)


class AbstractQuery : public Query  {

public:
   AbstractQuery();
   ~AbstractQuery();
   void setAbstractQuery (char* abstractQuery);
   void setConToAbsOp (char* theOperator);
   String& getAbsToKeyOp ();
};

#endif
```

```
//**********************************************************************
//*                                                                    *
//*                     Electronic Filing in C++                       *
//*                            Version 1.0                             *
//*                  Copyright (c) 1993 Kurt Derr                      *
//*                            absquery.cpp                            *
//**********************************************************************


#include <owl.h>
#include <stdio.h>
#include <strng.h>
#include "externs.h"
#include "absquery.h"

extern  abstractToKeywordOperator, contentToAbstractOperator;

//-----------------------------------------------------------------
// Creates the Abstract Query Object
//-----------------------------------------------------------------

AbstractQuery::AbstractQuery()
{
   queryElementsObj = new List;
   logicOperatorsObj = new List;
   queryEntered = FALSE;
}

//-----------------------------------------------------------------
// Disposes of the Abstract Query Object
//-----------------------------------------------------------------

AbstractQuery::~AbstractQuery(void)
{
   delete    queryElementsObj;
   delete    logicOperatorsObj;
}


//-----------------------------------------------------------------
// Set the query equal to the abstract query.
//-----------------------------------------------------------------

void AbstractQuery::setAbstractQuery(char* abstractQuery)
{
   queryObj = new const String (abstractQuery);
}

//-----------------------------------------------------------------
// Set the content-to-abstract operator equal to operator.
//-----------------------------------------------------------------

void AbstractQuery::setConToAbsOp(char* theOperator)
{
   contentToAbstractOperator = *theOperator;
}
```

```
//-------------------------------------------------------------------
// Get the abstract-to-keyword operator.
//-------------------------------------------------------------------

String& AbstractQuery::getAbsToKeyOp()
{
   return absToKeyOp;
}
//*********************************************************************
//*                                                                 *
//*                 Electronic Filing in C++                        *
//*                        Version 1.0                              *
//*              Copyright (c) 1993 Kurt Derr                       *
//*                        autquery.h                                    *
//*********************************************************************

#ifndef __AUTQRY_H
#define __AUTQRY_H
#include <strng.h>
#include "query.h"

_CLASSDEF(AuthorQuery)


class AuthorQuery : public Query {

public:
   AuthorQuery();
   ~AuthorQuery();
   void setAuthorQuery (char *authorQuery);
   void setKeywordToAuthorOperator (char *theOperator);
};

#endif

//*********************************************************************
//*                                                                 *
//*                 Electronic Filing in C++                        *
//*                        Version 1.0                              *
//*              Copyright (c) 1993 Kurt Derr                       *
//*                        autquery.cpp                             *
//*********************************************************************


#include <owl.h>

#include "autquery.h"
#include "query.h"

#include <stdio.h>
extern keywordToAuthorOperator;

//-------------------------------------------------------------------
// Creates the Author Query Object
//-------------------------------------------------------------------
```

```
AuthorQuery::AuthorQuery()
{
   queryElementsObj = new List;
   logicOperatorsObj = new List;
   queryEntered = FALSE;
}

//------------------------------------------------------------------
// Disposes of the Author Query Object
//------------------------------------------------------------------

AuthorQuery::~AuthorQuery(void)
{
   delete    queryElementsObj;
   delete    logicOperatorsObj;
}


//------------------------------------------------------------------
// Set the query equal to the author query.
//------------------------------------------------------------------

void AuthorQuery::setAuthorQuery(char *authorQuery)
{
   queryObj = new const String (authorQuery);
}

//------------------------------------------------------------------
// Set the keyword-to-author operator equal to operator.
//------------------------------------------------------------------

void AuthorQuery::setKeywordToAuthorOperator(char *theOperator)
{
   keywordToAuthorOperator = *theOperator;
}

//******************************************************************
//*                                                                *
//*               Electronic Filing in C++                         *
//*                      Version 1.0                               *
//*            Copyright (c) 1993 Kurt Derr                        *
//*                      conquery.h                                *
//******************************************************************

#ifndef __CONQRY_H
#define __CONQRY_H
#include <strng.h>
#include "query.h"


_CLASSDEF(ContentQuery)


class ContentQuery : public Query {
```

```
public:
    ContentQuery();
    ~ContentQuery();
    void setContentQuery (char *contentQuery);
    String& getContentToAbstractOperator ();
};

#endif

//**********************************************************************
//*                                                                    *
//*                     Electronic Filing in C++                       *
//*                           Version 1.0                              *
//*               Copyright (c) 1993 Kurt Derr                         *
//*                         conquery.cpp                               *
//**********************************************************************


#include <owl.h>
#include <stdio.h>
#include <strng.h>
#include "conquery.h"
#include "externs.h"

//------------------------------------------------------------------
// Creates the Abstract Query Object
//------------------------------------------------------------------

ContentQuery::ContentQuery()
{
    queryElementsObj = new List;
    logicOperatorsObj = new List;
    queryEntered = FALSE;
}

//------------------------------------------------------------------
// Disposes of the Abstract Query Object
//------------------------------------------------------------------

ContentQuery::~ContentQuery(void)
{
    delete    queryElementsObj;
    delete    logicOperatorsObj;
}


//------------------------------------------------------------------
// Set the query equal to the content query.
//------------------------------------------------------------------

void ContentQuery::setContentQuery(char *contentQuery)
{
    queryObj = new const String (contentQuery);
}

//------------------------------------------------------------------
```

```cpp
// Get the content-to-abstract operator.
//------------------------------------------------------------------

String& ContentQuery::getContentToAbstractOperator()
{
   return conToAbsOp;
}

//********************************************************************
//*                                                                  *
//*                   Electronic Filing in C++                       *
//*                         Version 1.0                              *
//*              Copyright (c) 1993 Kurt Derr                        *
//*                         keyquery.h                               *
//********************************************************************

#ifndef __KEYQRY_H
#define __KEYQRY_H
#include <strng.h>
#include "query.h"


_CLASSDEF(KeywordQuery)


class KeywordQuery : public Query  {

public:
    KeywordQuery();
    ~KeywordQuery();
    void setKeywordQuery (char *keywordQuery);
    void setAbsToKeyOp (char *theOperator);
    String& getKeyToAutOp ();
};
#endif


//********************************************************************
//*                                                                  *
//*                   Electronic Filing in C++                       *
//*                         Version 1.0                              *
//*              Copyright (c) 1993 Kurt Derr                        *
//*                         keyquery.cpp                             *
//********************************************************************


#include <owl.h>

#include "keyquery.h"

#include <stdio.h>
#include <strng.h>
#include "query.h"
#include "externs.h"

//------------------------------------------------------------------
```

```
// Creates the Keyword Query Object
//-------------------------------------------------------------------

KeywordQuery::KeywordQuery()
{
   queryElementsObj = new List;
   logicOperatorsObj = new List;
   queryEntered = FALSE;
}

//-------------------------------------------------------------------
// Disposes of the Keyword Query Object
//-------------------------------------------------------------------

KeywordQuery::~KeywordQuery(void)
{
   delete    queryElementsObj;
   delete    logicOperatorsObj;
}


//-------------------------------------------------------------------
// Set the query equal to the keyword query.
//-------------------------------------------------------------------

void KeywordQuery::setKeywordQuery(char *keywordQuery)
{
   queryObj = new const String (keywordQuery);
}

//-------------------------------------------------------------------
// Set the abstract-to-keyword operator equal to operator.
//-------------------------------------------------------------------

void KeywordQuery::setAbsToKeyOp(char *theOperator)
{
   absToKeyOp = theOperator;
}

//-------------------------------------------------------------------
// Get the keyword-to-author operator.
//-------------------------------------------------------------------

String& KeywordQuery::getKeyToAutOp()
{
   return keyToAutOp;
}

Hashing Subsystem

//*****************************************************************
//*                                                               *
//*              Electronic Filing in C++                         *
//*                    Version 1.0                                *
//*          Copyright (c) 1993 Kurt Derr                         *
//*                    hasheng.h                                  *
```

```
//**********************************************************************

#ifndef __HASHENG_H
#define __HASHENG_H
#include "defines.h"
#include "junkword.h"
#include <list.h>
#include "filgchrs.h"
#include <strng.h>
#include <fstream.h>

_CLASSDEF(HashEngine)

class HashEngine {

public:
    HashEngine();
    HashEngine (JunkWords *junkWordObject);
    ~HashEngine();
    void buildHashBlock (ofstream *indexFStream, ifstream *docFStream);
    void hash1stCharUsing (char aChar, char *theHashBlock);
    void hash2ndCharUsing (char aChar, char *theHashBlock);
    void hashOtherCharUsing (char aChar, char *theHashBlock);
    void hashTheWordUsing (String *theWord, String *theHashBlock);


private:
    void hashDocRec (char *documentRecord);
    void hash1stChar (char aChar);
    void hash2ndChar (char aChar);
    void hashOtherChar (char aChar);
    void hashTheWord (char *theWord);

    int     translateChar;
    int     offset;
    int     hashBlockIndex;
    JunkWords           *junkWordsObj;
    FilingCharacters    *filingCharsObj;
    char    hashBlock[YHashBlock * XHashBlock];
    int     recordsIndexedInBlock;
    int     totalRecordsIndexed;
    char    textBuffer[81];
    char    wordBuf[81];
    int     randomNumberTable[NumberOfRandomNumbers];
};

#endif

//**********************************************************************
//*                                                                    *
//*                  Electronic Filing in C++                          *
//*                        Version 1.0                                 *
//*              Copyright (c) 1993 Kurt Derr                          *
//*                       hasheng.cpp                                  *
//**********************************************************************
```

```
//#include "nowdefs.h"

#include <owl.h>
#include "defines.h"
#include "hasheng.h"
#include <stdio.h>
#include <fstream.h>
#include <strstrea.h>
#include "externs.h"

int  translateTable[NumberOfRandomNumbers];

//-------------------------------------------------------------------
// Creates the Search Engine
//-------------------------------------------------------------------

HashEngine::HashEngine()
{
   int  i, randomNumber;

   translateChar = 0;
   offset = 0;
   hashBlockIndex = 0;

   // Set up the random number table

   srand (1-19683+65536);

   for (i = 0; i <= (NumberOfRandomNumbers - 1); i++)
   {
      randomNumber = rand ();// generate a random number
      randomNumberTable[i] = randomNumber;
   }

   // create JunkWords and FilingCharacters objects once
   //     per index operation
   junkWordsObj = new JunkWords;
   filingCharsObj = new FilingCharacters;
   recordsIndexedInBlock = 0;
   totalRecordsIndexed = 0;
}

//-------------------------------------------------------------------
// Creates the Hash Engine using the specified junk word object
//-------------------------------------------------------------------

HashEngine::HashEngine (JunkWords *junkWordObject)
{
   int  i, randomNumber;

   translateChar = 0;
   offset = 0;
   hashBlockIndex = 0;

   // Set up the random number table
```

```
    srand (1-19683+65536);

    for (i = 0; i <= (NumberOfRandomNumbers - 1); i++)
    {
        randomNumber = rand ();// generate a random number
        randomNumberTable[i] = randomNumber;
    }

    // create JunkWords and FilingCharacters objects once
    //      per index operation
    junkWordsObj = junkWordObject;
    filingCharsObj = new FilingCharacters;
    recordsIndexedInBlock = 0;
    totalRecordsIndexed = 0;
}

//------------------------------------------------------------------
// Disposes of the Search Engine
//------------------------------------------------------------------

HashEngine::~HashEngine(void)
{

}

//------------------------------------------------------------------
// Build all hash blocks for the text document.
//------------------------------------------------------------------

void HashEngine::buildHashBlock(ofstream *indexFStream, ifstream *docFStream)
{
    int   eofCheck;

    // Initialize the hashBlock to all zeros
    fillBuffer (hashBlock, '0', XHashBlock * YHashBlock);

    docFStream->clear ();// reset eof

    // Position document file stream to the beginning of file
    docFStream->seekg (0, ios::beg);

    // Hash each record in a block
        // Read each record of the text document file and hash it
    while (!docFStream->eof())
    {
        fillBuffer (textBuffer, 0, sizeof (textBuffer));
        docFStream->getline (textBuffer, sizeof (textBuffer), '\n');
        hashDocRec (textBuffer);
        recordsIndexedInBlock++;
        totalRecordsIndexed++;

        // Check if the block is full
        if (recordsIndexedInBlock >= XHashBlock)
        {
            // Output the hashBlock to the Index file
            indexFStream->write (hashBlock, XHashBlock * YHashBlock);
```

```
            // Clear the hashBlock
            fillBuffer (hashBlock, '0', XHashBlock * YHashBlock);
        }
    }

    // Make sure that the text document file wasn't empty, and 2) that the
    //     last hashed block was not already output to the index file

    if ((recordsIndexedInBlock != 0) & (totalRecordsIndexed != 0))
            // Output the hashBlock to the Index file
            indexFStream->write (hashBlock, XHashBlock * YHashBlock);
    indexFStream->close ();
}

//------------------------------------------------------------------
// Hash the first character of the word and put it in the hashBlock.
//------------------------------------------------------------------

void HashEngine::hash1stCharUsing(char aChar, char *theHashBlock)
{
    div_t  x;
    int   maxIndexNumber;
    int   times;

    translateChar = 0;
    times = 6;
    maxIndexNumber = YHashBlock;
    while (times > 0)
    {
        times--;
        translateChar = translateChar + translateTable[(int) aChar];
        x = div (translateChar, NumberOfRandomNumbers);
        offset = x.rem;
        if (offset > 0)
        {
     x = div (randomNumberTable[offset], maxIndexNumber);
     hashBlockIndex = x.rem;  //this code replaces the following 2 lines
     *(theHashBlock + hashBlockIndex) = '1';
        }
    }
}

//------------------------------------------------------------------
// Hash the second character of the word and put it in the hashBlock.
//------------------------------------------------------------------

void HashEngine::hash2ndCharUsing(char aChar, char *theHashBlock)
{
    div_t  x;
    int   maxIndexNumber;
    int   times;

    translateChar = 0;
    times = 4;
    maxIndexNumber = YHashBlock;
    while (times > 0)
```

```
    {
       times--;
       translateChar = translateChar + translateTable[(int) aChar];
       x = div (translateChar, NumberOfRandomNumbers);
       offset = x.rem;
       if (offset > 0)
       {
    x = div (randomNumberTable[offset], maxIndexNumber);
    hashBlockIndex = x.rem;   //this code replaces the following 2 lines
    *(theHashBlock + hashBlockIndex) = '1';
       }
    }
}


//-----------------------------------------------------------------
// Hash the remaining characters of the word and put it in the hashBlock.
//-----------------------------------------------------------------

void HashEngine::hashOtherCharUsing(char aChar, char *theHashBlock)
{
    div_t   x;
    int   maxIndexNumber;
    int   times;

    translateChar = 0;
    times = 2;
    maxIndexNumber = YHashBlock;
    while (times > 0)
    {
       times--;
       translateChar = translateChar + translateTable[(int) aChar];
       x = div (translateChar, NumberOfRandomNumbers);
       offset = x.rem;
       if (offset > 0)
       {
    x = div (randomNumberTable[offset], maxIndexNumber);
    hashBlockIndex = x.rem;   //this code replaces the following 2 lines
    *(theHashBlock + hashBlockIndex) = '1';
       }
    }
}


//-----------------------------------------------------------------
// Hash a word and put it in the hashBlock.
//-----------------------------------------------------------------

void HashEngine::hashTheWordUsing(String *theWord, String *theHashBlock)
{
    char ch;
    unsigned intcount, index;
    int   firstFilingCharPosition, stringLength;
    const char*   stringPtr;
    const char*hashBlockPtr;

    // Hash the ASCII word. Words must be greater than 2 characters in length to be
    //   hashed. Non-filing characters may preceed a word and must be contiguous.
```

```cpp
     //    Non-filing characters  may not follow valid filing characters in a word.

     count = 0;
     index = 0;
     // count the number of filing characters in the word
     stringPtr = *theWord;
     hashBlockPtr = *theHashBlock;
     // try modifying hashTheWordUsing to iterate thru the string characters
     // rather than trying to determine its length

     stringLength = strlen(stringPtr);
     char *newWord = new char [stringLength];
     strcpy (newWord, stringPtr);


     ch = *(newWord + count);
     while (ch != 0)
     {
       if (filingCharsObj->checkIfFilingChar (ch) == TRUE)
      count++;
       index++;
       ch = *(newWord + index);
     }
     //
     // If the filing character count is greater than 2
     //
     if (count > 2)
     {
        firstFilingCharPosition = filingCharsObj->getFirstFilingChar(newWord);
      hash1stCharUsing (*(newWord + firstFilingCharPosition), (char *) hashBlockPtr);
        hash2ndCharUsing (*(newWord + firstFilingCharPosition + 1), (char *) hash-
                BlockPtr);
        count = count - 2;
        hashOtherCharUsing (*(newWord + firstFilingCharPosition + 2), (char *)
                hashBlockPtr);
        index = firstFilingCharPosition + 3;
        while (--count > 0)
        {
      hashOtherCharUsing (*(newWord + index), (char *) hashBlockPtr);
       index++;
        }
     }
}

//----------------------------------------------------------------
// Hash an 80 character record and put it in the hashBlock.
//----------------------------------------------------------------

void HashEngine::hashDocRec(char *documentRecord)
{
   long streamPos;
   int  numberOfCharsRead;

   // Initialize wordBuffer to all zeros
   fillBuffer (wordBuf, '0', sizeof (wordBuf));
```

```
   // Use an input string stream to read the document record
   istrstream inputStream (documentRecord, 80);

   // Get each word in the document record
   while ((streamPos = inputStream.tellg ()) < 80)
   {
      inputStream.getline (wordBuf, 80, ' ');
      numberOfCharsRead = inputStream.gcount();
      *(wordBuf + numberOfCharsRead - 1) = '\0';
      //
      // Check each word and make sure it is not a junk word. If it is not
      //    a junk word, then HASH the word
      //
      if ((junkWordsObj->checkIfJunkWord (wordBuf)) == FALSE)
    hashTheWord (wordBuf);
   }
}

//------------------------------------------------------------------
// Hash the first character of the word and put it in hashBlock.
//------------------------------------------------------------------

void HashEngine::hash1stChar(char aChar)
{
   div_t   x;
   int   maxIndexNumber;
   int   times;

   translateChar = 0;
   times = 6;
   maxIndexNumber = YHashBlock;
   while (times > 0)
   {
      times--;
      translateChar = translateChar + translateTable[(int) aChar];
      x = div (translateChar, NumberOfRandomNumbers);
      offset = x.rem;
      if (offset > 0)
      {
    x = div (randomNumberTable[offset], maxIndexNumber);
    hashBlockIndex = x.rem;   //this code replaces the following 2 lines
    hashBlock[hashBlockIndex] = '1';
      }
   }
}

//------------------------------------------------------------------
// Hash the second character of the word and put it in hashBlock.
//------------------------------------------------------------------

void HashEngine::hash2ndChar(char aChar)
{
   div_t   x;
   int   maxIndexNumber;
   int   times;
```

```
   translateChar = 0;
   times = 4;
   maxIndexNumber = YHashBlock;
   while (times > 0)
   {
      times--;
      translateChar = translateChar + translateTable[(int) aChar];
      x = div (translateChar, NumberOfRandomNumbers);
      offset = x.rem;
      if (offset > 0)
      {
   x = div (randomNumberTable[offset], maxIndexNumber);
   hashBlockIndex = x.rem;  //this code replaces the following 2 lines
   hashBlock[hashBlockIndex] = '1';
      }
   }
}

//-----------------------------------------------------------------
// Hash the remaining characters of the word and put it in hashBlock.
//-----------------------------------------------------------------

void HashEngine::hashOtherChar(char aChar)
{
   div_t   x;
   int   maxIndexNumber;
   int   times;

   translateChar = 0;
   times = 2;
   maxIndexNumber = YHashBlock;
   while (times > 0)
   {
      times--;
      translateChar = translateChar + translateTable[(int) aChar];
      x = div (translateChar, NumberOfRandomNumbers);
      offset = x.rem;
      if (offset > 0)
      {
   x = div (randomNumberTable[offset], maxIndexNumber);
   hashBlockIndex = x.rem;  //this code replaces the following 2 lines
   hashBlock[hashBlockIndex] = '1';
      }
   }
}

//-----------------------------------------------------------------
// Hash a word and put it in hashBlock.
//-----------------------------------------------------------------

void HashEngine::hashTheWord(char *theWord)
{
   char ch;
   unsigned int   count, index;
   int   firstFilingCharPosition;
```

```
// Hash the ASCII word. Words must be greater than 2 characters in length to
//   be hashed. Non-filing characters may preceed a word and must be contiguous.
//    Non-filing characters may not follow valid filing characters in a word.

count = 0;
// count the number of filing characters in the word

ch = *(theWord + count);
while (ch != 0)
{
  if (filingCharsObj->checkIfFilingChar (ch) == TRUE)
      count++;
  ch = *(theWord + count);
}
//
// If the filing character count is greater than 2
//
if (count > 2)
{
    firstFilingCharPosition = filingCharsObj->getFirstFilingChar(theWord);
    hash1stChar (*(theWord + firstFilingCharPosition));
    hash2ndChar (*(theWord + firstFilingCharPosition + 1));
    count = count - 2;
    hashOtherChar (*(theWord + firstFilingCharPosition + 2));
    index = firstFilingCharPosition + 3;
    while (count-- > 0)
    {
  hashOtherChar (*(theWord + index));
  index++;
    }
}
}

//********************************************************************
//*                                                                  *
//*                 Electronic Filing in C++                         *
//*                         Version 1.0                              *
//*             Copyright (c) 1993 Kurt Derr                         *
//*                        filgchrs.h                                *
//********************************************************************

#ifndef __FILGCHRS_H
#define __FILGCHRS_H
#include <list.h>
#include <strng.h>
#include <iostream.h>


_CLASSDEF(FilingCharacters)


class FilingCharacters {

public:
    FilingCharacters();
    ~FilingCharacters();
```

```
    void addFilingChar (char ch);
    void deleteFilingChar (char ch);
    List* getFilingChars ();
    void saveFilingChars ();
    int checkIfFilingChar (char ch);
    char getFirstFilingChar (char *aWord);

private:
    void replaceFilingCharsFile ();
    List*includedCharsObj;// Set of characters
};

#endif

//*******************************************************************
//*                                                                 *
//*                  Electronic Filing in C++                       *
//*                         Version 1.0                             *
//*                Copyright (c) 1993 Kurt Derr                     *
//*                        filgchrs.cpp                             *
//*******************************************************************


#include <owl.h>
#include "filgchrs.h"
#include <stdio.h>
#include <fstream.h>
#include <iostream.h>
#include "externs.h"
#include "defines.h"
#include <list.h>


//------------------------------------------------------------------
// Creates the Filing Characters Object
//------------------------------------------------------------------

FilingCharacters::FilingCharacters()
{
   ifstream filingCharFile ("c:/filechar.txt");
   char filingCharBuf[3];

   // Initialize filingCharBuf to all zeros
   fillBuffer (filingCharBuf, 0, sizeof (filingCharBuf));

   // Create a new List object to hold the filing characters from the file
   includedCharsObj = new List;

// Get all filing characters and add them to the includedChars List Object
   while (filingCharFile)
   {
      filingCharFile.getline (filingCharBuf, 2, ' ');
      filingCharBuf[1] = ' ';
      filingCharBuf[2] = '\0';
    . String *stringObj = new String (filingCharBuf);
      includedCharsObj->add (*stringObj);
   }
```

```
    filingCharFile.close ();

}
//-------------------------------------------------------------------
// Disposes of the Filing Characters Object
//-------------------------------------------------------------------

FilingCharacters::~FilingCharacters(void)
{
// delete all of the String objects that are in includedCharsObj
}

//-------------------------------------------------------------------
// Add the specified character to the list of filing characters.
//-------------------------------------------------------------------

void FilingCharacters::addFilingChar(char ch)
{

}

//-------------------------------------------------------------------
// Remove the filing character from the list of filing characters.
//-------------------------------------------------------------------

void FilingCharacters::deleteFilingChar(char ch)
{

}

//-------------------------------------------------------------------
// Answer the filing characters.
//-------------------------------------------------------------------

List* FilingCharacters::getFilingChars(void)
{

}

//-------------------------------------------------------------------
// Replace the filing characters file.
//-------------------------------------------------------------------

void FilingCharacters::saveFilingChars(void)
{

}

//-------------------------------------------------------------------
// Answer true if character is a filing character.
//-------------------------------------------------------------------

int FilingCharacters::checkIfFilingChar(char ch)
{
//
```

```
// Answer TRUE if a word is a filing character, else answer FALSE
//
     char    newString[3];

     newString[0] = ch;
     newString[1] = ' ';
     newString[2] = '\0';
     String *stringObj = new String (newString);
     if ((includedCharsObj->hasMember (*stringObj)) == 1)
     {
             delete stringObj;
             return TRUE;
     }
     else
     {
             delete stringObj;
             return FALSE;
     }

}


//-----------------------------------------------------------------
// Answer position of first filing character in the word.
//-----------------------------------------------------------------

char FilingCharacters::getFirstFilingChar(char *aWord)
{
     char newString[3];
     int  firstFilingCharPosition, stringLength;

   stringLength = strlen (aWord);
   firstFilingCharPosition = 0;
   while (stringLength > 0)
   {
     newString[0] = *(aWord + firstFilingCharPosition);
     newString[1] = ' ';
     newString[2] = '\0';
     String *stringObj = new String (newString);
     if ((includedCharsObj->hasMember (*stringObj)) == 1)
     {
             delete stringObj;
             return firstFilingCharPosition;
     }
     else
     {
             delete stringObj;
             firstFilingCharPosition++;
       stringLength--;
     }
   }
   return NOT_FOUND;// No filing character found
}


//-----------------------------------------------------------------
// Delete old filing characters file and create a new empty file.
//-----------------------------------------------------------------
```

```
void FilingCharacters::replaceFilingCharsFile(void)
{

}
//******************************************************************
//*                                                               *
//*                  Electronic Filing in C++                     *
//*                        Version 1.0                            *
//*                 Copyright (c) 1993 Kurt Derr                  *
//*                        junkword.h                             *
//******************************************************************

#ifndef __EJUNKWORDS_H
#define __EJUNKWORDS_H
#include <list.h>
#include <strng.h>

_CLASSDEF(JunkWords)


class JunkWords {

public:
    JunkWords();
    ~JunkWords();
    void addJunkWord (char *word);
    void deleteJunkWord (char *word);
    List* getJunkWords ();
    void saveJunkWords ();
    int checkIfJunkWord (String& aWord);


private:
    void replaceJunkWordFile ();
    List   *currentWordsObj; // Set of words from junk word file
};

#endif

//******************************************************************
//*                                                               *
//*                  Electronic Filing in C++                     *
//*                        Version 1.0                            *
//*                 Copyright (c) 1993 Kurt Derr                  *
//*                        junkword.cpp                           *
//******************************************************************


#include <owl.h>

#include "junkword.h"

#include <stdio.h>
#include "externs.h"
#include <list.h>
```

```cpp
#include <strng.h>
#include "defines.h"
#include <fstream.h>

//-------------------------------------------------------------
// Creates the Junk Words Object
//-------------------------------------------------------------

JunkWords::JunkWords()
{
    ifstream   junkWordFile ("c:/junkword.txt");
    char       junkWordBuf[20];
    int        itemCount, errorFlag;
               String*stringObj;

    // Initialize junkWordBuf to all zeros
    fillBuffer (junkWordBuf, 0, sizeof (junkWordBuf));

    // Create a List object to manage the junk words from the disk file
    currentWordsObj = new List;

    // Get all of the junk words and add them to the currentWords ListObj
    errorFlag = 0;
    itemCount = 0;
    while ((junkWordFile.eof () == 0) & (itemCount <= 95))
    {
        junkWordFile.getline (junkWordBuf, 20, ' ');
        stringObj = new const String (junkWordBuf);
        fillBuffer (junkWordBuf, 0, sizeof (junkWordBuf));
        if (stringObj != 0)
        {
            currentWordsObj->add (*stringObj);
        itemCount = currentWordsObj->getItemsInContainer();
        }
        else
            errorFlag = 1;
    }
    junkWordFile.close ();
}

//-------------------------------------------------------------
// Disposes of the Junk Words Object
//-------------------------------------------------------------

JunkWords::~JunkWords(void)
{
// delete all of the String objects that are in currentWordsObj
}

//-------------------------------------------------------------
// Add the junk word to the list of junk word.
//-------------------------------------------------------------

void JunkWords::addJunkWord(char *word)
{

}
```

```
//------------------------------------------------------------------
// Remove the junk word from the list of junk words.
//------------------------------------------------------------------

void JunkWords::deleteJunkWord(char *word)
{


}

//------------------------------------------------------------------
// Answer the junk words.
//------------------------------------------------------------------

List* JunkWords::getJunkWords(void)
{

}

//------------------------------------------------------------------
// Replace the junk words file.
//------------------------------------------------------------------

void JunkWords::saveJunkWords(void)
{

}

//------------------------------------------------------------------
// Answer true if word is a junk word.
//------------------------------------------------------------------

int JunkWords::checkIfJunkWord(String& aWord)
{
//
// Answer TRUE if a word is a junk word, else answer FALSE
//
      if ((currentWordsObj->hasMember (aWord)) == 1)
      {
   return TRUE;
      }
      else
      {
   return FALSE;
      }
}

//------------------------------------------------------------------
// Delete old junk words file and create a new empty file.
//------------------------------------------------------------------

void JunkWords::replaceJunkWordFile(void)
{

}
```

Miscellaneous Classes

```
//********************************************************************
//*                                                                  *
//*                    Electronic Filing in C++                      *
//*                         Version 1.0                              *
//*                 Copyright (c) 1993 Kurt Derr                     *
//*                         filedir.h                                *
//********************************************************************

#ifndef __FILEDIR_H
#define __FILEDIR_H
#include <strng.h>
#include <list.h>
#include <set.h>


_CLASSDEF(FilingDirectory)


class FilingDirectory {

public:
    FilingDirectory();
    ~FilingDirectory();
    void addIndexFile (String& indexFileName);
    void deleteIndexFile (String& indexFileName);
    List* retrieveIndexNames ();
    int numberOfIndexFiles ();

private:
    List*files;// Names of the index files
    int numberOfFiles;
};

#endif

//********************************************************************
//*                                                                  *
//*                    Electronic Filing in C++                      *
//*                         Version 1.0                              *
//*                 Copyright (c) 1993 Kurt Derr                     *
//*                         filedir.cpp                              *
//********************************************************************

#include <owl.h>
#include "filedir.h"
#include <stdio.h>
#include <list.h>


// Uses the Filing global to retain the Set of documents already filed

//-------------------------------------------------------------------
// Creates the Text Document Object
//-------------------------------------------------------------------
```

```
FilingDirectory::FilingDirectory()
{
    // Set up the Filing Set from the /Filing directory
    numberOfFiles = 0;
    files = new List;
}

//------------------------------------------------------------------
// Disposes of the Text Document Object
//------------------------------------------------------------------

FilingDirectory::~FilingDirectory(void)
{
    delete files;
}

//------------------------------------------------------------------
// Add a document name to the list of files for this directory.
//------------------------------------------------------------------

void FilingDirectory::addIndexFile(String& indexFileName)
{
    numberOfFiles++;
    files->add (indexFileName);
}

//------------------------------------------------------------------
// Delete the index file header and remove the index file name from
// the list of files for this directory.
//------------------------------------------------------------------

void FilingDirectory::deleteIndexFile(String& indexFileName)
{
    if (numberOfFiles > 0)
    {
        numberOfFiles--;
        files->findMember (indexFileName);
        files->detach (indexFileName);
    }
}

//------------------------------------------------------------------
// Answer the names of the index files in the filing directory.
//------------------------------------------------------------------

List* FilingDirectory::retrieveIndexNames()
{
    return files;
}

int FilingDirectory::numberOfIndexFiles()
{
    return numberOfFiles;
}
```

```
Miscellaneous Files
//REGEN_FILEHEADING
//REGEN_FILEHEADING

        /**********************************************************************
         *                                                                    *
         *      Source File: EF.rc                                            *
         *      Description: Resource file for EF application                 *
         *      Date:        Sun Jan 01 05:51:37 1995                         *
         *                                                                    *
         **********************************************************************/

#include <windows.h>
#include <bwcc.h>
#include "EFID.h"
#include "EF.h"
#include "EF.H"
//REGEN_RC
//REGEN_RC


#include "EF.mnu"
#include "file.dlg"
#include "dri.dlg"
#include "delete.dlg"
#include "search.dlg"
#include "srchres.dlg"
#include "view.dlg"
#include "print.dlg"
#include "charset.dlg"
#include "junkword.dlg"



//EF.DEF File
NAME                EF
DESCRIPTION         'ProtoGen Application'
EXETYPE             WINDOWS
STUB                'WINSTUB.EXE'
CODE                DISCARDABLE PRELOAD
DATA                PRELOAD
HEAPSIZE            4096
STACKSIZE           8192
EXPORTS
;DEF_BEGIN
;DEF_END
```

Metrics

K.1 PRODUCT-RELATED METRICS

Many of the outputs of the different phases of the object-oriented development process are measurable. Tables K.1 through K.5 list the measurable outputs of the OODP and the measures and metrics associated with them that we will use. The metrics are all product related.

Existing Metrics

Note that traditional metrics such as lines of code, McCabe cyclomatic complexity, and Halstead metrics are not included in our measurements and analysis. A line of code metric is not very useful in the object-oriented world because having a sizable class library and a programmer very familiar with that class library can significantly reduce the amount of written code and improve the quality of the program. So what does lines of code have to do with program complexity in a language such as Smalltalk? I have seen numerous examples of one programmer writing three or four times as much code as another programmer while achieving the same results. Line of code does not really tell us how complete or complex our program is and is not a meaningful measure for the system as a whole (Booch, 1994; Lorenz, 1993).

The McCabe cyclomatic complexity produces a number that is a measure of the complexity of a graph (i.e., a graph of the sequence your program may take showing all possible paths). The McCabe number is the number of test cases you need to do path testing. This number is less interesting in the object-oriented world than in the traditional software development world because of polymorphism. Polymorphism hides the number of operations in an untyped language such as Smalltalk (Jacobson et al., 1992), whereas "switch" (case) statements in a language such as "C" dramatically increase the McCabe number. However, some metrics tools are smart about the "C" switch statement. Booch (1994) also notes that the McCabe number does not give a meaningful measure of complexity when applied to the system as a whole. Some metrics experts do use average cyclomatic complexity for the entire system.

Halstead's metrics measure complexity by counting the number of operators and operands in source code. Halstead defined program effort as $E = V/L$, where V is potential volume and L is program level. Both V and L are calculated based on the number of operands and operators. A high value of E indicates that the software is complex. There is limited support for Halstead metrics on object-oriented systems (Welker, 1994).

Since managing complexity and improving productivity in the software development process are two of the major issues facing the software industry today (Winblad et al., 1990), we will attempt to use metrics to measure those attributes. We would like to choose metrics that focus on reuse, since reusing results from any/all phases of the OODP is one of the best opportunities for making productivity and quality improvements and for significantly reducing a product's life-cycle cost. However, our application has no artifacts to reuse, such as analysis and design documents, or office automation class libraries. Also, the software industry has no standard practices on how we should measure reuse. Therefore, we will select metrics that are espoused by other authors.

The Desired Measures column in the tables in this appendix shows what we would like to be able to compute. For example, in the analysis phase of the life cycle, we would like to be able to compare quantitatively the model complexity of two analysis models. In order to do this, we need a way of calculating model complexity directly from measurable aspects of the object model. However, there is no agreement in the industry as to the metrics or factors that affect complexity. For this and all of the other measures specified in Tables K.1 through K.4, we know of no formula that relates the metrics to an overall complexity indicator for object-oriented development. However, if we are ever to validate and calibrate metrics, we need to start collecting them and then refine the metrics as we learn more about them (Jacobson et al., 1992). From the standpoints of project management and software engineering, it would be useful to be able to compare analysis, design, and/or coding models quantitatively.

Analysis Phase

The outputs of the analysis phase that are measurable are the object model, dynamic model, and the functional model (see Table K.1). For the object model we would like to compute model complexity. We will measure model complexity by collecting data on several metrics: number of classes, number of operations, and number of associations.

For the dynamic model we would like to compute model complexity and transition complexity. The model complexity will be measured by collecting data on the number of scenarios. A scenario is just a sequence of events/transactions that represent a specific way of using the system. The minimum number of scenarios is the set of all scenarios that specify the complete functionality of the system. For our application we should have at least one normal scenario and one exception scenario for each major user interface function (i.e., file, search, delete, junk words, filing characters). So a minimum of 10 scenarios would be appropriate. As noted in Chapter 1, scenarios/use cases developed for the dynamic model form the basis for the testing processes; i.e, each scenario is a test case.

Table K.1. Product-Related Metrics for the Outputs of the Analysis Phase of the OODP.

Outputs	Desired Measures	Product Metrics
Object model	Model complexity	number of classes
		number of operations
		number of associations
Dynamic model	Model complexity	number of scenarios
	Transition complexity	number of states
		number of transitions
Functional model	Model complexity	number of primitive processes
		number of data flows

Transition complexity is associated with state transition diagrams. A transition in a state transition diagram is a change of state caused by an event. The directed arcs between states on a state transition diagram are transitions that are labeled by event names. Transition complexity will be measured by recording the number of states and the number of transitions.

The last output of the analysis phase in the OODP that we will want to measure is the functional model. Here again we would like to measure model complexity. The product metrics we will use to determine these measures are the number of primitive processes and the number of data flows. A process operates on or transforms data and is represented in a data flow diagram typically as a circle or round-cornered rectangle. The data flow shows the flow of data through a system of processes. The data flow diagram is a network representation of data flows and processes.

System Design Phase

The output of the system design phase that will be measured is the basic architecture (see Table K.2). We would like to compute the architectural complexity. The product metrics we will collect data on are the number of classes and the number of subsystems.

Table K.2. Product-Related Metrics for the System Design Phase of the OODP.

Outputs	Desired Measures	Product Metrics
Basic architecture	Architectural complexity	number of classes
		numer of subsystems

Table K.3. Product-Related Metrics for the Object Design Phase of the OODP.

Outputs	Measures	Metrics
Object model, dynamic model, functional model	Structural complexity	number of classes
		number of collaborations per class
		number of operations

Object Design Phase

The outputs of the object design phase are the detailed object model, dynamic, and functional models (see Table K.3). We would like to compute the structural complexity. The product metrics we will collect data on are the number of classes, the number of collaborations per class, and the number of operations. A collaboration represents a request from one object to another to provide a specific service. The number of collaborations per class is the number of publicly available services provided by an object class. "The pattern of collaborations within your application reveals the flow of control and information during its execution," according to Wirfs-Brock et al. (1990).

Testing Phase

The output of the testing phase is the number of scenarios (see Table K.4). We would like to compute the test complexity of the scenarios that are used to test the program/system. The product metrics we will collect data on are the number of normal scenarios and the number of scenarios with exceptions.

Table K.4. Product-Related Metrics for the Testing Phase of the OODP.

Outputs	Measures	Metrics
number of scenarios	test complexity	number of normal scenarios
		number of scenarios with exceptions

K.2 PROCESS-RELATED METRICS

In order to continuously improve our skills in object-oriented software development, or any type of development for that matter, you must define your work process, measure how you are doing, and then examine your processes to determine how they can be improved. The answers to how much time your team spends in each software development phase can lead you to a better software development process. According to DeMarco (1982), "you can't control what you can't measure." Therefore, it is important to start measuring and collecting data as soon as possible after your process has been defined.

Our process has already been defined in Chapter 1. We will measure various attributes of the object-oriented development process for the electronic filing application so that we can improve our process in the future and have a basis for future planning of software development projects. The process-related metrics that we will collect are shown in Table K.5. Some scheduling estimates for traditional development indicate that analysis and design together should take twice as long as coding. These same estimates also indicate that testing should take twice as long as coding (Sommerville, 1985). After completing our application, we'll see how these scheduling estimates relate to object-oriented development.

Table K.5. Process-Related Metrics for the Phases of the OODP.

Phase/Metric	Analysis	System design	Object design	Coding	Testing
Time	Analysis phase	Subsystem design	Object design phase	Coding phase	Testing normal scenarios
Time	Normal scenario development		Detailed object model development		Testing abnormal scenarios
Time	Abnormal scenario development		Detailed dynamic model development		
Time	Object model development		Detailed functional model development		
Time	Dynamic model development				
Time	Functional model development				

For each phase of the OODP, we will record the total time spent in that phase. For the analysis phase, we will also record the time spent for scenario development, object model development, dynamic model development, and functional model development. The time spent designing each subsystem will be recorded for the system design phase.

For the object design phase the time spent developing detailed object, dynamic, and functional models will be recorded. The time spent in the coding phase will also be noted.

The process-related metrics data will show us where we spend the most time in the OODP. After we have collected this information, we can analyze our process to determine how we can reduce the amount of time spent in a specific part of the OODP. Sometimes the application of automated tools and/or a change in the way we do our work are called for in order to improve our process.

K.3 RESULTS OF PROCESS METRICS COLLECTION

Process metrics were collected for the analysis, system design, object design, code, and test phases of the application development. The process measurements are strictly measurements of time for various aspects of these phases of development. I have recorded as accurately as possible the amount of time I spent on the many different activities that are within each of these phases. However, process measurements are very difficult to collect due to the iterative nature of software development (i.e., many overlapping activities occurring very close in time, such as doing some additional design to correct a problem discovered during testing and then adding some code and continuing the test), so there is some inaccuracy in the data collection process. But I think that the process measurements collected can still give us a feel for the amount of time spent in each phase and for the proportion of time spent in one phase relative to the total effort. Although these numbers might vary from one project to another, the data might be used as guidelines for future projects, while considering the circumstances of each project, by placing bounds on various aspects of the software development process.

The units of time shown in Table K.6 are hours. The Total Time row shows the total number of hours spent in each phase of the project and the percentage of time spent in each phase of the project relative to the total effort. The number of hours spent in the total development effort is

Table K.6. Number of Hours Spent in Each Phase of the Development of Electronic Filing Application.

	Analysis	System design	Object design	Code	Test
Object model	17		11		
Dynamic model	57		51		
Functional model	41		36		
Total Time	115 (25%)	14 (3%)	98 (21%)	160 (35%)	75 (16%)

462. One important point to note is that the coding effort includes the implementation of the electronic filing application in two computer languages: Smalltalk/V and C++. Also, the implementation in C++ is not 100% complete. A person with more experience in either or both of these languages could have reduced the coding time somewhat. I was a relative novice in both of these languages at the start of this project.

The data for traditional development versus object-oriented development for our electronic filing application is shown in Table K.7. We have added together the times for analysis, system design, and object design from Table K.6 to arrive at the 49% figure for electronic filing O-O development in Table K.7.

The O-O analysis and design effort took somewhat longer than the estimates for traditional development. Booch (1991) notes that more work is accomplished during this phase of development using object technology than using traditional techniques.

The O-O coding effort is slightly less than twice the guideline for traditional development. However, our O-O coding effort involved implementations in two languages: C++ and Smalltalk. The program was first implemented in Smalltalk and then later in C++. I believe that the second coding effort should have taken substantially less time than the first coding effort if the C++ environment had had a class library as comprehensive as the one for Smalltalk. Doing something the second time around is always faster and easier than the first time you do it. However, I believe that a good Smalltalk programmer is more productive than a good C++ programmer.

The O-O testing effort took significantly less time than in traditional development. Testing is not one monolithic activity in object-oriented development. Testing is more of a cumulative activity; (i.e., test each of the methods in a class, test the methods that call other methods in the same class, test the methods that call other methods in another class, test scenarios, etc.) (McGregor and Sykes, 1992). Because testing is a cumulative activity, it is difficult to measure. At times I may have forgotten to record the test activities.

I had to write an appreciable amount of test code for this application. The testing of the domain classes occurred in a bottom-up fashion starting with classes that depended upon classes in the class library. The testing of the application classes (i.e., user interface classes) occurred in a top-down fashion. Some of the times for developing the test code may also not have been recorded.

One lesson learned on process metrics collection is that at the beginning of a project, the project manager should develop a set of codes that will very specifically identify various development activities that the project wishes to track. The amount of time spent on the activities

Table K.7. Traditional Development Versus Electronic Filing Object-Oriented Development.

	Analysis and design	Coding	Testing
Traditional development	40%	20%	40%
Electronic filing object-oriented development	49%	35%	16%

identified by each of these codes should be recorded in a computer on a daily basis by each developer. Otherwise the accuracy of the data collection might be lost. A lot of discipline is required to do this for several months on a regular basis—and it can be a source of great annoyance to software developers. However, if we are to improve our work processes in software development, these measurements are critical. If we don't know where we are spending our time, how can we improve our efficiencies in the most time-consuming phases of our development effort?

K.4 RESULTS OF PRODUCT METRICS COLLECTION

Product metrics are determined by measuring various aspects of the object-oriented development process (see Chapter 1). The metrics data for the object model in the analysis phase of development are shown in Table K.8. The metrics data here do not include any measurements from the user interface classes. If we were to include user interface information, the number of classes would increase by 10, the number of methods by at least 50, and the number of associations by 10.

The metrics data for the dynamic model in the analysis phase of development are shown in Table K.9. The number of scenarios in this table includes both normal scenarios and scenarios with exceptions. The number of states and transitions is measured in the scenario with

Table K.8. Metrics Data for Object Model in Analysis Phase.

Outputs	Desired measures	Product metrics	Data
Object model	Model complexity	number of classes	24
		number of methods	14
		number of associations	18

Table K.9. Metrics Data for Dynamic Model in Analysis Phase.

Outputs	Desired measures	Product metrics	Data
Dynamic model	Model complexity	number of scenarios	15
	Transition complexity	number of states	31
		number of transitions	75

exceptions only, since these scenarios are inclusive of the states and transitions in a normal scenario. Additional scenarios are possible, of course. These numbers reflect the minimum number of scenarios to exercise the basic functionality of the application. Note that we were not able to find any existing object-oriented analysis documents, design documents, or implementations and class libraries in the electronic filing domain, so no reuse of electronic filing artifacts is indicated in our data.

The metrics data for the functional model in the analysis phase of development are shown in Table K.10. Note that the data flows that were counted in a parent diagram were not counted again in the child diagram owing to the required balancing. However, all primitive and nonprimitive processes were counted in the total number of processes. The closeness of these two numbers indicates that there may not be many levels in the data flow diagrams.

The metrics data collected for the system design phase of development are shown in Table K.11. These data represent the number of classes and the number of subsystems reflected in the final design. At the actual completion of the system design phase, 32 classes and seven subsystems were part of the system.

The metrics data collected for the object design phase of development are shown in Table K.12. The number of classes is the total number of classes, including user interface, for the entire application. Remember that a collaboration is a request from a client class to a supplier class to help

Table K.10. Metrics Data for Functional Model in Analysis Phase.

Outputs	Desired measures	Product metrics	Data
Functional model	Model complexity	number of processes	29
		number of primitive processes	22
		number of data flows	32

Table K.11. Metrics Data for System Design Phase.

Outputs	Desired measures	Product metrics	Data
Basic architecture	Architectural complexity	number of classes	32
		number of subsystems	7

Table K.12. Metrics Data for Object Design Phase.

Outputs	Desired measures	Product metrics	Data
All models	Structural complexity	number of classes	32
		number of collaborations per class	1
		number of methods	55

it carry out its responsibility. The number of collaborations internal to a class are not reflected in these statistics. Only a request or message sent from one class to another class is counted as a collaboration.

The metrics data collected for the testing phase of development are shown in Table K.13. Eight normal scenarios and seven scenarios with exceptions were developed to exercise the functionality of the system.

Table K.13. Metrics Data for Testing Phase.

Outputs	Desired measures	Product metrics	Data
number of scenarios	Test complexity	number of normal scenarios	8
		number of scenarios with exceptions	7

User Interface

L.1 DETAILED USER INTERFACE OBJECT MODEL

The object model of the GUI for electronic filing will be developed by (1) examining the code generated from the Window Builder and ProtoGen user interface design tools and picking out classes and their associations, operations, etc., and (2) examining the Digitalk Smalltalk/V and Borland ObjectWindows class libraries as needed to gain a better understanding of the code and to fill out the GUI implementation. The design of the user interface is heavily dependent upon the user interface objects of these class libraries. All of the objects of the user interface are defined as instances of existing classes whose methods may be inherited. Without such class libraries of reusable and extensible graphical objects, user interface programming would be much more difficult and time consuming.

L.2 OBJECT MODEL USING BORLAND'S OBJECTWINDOWS

The ObjectWindows class hierarchy is shown in Figure L.1 (Borland, 1991). The vertical arrow is used to show inheritance in the ObjectWindows hierarchy. This follows the notation used in the Borland manuals to show inheritance. The base class for all of the ObjectWindows derived classes is *Object*. *TModule* defines the behavior shared by both library and application modules. The member functions of *TModule* support window memory management and error processing. All applications that are written using ObjectWindows must define their own application class from *TApplication*. The methods of *TApplication* perform initialization, message processing, and creation of a main window.

All of the remaining classes of the ObjectWindows hierarchy are user interface, or interface objects; i.e., they represent windows, dialog boxes, and controls. These remaining classes represent objects that interface between your application code and the Windows environment. Windows, dialog boxes, and controls are the three main types of ObjectWindows interface objects. *TWindows-Object* is the base class for these types of interface objects. *TWindowsObject* has methods for creating and destroying window objects, and message processing.

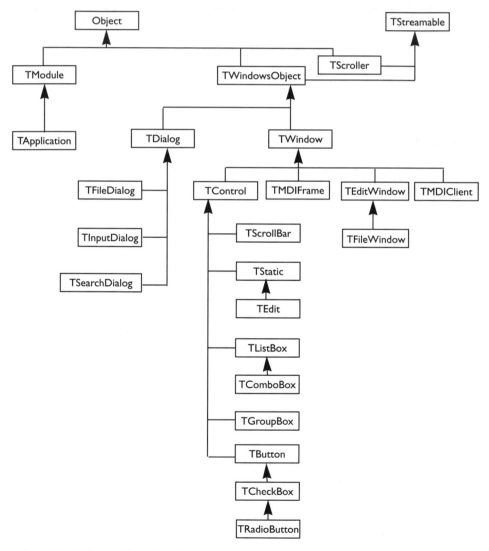

Figure L.1. ObjectWindows Class Hierarchy.

TDialog is the base class for Windows dialog boxes. This class has methods to handle communications between a dialog and its controls. *TWindow* is a general purpose Window class. Control objects allow users to enter data and select options. *TControl* is a base class for many different types of control object. *TEdit* and *TListBox* are derived from *TControl* and are part of the code for many of the dialog boxes that were developed using Resource Workshop and that had code generated using ProtoGen.

The user interface class diagram, shown in Figure L.2, is developed using the code generated by ProtoGen. Note that *TApplication, TWindow,* and *TDialog* are the object classes from the ObjectWindows class library that our program must use. The *TEF* object class represents our electronic filing application and inherits the behavior of *TApplication*. *TMainWindow* is the main application menu for electronic filing and inherits the behavior of *TWindow*. TDialog_*n*D1g, where *n* is 1, 2, 3, 5, 7, or 8, represents our dialog boxes. The dialog boxes inherit the behavior of *TDialog*.

Notice that each dialog box is composed of *TEdit* and *TListBox* controls. This represents an aggregation relationship between the dialog box and the *TEdit* and *TListBox* object classes. Some of the dialog boxes have multiple instances of *TEdit* or *TListBox* controls. The *TEdit* control is an interface object that represents an edit control interface element in Windows. This object is used

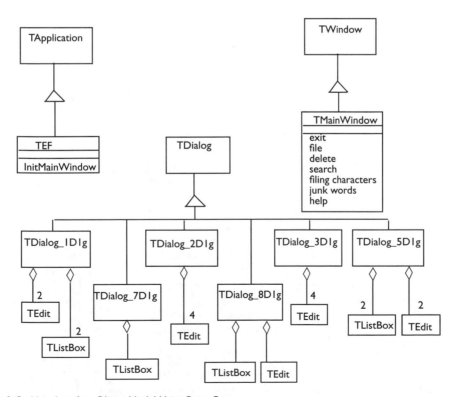

Figure L.2. User Interface Object Model Using ProtoGen.

to retrieve text input from a user. The *TListBox* interface object represents a list box element in Windows. A list box element enables a user of a Windows program to pick something from a list.

We can determine which TDialog*n*D1g dialog box represents which electronic filing function by examining each numbered dialog box in the .RC file in Resource Workshop. The number of the dialog box in the .RC file corresponds to *n* in TDialog*n*D1g.

Several components of the application user interface have not yet been linked into the rest of the menu. These components are the search results dialog box, print dialog box, view a document dialog box, and the message boxes. The print and view functions are tied to the search results dialog box. The search results dialog box has not been linked to the search dialog box because it is displayed only if search results are found by the program. However, we will link the search results dialog box to the search dialog box and insert the conditional code later. The print and view dialog boxes are now linked to the search results dialog box. Figure L.3 shows the new user interface class diagram combined with the ObjectWindows class library. *TEF* is the elec-

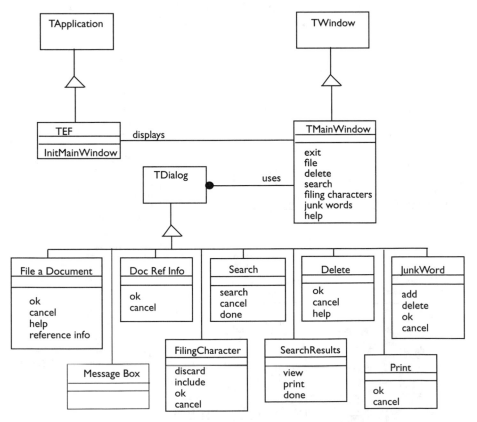

Figure L.3. User Interface Object Model Combined with ObjectWindows Class Library.

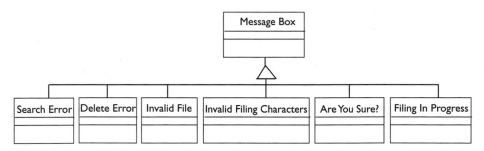

Figure L.4. User Interface Message Box Classes.

tronic filing application class, and *TMainWindow* represents the main application window and menu for electronic filing. The push-button functions for each dialog box are shown as operations associated with each dialog class. The various types of message boxes associated with the user interface are shown in Figure L.4. The edit and list boxes associated with each dialog box are shown in Figure L.5. The edit and list boxes for the search and search results user interface classes, or dialog boxes, are shown in Figure L.6.

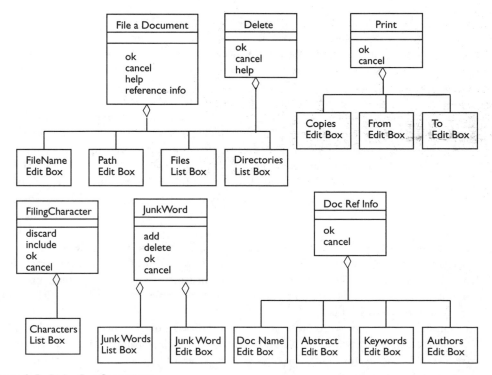

Figure L.5. Dialog Box Components.

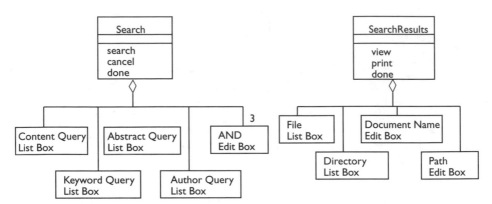

Figure L.6. Search and Search Results Dialog Box Components.

L.3 OBJECT MODEL USING DIGITALK'S SMALLTALK/V ENCYCLOPEDIA OF CLASSES

A partial Smalltalk/V class hierarchy is shown in Figure L.7 (Digitalk, 1992a). The class *Object* is the most general Smalltalk class and the parent of all other classes. The *ViewManager* class handles the user interface portion of an application and provides a buffer between our application and the underlying GUI processing. This means that you can treat windows as reusable objects that you plug into the electronic filing application without having to deal with things such as scroll bar action, window resizing and movement, mouse movements, clicks of the left and right mouse buttons, etc. The Window Builder tool subclasses *ViewManager* as the starting point for application construction. The *open* method for our application window, *Efiling* class, is the primary output of Window Builder, containing all of the code to create the window we designed.

The user interface class diagram using the Smalltalk class library and the Window Builder design tool is shown in Figure L.8. The class diagram for the dialog boxes that are part of the user interface is shown in Figure L.9. The various types of message boxes for the Smalltalk implementation are the same as shown in Figure L.4 for the C++ Application Frameworks implementation.

A dialog box is a type of window. In Smalltalk, windows are composed of one or more panes. The most prevalent types of Smalltalk pane are text, list, group, and push-button panes. Each electronic filing dialog box will contain multiple panes. In the Borland C++ Application Frameworks environment, these panes are referred to as control elements or objects. Control elements or panes facilitate the transfer of user input.

An example of the panes within the *FileADocument* dialog box is shown in Figure L.10. The *FileADocument* dialog box has four push-button panes, two list box panes, four static text panes, and two entry field panes. This example is typical of the types of pane contained within the other electronic filing dialog boxes.

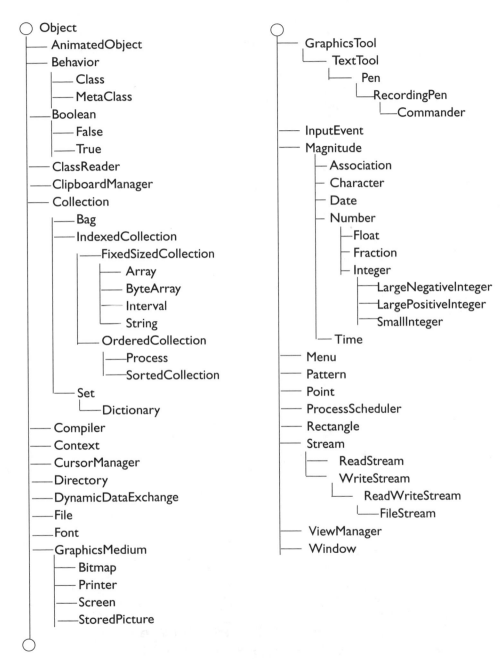

Figure L.7. Partial Smalltalk/V Version 2.0 Class Hierarchy.

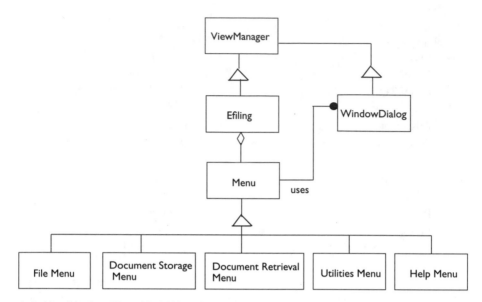

Figure L.8. User Interface Object Model Using Smalltalk/V and Window Builder.

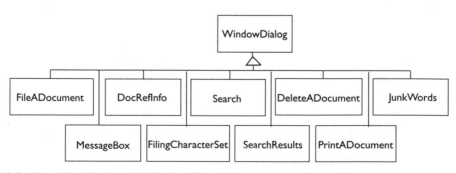

Figure L.9. Object Model for Smalltalk Window Dialog Boxes

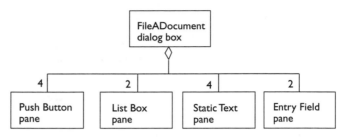

Figure L.10. FileADocument Dialog Box Components.

Smalltalk and C++ Implementation Models

M.1 SMALLTALK IMPLEMENTATION

The Smalltalk/V implementation for electronic filing will be discussed on a subsystem basis. Classes that are not part of a subsystem will be discussed individually following the subsystem discussions. Each class will be discussed in terms of the fundamental elements of a class description protocol. A class description protocol is described by properties, features, and methods that describe any instantiation of that class.

Note that all methods in Smalltalk are *public* by definition. However, our methods in the electronic filing program are commented as either *public* or *private*. The methods commented as *public* should be accessible to other objects. The methods commented as *private* should not be used by other objects. Callback methods are also noted in the method description. Any methods commented as being *private* remain *private* as long as the programmer respects the privacy.

We will attempt to reuse code to the maximum practical extent. As with the C++ implementation of the electronic filing program, the developer relies heavily on a class library to scavenge for reusable code. Code is reused (1) through inheritance by creating subclasses of existing classes and overriding some of its methods, (2) by composition, or (3) by copying and pasting methods from an existing class to your new class that is not part of the same hierarchy.

The following format will be used to discuss each class:

❑ *Definition*—identify the location of the class in the Smalltalk class hierarchy. Also identify the elements of the class such as private data (instance variables), shared data (class variables), pool dictionaries, and number of instance and class methods. Private and shared data names will be shown in **bold**, while instance and class method names will be shown in *italics*.

❑ *Private data*—a description of each instance variable type.

❑ *Shared data*—a description of each class variable type.

❑ *Pool dictionaries*—a description of each pool dictionary variable type.

❑ *Instance methods*—a description of each instance method and what it does.

❑ *Class methods*—a description of each instance method and what it does.

❑ *Inherited protocol*—a description of any protocol inherited by an application class.

❑ *Discussion on programming style*—if programming style improvements are suggested.

❑ *Design versus implementation differences* (the implementation model will be compared against the design object model shown).

Full code listings for each class within a subsystem for the current implementation are shown in Appendix I. Some class and instance methods have been deleted or renamed. The deleted methods were found not to be needed, and some methods were renamed to more accurately reflect what they actually do. The following discussions in are based on the code in Appendix I.

M.1.1 User Interface Subsystem

The structure and operation of the user interface for the electronic filing program centers around user-generated events; e.g., mouse clicks and keystrokes. This is true for both the Smalltalk and C++ implementations: whenever a push-button is selected or data characters are entered, an event is generated, and whenever an event is generated, a message is sent to the current window or dialog box object. The message is defined by the name of the method to invoke that is part of the behavior of the current window or dialog box. This method is generally referred to as an *event method, event handler, message-response member function*, or *callback* function. Many of the methods for the user interface classes are event handlers. Other methods may exist to support the event handlers.

At this point in our design we'll pause and implement the user interface methods to increase our understanding of the design of the application. The main purpose in doing this is to gain new insights into the design that will become evident due to our increased understanding of the implementation.

The following steps must be taken next to completely fill out the user interface code for the Smalltalk implementation:

1. Add comments to the user interface code generated by Window Builder as deemed appropriate.

2. Add code to each dialog box class so that all of the radio buttons and push-buttons are functional and so that dialog boxes are erased from the screen when they are supposed.

3. Include code to add items to the list boxes that are part of each dialog box. Code must also be added to get selections from a list box that have been chosen by the user.

4. Add code to retrieve and paste/insert text from and into an edit control box, respectively.

5. Declare and implement any additional objects from the Smalltalk class library necessary to complete the implementation of the user interface.

Steps 2 through 5 require flushing out the code for the event handlers, or callbacks, in Smalltalk. Code has already been added to the user interface to close each dialog box when either the OK or Done push-button has been selected by the user. The remaining user interface code needs to be completed now.

The user interface subsystem classes were generated with the use of WindowBuilder. All callback or event handler stubs are also generated by WindowBuilder. Additional programming was necessary to close dialog boxes, fill the contents of a list box, write code to deal with text edit boxes and push-buttons, and add code to the callbacks or event handlers to perform the necessary event processing. The **FileADocument** user interface class will be discussed here as an example of a user interface class implementation. The implementation model for the user interface classes is shown in Figures M.1 and M.2. Note that this model has been divided into two figures owing to the lack of space on a single diagram. Also note that the print and view dialog boxes are not shown as part of this model. The print dialog box and the view dialog box will be implemented using the **PrintDialog** and **WindowDialog** classes, respectively, in the Smalltalk/V class library.

FileADocument *Class Description*

Definition—The hierarchy for class **FileADocument** is **Object-ViewManager-WindowDialog**. It has no shared data (class variables). Objects of class **FileADocument** represent the File a Document dialog box. The **FileADocument** class has 1 class method and 12 instance methods.

Private data—Class **FileADocument** has four instance variables.

selectedDirectory—an instance of **Directory** representing the current directory selected by the user from the Directories scrolling list box.

selectedFile—an instance of **String** representing the current file selected by the user from the Files scrolling list box.

directoryList—an instance of **OrderedCollection** representing the list of current directories in the Directories scrolling list box.

pathNameArray—an instance of **OrderedCollection** representing the list of path names for each of the directory names shown in the Directories scrolling list box.

Pool dictionaries:

ColorConstants—Associates color names to system color palette indices.

WBConstants—Constants used by the WindowBuilder tool.

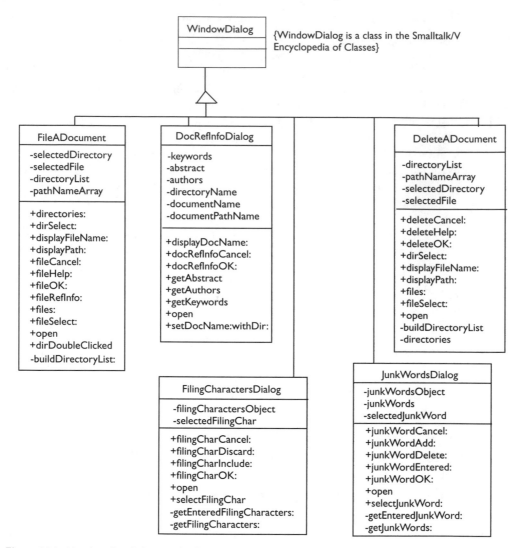

Figure M.1. User Interface Subsystem Implementation Model (Part A).

Instance methods:

buildDirectoryList—Private. Builds an **OrderedCollection** of directory name strings for all directories on the disk. Precedes names with spaces to indicate directory hierarchy.

directories: directoryListBox—Callback for the #getContents event in an unnamed **ListBox**. Fills the directoryListBox pane with the list of directories for the selected device.

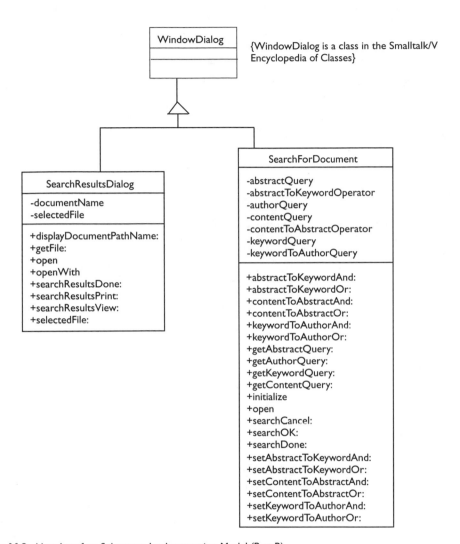

Figure M.2. User Interface Subsystem Implementation Model (Part B).

dirSelect: aPane—Callback for the #select event in directoryListBox. Gets the directory name selected by the user.

displayFileName: aPane—Callback for the #getContents event in the **EntryField** named 'file-NameEntryField.' Inserts the file name in the **EntryField**.

displayPath: aPane—Callback for the #getContents event in the **EntryField** named 'pathEntry-Field.' Inserts the path name in the **EntryField**.

fileCancel: aPane—Callback for the #clicked event in an unnamed **Button** (contents is 'Cancel'). Confirms if a user wants to cancel the operation.

fileHelp: aPane—Callback for the #clicked event in an unnamed **Button** (contents is 'Help'). Displays help information to the user.

fileOK: aPane—Callback for the #clicked event in an unnamed **Button** (contents is 'OK'). Add document name (selectedFile) to **Filing** dictionary. There is one directory for the electronic filing application, '**Filing**.' Documents filed in the system have their names in the **Filing** dictionary.

fileRefInfo: aPane—Callback for the #clicked event in an unnamed **Button** (contents is 'Reference Information'). Adds document name (selectedFile) to **Filing** dictionary.

files: aPane—Callback for the #getContents event in the **ListBox** named 'fileListBox.' Fills the **ListBox** with a sorted list of files for the selected directory.

fileSelect: aPane—Callback for the #select event in an unnamed **ListBox**.

open—Public. Creates the **FileADocument** dialog box. Entirely generated by Window-Builder.

dirDoubleClicked—Callback for the #doubleClickSelect event. A directory name was double clicked. Gets the directories' subdirectories, if any.

Class methods:

wbCreated—This is generated by WindowBuilder and used by the **ViewManager** class.

Programming Style

The user interface classes are almost entirely generated by WindowBuilder. Many of the methods are *callbacks*. The *open* method in the **FileADocument** class is rather large, but it is cohesive. It builds the File a Document dialog box. WindowBuilder uses inheritance to build the dialog box, subclassing the **WindowDialog** class.

This class uses a global variable, *Filing*, which retains the filing directory name and an **OrderedCollection** of files that have been indexed by the program. This allows the program to maintain a reference to all indexed documents. The use of global variables should be minimized in the implementation of any program.

The **FileADocument** class doesn't check against all user errors, such as ensuring that the user has selected a file/document that this program recognizes and is able to file. This code should be added to protect the program from trying to process invalid data and generating erroneous results.

Future implementations should drop "get" from the front of the method names to improve readability (Lorenz, 1993). For example, the *getKeywords* method of the **DocRefInfoDialog** class should be changed to *keywords*.

M.1.2 Document Subsystem

The document subsystem classes are **TextDocument** and **DocRefInfo** (short for document reference information).

TextDocument *Class Description*

Definition—The hierarchy for class **TextDocument** is **Object**. It has neither shared data nor pool dictionaries. Objects of class **TextDocument** represent a text document that is filed in the system. The **TextDocument** class has no class methods and 2 instance methods.

Private data:

> *name*—The name variable represents the name of the document. This variable is not used.

> *directory*—The directory variable represents the name of the document. This variable is not used.

Instance methods:

> *fileDoc: documentName with: directoryName*—Public. Files a document with no document reference information.

> *fileDoc: documentName with: directoryName with: theDriObject*—Public. Files a document with document reference information.

> *Protocol inherited from* **Object** *and used*—class **Object** is the immediate superclass of **Text-Document**. **TextDocument** inherits all of the protocol from class **Object,** as do all of the classes in the Smalltalk hierarchy. However, none of the inherited methods has any meaning for objects of **TextDocument**.

Programming Style

Neither instance variable is used. They can be deleted by changing the *fileDoc:with:* and *fileDoc:with: with:* methods to use their arguments rather than using the instance variables. The instance methods are small, cohesive, and use no global information. However, no argument validation is performed for these *public* methods. Argument validation code should be added to the methods of **Text-Document** prior to releasing this class for general use.

Design Versus Implementation Differences

The design showed an association between the **TextDocument** and the **DocRefInfo** classes. No such association is necessary.

Some of the names of the attributes changed during the implementation: *directory name* to *directory, document name* to *name*, and both *creation date* and *record number* were discarded as unnecessary attributes of this class.

Some of the methods of this class changed during the implementation. *fileDocument* changed to *fileDoc:with:* and *fileDoc:with:with:*. Two methods were necessary for filing a document: one for filing just a text document itself and the other for filing the text document with document reference information. The *get document record*, *viewDocument*, *printDocument*, *create text doc index*, and *validateFile* methods were not necessary as part of the **TextDocument** class.

Index *Class Description*

Definition—The hierarchy for class **Index** is **Object**. Objects of class **Index** represent entities that index a document specified by a user. The **Index** class has three instance methods. It has neither shared data nor pool dictionaries.

Private data—Class **Index** has three instance variables.

indexFileName—an instance of **String** representing the name of the index file.

name—an instance of **String** representing the name of the text document file.

directory—an instance of **String** representing the directory name of the text document file.

Instance methods:

buildIndexFileHeader: indexFileWriteStream with: documentName with: directoryName—Private. Builds the index file header and outputs it to the index file.

createDocIndex: documentName withDir: directoryName—Public. Creates the actual text document index and its file.

createIndex: indexFileStream with: docFileStream with: documentName with: directoryName—Private. Creates an index of the contents of the text document.

Protocol inherited from **Object** *and used*—None.

DocRefInfo *Class Description*

Definition—The hierarchy for class **DocRefInfo** is **Object**. Objects of class **DocRefInfo** represent document reference information associated with a specific **TextDocument** object. Class **DocRefInfo** has neither shared data nor pool dictionaries. The **DocRefInfo** class has one class method and seven instance methods.

Private data—Class **DocRefInfo** has six instance variables.

abstract—an instance of **String** representing the abstract information entered by a user about a document.

authors—an instance of **String** representing the author information entered by a user about a document.

keywords—an instance of **String** representing the keyword information entered by a user about a document.

textDocument—an instance of **TextDocument** representing the document filed in the system.

documentName—an instance of **String** representing the name of the text document filed by the user.

pathAndDocumentName—an instance of **String** representing the path and document name of the text document filed by the user.

Instance methods:

getAbstract—Public. Answers with the abstract **String** for this text document.

getAuthors—Public. Answers with the authors **String** for this text document.

getKeywords—Public. Answers with the keywords **String** for this text document.

getDocumentName—Public. Answers with the documentName **String** for this text document.

setDRI: allAuthors with: theAbstract with: allKeywords with: textDocumentName with:

docAndPathName—Sets the authors, abstract, keywords, documentName, and documentAndPathName for this **DocRefInfo** object.

initialize: theTextDocument—Private. Sets up a reference to the **TextDocument** object associated with the **DocRefInfo** object.

getDocumentAndPathName—Public. Answers with the documentAndPathName **String** for this text document.

Class methods:

new: theTextDocument—Creates a new **DocRefInfo** object, passing along the **TextDocument** object associated with the **DocRefInfo** object.

Protocol inherited from **Object** *and used*—None.

Programming Style

No argument validation is performed for the *public* methods of this class. Argument validation code should be added to the public methods of **DocRefInfo** prior to releasing this class for general use.

Design Versus Implementation Differences

Several additional attributes were added to the class to facilitate the implementation: **textDocument**, **documentName**, and **pathAndDocumentName**.

The *checkForLogicalQueryMatch* and *checkForDRIMatches* methods were moved to the SearchEngine class. The *getAbstract, getAuthors, getKeywords, getDocumentName, setDRI:with:with:with:with:, initialize,*

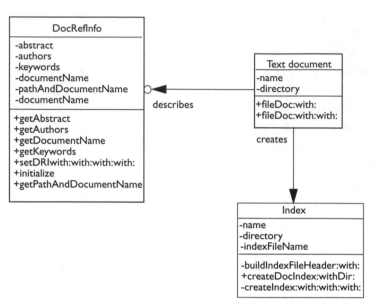

Figure M.3. Document Subsystem Implementation Model.

and *getDocumentAndPathName* are now instance methods for the **DocRefInfo** object.

An implementation model for the document subsystem is shown in Figure M.3.

M.1.3 Search Results Subsystem

The search results subsystem classes are **DocumentNameList** and **DocumentRecordsList**.

DocumentNameList *Class Description*

Definition—The hierarchy for class **DocumentNameList** is **Object**. Objects of class **Document-NameList** represent lists of document names associated with a specific search request. The **DocumentNameList** class has one class method and nine instance methods. It has neither shared data nor pool dictionaries.

Private data—Class **DocumentNameList** has two instance variables.

documentNameList—an instance of **OrderedCollection** representing the list of documents that satisfy the user-specified search criteria.

recordDictionary—an instance of **Dictionary** representing the list of record numbers where the search criteria was satisfied within a document.

Instance methods:

addToDNL: anObject—Public. Adds anObject to the documentNameList.

do: aBlock—Public. For each document name in the documentNameList, evaluates aBlock with a document name as the argument.

getRecordsList: indexFileName—Public. Answers with an **OrderedCollection** representing the list of record numbers for the indexFileName.

initialize—Private. Sets up the documentNameList and recordDictionary instance variables.

removeFromDNL—Public. Answers with a **String** representing a document name removed from the head of the documentNameList.

size—Public. Answers with an **Integer** that is the number of entries in the documentNameList.

includes: anObject—Public. Answers True if anObject is included in the DNL, else answers False.

putRecordsList: theRecordsListObject with: indexFileName—Public. Associates a **Document-RecordsList** object with the indexFileName.

retrieveDocumentNames—Public. Answers with the documentNameList.

Class methods:

new—Public. Create a new **DocumentNameList** object.

*Protocol inherited from **Object** and used*—None. The method size is polymorphically redefined in class **DocumentNameList**.

Programming Style

The methods for this class are small and cohesive. However, some of the names for arguments, such as *anObject*, could have been better chosen so that the methods stay consistent across the application.

Design Versus Implementation Differences

The name list attribute has been renamed to **documentNameList**, an instance variable. Another instance variable, **recordDictionary**, has been added to represent the document names and document record lists associated with those documents.

DocumentRecordsList *Class Description*

Definition—The hierarchy for class **DocumentRecordsList** is **Object**. Objects of class **Document-RecordsList** represent lists of document records associated with a specific document name that satisfied a search request. The **DocumentRecordsList** class has one class method and eight instance methods. It has neither shared data nor pool dictionaries.

Private data—Class **DocumentRecordsList** has one instance variable.

    documentRecordsList—an instance of **OrderedCollection** representing the list of document record numbers that specify the record numbers where the search criteria was satisfied within a specific document.

Instance methods:

    addToDRL: anObject—Public. Adds anObject to the documentRecordsList.

    do: aBlock—Public. For each document record number in the receiver, evaluates aBlock with that document record number as the argument.

    at: anInteger put: aRecordNumber—Public. Replaces the element of the receiver at index position anInteger with *aRecordNumber*.

    initialize—Private. Sets up the **DocumentRecordsList** instance variable—*documentRecordsList*.

    removeFromDRL—Public. Answers with a removed object from the head of the *documentRecordsList*.

    removeIndex: anInteger—Public. Removes a document record number at index position anInteger in the *documentRecordsList*.

    size—Public. Answers with an **Integer** that is the number of entries in the *documentRecordsList*.

    removeRecordNumber: recordNumber—Public. Removes the document record number at index position *anInteger*.

Class methods:

    new—Public. Answers with an instance of the **DocumentRecordsList** class.

    Protocol inherited from **Object** *and used*—None. (The methods *size* and *at:put:* are polymorphically redefined in class **DocumentNameList**.)

Programming Style

Same comments as noted for the **DocumentNameList** class. An implementation model for the search results subsystem is shown in Figure M.4.

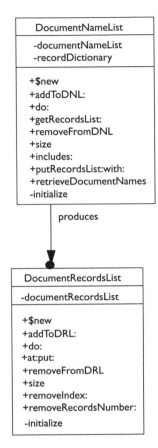

Figure M.4. Search Results Subsystem Implementation Model.

M.1.4 Query Subsystem

The query subsystem classes are **Query, AuthorQuery, AbstractQuery, KeywordQuery,** and **ContentQuery.**

Query *Class Description*

Definition—The hierarchy for class **Query** is **Object**. It has no pool dictionaries. **Class Query** has five instance methods and no class methods. **Query** is an abstract class. There are no instances of **Query**, only instances of subclasses of **Query**. The protocol in class **Query** is common to all of its subclasses.

Private data—Class **Query** has three instance variables.

queryElements—an instance of **Queue** representing words or phrases that are part of a query.

logicalOperators—an instance of **Queue** representing the logical operators that connect words or phrases in a query.

query—an instance of **String** representing a query entered by a user.

Shared data—Class **Query** has three class variables.

ContentToAbstractOperator—an instance of **String** representing a logical operator between a content query and an abstract query.

KeywordToAuthorOperator—an instance of **String** representing a logical operator between a keyword query and an author query.

AbstractToKeywordOperator—an instance of **String** representing a logical operator between an abstract query and a keyword query.

Instance methods:

checkForElementMatch: type OfQueryElements—Public. Answers **True** or **False** based on a match between a keyword/abstract/author query and document reference information for each and every filed document.

getLogicalOperators—Public. Answers with an **Array** of substrings of logical operators.

getQueryElements—Public. Answers with an **Array** of substrings of query elements.

parseQuery—Public. Parses a query into queryElements and logicalOperators.

query—Public. Answers with a **String**, which is the query.

Protocol inherited from **Object** *and used*—None.

AuthorQuery *Class Description*

Definition—The hierarchy for class **AuthorQuery** is **Object-Query**. Objects of class **Author-Query** represent the author query entered by a user for conducting a search operation. **AuthorQuery** has neither private nor shared data and has no pool dictionaries. The **Au-thorQuery** class has two instance methods.

Instance methods:

setAuthorQuery: authorQuery—Public. Sets the query equal to the *authorQuery* **String**.

setKeywordToAuthorOperator: operator—Public. Sets the **KeywordToAuthorOperator** equal to operator, which is a **String**.

Protocol inherited from **Query** *and used:*

> *Private data*—Class **Query** has three instance variables that are inherited: **queryElements, logicalOperators,** and **query.**

> *Shared data*—Class **Query** has three class variables that are inherited: **KeywordToAuthorOperator, ContentToAbstractOperator,** and **AbstractToKeywordOperator.**

> *Instance methods*—checkForElementMatch: type *OfQueryElements, getLogicalOperators, getQueryElements, parseQuery,* and *query.*

All of the protocol from class **Query** is useful in the **AuthorQuery** subclass.

Protocol inherited from **Object** *and used*—None. The higher in the class hierarchy the protocol lies, the less likely that all of the protocol will be useful at the lower levels. This is because the classes at the top of the class hierarchy have a very general protocol, while the classes at the bottom of the class hierarchy have a very specialized protocol.

Programming Style

No argument validation is performed for the *public* methods of this class. Argument validation code should be added to the public methods of **AuthorQuery** prior to releasing this class for general use.

AbstractQuery *Class Description*

Definition—The hierarchy for class **AbstractQuery** is **Object-Query.** Objects of class **AbstractQuery** represent a user-entered abstract query for a search operation. The **AbstractQuery** class has three instance methods. It has neither shared data nor pool dictionaries.

Instance methods:

> *setAbstractQuery: abstractQuery*—Public. Sets the query equal to the abstractQuery **String.**

> *setContentToAbstractOperator: operator*—Public. Sets the **ContentToAbstractOperator** equal to operator, which is a **String.**

> *getAbstractToKeywordOperator*—Public. Answers with the **AbstractToKeywordOperator String.**

Protocol inherited from **Query** *and used*—All of the protocol from class **Query** is useful in the **AbstractQuery** subclass.

Protocol inherited from **Object** *and used*—None.

Programming Style

No argument validation is performed for the *public* methods of this class. Argument validation code should be added to the public methods of **AbstractQuery** prior to releasing this class for general use.

KeywordQuery *Class Description*

Definition—The hierarchy for class **KeywordQuery** is **Object-Query**. Objects of class **KeywordQuery** represent a user-entered keyword query for a search operation. The **KeywordQuery** class has three instance methods. It has neither shared data nor pool dictionaries.

Instance methods:

> *setKeywordQuery: keywordQuery*—Public. Sets the query equal to the authorQuery **String**.

> *setAbstractToKeywordOperator: operator*—Public. Sets the **AbstractToKeywordOperator** equal to operator, which is a **String**.

> *getKeywordToAuthorOperator*—Public. Answers with the **AbstractToKeywordOperator**, which is a **String**.

> *Protocol inherited from* **Query** *and used*—All of the protocol from class **Query** is useful in the **KeywordQuery** subclass.

> *Protocol inherited from* **Object** *and used*—None.

Programming Style

No argument validation is performed for the *public* methods of this class. Argument validation code should be added to the public methods of **KeywordQuery** prior to releasing this class for general use.

ContentQuery *Class Description*

Definition—The hierarchy for class **ContentQuery** is **Object-Query**. Objects of class **ContentQuery** represent a user-entered content query for a search operation. The **ContentQuery** class has two instance methods. It has neither shared data nor pool dictionaries.

Instance methods:

> *setContentQuery: contentQuery*—Public. Sets the query equal to the contentQuery **String**.

> *getContentToAbstractOperator*—Answers with the **ContentToAbstractOperator**, which is a **String**.

> *Protocol inherited from* **Query** *and used*—All of the protocol from class **Query** is useful in the **ContentQuery** subclass.

> *Protocol inherited from* **Object** *and used*—None.

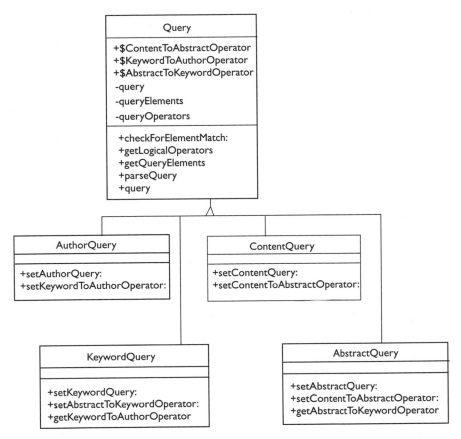

Figure M.5. Query Subsystem Implementation Model.

Programming Style

No argument validation is performed for the *public* methods of this class. Argument validation code should be added to the public methods of **ContentQuery** prior to releasing this class for general use. An implementation model of the query subsystem is shown in Figure M.5.

M.1.5 Hashing Subsystem

The hashing subsystem classes are **HashEngine**, JunkWords, and **FilingCharacters**. The **Hash-Engine** class uses the **JunkWords** and **FilingCharacters** classes in hashing a document.

HashEngine *Class Description*

Definition—The hierarchy for class **HashEngine** is **Object**. Objects of class **HashEngine** represent agents that do work on behalf of an **Index** object. The **HashEngine** class has 13 instance methods and one class method. It has no pool dictionaries.

Private data—Class **HashEngine** has 7 instance variables.

hashBlock—a **String** of size **YHashBlock * XHashBlock** representing **YHashBlock** number of 80 character records that have been hashed.

translateChar—an **Integer** used to represent an ASCII character that is hashed.

offset—an Integer offset into a **RandomNumberTable**.

hashBlockIndex—an **Integer** index into the **hashBlock**.

seed—an **Integer** that is used to generate a random number.

recordsIndexed—an **Integer** representing the number of records indexed within the current **hashBlock**.

junkWords—an instance of the **JunkWords** class.

filingCharacters—an instance of the **FilingCharacters** class.

Shared data—Class **HashEngine** has three class variables.

RandomNumberTable—an **OrderedCollection** of numbers.

TranslateTable—an **OrderedCollection** of numbers representing hashed ASCII characters.

Instance methods:

buildHashBlock: indexFileStream with: docFileStream—Public. Builds every *hashBlock* for the text document.

hashDocumentRecord: documentRecord—Private. Hashes an 80-character record and puts it in the *hashBlock*.

hashFirstChar: aChar—Private. Hashes the first character of a word represented by a **String** and puts it in the *hashBlock*.

hashFirstChar: aChar using: theHashBlock—Public. Hashes the first character of a word represented by a **String** and puts it in *theHashBlock*.

hashOtherChar: aChar—Private. Hashes the third or subsequent character of a word represented by a **String** and puts it in the *hashBlock*.

hashOtherChar: aChar using: theHashBlock—Public. Hashes the third or subsequent character of a word represented by a **String** and puts it in *theHashBlock*.

hashSecondChar: aChar—Private. Hashes the second character of a word represented by a **String** and puts it in the hashBlock.

hashSecondChar: aChar using: theHashBlock—Public. Hashes the second character of a word represented by a **String** and puts it in *theHashBlock*.

hashTheWord: word—Private. Hashes a word represented by a **String** and puts it in the *hashBlock*.

hashTheWord: word using: theHashBlock—Public. Hashes a word represented by a **String** and puts it in *theHashBlock*.

initialize—Private. Sets up the **TranslateTable** and **RandomNumberTable**.

randomNumber—Private. Generates a random number based on a **seed**.

setUpTranslateTable—Sets up the **TranslateTable**.

Class methods:

new—Public. Answers with an instance of the **HashEngine** class.

Protocol inherited from **Object** *and used*—None.

Programming Style

This class is not entirely cohesive—it performs more than one function. The random number generation should be broken out as a separate class with the appropriate methods. Also, the part of the *buildHashBlock* that creates an empty hash block and initializes it to all zeros could be broken out into a separate method.

JunkWords *Class Description*

Definition—The hierarchy for class **JunkWords** is **Object**. Objects of class **JunkWords** represent the set of junk words associated with a document that are skipped over during the filing of the document. The **JunkWords** class has seven instance methods. It has no pool dictionaries.

Private data—Class **JunkWords** has one instance variables.

junkWordFileStream—an instance of **FileStream** representing the file of the junk words.

Shared data—Class **JunkWords** has one class variable.

CurrentWords—a **SortedCollection** of words from the junk words file.

Instance methods:

addJunkWord: word—Public. Adds a word in the form of a **String** to the **CurrentWords**.

deleteJunkWord: word—Public. Deletes a word in the form of a **String** from the **CurrentWords**.

getJunkWords—Public. Answers with the **CurrentWords**.

initialize—Private. Reads the entire junk words file from disk and establishes a **SortedCollection** of junk words.

replaceJunkWordFile—Private. Deletes the old junk word file and creates a new empty junk word file.

saveJunkWords—Public. Replace the current junk word file and then save the **CurrentWords** in the junk word file via the **junkWordFileStream**.

checkIfJunkWord: aWord—Public. Answer True if aWord is a junk word, else answer False.

Class methods:

new—Public. Answer an instance of the **JunkWords** class.

Protocol inherited from **Object** *and used*—None.

Programming Style

The methods of this class are small and cohesive. However, no argument validation is performed for the *public* methods. Argument validation code should be added to the methods of **JunkWords** prior to releasing this class for general use.

FilingCharacters *Class Description*

Definition—The hierarchy for class **FilingCharacters** is **Object**. Objects of class **FilingCharacters** represent the set of filing characters associated with a document that are processed during the filing of the document. The **FilingCharacters** class has eight instance methods. It has no pool dictionaries.

Private data—Class **FilingCharacters** has one instance variable.

filingCharactersFileStream—an instance of **FileStream** representing the file of filing characters.

Shared data—Class **FilingCharacters** has one class variable.

IncludedCharacters—a **SortedCollection** of characters from the filing characters file.

Instance methods:

addFilingChar: aChar—Public. Adds the specified character to the *IncludedCharacters*.

deleteFilingChar: aChar—Public. Removes the specified character from the *IncludedCharacters*.

getFilingChars—Public. Answers with the **IncludedCharacters**.

initialize—Private. Reads the entire filing characters file from disk and establishes a **Sorted-Collection** of filing characters.

replaceFilingCharactersFile—Private. Deletes the old filing characters file and creates a new empty filing characters file.

saveFilingCharacters—Public. Replaces the filing characters file and then saves the **Included-Characters** in the filing characters file via the *filingCharactersFileStream*.

checkIfFilingCharacter: aChar—Public. Answers **True** if *aChar* is a filing character, else answer **False**.

getFirstFilingCharacter: aWord—Public. Answers with the position of the first filing character in the word. Answer 0 if not found.

Class methods:

new—Public. Answers with an instance of the **FilingCharacters** class.

Protocol inherited from **Object** *and used*—None.

Programming Style

The methods of this class are small and cohesive. However, no argument validation is performed for the *public* methods. Argument validation code should be added to the methods of **Filing-Characters** prior to releasing this class for general use. An implementation model for the hashing subsystem is shown in Figure M.6.

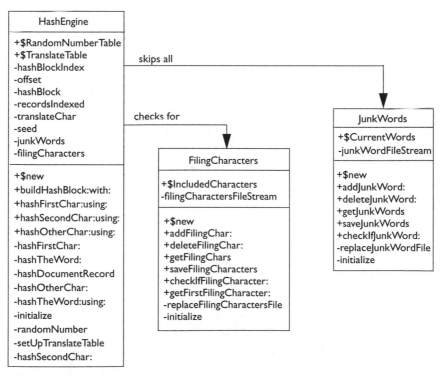

Figure M.6. Hashing Subsystem Implementation Model.

M.1.6 Search Subsystem

The search subsystem classes are **SearchEngine** and **SearchVector**.

SearchEngine *Class Description*

Definition—The hierarchy for class **SearchEngine** is **Object**. Objects of class **SearchEngine** represent entities that act as a user's agent, looking for documents that satisfy specified search criteria. The **SearchEngine** class has 8 instance methods. It has neither shared data nor pool dictionaries.

Private data—Class **SearchEngine** has three instance variables.

aAuthorQueryObject—an instance of the **AuthorQuery** object representing the user entered author query.

aKeywordQueryObject—an instance of the **KeywordQuery** object representing the user entered keyword query.

aAbstractQueryObject—an instance of the **AbstractQuery** object representing the user entered abstract query.

Instance methods:

calculateDocRecNumbers: indexFileStream with: searchVectorStream—Private. Calculates the document record numbers where hits are possible and answers with a **DocumentRecordsList** object.

checkForDocumentMatches: theSearchVector—Private. Determines the documents that satisfy the search criteria and answers with a **DocumentNameList** object.

checkForDRIMatches—Private. Determines what document reference information satisfies the search criteria and answers with a **DocumentNameList** object.

checkForLogicalQueryMatch: authorMatchIndicator with: keywordMatchIndicator with:

abstractMatchIndicator—Private. Performs logical operations between queries using query logical operators. Answers with a **True** or **False** object.

findDocument: contentQueryObject—Searches for documents based only on a content search. Activates the Search Results dialog box if the search query is satisfied.

findDocument: authorQueryObject with: keywordQueryObject with: abstractQueryObject—Searches for documents based only on a document reference information search. Activates the Search Results dialog box if the search query is satisfied.

findDocument: authorQueryObject with: keywordQueryObject with: contentQueryObject with:

abstractQueryObject—Searches for documents based on both a content search and a document reference information search. Activates the Search Results dialog box if the search query is satisfied.

verifyMatches: docRecordNumberList with: indexFileStream using: contentQuery—Private. Uses the *docRecordNumberList* and *contentQuery* to verify that a content query actually exists in a document. Answers with the document and path name.

Protocol inherited from **Object** *and used*—None.

Programming Style

The *findDocument*, *checkForLogicalQueryMatch*, and *verifyMatches* methods are reasonable in size and cohesive in function. However, *calculateDocRecNumbers* is a large method and could be broken into several methods. No argument validation is performed for the *public* methods of this class. Argument validation code should be added to the *public* methods of **SearchEngine** prior to releasing this class for general use.

SearchVector *Class Description*

Definition—The hierarchy for class **SearchVector** is **Object**. Objects of class **SearchVector** represent a search vector, which is a **String** of characters that indicates which parts of an index file point to the search criteria within a document. The **SearchVector** class has two instance methods. It has neither private nor shared data and it has no pool dictionaries.

Instance methods:

buildSearchVector: contentQueryObject—Public. Answers with a search vector, which is a **String**.

constructVector: queryVectorString with: elementVectorString using: operator—Private. Performs the required logical operation between query and element vectors. The result is placed in the *queryVector*.

Protocol inherited from **Object** *and used*—None.

Programming Style

One of our goals is to keep methods consistent; e.g., similar methods should use the same names, conditions, arguments, etc. The name *constructVector* is not meaningful for the function that this method is performing. This method performs two different logical operations, AND and OR, on vectors; the *constructVector* method can be broken into two methods, *orVectors* and *andVectors*, which will then both be invoked from *buildSearchVector*. This helps to separate policy from implementation. Both *orVectors* and *andVectors* are implementation methods, and *buildSearchVector* is a policy method.

M.1.7 Miscellaneous Classes

The miscellaneous class that is not part of another subsystem is **FilingDirectory.**

FilingDirectory *Class Description*

Definition—The hierarchy for class **FilingDirectory** is **Object**. Objects of class **FilingDirectory** represent a directory and the index files used by the application in storing and retrieving document indexes. The **FilingDirectory** class has four instance methods and one class method. It has neither shared data nor pool dictionaries.

Private data—Class **FilingDirectory** has two instance variables.

    directoryName—an instance of **String** representing the name of the filing directory.

    files—an instance of **OrderedCollection** used to contain the names of the index files.

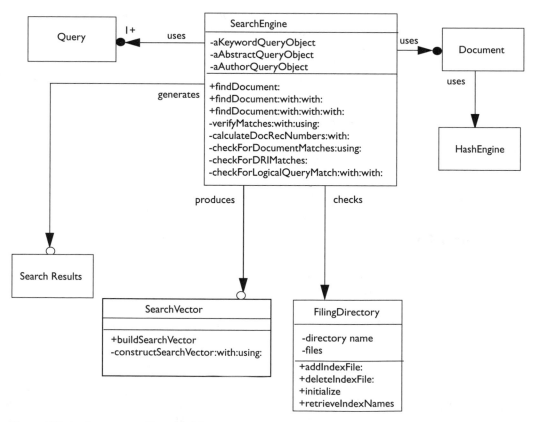

Figure M.7. Implementation Object Model.

Instance methods:

    addIndexFile: fileName—Public. Adds a file name in the form of a **String** to *files*.

    deleteIndexFile: indexName—Public. Deletes the specified index file from disk and removes the *indexName* from *files*.

    initialize—Private. Sets up **directoryName** and **files**.

    retrieveIndexNames—Public. Answers with **files**.

Class methods:

    new—Public. Creates a new **FilingDirectory** object.

Protocol inherited from **Object** *and used*—None.

An implementation model (a class diagram) showing the filing directory class, search subsystem, and other subsystems in the model is shown in Figure M.3. The implementation model has many more elements, operations, and attributes than the preceding object model (design model) from Chapter 8. Note that the implementation model has involved changing the contents of the object model to observe the syntax and restrictions of the programming language.

M.2 C++ IMPLEMENTATION

Some of the terms used throughout the text, such as methods and messages, are seldom used in some language texts such as C++. A method is described in C++ books as a *member function*, and sending a message to an object is referred to as *invoking a member function*. Variables are referred to as *data members* in C++. The data members, member functions, and the levels of information hiding are specified within the C++ class body. This terminology will be used throughout the discussion of the C++ implementation.

    Note that, unlike Smalltalk, there are multiple levels of information hiding for the data members and member functions of each class—*public, protected,* and *private.* Only the member functions that provide the external interface to the class are declared as *public.* The data members and the member functions used internally by the class are typically declared as *private.* Any member functions or data members declared as protected are accessible only to derived classes and to the base class in which they are declared.

    As with the Smalltalk implementation, we will attempt to reuse code to the maximum practical extent. We will rely heavily upon the Borland C++ class libraries to scavenge for reusable code. These class libraries are for the streamable classes, Windows classes, and the container classes. Additionally, we will make use of the Windows functions and the run-time library that are provided with our C++ environment.

    Each class will be discussed in terms of the data members and member functions provided at each level of information hiding. The following format will be used to discuss each class:

❑ *Definition*—identify the location of the class in the C++ class hierarchy. Also identify the elements of the class such as data members and member functions. Data member names will be shown in **bold**, while member function names will be shown in *italics*.

❑ *Public*—a description of each data member and member function defined at this level of information hiding.

❑ *Protected*—a description of each data member and member function defined at this level of information hiding.

❑ *Private*—a description of each data member and member function defined at this level of information hiding.

❑ *Data members*—the data members specified at a specific level of information hiding.

❑ *Member functions*—the member functions specified at a specific level of information hiding.

❑ *Inherited protocol*—a description of any protocol inherited by an application class

❑ *Discussion on programming style*—if programming style improvements are suggested.

❑ *Design versus implementation differences* (the implementation model will be compared against the design object model).

Full code listings for each class within a subsystem for the current implementation are shown in Appendix J. Some member functions have been deleted or renamed. The deleted member functions were found not to be needed, and some member functions were renamed to more accurately reflect what they actually do.

The following discussions are based on the code in Appendix J. Each level of information hiding for a class is discussed only if there are data members or member functions defined for that level of access. Also, the constructors and destructors for each class will not be discussed unless they contribute such unique behavior to the program that they warrant discussion.

M.2.1 User Interface Subsystem

The following steps must be taken next to completely fill out the user interface code for the C++ implementation:

1. Add comments to the user interface code (ef.cpp) generated by Protogen. The comments should note the various dialog boxes, push-buttons, etc.

2. Add code to the ef.cpp file so that all of the radio buttons and push-buttons are functional and that dialog boxes are erased from the screen when they are supposed to be.

3. Provide code that adds items to the list boxes that are part of each dialog box. Code must also be added to get selections from a list box as chosen by the user.

4. Add code to retrieve from and paste/insert text into an edit control box.

5. Declare and implement any objects from the container class library that are necessary to implement the user interface.

Steps 1 and 2 have previously been completed and are reflected in the code. Note that for the C++ implementation, when the electronic filing program closes a window/dialog element, ObjectWindows will automatically delete the dialog object. Steps 3 through 5 need to be completed now.

The user interface subsystem classes were generated with the use of ProtoGen. Some callback or event handler stubs are also generated by ProtoGen. Additional programming was necessary to close dialog boxes, fill the contents of a list box, write code to deal with text edit boxes and pushbuttons, and add code to the callbacks or event handlers to perform the necessary event processing. The **FileADocument** user interface class will be discussed here as an example of a user interface class implementation. Many of the names of member functions generated by ProtoGen were changed to make them more meaningful.

FileADocument *Class Description*

Definition—The TDIALOG_1Dlg class generated by ProtoGen has been renamed to **FileADocument**. The hierarchy for class **FileADocument** is **Object-TWindowsObject/TStreamable-TDialog**. Note that TDialog multiply inherits from both **TWindowsObject** and **TStreamable**. Objects of class **FileADocument** represent the File a Document dialog box. The **FileADocument** class has six data members and nine member functions.

Public:

Class **FileADocument** has six data members. Two of those data members are edit control boxes. Another two of those data members are list box elements.

selectedDirectory—a character string representing the current directory selected by the user from the Directories' scrolling list box.

selectedFile—a character string representing the current file selected by the user from the Files scrolling list box.

Class **FileADocument** has nine member functions. This includes both a constructor and a destructor.

handleFileListBoxMsg ()—Callback for any event associated with the file list box.

handleDirListBoxMsg ()—Callback for any event associated with the directory list box.

setUpWindow ()—Sets up the dialog box.

refInfoPushButton ()—Callback for any event associated with the Reference Information **pushbutton**.

helpPushButton ()—Callback for any event associated with the Help **push-button**.

cancelPushButton ()—Callback for any event associated with the Cancel **push-button**.

okPushButton ()—Callback for any event associated with the OK **push-button**.

Programming Style

The user interface classes are almost entirely generated by ProtoGen. (Note that ProtoGen places regeneration brackets in their output code. The developer can add code between these regeneration brackets, and ProtoGen will not destroy that code unless the developer deleted the basic entity associated with that code, such as a dialog box. This allows the developer to go back and forth between the GUI builder and the code for maintenance.)

Several of the member functions are *callbacks*. Many of the names generated by ProtoGen for user interface class names and member function names are not meaningful to the programmer. This is typical of user interface generation tools. These names have been manually changed to improve the clarity of the code and our understanding of the program. ProtoGen uses inheritance to build the dialog box, subclassing the **TDialog** class. All of the member functions are fairly small, i.e., less than one page of code.

The **FileADocument** class doesn't check against all user errors, such as ensuring that the user has selected a file/document that this program recognizes and is able to file. Thus, code should be added to protect the program from trying to process invalid data and generating erroneous results.

The user interface code developed by the graphical user interface (GUI) builder tool for C++ is much more difficult to follow than the code developed for the Smalltalk GUI. Callback or event handler names are combinations of alphabetic and numeric characters rather than meaningful names/labels. The Smalltalk GUI tool allows the developer to specify each event handler name, and the C++ tool does not. Therefore, no implementation model was developed for the user interface subsystem.

M.2.2 Document Subsystem

The document subsystem classes are **TextDocument**, **Index**, and **DocRefInfo** (short for document reference information).

TextDocument *Class Description*

Definition—**TextDocument** is a stand-alone class that is not part of the existing class hierarchy. Objects of class **TextDocument** represent a text document that is filed in the system.

Public:

The **TextDocument** class has no data members and four member functions.

TextDocument ()—TextDocument is a constructor for the **TextDocument** class.

~TextDocument ()—~TextDocument is a destructor for the **TextDocument** class.

fileDoc (file, directory)—File a document in the absence of document reference information.

fileDocAndDRI (file, directory, docRefInfoObj)—File a document with document reference information.

Programming Style

The member functions are small, are cohesive, and use no global information.

Design Versus Implementation Differences

The design showed an association between the **TextDocument** and the **DocRefInfo** classes. No such association is necessary. None of the attributes specified during design were returned during the implementation.

Some of the methods of this class changed during the implementation; (e.g., *fileDocument* changed to *FileDoc*). Two methods were necessary for filing a document: *FileDoc* for filing just a text document and *FileDocAndDRI* for filing the text document along with document reference information. The *FileDocAndDRI* member function required some additional functionality not specified in the original algorithm to deal with the lack of persistence in the C++ language. Some code was added to write the document reference information to a *.dri* file that could be used later during a search.

The *get document record, viewDocument, printDocument, create text doc index*, and *validateFile* methods were not necessary as part of the **TextDocument** class.

Index *Class Description*

Definition—**Index** is a stand-alone class that is not part of the existing class hierarchy. Objects of class **Index** represent entities that index a document specified by a user.

Public:

The **Index** class has no public data members and one public member function.

Index ()—*Index* is a constructor for the **Index** class.

~Index ()—*~Index* is a destructor for the **Index** class.

createDocIndex (file, directory)—Create the actual text document index and its file.

Private:

Class **Index** has three private data member.

indexFileName—an instance of **String** representing the name of the index file.

name—an instance of **String** representing the name of the text document file.

directory—an instance of **String** representing the directory name of the text document file.

The **Index** class has two private member functions.

buildIndexFileHeader (indexFileStream, docFileStream, pathName)—Builds the index file header and outputs it to the index file.

createIndex (indexFileStream, docFileStream, pathName)—Creates an index of the contents of the text document.

Programming Style

All of the member functions are cohesive.

DocRefInfo *Class Description*

Definition—**DocRefInfo** is a stand-alone class that is not part of the existing class hierarchy. Objects of class **DocRefInfo** represent document reference information associated with a specific **TextDocument** object. Class **DocRefInfo** has neither shared data nor pool dictionaries. The **DocRefInfo** class has one class method and seven instance methods.

Public:

The **DocRefInfo** class has no data members and 4 member functions.

DocRefInfo ()—*DocRefInfo* is a constructor for the **DocRefInfo** class.

~DocRefInfo ()—*~DocRefInfo* is a destructor for the **DocRefInfo** class.

getAbstract ()—Answers with the abstract **String** for this text document.

getAuthors ()—Answers with the authors **String** for this text document.

getKeywords ()—Answers with the keywords **String** for this text document.

getDocumentName ()—Answers with the documentName **String** for this text document.

setDRI (theAuthors, theAbstract, theKeywords, documentName, theDocPath)—Sets the authors, abstract, keywords, documentName, and theDocPath for this **DocRefInfo** object.

getDocumentAndPathName ()—Answers with the theDocPath **String** for this text document.

Private:

Class **DocRefInfo** has five data members.

abstract—an instance of **String** representing the abstract information about a document entered by a user.

authors—an instance of **String** representing the author information about a document entered by a user.

keywords—an instance of **String** representing the keyword information about a document entered by a user.

documentName—an instance of **String** representing the name of the text document filed by the user.

pathAndDocumentName—an instance of **String** representing the path name and document name of the text document filed by the user.

Programming Style

All of the member functions are small and cohesive. The member functions store and retrieve data only.

Design Versus Implementation Differences

Several additional attributes were added to the class to facilitate the implementation: **docName** and **pathAndDocName**. The checkForLogicalQueryMatch and checkFor DRIMatches methods were moved to the **SearchEngine** class. The *getAbstract, getAuthors, getKeywords, getDocumentName, setDRI,* and *getDocumentAndPathName* are now member functions for the **DocRefInfo** object. An implementation model for the document subsystem is shown in Figure M.3.

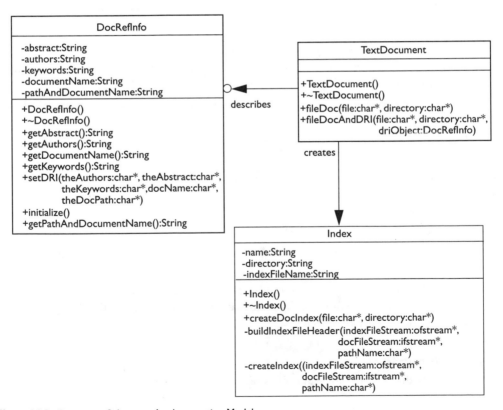

Figure M.8. Document Subsystem Implementation Model.

M.2.3 Search Results Subsystem

The search results subsystem classes are **DocumentNameList** and **DocumentRecordsList**.

DocumentNameList *Class Description*

Definition—**DocumentNameList** is a stand-alone class that is not part of the existing class hierarchy. Objects of class **DocumentNameList** represent lists of document names associated with a specific search request.

Public:

Class **DocumentNameList** has seven member functions.

DocNameL ()—*DocNameL* is a constructor for the **DocNameL** class.

~DocNameL ()—*~DocNameL* is a destructor for the **DocNameL** class.

addToDNL (documentName)—Adds a documentName to the docNameList.

getRecordsList (documentName)—Answers with a **Set** representing the list of record numbers for the documentName.

size ()—Answers with an **Integer,** which is the number of entries in the *documentNameList.*

removeFromDNL (documentName)—Answers with a **String** representing a document name removed from the head of the *documentNameList.*

includes (documentName)—Answers **True** if documentName is included in the DNL, else answers **False.**

putRecordsList (docRecListObj, indexName)—Associates a **DocumentRecordsList** object with the *indexName.*

retrieveDocumentNames ()—Answers with the *documentNameList.*

Private:

Class **DocumentNameList** has two data members.

documentNameList—an instance of **Set** representing the list of documents that satisfy the user-specified search criteria.

recordDictionary—an instance of **Dictionary** representing the list of record numbers associated with each document name in the **documentNameList** where the search criteria was satisfied within a document.

Programming Style

The methods for this class are small and cohesive.

Design Versus Implementation Differences

The name list attribute has been renamed to **documentNameList**, a private data member. Another data member, **recordDictionary**, has been added to represent the document names and document record lists associated with those documents.

DocumentRecordsList *Class Description*

Definition—**DocumentRecordsList** is a stand-alone class that is not part of the existing class hierarchy. Objects of class **DocumentRecordsList** represent lists of document records associated with a specific document name that satisfied a search request.

Public:

Class **DocumentRecordsList** has five public member functions.

DocRecdL ()—*DocRecdL* is a constructor for the **DocRecdL** class.

~DocRecdL ()—*~DocRecdL* is a destructor for the **DocRecdL** class.

addToDRL (recordNumber)—Adds a recordNumber to the *documentRecordsList*.

atPut (anInteger, aRecordNumber)—Replaces the element of the receiver at index position *anInteger* with *aRecordNumber*.

size ()—Answers with an **Integer,** which is the number of entries in the *documentRecordsList*.

removeRecordNumber (recordNumber)—Removes the *recordNumber* from the *documentRecordsList*.

getRecordsList ()—Answers with the **Set** of record numbers in the *documentRecordsList*.

Private:

Class **DocumentRecordsList** has one private data member.

documentRecordsList—an instance of **Set** representing the list of document record numbers, which specify the record numbers where the search criteria was satisfied within a specific document.

Class **DocumentRecordsList** has two private member functions.

getFirstRecord ()—Answers with the first record number in the *documentRecordsList*.

getNextRecord ()—Answers with the next record number in the *documentRecordsList*.

Programming Style

Same comments as noted for the **DocumentNameList** class. An implementation model for the search results subsystem is shown in Figure M.9.

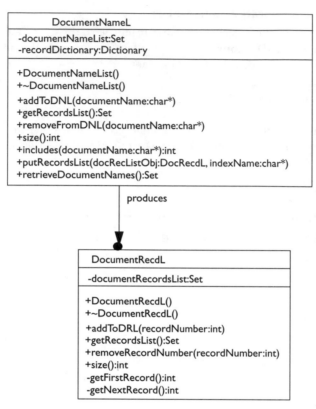

Figure M.9. Search Results Subsystem Implementation Model.

M.2.4 Query Subsystem

The query subsystem classes are **Query**, **AuthorQuery**, **AbstractQuery**, **KeywordQuery**, and **ContentQuery**.

Query *Class Description*

Definition—**Query** is a stand–alone class that is not part of the existing class hierarchy. **Query** is an abstract class. There are no instances of **Query**; there are only instances of subclasses of **Query**. The protocol in class **Query** is common to all of its subclasses.

Public:

Class **Query** has seven member functions. Class **Query** has no constructor or destructor.

checkForElementMatch (element)—Answers **True** or **False** based on a match between a keyword/ abstract/author query and document reference information for each and every filed document.

getLogicalOperators ()—Answers with an **Array** of substrings of logical operators.

getQueryElements ()—Answers with an **Array** of substrings of query elements.

parseQuery ()—Parses a query into **queryElements** and **logicalOperators**.

query ()—Answers with a **String,** which is the query.

Protected:

Class **Query** has three *protected* data members. Each of these data members are declared as *static* data members. *Static* data members in C++ are analogous to *class* variables in Smalltalk. There is only one instance of a static data member for the Query class or any of its subclasses.

ContentToAbstractOperator—an instance of **String** representing a logical operator between a content query and an abstract query.

KeywordToAuthorOperator—an instance of **String** representing a logical operator between a keyword query and an author query.

AbstractToKeywordOperator—an instance of **String** representing a logical operator between an abstract query and a keyword query.

Private:

Class **Query** has three private data members.

queryElements—an instance of **Queue** representing words or phrases that are part of a query.

logicalOperators—an instance of **Queue** representing the logical operators that connect words or phrases in a query.

query—an instance of **String** representing a query entered by a user.

AuthorQuery *Class Description*

Definition—The hierarchy for class **AuthorQuery** is **Query**. Objects of class **AuthorQuery** represent the author query entered by a user for conducting a search operation.

Public:

AuthorQuery has no data members. The **AuthorQuery** class has four member functions, which include a constructor and a destructor.

AuthorQuery ()—*AuthorQuery* is a constructor for the **AuthorQuery** class.

~AuthorQuery ()—*~AuthorQuery* is a destructor for the **AuthorQuery** class.

setAuthorQuery (authorQuery)—Sets the query equal to the *authorQuery* String.

setKeywordToAuthorOperator (theOperator)—Sets the **KeywordToAuthorOperator** equal to *theOperator*, which is a **String**.

Protected:

Protocol inherited from **Query** *and used*—

Class **Query** has three static data members that are inherited: **KeywordToAuthorOperator**, **ContentToAbstractOperator**, and **AbstractToKeywordOperator**.

Private:

Class **Query** has three data members that are inherited: **queryElements**, **logicalOperators**, and **query**. Class **AuthorQuery** also inherits five member functions from class **Query**: *CheckForElementMatch*, *GetLogicalOperators*, *GetQueryElements*, *ParseQuery*, and *Query*.

All of the protocol from class **Query** is useful in the **AuthorQuery** subclass.

AbstractQuery *Class Description*

Definition—The hierarchy for class **AbstractQuery** is **Query**. Objects of class **AbstractQuery** represent a user-entered abstract query for a search operation.

Public:

AbstractQuery has no data members. The **AbstractQuery** class has five member functions, which include a constructor and a destructor.

AbstractQuery ()—*AbstractQuery* is a constructor for the **AbstractQuery** class.

~AbstractQuery ()—*~AbstractQuery* is a destructor for the **AbstractQuery** class.

setAbstractQuery (abstractQuery)—Sets the query equal to the abstractQuery **String**.

setContentToAbstractOperator (theOperator)—Sets the **ContentToAbstractOperator** equal to *operator*, which is a **String**.

getAbstractToKeywordOperator ()—Answers with the **AbstractToKeywordOperator String**.

Protected:

Protocol inherited from **Query** *and used*—

Class **Query** has three static data members that are inherited: **KeywordToAuthorOperator**, **ContentToAbstractOperator**, and **AbstractToKeywordOperator**.

Private:

Class **Query** has three data members that are inherited: **queryElements**, **logicalOperators**, and **query**. Class **AbstractQuery** also inherits five member functions from class **Query**: *CheckForElementMatch*, *GetLogicalOperators*, *GetQueryElements*, *ParseQuery*, and *Query*.

All of the protocol from class **Query** is useful in the **AbstractQuery** subclass.

KeywordQuery *Class Description*

Definition—The hierarchy for class **KeywordQuery** is **Query**. Objects of class **KeywordQuery** represent a user entered keyword query for a search operation.

Public:

KeywordQuery has no data members. The **KeywordQuery** class has five member functions, which include a constructor and a destructor.

> *KeywordQuery ()*—*KeywordQuery* is a constructor for the **KeywordQuery** class.

> *~KeywordQuery ()*—*~KeywordQuery* is a destructor for the **KeywordQuery** class.

> *setKeywordQuery (keywordQuery)*—Sets the query equal to the keywordQuery **String**.

> *setAbstractToKeywordOperator (theOperator)*—Sets the **AbstractToKeywordOperator** equal to *operator*, which is a **String**.

> *getAbstractToKeywordOperator ()*—Answer with the **AbstractToKeywordOperator**, which is a **String**.

Protected:

Protocol inherited from **Query** *and used*—
Class **Query** has three static data members that are inherited: **KeywordToAuthorOperator**, **ContentToAbstractOperator**, and **AbstractToKeywordOperator**.

Private:

Class **Query** has three data members that are inherited: **queryElements**, **logicalOperators**, and **query**. Class **KeywordQuery** also inherits five member functions from class **Query**: *CheckForElementMatch*, *GetLogicalOperators*, *GetQueryElements*, *ParseQuery*, and *Query*.
All of the protocol from class **Query** is useful in the **KeywordQuery** subclass.

ContentQuery *Class Description*

Definition—The hierarchy for class **ContentQuery** is **Object-Query**. Objects of class **ContentQuery** represent a user-entered content query for a search operation. The **ContentQuery** class has two instance methods. It has neither shared data nor pool dictionaries.

Public:

ContentQuery has no data members. The **ContentQuery** class has four member functions, which include a constructor and a destructor.

ContentQuery ()—*ContentQuery* is a constructor for the **ContentQuery** class.

~ContentQuery ()—*~ContentQuery* is a destructor for the **ContentQuery** class.

setContentQuery (contentQuery)—Sets the query equal to the contentQuery **String**.

getContentToAbstractOperator ()—Answers with the **ContentToAbstractOperator**, which is a **String**.

Protected:

Protocol inherited from **Query** *and used*—

Class **Query** has three static data members that are inherited: **KeywordToAuthorOperator**, **ContentToAbstractOperator**, and **AbstractToKeywordOperator**.

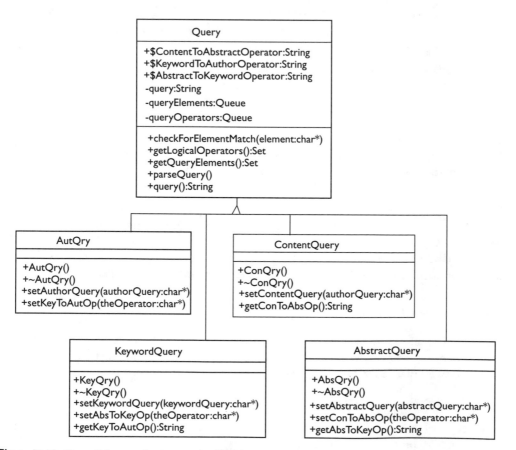

Figure M.10. Query Subsystem Implementation Model.

Private:

Class **Query** has three data members that are inherited: **queryElements**, **logicalOperators**, and **query**. Class **ContentQuery** also inherits five member functions from class **Query**: *CheckForElementMatch*, *GetLogicalOperators*, *GetQueryElements*, *ParseQuery*, and *Query*.

    All of the protocol from class **Query** is useful in the **ContentQuery** subclass.

Protocol inherited from **Query** *and used*—All of the protocol from class **Query** is useful in the **Content-Query** subclass.

An implementation model for the query subsystem is shown in Figure M.10.

M.2.5 Hashing Subsystem

The hashing subsystem classes are **HashEngine**, **JunkWords**, and **FilingCharacters**. The **Hash-Engine** class uses the **JunkWords** and **FilingCharacters** classes in hashing a document.

HashEngine *Class Description*

Definition—**HashEngine** is a stand-alone class that is not part of the existing class hierarchy. Objects of class **HashEngine** represent agents that do work on behalf of an **Index** object.

Public:

Class **HashEngine** has seven public member functions, which include both a constructor and a destructor.

    HashEng ()—*HashEng* is the **HashEngine** constructor. It sets up the **TranslateTable** and **RandomNumberTable** that are used during the hashing process.

    ~HashEng ()—*~HashEng* is the **HashEngine** destructor.

    buildHashBlock (indexFileStream, docFileStream)—Builds every *hashBlock* for the text document.

    hashFirstCharUsing (aChar, theHashBlock)—Hashes the first character of a word represented by a **String** and puts it in *theHashBlock*.

    hashOtherCharUsing (aChar, theHashBlock)—Hashes the third or subsequent character of a word represented by a **String** and puts it in *theHashBlock*.

    hashSecondCharUsing (aChar, theHashBlock)—Hashes the second character of a word represented by a **String** and puts it in *theHashBlock*.

    hashTheWordUsing (theWord, theHashBlock)—Hashes a word represented by a **String** and puts it in *theHashBlock*.

Private:

Class **HashEngine** has five private member functions.

hashDocumentRecord (documentRecord)—Hashes an 80-character record and puts it in the hash-Block.

hashFirstChar (aChar)—Hashes the first character of a word represented by a **String** and puts it in the *hashBlock*.

hashOtherChar (aChar)—Hashes the third or subsequent character of a word represented by a **String** and puts it in the *hashBlock*.

hashSecondChar (aChar)—Hashes the second character of a word represented by a **String** and puts it in the *hashBlock*.

hashTheWord (theWord)—Hashes a word represented by a **String** and puts it in the *hashBlock*.

Class **HashEngine** has 12 private data members.

randomNumberTable—an array of random numbers.

hashBlock—an array of characters of size **YHashBlock * XHashBlock**, representing **YHashBlock** number of 80-character records that have been hashed.

translateChar—an **Integer** used to represent an ASCII character that is hashed.

offset—an **Integer** offset into a **randomNumberTable**.

hashBlockIndex—an **Integer** index into the **hashBlock**.

recordsIndexedInBlock—an **Integer** representing the number of records indexed within the current **hashBlock**.

totalRecordsIndexed—an **Integer** representing the total number of records indexed for this document.

junkWordsObj—a pointer to an instance of the **JunkWords** class.

filingCharsObj—a pointer to an instance of the **FilingCharacters** class.

textBuffer—a buffer consisting of an array of characters for reading text document records.

wordBuf—a buffer consisting of an array of characters for processing words within text document records.

Programming Style

The part of the *BuildHashBlock* member function that creates an empty hash block and initializes it to all zeros could be broken out into a separate member function. This would make the member function more cohesive and smaller in size.

JunkWords *Class Description*

Definition—**JunkWords** is a stand-alone class that is not part of the existing class hierarchy. Objects of class **JunkWords** represent the set of junk words associated with a document that are skipped over during the filing of the document.

Public:

Class **JunkWords** has 7 public member functions, which include both a constructor and a destructor.

JunkWords ()—*JunkWords* is the constructor for the **JunkWords** class. The constructor reads the entire junk words file from disk and creates a **Set** of junk words.

~JunkWords ()— *~JunkWords* is the destructor for the **JunkWords** class.

addJunkWord (word)—Adds a word to the **currentWordsObj**.

deleteJunkWord (word)—Deletes a word in the form of a **String** from the **currentWordsObj**.

getJunkWords (word)—Answers the **currentWordsObj**.

saveJunkWords ()—Replaces the current junk word file and then saves the **currentWordsObj** in the junk word file via the **junkWordFileStream**.

checkIfJunkWord (word)—Answer **True** if a word is a junk word; otherwise, answer **False**.

Private:

Class **JunkWords** has two private data members.

junkWordFileStream—an instance of **ostream** representing the file of the junk words.

currentWordsObj—a **Set** of words from the junk words file.

Class **JunkWords** has one private member function.

replaceJunkWordFile ()—Deletes the old junk word file and creates a new empty junk word file.

Programming Style

The methods of this class are small and cohesive.

FilingCharacters *Class Description*

Definition—**FilingCharacters** is a stand-alone class that is not part of the existing class hierarchy. Objects of class **FilingCharacters** represent the set of filing characters associated with a document that are processed during the filing of the document.

Public:

Class **FilingCharacters** has seven public member functions, which include both a constructor and a destructor.

FilgChrs ()—*FilgChrs* is the constructor for the **FilingCharacters** class. The constructor reads the entire filing characters file from disk and creates a **Set** of filing characters.

~FilgChrs ()— *~FilgChrs* is the destructor for the **FilingCharacters** class.

addFilingChar (aChar)—Adds the specified character to the **includedCharactersObj**.

deleteFilingChar (aChar)—Removes the specified character from the **includedCharactersObj**.

getFilingChars ()—Answers the **includedCharactersObj**.

saveFilingCharacters ()—Replaces the filing characters file and then saves the **includedCharactersObj** in the filing characters file via the *filingCharactersFileStream*.

getFirstFilingCharacter (aWord)—Answers with the position of the first filing character in the word. Answer 0 if not found.

checkIfFilingCharacter (aChar)—Answer **True** if *aChar* is a filing character, else answer **False**.

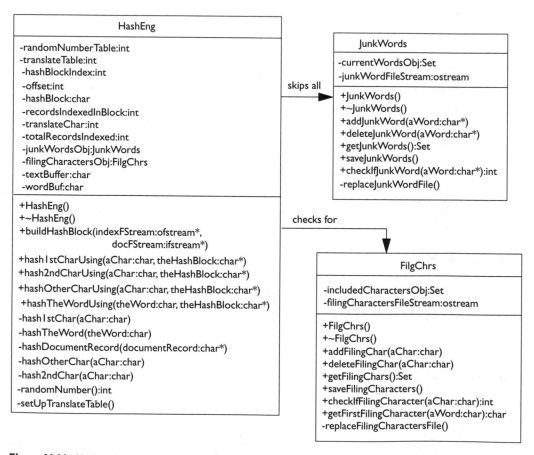

Figure M.11. Hashing Subsystem Implementation Model.

Private:

Class **FilingCharacters** has 2 private data members.

  filingCharactersFileStream—an instance of **ostream** representing the file of filing characters.

  includedCharactersObj—a **Set** of characters from the filing characters file.

Class **FilingCharacters** has one private member function.

  replaceFilingCharactersFile ()—Deletes the old filing characters file and creates a new empty filing characters file.

Programming Style

The methods of this class are small and cohesive. An implementation model for the hashing subsystem is shown in Figure M.6.

M.2.6 Search Subsystem

The search subsystem classes are **SearchEngine** and **SearchVector**.

SearchEngine *Class Description*

Definition—**SearchEngine** is a stand-alone class that is not part of the existing class hierarchy. Objects of class **SearchEngine** represent entities that act as a user's agent, looking for documents that satisfy a search criteria.

Public:

Class **SearchEngine** has five public member functions.

  SrchEng ()—*SrchEng* is the constructor for the **SearchEngine** class.

  ~SrchEng ()— *~SrchEng* is the destructor for the **SearchEngine** class.

  findDocument (contentQueryObject)—Searches for documents based only on a content search. Activates the Search Results dialog box if the search query is satisfied.

  findDocument (authorQueryObject, keywordQueryObject, abstractQueryObject)—Searches for documents based only on a document reference information search. Activates the Search Results dialog box if the search query is satisfied.

  findDocument (authorQueryObject, keywordQueryObject, contentQueryObject, abstractQueryObject)— Searches for documents based on both a content search and a document reference information search. Activates the Search Results dialog box if the search query is satisfied.

Private:

Class **SearchEngine** has 7 private data members.

aAuthorQueryObject—an instance of the **AuthorQuery** object representing the user-entered author query.

aKeywordQueryObject—an instance of the **KeywordQuery** object representing the user-entered keyword query.

aAbstractQueryObject—an instance of the **AbstractQuery** object representing the user-entered abstract query.

aContentQueryObject—an instance of the **ContentQuery** object representing the user-entered content query.

aDocumentNameListObject—an instance of the **DocumentNameList** object representing the names of those documents found that meet the search criteria.

resultVector—the search result vector.

recListObj—an instance of the **DocumentRecordsList** object.

Class **SearchEngine** has five private member functions.

calculateDocRecNumbers (indexStream, vectorStream)—Calculates the document record numbers where hits are possible and answers with a **DocumentRecordsList** object.

checkForDocumentMatches (theSearchVector)—Determines those documents that satisfy the search criteria and answers with a **DocumentNameList** object.

checkForDRIMatches ()—Determines what document reference information satisfies the search criteria and answers with a **DocumentNameList** object.

checkForLogicalQueryMatch (authorMatchIndicator, keywordMatchIndicator, abstractMatchIndicator)—Performs logical operations between queries using query logical operators. Answers **True** or **False**.

verifyMatches (docRecordNumberList, indexStream, contentQuery)—Uses the *docRecordNumberList* and *contentQuery* to verify that a content query actually exists in a document. Answers with the document name and path name.

checkEachIndex (indexDocName)—Checks each document index for a match against the search criteria.

Programming Style

The *FindDocument*, *CheckForLogicalQueryMatch*, and *VerifyMatches* member functions are reasonable in size and cohesive in function. *CalculateDocRecNumbers* is a large member function and could be broken into several member functions.

SearchVector *Class Description*

Definition—**SearchVector** is a stand-alone class that is not part of the existing class hierarchy. Objects of class **SearchVector** represent a search vector, which is a **String** of characters that indicates what parts of an index file point to the search criteria within a document.

Public:

Class **SearchVector** has four public member functions.

SrchVect ()—*SrchVect* is the constructor for the **SearchVector** class.

~SrchVect ()—*~SrchVect* is the destructor for the **SearchVector** class.

buildSearchVector (contentQueryObject)—Answers with a search vector, which is a **String**.

returnVector ()—Returns the actual search vector string

Private:

Class **SearchVector** has one private data member.

queryVector—a string of characters representing the query search vector.

Class **SearchVector** has one private member function.

constructVector (queryVectorString, elementVectorString, operator)—Performs the required logical operation between query and element vectors. The result is placed in the *queryVector*.

Programming Style

One of our goals is to keep member functions consistent; e.g., similar member functions should use the same names, conditions, arguments, etc. The name *ConstructVector* is not meaningful for the function this member function is performing. This member function performs two different logical operations, AND and OR, on vectors. *ConstructVector* can be broken into two member functions, *OrVectors* and *AndVectors*, which will then both be invoked from *BuildSearchVector*. This helps to separate policy from implementation. *OrVectors* and *AndVectors* are both implementation member functions, and *BuildSearchVector* is a policy member function.

M.2.7 Miscellaneous Classes

The data storage subsystem classes are **Index** and **FilingDirectory**.

FilingDirectory *Class Description*

Definition—The hierarchy for class **FilingDirectory** is **Object**. Objects of class **FilingDirectory** represent a directory and the index files used by the application in storing and retrieving document indexes.

Public:

Class **FilingDirectory** has six public member functions, which include both a constructor and a destructor.

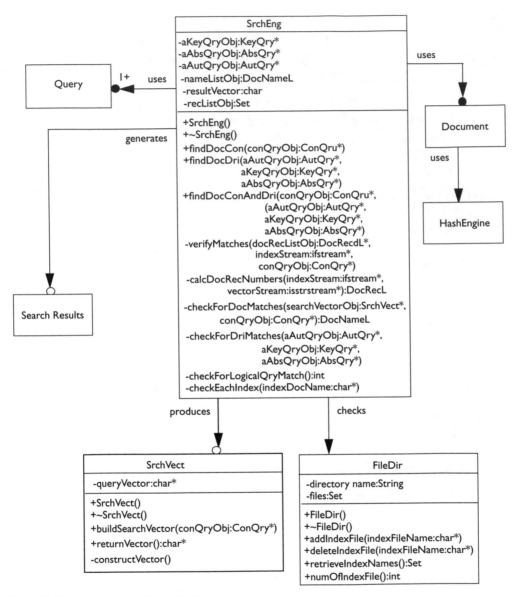

Figure M.12. Implementation Object Model.

FileDir ()—*FileDir* is the constructor for the **FilingDirectory** class.

~FileDir ()— *~FileDir* is the destructor for the **FilingDirectory** class.

addIndexFile (fileName)—Adds a file name in the form of a **String** to *files*.

deleteIndexFile (indexName)—Deletes the specified index file from disk and removes the *index-Name* from *files*.

retrieveIndexNames ()—Answers with **files**.

numberOfIndexFiles ()—Answers with the number of index files.

Private:

Class **FilingDirectory** has two private data members.

directoryName—an instance of **String** representing the name of the filing directory.

files—an instance of **Set** used to contain the names of the index files.

Abbott, R. *Program Design by Informal English Descriptions.* New York: ACM, 1983.

Blaha, M. Finding objects in object diagrams, *Journal of Object-Oriented Programming,* 5(9): (1994).

Booch, G. *Object-Oriented Analysis and Design.* Redwood City, CA: Benjamin Cummings, 1994.

Booch, G. *Object-Oriented Design.* Redwood City, CA: Benjamin Cummings, 1991

Borland. *C++ 3.1 Programmer's Guide.* Borland International, 1992.

Borland. *ObjectWindows for C++ Reference Guide.* Borland International, 1991.

Budd, T. *Object-Oriented Programming.* Reading, MA: Addison-Wesley, 1991.

Coad, P. and E. Yourdon. *Object-Oriented Analysis.* Englewood Cliffs, NJ: Yourdon Press, 1991.

Coad, P. and E. Yourdon. *Object-Oriented Design.* Englewood Cliffs, NJ: Yourdon Press, 1991.

Constantine, L. and E. Yourdon. *Structured Design.* Englewood Cliffs, NJ: Yourdon Press, 1978.

DeMarco, T. *Structured Analysis and System Specification.* New York: Yourdon Press, 1979.

DeMarco, T. *Controlling Software Projects.* New York: Yourdon Press, 1982.

Digitalk. *Smalltalk V for Windows Encyclopedia of Classes Handbook.* Los Angeles: Digitalk, 1992a.

Digitalk. *Smalltalk V for Windows Tutorial and Programming Handbook.* Los Angeles: Digitalk, 1992b.

Goldberg, A. and K. Rubin. *Object Behavior Analysis.* New York: ACM, September 1992.

Graham, I. *Object Oriented Methods.* Reading, MA: Addison-Wesley, 1991.

Grady, R. B. and D. L. Caswell. *Software Metrics: Establishing a Company-Wide Program.* Englewood Cliffs, NJ: Prentice Hall, 1987.

Harel, D. Statecharts: A visual formalism for complex systems. *Science of Computer Programming* 8: 231–274. North Holland, 1987.

Humphrey, W. S. *Managing the Software Process.* Reading, MA: Addison-Wesley, 1990.

Jacobson, I. M. Christerson, P. Jonsson, and G. Overgaard. *Object-Oriented Software Engineering.* Reading, MA: Addison-Wesley, 1992.

Jacobson, I. M. Ericsson, and A. Jacobson. *The Object Advantage.* Reading, MA: Addison-Wesley, 1995.

Kirkpatrick, D. Developing a commercial engineering application in Smalltalk. *Journal of Object-Oriented Programming,* (Oct.) 1994.

Knuth, D. E. *Searching and Sorting.* Vol. 3, Reading, MA: Addison-Wesley, 1973.

Kuhn, T. *The Structure of Scientific Revolutions,* 2nd ed. Chicago: University of Chicago Press, 1970.

Lorenz, M. *Object-Oriented Software Development.* Englewood Cliffs, NJ: Prentice Hall, 1993.

Love, T. *Object Lessons.* New York: SIGS Books, 1993.

McGregor, J. D, and D. A. Sykes. *Object-Oriented Software Development: Engineering Software for Reuse.* New York: Van Nostrand Reinhold, 1992.

Meyer, B. *Object-Oriented Software Construction.* Hertfordshire, UK: Prentice Hall International, 1988.

Norton, P. and P. L. Yao. *Borland C++ Programming for Windows.* Version 3.0, New York: Bantam Books, 1992.

Page-Jones, M. *The Practical Guide to Structured Systems Design.* Englewood Cliffs, NJ: Prentice Hall, 1980.

Poston, R. M. *Automated Testing from Object Models.* New York: ACM, 1994.

Rumbaugh, J., M. Blaha, W. Premerlani, F. Eddy, and W. Lorensen. *Object-Oriented Modeling and Design.* Englewood Cliffs, NJ: Prentice Hall, 1991

Rumbaugh, J. Going with the flow. *Journal of Object-Oriented Programming,* 7(3): (1994b).

Rumbaugh, J. The life of an object model. *Journal of Object-Oriented Programming,* 7(1): (1994c).

Rumbaugh, J. Controlling code. *Journal of Object-Oriented Programming,* 6(2): (1993a).

Rumbaugh, J. Objects in the Twilight Zone. *Journal of Object-Oriented Programming,* 6(3): (1993b).

Rumbaugh, J. Getting Started. *Journal of Object-Oriented Programming,* 7(5): (1994a).

Sommerville, I. *Software Engineering.* Reading, MA: Addison-Wesley, 1995.

Welker, K. *Application of Software Metrics to Object-Based Re-engineered Code Implemented in Ada.* Masters Thesis. Moscow, ID: University of Idaho, 1994.

White, I. *Using the Booch Method.* Redwood City, CA: Benjamin Cummings, 1994.

Wiegers, K. Work metrics. *Software Development Magazine,* (Oct.) (1994).

Winblad, A. L., S. Edwards, and D. R. King. *Object-Oriented Software.* Reading, MA: Addison-Wesley, 1990.

Wirfs-Brock, R., B. Wilkerson, and L. Wiener. *Designing Object-Oriented Software.* Englewood Cliffs, NJ: Prentice Hall, 1990.

Object Model Notation
Advanced Concepts

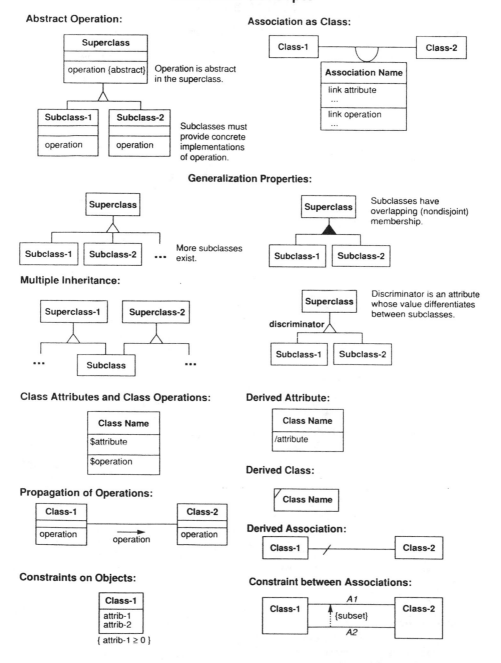

Abstract Operation:

Operation is abstract in the superclass.

Subclasses must provide concrete implementations of operation.

Association as Class:

Generalization Properties:

More subclasses exist.

Subclasses have overlapping (nondisjoint) membership.

Multiple Inheritance:

Discriminator is an attribute whose value differentiates between subclasses.

Class Attributes and Class Operations:

Derived Attribute:

Propagation of Operations:

Derived Class:

Derived Association:

Constraints on Objects:

Constraint between Associations:

This section is reprinted, with permission of Prentice Hall (Englewood Cliffs, NJ) and James Rumbaugh, Michael Blaha, William Premerlani, Frederick Eddy, and William Lorensen, from *Object Modeling and Design* (1991).

Object Model Notation
Basic Concepts

Class:

Class Name

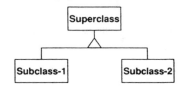

Generalization (Inheritance):

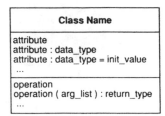

Aggregation:

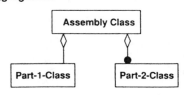

Aggregation (alternate form):

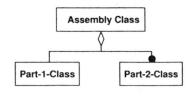

Object Instances:

Association:

Qualified Association:

Multiplicity of Associations:

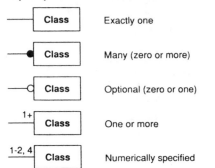

Ordering:

Link Attribute:

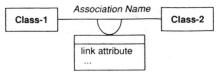

Ternary Association:

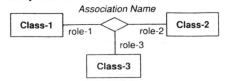

Instantiation Relationship:

Functional Model Notation

Process:

Data Flow between Processes:

Data Store or File Object:

Data Flow that Results in a Data Store:

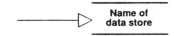

Actor Objects (as Source or Sink of Data):

Control Flow:

Access of Data Store Value:

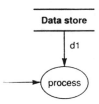

Update of Data Store Value:

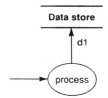

Access and Update of Data Store Value:

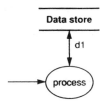

Composition of Data Value:

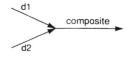

Duplication of Data Value:

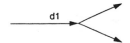

Decomposition of Data Value:

Dynamic Model Notation

Event causes Transition between States:

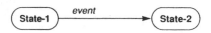

Event with Attribute:

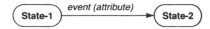

Initial and Final States:

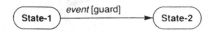

Action on a Transition:

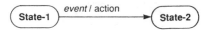

Guarded Transition:

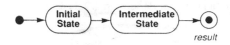

Output Event on a Transition:

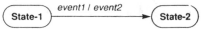

Actions and Activity while in a State:

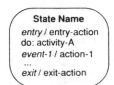

Sending an event to another object:

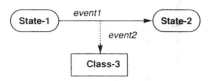

State Generalization (Nesting):

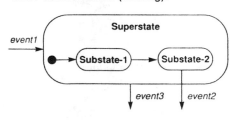

Concurrent Subdiagrams:

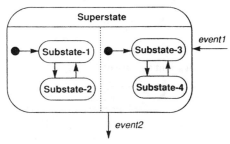

Splitting of control: **Synchronization of control:**

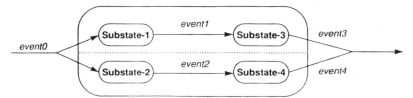